Thought and Reference

for Claire

Thought and Reference

KENT BACH

CLARENDON PRESS · OXFORD

Oxford University Press, Walton Street, Oxford OX2 6DP

Oxford New York Toronto
Delhi Bombay Calcutta Madras Karachi
Kuala Lumpur Singapore Hong Kong Tokyo
Nairobi Dar es Salaam Cape Town
Melbourne Auckland Madrid
and associated companies in
Berlin Ibadan

Oxford is a trade mark of Oxford University Press

Published in the United States
by Oxford University Press Inc., New York

British Library Cataloguing in Publication Data
Bach, Kent
Thought and reference.
1. Reference (Philosophy   2. Semantics
(Philosophy)
I. Title
401'.41   B105.R25
ISBN 0-19-824983-7
ISBN 0-19-824077-5 (pbk.)

Library of Congress Cataloging-in-Publication Data
Bach, Kent.
Thought and reference
Bibliography: p.
Includes index.
1. Reference (Philosophy)   I. Title.
B105.R25B33 1987   149'.946   87-24884
ISBN 0-19-824983-7
ISBN 0-19-824077-5 (pbk.)

Printed in Great Britain
on acid-free paper by
Biddles Ltd. Guildford and King's Lynn

Preface to the Paperback Edition

The seemingly simple fact that we can think and talk about particular persons, places, and things has given rise to some not so simple philosophical problems. In taking on these problems, I have adopted the general strategy of locating the various issues at different levels of analysis. I distinguish three levels—cognitive, semantic, and pragmatic—and offer split-level solutions. Although the specific solutions may be controversial, the general strategy seems to be gaining acceptance, probably through the influence of Paul Grice's work. More and more philosophers are coming to appreciate that the theory of mental contents, the semantics of sentences, and the pragmatics of utterances are but loosely connected and, in particular, that the issues of singular thought, singular terms, and singular reference should not be conflated.

The main topics addressed here have received considerable attention since the book appeared in 1987. Although some remain in dispute, proper names and belief reports, for example, it is encouraging to observe that on others, such as singular thought, definite descriptions, and the pragmatics of reference, there has developed if not a consensus at least a growing convergence of opinion along lines followed here. More than enough ideas and arguments have appeared in recent years to warrant adding a Postscript (it appears after Chapter 13). It gives an update on work that bears, either explicitly or by implication, on views proposed here. It describes and documents developing trends and continuing controversies, and provides, I hope, some useful explanation and clarification.

San Francisco
September 1993

Acknowledgements

The first half of Chapter 1 is adapted from parts of 'De re belief and methodological solipsism', which appeared in *Thought and Object: Essays on Intentionality*, edited by Andrew Woodfield, Oxford University Press (1982), pp. 121–51; the remainder of Chapter 1 and all of Chapter 2 are reprinted with minor changes from 'Thought and object: *de re* representations and relations', which appeared in *The Representation of Knowledge and Belief*, edited by Myles Brand and Robert M. Harnish, University of Arizona Press (1986), pp. 187–218; the Speech Act Schema in Chapter 3, pp. 53–5, is reprinted from *Linguistic Communication and Speech Acts*, co-authored by Robert M. Harnish, MIT Press (1979), pp. 76–7; Chapter 6 is based on 'Referential/attributive', *Synthese* 49 (1981), D. Reidel Publishing Co., pp. 219–44; Chapters 7 and 8 are based on 'What's in a name', *Australasian Journal of Philosophy* 59 (1981), pp. 371–86; Section 5 of Chapter 10 is based on a portion of 'Feigned reference and failed reference: much ado about nothing', *Grazer Philosophische Studien* 25/26 (1985/1986), pp. 359–74. I wish to thank the respective publishers and editors for permission to reprint or adapt the above material.

Contents

Introduction: Meaning and Reference 1

 1. Two Kinds of Reference 3
 2. Semantics and Pragmatics 4
 3. Thoughts, Words, and Things 6

PART ONE: SINGULAR THOUGHT

1. The Nature of *de re* Thought 11

 1. Characterizing *de re* Thought 12
 2. What *de re* Thought is not 13
 3. The Form of *de re* Thought 17
 4. *De re* Representations and Relations 19

2. Varieties of *de re* Thought 27

 1. Memory-based *de re* Thoughts 27
 2. Communication-based *de re* Thoughts 31
 3. Thinking of and Identifying: A Comparison with Evans 39

PART TWO: SINGULAR REFERENCE

3. Varieties of Reference 49

 1. What is Speaker Reference? 49
 2. Referring Expressions 55
 3. Russell and Reference 59
 4. Meaning and Reference 62
 5. Types of Referring 66

4. Semantics, Pragmatics, and Reference 69

 1. Beyond Literality: Grades of Inexplicitness 69
 2. Semantic Indeterminacy and Ambiguity 74
 3. Ockham's Semantic Razor 77
 4. Inexplicitness and Standardized Non-literality 79
 5. Singular Terms and Standardized Non-literality 82
 6. Against Token Semantics 85

Contents

PART THREE: SINGULAR TERMS

5. Definite Descriptions I: Vindicating Russell   91

    1. Russell's Theory   91
    2. Strawson's Objection   96
    3. Donnellan's Objection   98
    4. The Incomplete Description Objection   103

6. Definite Descriptions II: The Referential/Attributive
    Distinction   109

    1. Donnellan's Account   109
    2. Searle's Account   115
    3. Referential Uses   117
    4. Incomplete Definite Descriptions   124
    5. Loose Ends: Near Misses, Misfits, and Fall-backs   126

7. Proper Names I: The Nominal Description Theory   130

    1. Russell on Names   131
    2. NDT and the Descriptive Contents of Names   133
    3. Explaining Literal Uses of Names: Alternatives to NDT   138
    4. Objections to NDT   140

8. Proper Names II: Answering Kripke   149

    1. Kripke's First Objection: The Modal Argument   149
    2. Kripke's Second Objection: The Argument from Ignorance
       and Error   157
    3. Kripke's Objection to NDT: The Circularity Argument   159
    4. Four Familiar Problems for RDT   162
    5. The Illusion of Rigidity   167

9. Reference and Pronouns   175

    1. Reference and Context   176
    2. Referring and Saying   179
    3. Intending and Demonstrating   182
    4. The Semantics of Indexicals: Referential Constraints   186
    5. Objectual and Descriptive Reference with Indexicals   193

10. Singular Terms in Belief and in Fictional Contexts   195

    1. Descriptions in Belief Contexts   195
    2. Names and Indexicals in Belief Contexts   202
    3. Scope and Ambiguity   206
    4. The Semantic Indeterminacy of Belief Sentences   210
    5. Fictional Contexts   214

Contents

PART FOUR: OTHER KINDS OF REFERENCE

11. Anaphoric Reference: Grammatical or Pragmatic?   221

    1. Anaphoric and Other Uses of Personal Pronouns   222
    2. Evans vs. Lasnik   225
    3. A Rule of Non-co-reference?   230
    4. Pronouns and their 'Antecedents'   235

12. Quantifier Phrases and Pronouns: Plural Reference
    and Anaphora   238

    1. Quantifier Phrases   240
    2. Using Quantifier Phrases to Refer   244
    3. Plural Pronouns   248
    4. Quantifier Phrases and 'Bound' Pronouns   250
    5. 'Binding' as Referential Dependence   255
    6. Quantifier Phrases and 'E-type' Pronouns   258

13. Reference and Natural Kinds   262

    1. Belief and Meaning   264
    2. Concepts and Context   274
    3. Uses and Extensions   280
    4. Relevant Similarity   285
    5. The Division of Linguistic Labour   286
    6. Semantic Natural Kinds?   290

Bibliography   293

Glossary   298

Postscript to the paperback edition   302

Index   321

Introduction: Meaning and Reference

At first glance the problems of reference do not seem hopelessly difficult: challenging, yes, but not impossible. Yet since the days of Mill and of Frege the subject has been fraught with controversy. The diversity of competing theories which philosophers have devised, often with more complexity than the subject would seem to demand, could well make an impartial observer wonder whether the problems of reference are too difficult to be solved or even too deep to be comprehended. I am not that discouraged, but then I am not exactly an impartial observer. As I see it, the constant competition among theories, though not unhealthy, is symptomatic of something having gone awry. I do not deny that the problems are more difficult than they seem at first glance, but I believe their treatment could use a good dose of common sense. For example, proper names, which strike people initially as rather unproblematic linguistic items, have given rise to problems apparently more intractable than the common cold. One might have thought the everyday phenomenon of referring to an individual by name to be something less than a mystery, but the debate on proper names keeps spreading and the epidemic of theories goes unabated.

Without promising a cure-all, I cannot believe that solving the problems of reference should compete in difficulty with the problem of curing the common cold. Lest it seem that I am joking, recall the chestnut about the mathematician G. H. Hardy. While trying to demonstrate a theorem to a class of astute students, he remarked that a certain lemma was obvious. One student, no slower than the rest, found it less than obvious and said so. Hardy looked puzzled and stormed out of the room, returning some time later with the pronouncement 'Yes, it *is* obvious.' I believe that the solutions to the problems of reference, some of them anyway, are no less obvious.

To anticipate the complaint that there is no excuse for a book to belabour the obvious, I answer, first, that much in this book will be far from obvious and often downright controversial, and second, that many things are obvious but only after you see them.

We cannot deny that Wittgenstein was right, at least about some problems, when he remarked, 'The problems are solved, not by giving new information, but by arranging what we have already known. Philosophy is a battle against the bewitchment of our intelligence by means of language.' (1953, sec. 109) For us language *is* the problem, not just the source of it, but Wittgenstein's dictum still applies, if only to some of the problems. Others will require substantive, not just cosmetic solutions, but collectively they demand the kind of intellectual housekeeping Wittgenstein had in mind. Doing this will require not only putting things in their place but appreciating how the mess got there.

I recognize the need also for some Aristotelian taxonomy and Rylean logical geography. In this vein I will suggest that many of the problems of reference can be solved if we heed certain fundamental distinctions. Many of them are familiar but have been neglected or at least not fully appreciated. Even when the confusion resulting from their neglect is more terminological than substantive (in philosophy these are often not readily distinguishable), clarifying our terms will help us locate the problems. As I see them, the problems of reference fall into three main domains: semantics, pragmatics, and epistemology. I believe that many (certainly not all) have eluded solution largely because they have not been put in their proper place. For example, the main problems concerning names have been placed erroneously in the area of semantics and, as I see them, belong partly to epistemology and partly to pragmatics. Knowing where they belong will help us solve them.

I will be taking on certain currently influential theories, and my criticisms of them will depend heavily on the distinctions I draw. So it might seem that if these distinctions are as fundamental and familiar as I claim, I must be either misconstruing these theories or underestimating the force of the arguments behind them. Even an impartial observer might dismiss my criticisms outright, thinking that no proponent of a given theory could have been so silly as to leave it vulnerable to such an elementary objection. Well, I certainly do not take these philosophers for fools. Quite the contrary: the basic insights of philosophers like Evans, Strawson, Donnellan, and Kripke deserve considerable admiration—but not without qualification. For I believe that in many cases these insights, though not misguided, are misplaced. They are correct in their essentials, but not about what they purport to be about. I will explain what I mean in due course.

For now suffice it to say that gaining full benefit from the insights of these philosophers requires distinguishing different sorts of facts: facts about language, facts about language use, and facts about the thoughts of language users. To make these distinctions we will need to engage in plenty of conceptual house-cleaning or logical geography, call it what you will. In this regard I should make the following disclaimer. Although I will often be appealing to concrete examples, my claims (with a few exceptions) should not be construed as empirical. I am concerned primarily to demarcate the relevant empirical facts, not to discover and delineate them from the comfort of an armchair, and my occasional excursions into psychology or linguistics should be understood accordingly.

1. TWO KINDS OF REFERENCE

I embarked on this book with the idea of developing a theory of singular reference. But the more I thought about it, the less it struck me as suitable for a unitary theory. Recalling Wittgenstein's dictum quoted above, I came to see reference as a topic that cuts across familiar theoretical boundaries. I noticed its intimate ties to other notions, which in turn belong to diverse theoretical domains. These notions seemed to deserve consideration in their own right, and of course their connections with reference had to be explained. But important as these other notions seemed, there was something even more important, about reference itself, that had to be reckoned with.

Most philosophers recognize the fact, even if they merely pay it lip-service, that there are two different notions of reference, SPEAKER REFERENCE and LINGUISTIC REFERENCE.[1] These must be distinguished, because, after all, we can just as well say that a speaker uses a term to refer as that the term itself refers. Once distinguished, these two kinds of referring raise obvious questions. How are they related, both to each other and to other notions? Is one kind of referring to be explained in terms of the other? How is

---

[1] Here I am limiting myself to singular reference. That is what I will always mean by 'reference' unless otherwise indicated, as in our discussion later of plural reference.

speaker reference related to speaker meaning (communication) and how is linguistic reference related to linguistic meaning? In one form or another, these are questions that will present themselves again and again.

2. SEMANTICS AND PRAGMATICS

The difference between linguistic and speaker reference corresponds to the distinction between SEMANTICS and PRAGMATICS. What these theoretical domains are and how they differ has led to considerable confusion. Pragmatics, or the theory of language use,[2] is often regarded as the waste-bin for semantics: whatever does not belong to semantics goes into pragmatics. Having collaborated on an entire book on the subject (Bach and Harnish 1979), I view it in more positive terms, as the theory of communication (speaker meaning) and speech acts. As for semantics, we think of it as covering truth and reference as well as (or instead of, for Quinean semantic sceptics) meaning and synonymy. Indeed, meaning is peripheral to most approaches in formal semantics, including truth theory (*à la* Tarski) and model-theoretic and possible-worlds semantics, all of whose primary goal is to give a systematic account of entailment in terms of notions like 'true/refers under an interpretation'. Whether or not truth and reference are the semantic properties of choice for a given theory, for all semantic theories they are properties that belong to linguistic expressions. Unfortunately, many philosophers seem to regard truth and reference as semantic no matter what they are properties of. One finds them speaking of truth (or falsity) as a semantic property of utterances and of beliefs, not just of sentences. This would be harmlessly misleading but for the suggestion that the domain of the discipline of semantics includes utterances and even beliefs.

It is important to resist this suggestion, and to do this we might recall the goal of grammar (syntax-cum-semantics) in linguistics. This goal is systematically to specify 'what every speaker knows',[3]

---

[2] Adding to the confusion is that for Montague (1974) and his followers, 'pragmatics' is the word for indexical semantics, but that is not what is generally meant by the term and certainly not what I will mean by it.

[3] This is an idealization, since no speaker has full command of the language.

that is, to characterize speakers' ability to distinguish sentences of the language from non-sentences and to understand them. Simply put, the grammar must specify the relation between form and meaning. Put more abstractly, its goal is to specify the sentences of the language in some recursive fashion, by way of a function mapping sentences, as specified by their syntactic structure and lexical content, on to meanings. Without getting into the many controversies surrounding the precise nature and goal of the linguistic enterprise, I think it is safe to say that for linguists the semantics of an expression gives the information that a competent speaker can glean from it independently of any context of utterance. Whenever he hears a particular utterance of it in a given context, he uses this information, in tandem with specific information available in the context, to understand the speaker's communicative intent.

That this information is independent of contexts of utterance is a consequence of the fact that grammar, semantics in particular, is concerned with linguistic types, not tokens. If a token of an expression carries any information not encoded by the type of which it is a token, that information is not *linguistic* information, hence not semantic. So to the extent that such non-linguistic information is relevant to the truth of a sentence token and/or to the reference of a token of a singular term, truth and reference, as properties of tokens, are not semantic properties, at least not in the linguistic sense. If someone utters sentence type (1), for example,

> The president of France is bald. (1)

the token of (1) being produced is true in virtue of (1)'s being true, and the token of 'the president of France' refers to whatever the type refers to. If, however, (2) is uttered,

> The king of France is bald. (2)

and 'the king of France' is being used non-literally to refer to Mitterand, then whereas the sentence type is not true and the description does not refer, we could still regard the token of (2) as true and the token of 'the king of France' as referring to Mitterand, but these would not be semantic properties of those tokens. Similar points would apply to an utterance of (3), (3)

> He is bald.

except that even if there were a king of France and 'he' were being used to refer to him, as a type (3), unlike (2), would have no truth value, and as a type 'he', unlike 'the king of France', would still not refer. Thus I say that, in the strict sense relevant to linguistic semantics, such properties as truth and reference are semantic properties only as properties of expression types. Only when a token inherits from its type the property of being true or of referring to a certain individual is this a *semantic* property of the token, though even then it belongs to the token only derivatively, by inheritance from the type of which it is a token.

Although much of what goes by the name 'philosophical semantics' concerns tokens (or utterances), the province of semantics is linguistic types only. Utterances are the acts of producing tokens of those types and belong to the domain of pragmatics. The job of pragmatics is to reckon with the fact that the properties of these tokens depend on much more than the properties of their types. In speech act theory, a central part of pragmatics, it is well known that utterances of complete sentences can be described at different levels, as locutionary, illocutionary, or perlocutionary acts (Austin 1962). Acts of referring, of using expressions to refer one's audience to certain individuals, are components of speech acts, specifically of illocutionary acts. When the illocutionary act is a statement, a prediction, or any other 'constative' act (Bach and Harnish 1979, 42–46), it can be true or false, but since the meaning of a sentence generally does not determine the content of the illocutionary act performed in uttering it, truth or falsity should not be regarded here as a semantic property. An analogous point applies to reference in connection with singular terms and their use to refer: linguistic reference belongs to semantics and speaker reference to pragmatics.

3. THOUGHTS, WORDS, AND THINGS

Failing to distinguish speaker reference from linguistic reference (or, correlatively, pragmatics from semantics) inevitably leads to theoretical confusion. Matters become further confused when philosophers take up the question of what it is to think of an object (singular thought), and describe it, as some do, as 'mental' reference.[4] In thinking of something, surely one is not 'referring'

---

[4] This last usage, though rare, is symptomatic of something more common, a confusion that goes beyond terminology. This is the supposition that the problem of

an audience to it, nor, for that matter, is one referring oneself to it. At least it can be said that the misnomer 'mental reference' serves to provoke an important question to add to our earlier question about the connection of speaker reference to linguistic reference: what is the connection between a speaker's thinking of something and referring to it?

When we think and speak about the world around us, we commonly form and express thoughts about particular items in it. First and foremost, these are the persons, places, and things we encounter in perception. Then there are the ones we have perceived before and now recall, as well as those we are told of by others. Perhaps this is a platitude, but without singular thoughts and our ability to express them, all our thought and talk about the world could only be qualitative. We could think and speak only of its character, of what it is like, but we could not think or speak of anything in particular.

The problems of singular thought and reference have drawn a great deal of attention in recent philosophy. Not only do they bear on a wide range of issues, which cut across philosophy of mind and of language, epistemology, and even metaphysics, they have provoked considerable controversy and have inspired numerous competing theories. Commonly addressed by the title DE RE BELIEF, singular thought strikes some as a mystery and others as a myth. Does thinking of something involve a distinctively intimate cognitive relation ('rapport' is one word that has been used for it) of subject to object, or can it be given a descriptive treatment and thereby be reduced to so-called DE DICTO BELIEF? As for singular reference, especially where proper names are involved, there is a similar opposition, although the position on one extreme currently enjoys more favour. The fashionable one is the 'CAUSAL THEORY OF REFERENCE' (really a family of theories), according to which reference, at least when the singular term being used is a name, is a direct relation between word and object, unmediated by a concept (its would-be sense). According to traditional theories like Frege's, every such expression possesses a sense (or meaning), which it has whether or not it refers and in virtue of which it refers when it does refer.

singular thought and the problem of the occurrence of singular terms in belief contexts are merely two versions of the same problem. Why this is not so will be explained in Chapter 1.

Even its champions realize that the causal theory, because it denies names Fregean treatment, has trouble explaining the role of names in existence, identity, and belief contexts. Traditional theories are free from this problem, but, as their critics keep reminding us, the descriptions these theories associate with names are too rich in their contents to be plausible candidates for senses of names. Take any description putatively equivalent to the name of a given individual, and one can easily see that it is not necessary (sometimes not even true) that the description be satisfied by this individual.

So on the topics both of singular thought and of singular reference, there has been a continual conflict between descriptive and non-descriptive theories (never mind the internal squabbles within each camp). Each type of theory has its attractions and its drawbacks, though sometimes these are not acknowledged equally. Indeed, some philosophers seem to think that the way to resolve the conflict, whether on thought or reference, is to adopt the theory whose merits outweigh its difficulties. But surely resolving a conflict between theories is not like resolving indecision. It is not like trying to decide whether, for example, to go from New York to Boston by plane or by train. Besides, perhaps there is a middle road (one can also drive to Boston), though the simplistic labels 'descriptive' and 'non-descriptive' obscure this possibility. Whatever the choice, paving the way will require steering clear of certain terminological obstacles, such as the one already encountered with the word 'reference'. We will begin with the problem of singular thought.

PART ONE

SINGULAR THOUGHT

1

The Nature of *de re* Thought

When we perceive something, we can think about it in a fundamentally different way than if we thought of it merely by description. To think of something by description is just to think of whatever happens to have the properties expressed by the description. But to perceive something is to be in a real relation to it, to be in a position to think of that object in particular, no matter what its properties. While attending to it, somehow (I hope to explain just how) we can think of it as 'that', not merely, under some individual concept, as 'the F'. Our thoughts about it are not DESCRIPTIVE[1] but *DE RE*.

Thoughts about objects of perception make up the basic but not the only kind of *de re* thought.[2] We can have *de re* thoughts also about things we have perceived before and now remember and even about things others have perceived and have informed us of. Still, any object of *de re* thought must be or have been an object of perception, if not one's own then someone else's. Of course this does not apply to *de re* thoughts about oneself or about abstract objects, but these will not be taken up here. My theory is intended to apply only to *de re* thoughts about concrete individuals other than oneself. I will first schematize the general form of *de re* thought and then characterize the *de re* representations and relations associated with each of the three kinds of *de re* thought: perception-based, memory-based, and communication-based. I know all three have been recognized by others, but I believe that my view is different, and not just in detail. Accordingly, I will indicate how it differs from various other conceptions. One theme that will gradually emerge here will prove relevant to our inquiry later into the theory of singular reference: the main insights that underlie the

---

[1] I prefer the term 'descriptive' over the usual '*de dicto*', which misleadingly suggests that descriptive thoughts are about sentences (*dicta*).

[2] I intend the phrase '*de re* thought' to apply not just to (occurrent) *de re* beliefs but to *de re* attitudes of any kind, though my examples will mainly be beliefs. Also, *de re* thoughts include occurrences too fleeting to qualify as attitudes at all.

causal theory of names properly belong to the theory of singular thought.

1. CHARACTERIZING *DE RE* THOUGHT

If you could not have *de re* thoughts about things in the world, you could think of them only by description, each merely as something of a certain sort. If *all* your thoughts about things could only be descriptive, your total conception of the world would be merely qualitative. You would never be related in thought to anything in particular. Thinking of something would never be a case of having it 'in mind', as we say colloquially, or as some philosophers have said, of being *'en rapport'*, in 'cognitive contact', or 'epistemically intimate' with it. But picturesque phrases aside, just what is this special relation? Whatever it is, it is different from that involved in thinking of something under a description. If we can even speak of a relation in the latter case, it is surely not a real (or natural) relation. Since the object of a descriptive thought is determined SATISFACTIONALLY, the fact that the thought is of that object does not require any connection between thought and object. However, the object of a *de re* thought is determined RELATIONALLY. For something to be the object of a *de re* thought, it must stand in a certain kind of relation to that very thought.

The relation that makes something the object of a *de re* thought is a causal relation, of a special kind to be explained in due course. We do not need to know its precise nature to appreciate the crucial fact that, being causal, it can connect objects with thought *tokens* only, not with thought *types*. Abstract entities simply cannot enter into causal relations. This fact has the important consequence that different tokens of the same type can have different objects, hence different truth conditions. Of course this cannot be true if types of *de re* thoughts are individuated in part by their objects, but I will defend the view that they can (and should) be individuated narrowly, without mention of their objects.[3] The idea is that a type of *de re* thought consists in a way of thinking of an object, together with a way of thinking of a property.[4] When I am claiming, then, is that a

[3] For the distinction between narrow and wide content and the corresponding ways of individuating types of thoughts, see Fodor (1980) or McGinn (1982).

[4] This is for the monadic case, but obviously the same idea can be extended to individuating *de re* thoughts about *n* objects in an *n*-ary relation. For simplicity, in

way of thinking of an object does not determine the object of a thought token. In other words, if we call (following Frege) a way of thinking of something its MODE OF PRESENTATION, the object is not determined by its mode of presentation alone.

De re modes of presentation function as mental indexicals. They determine the contextual relation that something must bear to a thought to be the object of that very thought. And as McGinn so aptly puts it, the object 'is determined by the occurrence of a representation *in* a context, not by way of a representation *of* the context' (1982, 209). As we will see, the way in which the object is thus determined is remarkably similar to the way in which, according to proponents of the so-called causal theory of reference, the referents of proper names are determined.

Since *de re* modes of presentation function as indexicals, the thoughts in which they occur are not propositional. All I mean by this (I am making no assumptions about the ontological status of propositions) is that they do not have context-independent truth conditions. As Burge (1977) first pointed out, they must be contextually related to an object for a truth condition to be determined. That is, there is nothing internal to a non-descriptive, *de re* thought that makes it about some object in particular. There is no kind of thought symbol, as Burge says, that must designate a certain object and no other. The same thought symbol can pick out different objects in different contexts.[5]

2. WHAT *DE RE* THOUGHT IS NOT

Before spelling out my conception of *de re* thought, I will try to motivate it further by way of dispelling some common misconceptions. Since I have discussed them in some detail before

this chapter I will stick to the monadic case. Also, I will not take up the subject of predicative contents of thoughts, of what it is to employ a concept of a property (or a relation).

[5] If I may wax metaphysical, there is no such thing as a representation (linguistic or mental) of an object's essence, particularity, or haecceity (to use some old terms enjoying undeserved revivals). There is nothing internal to a *de re* thought about an object that makes the thought about *that* object. There is no way to capture in thought the 'particularity' of an object, for as far as the content of the thought is concerned, the thought could just as well have been about a different object, had a different object been in its place.

(Bach 1982), here my description of them and their defects will be brief.

(*a*) Intuitively, thinking of an object *de re* is having it 'in mind', which if construed literally is a rather more intimate relation than the one I am suggesting. Then it can only mean that the object itself is a constituent of the thought. This is reminiscent of Russell, who held that the basic constituents of propositions must be objects of acquaintance, in his special sense. The trouble is that for Russell physical objects do not qualify, and the only particulars that can be constituents of one's thoughts are oneself (at least as Russell sometimes held) and one's sense data.

(*b*) However, we do not have to take 'having an object in mind' literally. It can be taken merely to suggest the familiar idea that the content of a *de re* thought is a singular proposition, as expressed by a sentence of the form '*a* is G'. Here '*a*' is an individual constant of standard first-order logic, what Russell called a 'logically proper name', whose sole semantic role is to introduce an object into a proposition. If it fails to denote, any sentence containing it fails to express a proposition.[6] The trouble with the view that the complete content of a *de re* thought is a singular proposition is that it violates what Schiffer calls Frege's Constraint (1978, 180).[7] It fails to account for the fact that one can think contradictory things of the same object without being guilty of logical inconsistency—one can think of the same object in different ways, under distinct modes of presentation. For example, you might think that a vegetable you see is clean and that one you smell is filthy without realizing that the one you are looking at is the one you are smelling. In general, without inconsistency you can think of *a* under m_1 and take it to be

6 As Russell showed, his 'denoting phrases' do not have this feature. If we replace '*a*' with a definite description, the resulting sentence, of the form 'The F is G', expresses a proposition even if nothing fits the description. Since 'the F' introduces not an individual but an individual concept into the proposition, this is not a singular but a general proposition.

7 It is similar to what Evans calls the Intuitive Criterion of Difference (1982, 18 ff.). I should note here that Evans's view of *de re* thought, though observant of Frege's constraint, does have the feature that the object enters into the type individuation of the thought. Whereas for me modes of presentation are individuated independently of the objects they present, Evans's 'modes of identification' are not, as we will see when we take up his view later.

As for Schiffer, not only does he reject the singular proposition view of *de re* thought, he claims that the only way one can think of an object (other than oneself) is under a description, hence that one can have 'irreducibly' *de re* thoughts only about oneself (and the present moment).

F while thinking of a under m_2 and taking it to be not-F, provided you are ignorant of the fact that $m_1 = m_2$. As Schiffer points out, since the singular proposition theory provides no place for modes of presentation, it can represent what you think only as the blatantly inconsistent 'a is F' and 'a is not F' and what you are ignorant of as '$a = a$'. It neglects the fact that for an object to be thought of at all it must be thought of in some way or another, and that a physical object can be thought of in various ways.[8]

(c) Then there is the idea that *de re* thoughts, unlike descriptive ones, are essentially about their objects. Though true in one respect, it does not qualify as an adequate conception of *de re* thought since, as is typical with essentialist claims, it is false in another respect. It is true of *de re* thought tokens since the object enters into the token's truth condition. However, it is not true of *de re* thought types, since different tokens of the same type can have different objects. In so far as *de re* thought tokens are type-individuated by their narrow contents, as they should be for psychological purposes, they are not essentially of their objects. Their narrow contents do not fix their truth conditions (wide contents). From a semantic standpoint, of course, they can be individuated by their truth conditions, and in this respect they are essentially about their objects.[9] True though that is, it doesn't help us with the problem of characterizing their contents and of explaining how their objects are determined.

(d) Sometimes it is suggested that having a *de re* thought about an object is to be in some special cognitive relation to it. This is not as intimate a relation as acquaintance in Russell's sense, but it is

[8] This suggests a corollary to Russell's view, noted earlier, that physical objects do not qualify as objects of acquaintance. Since a physical object can be thought of in different ways, these ways of thinking of it cannot be expressed by logically proper names for it. For if one thing has two names, the same proposition is expressed no matter which name is used (1919, 175).

[9] Distinguishing psychologically from semantically motivated ways of individuating types of beliefs provides a ready reply to Stich's (1978) and Perry's (1979) denial that belief is a properly psychological notion. They both rely on the arbitrary assumption that beliefs are or ought to be type-individuated by truth conditions only. However, like anything else beliefs can be type-individuated in different ways for different purposes. Rather than conclude that for the purposes of explanation and prediction psychology does not need belief, Stich and Perry ought to have concluded that psychology should individuate types of beliefs in a way suitable to these purposes, namely by narrow contents. People's behaviour is intelligible only if we understand how they represent the world and particular things in it. How they do that consists in the narrow contents of their beliefs and other attitudes, not in objects of these attitudes.

cosy enough to have been called such things as 'rapport' (Kaplan 1968), 'direct cognitive contact' (Kim 1977), and 'epistemic intimacy' (Chisholm 1980). Chisholm and Pollock (1980) have each offered what they take to be necessary and sufficient conditions for thinking of an object in what Pollock calls a '*de re* way'. According to Pollock (1980, 492–3), for example, one has epistemic contact with a unique object of a certain sort just in case one believes there to be an object of that sort and one's reason for the belief is 'logically good' and 'non-defective' (Pollock defines these technical terms). According to another epistemic conception that some have found attractive (I have seen no precise formulation), to think *de re* of something is to think of it in such a way that one can identify it. I cannot go into the details of these or other epistemic approaches, but a simple example will show why they are on the wrong track.

Suppose you see a tomato and take it to be red. Later you look back at the same spot, again see a tomato, and take it to be red. Unbeknownst to you, however, it is not the same one. Your two thoughts, being of the same psychological type, have the same (narrow) content but not the same objects (even if you believe that they do).[10] Still, they are paradigmatic cases of *de re* thoughts. However, they do not meet the requirements of any version of the epistemic approach to *de re* thought. For example, contrary to the last version mentioned above, one would be unable to distinguish the two objects. And Pollock's version imposes the further requirement, also unnecessary, that one have beliefs about the (unique) kind of object involved. All in all, the requirements of the epistemic approach are too strong.

(*e*) Perhaps the most widespread misconception is that *de re* thoughts are what *de re* ascriptions ascribe, while *de dicto* (descriptive) thoughts are what *de dicto* ascriptions ascribe. This misconception comes in two forms, that 'believes-that' locutions can be used literally only to ascribe *de dicto* beliefs, while 'believes-of' (or 'believes-to-be') locutions can be used literally only to ascribe *de re* beliefs, and that whether a singular term in the 'that'-clause of an ascription occurs opaquely or transparently determines whether the belief being ascribed is *de dicto* or *de re*.

---

[10] Of course if you believe the tomato you are now looking at is the one you saw before, you may make false inferences, such as that it mysteriously changed shape.

It is easy to show (Bach 1982, 129–31) that these distinctions in belief ascriptions do not reflect the *de re/de dicto* distinction in beliefs ascribed. An ascriber can use a singular term (in subject position of a 'that'-clause) either to express an element in the content of the ascribed belief, i.e. how the believer is thinking of an object, *or* to express how he the ascriber is thinking of the object. And the belief can just as well be *de re* as *de dicto*. Similarly, using a singular term opaquely in a 'believes-that' ascription does not imply that the belief being ascribed is *de dicto*. Its occurring opaquely means only that the ascriber is not using it to refer. Even then, he need not be using it to exhibit an element of the content of the thought being ascribed. He could be using it to express a concept (that he takes to be) coextensive with that element. And even if the singular term occurs transparently, the thought being ascribed could still be *de dicto*. The ascriber could be using the singular term to refer to the object of a *de dicto* thought, whose content he is not fully specifying.

In short, different forms of belief ascription do not mark differences in kind of belief. Neither the grammatical form of a belief sentence nor how a singular term occurs in it determines the kind of belief ascribed. So it is a mistake to suppose, as Searle does for example, that the distinction between *de re* and *de dicto* belief is an illusion arising 'from a confusion between reports of beliefs and features of the beliefs being reported' (1979, 157). Rather, we must be careful to distinguish *de-re*-belief ascriptions from *de re* belief-ascriptions and *de-dicto*-belief ascriptions from *de dicto* belief-ascriptions.

3. THE FORM OF *DE RE* THOUGHT

Recognizing the indexical character of *de re* thoughts, Burge suggests we represent them with predicates or open sentences. '*De re* locutions are about predication broadly conceived. They describe a relation between open sentences (or what they express) and objects.' (1977, 343) However, as Burge then points out, there is more than one kind of *de re* relation, and a representation giving only the predicative content does not specify how that content is being applied to an object. If a *de re* locution is to give the complete content of a *de re* thought, it must specify the element of content that determines the relevant relation. Otherwise, there would be no difference in content between, for example, believing of a certain object you are looking at that it is G and believing of a certain object you are recalling, which happens to be the same object, that it is G. Accordingly, the complete content of a *de re* thought cannot be expressed simply by a predicate or an open sentence. Its content must also include an indexical element expressing the mode of presentation determining the relation which, in the context of thought, determines the object (if any) the thought is about. So, letting t be the time of the belief and R be the relation, as determined by m_R, that contextually fixes the object of the belief, the natural way to specify the belief is by 's believes (at t) under m_R that x is G.' For simplicity I am assuming a present-tensed belief content ('is G'), but allowances could easily be made here and in (DR) below for past-tensed ('was G'), future-tensed ('will be G'), and time-indexed ('is G at t_0') belief contents. The object of a *de re* belief need not still exist at the time of the belief, but of course such a belief cannot be of something that does not yet exist.

A *de re* belief is true iff there is (was) a unique object fixed by R and this object is (was/will be) G. Its truth condition can be expressed in Russellian style by (DR).[11]

At t, s's belief under m_R that x is G is true iff
$$(\mathrm{E}x)(Rx[m_R s] \ \& \ (y)(\text{if } Ry[m_R s] \text{ then } y = x) \ \& \ Gx), \qquad \text{(DR)}$$
or, in a more perspicuous form, which will be applied later,

At t, s's belief under m_R that x is G is true iff
$$G(\text{the } x \text{ such that } Rx[m_R s]). \qquad \text{(DR)}$$

(DR) does *not* imply that in order for s to have this belief, the belief must have an object. Quite the contrary, it allows for the possibility that s could have had just that belief without thinking of any object. Equally, if the belief does have an object, (DR) allows for the possibility that it could have had a different object, had something else been the unique object bearing R to the belief token. (DR) specifies the object descriptively, but of course that is not how the object (if any) is represented by s. Something is the object of s's

---

[11] For simplicity (but, as they say, without loss of generality) I am sticking to one-place predicates and to *de re* beliefs about one object. (DR) could be suitably elaborated to cover *de re* thoughts about more than one object, as when you believe of two objects you are looking at that one is larger than the other.

belief not by being represented in *s*'s belief token by an individual concept but by actually bearing R to that very belief token.

In this way, then, (DR) captures the fact that *de re* thoughts are indexical. '*x* is G' is the open sentence that Burge took to express the full content of such a thought, while 'm_R' represents the mode of presentation that determines the relation in which the token of that mode of presentation must stand to an object such that this object is the object of *s*'s thought token.[12]

4. *DE RE* REPRESENTATIONS AND RELATIONS

Now I will distinguish the various types of *de re* representations and the *de re* causal relations they determine. If we can have *de re* thoughts about objects we are presently perceiving, objects we have perceived before, and objects we have been informed of,[13] for each kind of thought there should be a specific *de re* relation. For the purpose of formulating a specific version of (DR) for each, along with a recursive definition of the *of* relation, in this section I will merely sketch my accounts of each. I have stated my account of the first previously (Bach 1982), and so I will go into detail later (in Chapter 2) only on the second and third cases.

[12] Here I should mention a recent argument of Searle's against 'irreducibly' *de re* beliefs, on the grounds that their 'contents are sufficient to determine the entire sets of conditions of satisfaction . . . not by setting purely general conditions, but rather by indicating relations in which the rest of the conditions of satisfaction must stand to the Intentional state or event itself.' (1983, 213–14) Searle's view sounds so similar to mine that at first I thought we differed only in his unwillingness to call beliefs '*de re*' because they contain modes of presentation of their objects rather than the objects themselves. Obviously I agree that 'a change in the world would [not] necessarily mean a change in the [content of a] belief', but I would qualify his claim that 'all of our beliefs consist entirely in an Intentional content' (1983, 214). For as (DR) makes explicit, the narrow content of a *de re* belief does not determine its truth condition. Searle holds that it does, evidently because the content represents the 'relation in which the rest of the conditions of satisfaction must stand to the Intentional state or even itself' and is thereby 'self-referential'. I agree that the condition of satisfaction (truth condition) refers to the state itself, but I deny that this condition of satisfaction is represented in the state. That is why I claim, contrary to Searle, that the object of such a belief is determined relationally, not satisfaction-ally. So far as I can tell, this is the main difference between my view and his. But it is a big one.

[13] Burge (1977), Beebe (1979), and Evans (1982) accept all three, but as we will see in Section 2 of the next chapter, the third case can seem dubious, even to those not generally sceptical of *de re* thought about external objects.

Perception

Beliefs about objects being perceived are the paradigm case of *de re* belief, and yet even they, like *de re* beliefs generally, can fail to have objects, as in realistic hallucinations. Accordingly, we should describe their contents so as to allow that a person could be in the same belief state whether or not he was actually perceiving a physical object.[14] Without committing ourselves to any particular philosophical theory of perception, we can do this by applying Chisholm's 'adverbial' method (1957), whereby types of perceptual states are individuated by the way in which the perceiver is 'appeared to'.[15] Let us call these contents of perceptual states PERCEPTS, which for our purposes should be limited to ways in which individual physical objects can appear. With the schema 's is appeared$_k$ to f-ly' we can represent a person's being in a certain type of perceptual state, as determined by the kind k of percept (its sense modality) and the value of 'f',[16] and abbreviate the whole schema by '$A_k fs$'.

This schema applies equally to perceptions of physical objects and to realistic hallucinations. If the content of a perceptual state, the percept, is represented by '$A_k fs$', we can represent the state of affairs in which a physical object x actually appears$_k$ f to s as '$Cx(A_k fs)$', where 'C' means, roughly, 'causes in the way appropriate to perception'. Explaining what *that* means would be tantamount to formulating a causal theory of perception which satisfactorily handles the notorious problem of deviant causal chains, but not knowing the solution I can only assume the causal theory to be correct in principle.[17] With that understood, for

[14] As Descartes let us never forget, you cannot tell merely from having a perceptual experience that you are not hallucinating: any perception of a physical object can be matched by a qualitatively indistinguishable hallucination. This may or may not lead to scepticism, but here we are concerned with the content of perception-based beliefs, not their justification.

[15] The adverbial *method* does not commit us to Chisholm's adverbial *analysis*. It is compatible with such other ontological analyses of perception as sense-data theories, whether representative (causal) or phenomenalist, and direct realist theories, be they act-object or adverbial. The adverbial analysis may make the least ontological commitment, but that does not make it right (the claim that nothing exists is ontologically parsimonious).

[16] We need not limit the range of 'f' to purely sensible qualities, as the classical empiricists would have insisted, but can let it include properties like being waxen, rotten, or tomato-ish. There seems to be no definite psychological limit on the complexity of values of 'f'.

[17] I cannot take seriously the objection to my view based merely on the absence to

convenience I will paraphrase 'C' simply as 'causes'. Then '$Cx(A_kfs)$' says 'x causes s to be appeared$_k$ to f-ly', or 'x appears$_k$ (looks, feels, etc.) f to s'. Along the lines of (DR) above, the truth condition of s's belief of the object that appears$_k$ to him that it is G may be represented as (PB).

> At t, s's belief under A_kf that x is G is true iff $\qquad$ (PB)
> G(the x such that $Cx[A_kfs]$).

(PB) makes clear that a perceptual or other PERCEPTION-BASED belief[18] can be true or false of something only if s is perceiving it, but that s can be in his belief state without even perceiving anything. That is, specifying the perceptual and conceptual contents of s's belief is enough to identify the type of belief state he is in. It is possible for there to be nothing that he is believing to be G, because the content of the belief is not a singular proposition. Indeed its content is not a proposition at all, since its perceptual component functions as a mental indexical.

To appreciate (PB) contrast it with its descriptive counterpart, formerly endorsed by Schiffer (1978), according to which the narrow content of a perception-based belief is the same as its truth condition, G(the x such that $Cx[A_kfs]$). The trouble with this view is that to believe something of an object one is perceiving does not require thinking of it under any description—the object is already singled out perceptually. By suggesting that there must be an individual concept, formed from the percept, that determines (satisfactionally) the object of belief, the descriptive view gets things backwards.[19] For by having the percept, the perceiver is already in a position (assuming the percept is appropriately caused by the object) to form beliefs about the object, which is determined relationally. Percepts function in belief as mental indexicals, and the object of a percept token is whatever bears C to it. To be the object of a perception-based belief, an object need not be represented as being in that relation; it need merely be in that relation.

date of an adequate formulation of the causal theory of perception, but I would take seriously any plausible in-principle objection or alternative to the causal theory. In any case, I think something like Peacocke's (1979) notion of differential explanation could well lead to an adequate formulation.

[18] It should be noted that what I am calling 'perception-based' beliefs are not limited to perceptual beliefs proper, whose predicative contents (schematized by 'G') are formed solely as the result of how the object of perception appears. There is no limit to the predicative contents of perception-based beliefs.

[19] For further discussion see Bach (1982, 139–43) and Evans (1982, 173 n.).

How does (PB) deal with problem cases, such as believing contradictory things about the same object but without being irrational? Suppose s is perceiving an object twice at the same time but does not realize this. He might be feeling it as well as seeing it; he might be seeing it straight on and in a mirror; he might be 'seeing double'. Suppose he is perceiving it in the same modality but that it appears in two distinct ways f and f'. Then, according to (PB), s believes of the x such that $Cx(A_k fs)$ that it is G and of the y such that $Cy(A_k f's)$ that it is not G. (PB) does not imply or even suggest that s believes that $x = y$. He might have no belief about the identity or even disbelieve it. In any case, so long as s is ignorant of the identity, it is not irrational of him to believe of what in fact is one and the same object that it is G and that it is not G.

Now recall the example in which you see a tomato and take it to be red, later see a tomato in the same spot and take it to be red, but fail to realize that it is not the same one. Then s believes at t_1 of the x such that $Cx(A_k fs)$ that it is G (red) and at t_2 of the y such that $Cy(A_k fs)$ that it is G (red). The first belief is true iff at t_1 G(the x such that $Cx[A_k fs]$), and the second belief is true iff at t_2 G(the y such that $Cy[A_k fs]$). The (narrow) contents of the two beliefs are the same, and the difference in their truth conditions is due entirely to the different times of the beliefs. And because there is no implication as to the identity or distinctness of the objects being perceived, the first belief could be true of one object and the second false of another without s being any the wiser.

A perception-based belief is about an object without being about the identity of its object, but of course we may have beliefs about the latter as well. Otherwise, since perception-based beliefs are as short-lived as the perceptual states they involve, their contents could not be integrated into our system of beliefs. That requires conceptualizing or in some other way transforming their perceptual contents so that the information they provide can be retained beyond the context of perception.[20] However, if we are to maintain over time a coherent model of things in the world, we must be able to form beliefs about objects we have previously encountered in

[20] I believe that Schiffer's argument against irreducibly *de re* thought about objects of perception (1978, 194–6) depends on a conflation of perceptual beliefs with their conceptualization. And even if he is right in maintaining that our *knowledge* of such objects can only be under (indexical) descriptions, like 'the tomato I am now looking at', it does not follow that our *thoughts* of them can only be under such descriptions.

perception. Although I have rejected the descriptive theory of perception-based belief, I recognize that descriptive beliefs, namely those cited by this theory, can play a role here, since they are beliefs about objects represented *as* objects of current perception. Also, such beliefs can be updated and thereby represent things as objects of past perceptions. However, we can also have *de re* beliefs about objects we have perceived before, in so far as we can *remember* them.

Memory

Without either endorsing or proposing a theory of what it is to remember an object, I will simply make three assumptions about this, I hope safely.[21] First, we can remember an object only if we have perceived it before. For example, I remember my father Karl Bach but not the composer Karl P. E. Bach. I remember *that* the composer was the second surviving son of J. S. Bach, but I don't remember *him*. Next, to misremember something is still to remember *it*. What makes a memory a (mis-) representation of a certain object is that it is a TRACE of a perception of that object. Finally, remembering something often consists in but does not require having (or being able to have) an image of it. Instead, we can conceptualize how it appeared. Either way, however, the object remembered is the object whose perception led causally to the memory, not necessarily the one that best fits the memory. A MEMORY-BASED[22] belief can derive either from a perception-based belief (though perhaps with not the same predicative content) or from a mere perception. After all, even if one formed no beliefs about the object when originally perceiving it, one could still form beliefs about it upon remembering it. And as we will see in the next chapter, any beliefs you might form about the identity of the object of a memory-based belief have no bearing on which object that belief is about—but they can readily lead to false inferences about that object.

The truth-conditional schema for memory-based *de re* belief parallels the one for perception-based belief (PB):

At t, s's belief under $W_k f$ that x is G is true iff
$$G(\text{the } x \text{ such that } Mx[W_k fs]). \qquad \text{(MB)}$$

---

[21] They recall Martin and Deutscher's (1966) well-known causal account.

[22] Just as not all perception-based beliefs are perceptual beliefs, so not all memory-based beliefs are memories-that. But they all must contain memories-*of* (their objects).

'M' stands for the relation *causes in the way appropriate to memory*[23] (the converse of the relation *being a memory of*), and '$W_k f$' schematizes a way of having been appeared$_k$ to, i.e. a memory mode of presentation. Thus '$Mx[W_k fs]$' abbreviates '*s* remembers *x* having appeared$_k f$'.

I am supposing that *being a memory of* is a causal relation between memory tokens and objects of past perception. I may have suggested that this relation is the relative product of the relation *being a trace of*, which we took to be between memory tokens and prior percept tokens, and *being a percept of*, holding between percept tokens and objects of perception, but surely *being a trace of* can just as well hold between two memory tokens. In general, then, a memory token of an object is a trace of a memory token which . . . is a trace of a memory token which is a trace of a percept token of the object. So letting 'T' represent *being a trace of*, 'P' *being a percept of*, 'O' the *of* relation, and '*m*' and '*m'*' modes of presentation, we can recursively define the *of* relation for memories:

$$(m)(\text{if } mPx, \text{ then } mOx), \text{ and}$$
$$(m')(m)(\text{if } m'Tm \text{ and } mOx, \text{ then } m'Ox). \tag{OF$_M$}$$

This recursive definition will be generalized later to cover the case of communication.

Communication

We can have *de re* thoughts not only about things we perceive or remember but also about things of which we have been informed. If a speaker refers to something by name and expresses a *de re* thought about it, he thereby puts his audience, who may have never perceived it, in a position to form *de re* thoughts about it himself. If the hearer is in that position already, either because he has perceived and not forgotten it or because he knows it by some other name, at least the speaker is putting him in the position of thinking of it under a new *de re* mode of presentation. In any event, to understand the speaker fully the audience must think of the referent in the same way as the speaker.[24]

---

[23] Obviously I am assuming, as I did earlier in regard to the causal theory of perception, that the causal theory of memory is correct in principle, though it too awaits a formulation that solves the problem of deviant causal chains.

[24] When indexicals, demonstratives, or descriptions containing them are used,

When the audience has no independent *de re* way to think of the referent (call this the 'pure' case), the speaker must use a name[25] to succeed in expressing a *de re* attitude about it. The reason, as I will explain more fully in the next chapter, is that names make up the only kind of *de re* mode of presentation that a speaker can actually display to a hearer. You can *express* a percept or a memory but you cannot *display* one—you cannot produce a public token of a percept or a memory. In thinking of something by name, a speaker entertains a mental token of the name; in using it to refer, he produces a physical token of it; in hearing that token, the hearer forms a mental token of the same name. If instead of using a name the speaker used a definite description referentially, even if the hearer took the speaker to be expressing a *de re* thought[26] he could think of the referent only descriptively (at least in the pure case).

Again we can follow the pattern of (DR) to give truth conditions of COMMUNICATION-BASED *de re* thoughts. Letting '*n*' schematize a name (or any singular term used as a name) and 'H' represent the relation *having*, the converse of the *of* relation for names, we have:

At *t, s*'s belief under *n* that *x* is G is true iff
G(the *x* such that H*x*[*ns*]). (CB)

I can make (CB) clearer by extending our recursive definition of the *of* relation. Let us distinguish two relations, the relation *being dubbed* (D), between the object and the initial token of the name,[27] and the relation *being linked to* (L), between a token of the name and its immediate predecessor in the causal process. Ordinarily, an individual is dubbed while being perceived, but not always. It can be dubbed by virtue of still being remembered, and even if no longer remembered it can be given one name by virtue of already being thought of by some other name. In any case, a name can function as a *de re* mode of presentation only of something that has been perceived.[28] Tokens of a name can be linked inter- or

---

full understanding requires thinking of the referent only in the same kind of way. For allowances must be made for person (e.g. 'you' for 'I'), perspective ('there' for 'here'), etc.

[25] Or use a singular term 'as a name', in the sense of Chapter 2, Section 2.

[26] It is not necessary, as we will see in Chapter 5, for a thought expressed when one uses a description referentially to be *de re*.

[27] This label is convenient but strictly speaking it is a bit misleading, since it normally applies to a relation between an object and a name *type*.

[28] A name can be given to something known only by description but then it does not qualify as a *de re* mode of presentation of that object.

intrapersonally: L can hold between an uttered (or written) physical token and a mental token, or between two mental tokens. Now we can extend our recursive definition of the *of* relation. Let us restrict the '*m*'s to percepts and memories, and for clarity use '*n*' and '*n*' ' for tokens (physical or mental) of the same name and subscripts to indicate different names. With (R_M) repeated as the first two lines, we have a branching recursive definition:

(m)(if mPx, then mOx),
$(m')(m)$(if m'Tm and mOx, then m'Ox),
$(n)(m)$(if nDx by virtue of mOx, then nOx),
$(n_1)(n_2)$(if n_2Dx by virtue of n_1Ox, then n_2Ox), and
$(n')(n)$(if n'Ln and nOx, then n'Ox).   (OF)

I have not yet said what it is to think of something by name. In the next chapter, we will investigate the psychological role of names and of expressions used as names. We will also take a closer look at memory-based *de re* thoughts. So far we have seen that *de re* thoughts do not literally contain their objects, and their contents are not singular propositions in that or any other sense. Indeed, they are not propositional at all. For they include modes of presentation that function as mental indexicals, and different tokens of a mode of presentation of the same type can present different objects. The object of a *de re* thought is determined not satisfactionally but relationally, as the one standing in the appropriate causal relation to the very token of the mode of presentation contained in the thought. Which relation this is depends on the kind of mode of presentation, but whether it is a percept, a memory, or a name, one does not have to know what he is thinking of in order to be thinking of it.

2

Varieties of *de re* Thought

So far I have proposed a way of schematizing the general form of *de re* thought and have characterized the *de re* representations and relations associated with each of the three kinds of *de re* thought: perception-based, memory-based, and communication-based. In this chapter I will take up the last two cases in more detail. They are interesting in their own right and will also serve to clarify my account. Our discussion of them will include some concrete illustrations of why I believe that the insights underlying the causal theory of names properly belong to the theory of singular thought. At the end of the chapter, in order to highlight certain of the distinctive features of my view, I will compare it with the approach taken by Evans, which might seem at first glance to be similar. The underlying difference arises from the distinction between identifying an object and merely thinking of one, and I will argue that the identity of the object of a *de re* thought does not depend on one's belief about its identity.

1. MEMORY-BASED *DE RE* THOUGHTS

I remember very little about a certain boyhood friend of mine. I am pretty sure that his name was 'Dick Holloway', and I seem to recall that he lived about three doors down the block, that he and I were in the same third- or fourth-grade class, and that he believed the largest number in the world to be infinity twelve (how could I forget *that*?). These beliefs are about him not because they contain an individual concept that applies to him alone, a concept expressed by a description like 'my boyhood friend who thought the largest number to be infinity twelve'. For I *remember* Dick Holloway, and that is not a matter of thinking of him descriptively.

It might be suggested that if we construe individual concepts so broadly as to include images, then my beliefs about Dick Holloway *are* descriptive: I think of him as 'the boy who looked thus-and-so', where 'thus-and-so' expresses a certain way of looking.[1] My visual image of him may be dim and vague, but I am pretty sure I could pick him out of our class picture. I think I would recognize him if, somehow, I saw him unchanged from when I knew him, but I do not doubt that I could mistake many other boys for him. So his looking thus-and-so cannot be what makes the above beliefs about him. Even if my image matched him and him alone, only a causal connection would make it an image of him. Besides, he might not have looked the way I remember him as much as some other boy, but this would not make my beliefs about the other boy instead. So when I think of him under an image, his fitting that image (or a description verbalizing that image) is not what makes my beliefs about him. Rather, it is the fact that this memory image is causally connected in a certain way to how I perceived him. It is a *trace* of my percept of him.[2] Whatever the causal relation appropriate to memory is exactly, it explains the way in which an image can literally be a preservation in memory of a percept of a certain individual. Whatever the psychological story of how memories change over time, surely there must be some set of facts in virtue of which a certain one of my memory images, inaccurate though it may be, counts as the trace of my percept of Dick Holloway. Only thus can the image function in thought as a mode of presentation of *him*.

   To be a memory of some individual in particular, a memory need not include anything about the identity of its object (nor must one be able to 'place' that individual). Any beliefs I have about the identity of the object of the memory-based beliefs I take to be about a boy named 'Dick Holloway' have no bearing on who those

---

[1] Schiffer suggests a different description, 'the person your image is a memory of' (1978, 197), and proceeds to argue that your knowledge of the person must be under such a description rather than under the image itself (he seems to suppose that such a description is always available, even though it is clearly much too sophisticated for small children and for many larger people). Even if Schiffer is right to insist that having the description is necessary for knowledge of the person, nothing he says even suggests that you could not use the image itself merely to *think* of the person.

[2] Strictly speaking I should say 'percepts', since he did, after all, appear to me in many ways. But these ways of appearing were close enough (he didn't wear disguises, for example) that I could always recognize him. Thus it seems that my image of him then was an abstraction from those percepts (yes, there is the still unsolved problem of abstraction posed long ago by Berkeley), which though not identical were of a certain general type (I mean qualitative type, not the type *being of Dick Holloway*). So to be precise I should say that my image now is a trace of my image then, not of the various percepts, and that my image then was of him because it was an abstraction from percepts of him.

beliefs are about. So, for example, I believe that Dick Holloway was my only friend who said that the largest number in the world is infinity twelve, but this is not what makes my memory-based beliefs about Dick Holloway. For among those memory-based beliefs is the belief of someone I am thinking of under a certain memory image that *he* was Dick Holloway and that *he* was my only friend who said the largest number in the world is infinity twelve.

However, despite the fact that one can be ignorant or even mistaken about the identity of the object of a memory-based belief, identity beliefs are still important. For they enable these memory-based beliefs to be integrated with other beliefs inferentially. For example, I believe of Dick Holloway, whom I think of under an image, that he was Dick Holloway, that he was my boyhood chum who lived three doors down the block, that he was in my third- or fourth-grade class, and that he said the largest number is infinity twelve. I believe them all of the same individual, but without the appropriate identity beliefs I would fail to realize that. Now it might be objected, considering all the combinations of pairs of things I believe of Dick Holloway, that to ascribe the required number of identity beliefs is psychologically implausible. This would be so if they were all individually represented, but I do not mean to suggest that. Rather, these identity beliefs are jointly constituted by the fact that all the memory-based beliefs in question are stored in one FILE.[3] I will develop this idea, which to me is intuitively attractive, when we take up the subject of thinking of an individual by name.

A Case of Mistaken Identity. Suppose you once knew the tennis player Tim Gullikson. You didn't know then and still don't know that he has a twin brother Tom, also a tennis pro, who is not quite identical: Tom is left-handed, Tim right-handed. One afternoon you show up late for a tournament and see what you take to be the player you remember (Tim) in the midst of a tennis match. To your amazement he is playing left-handed and winning, the scoreboard showing Gullikson leading Glickstein, 6–3, 4–1. What do you believe about whom?

Because you are already acquainted with Tim and have *de re* beliefs about him, as you watch what you take to be Tim,[4] you

---

[3] This is Perry's (1980) term, which I prefer over Grice's (1969) 'dossier' and Beebe's (1979) 'cluster'. One is too suggestive and the other not suggestive enough.

[4] I will assume that you remember Tim Gullikson under an image, even if not by

form many new beliefs about him, including the belief that he has developed a remarkable left-handed tennis game. It simply does not occur to you that he might have a left-handed twin. Now these new beliefs are about Tim under a memory image (how you visualize Tim), and each is the result of a perception-based belief about Tom and the identity belief that the player you are watching is the player you remember. That is, for each perception-based belief (about Tom) there is a memory-based belief (about Tim) with the same predicative content. I do not mean to suggest that there are two distinct sets of mental representations in your head, one functioning as the contents of your new beliefs about Tim and the other as the contents of your beliefs about Tom. Rather, your identity belief has led your perception-based beliefs about Tom to have become MERGED with your memory-based beliefs about Tim.[5]

Notice that your having two sets of *de re* beliefs, memory-based and perception-based, does not depend on the fact that the player you remember is distinct from the one you are watching. Even if Tim had developed a left-handed game and it was he you were watching, you would still have distinct memory- and perception-based beliefs, even though their objects (as well as their predicative contents) would now be the same. Only this time both sets of beliefs would be about Tim, your identity belief would be true, and the merger resulting from it would not lead to confusion. As things are, however, your identity belief is false, as are your new memory-based beliefs about Tim (unless true fortuitously, for example that Tim is still playing tennis). So, for example, you believe falsely of Tim that he is beating Glickstein but truly of Tom that he is beating Glickstein (under different modes of presentation, of course, a memory and a percept).

Now suppose a friend comes by and says, 'That's one of the Gullikson twins, whom I can tell apart only because Tom is left-

name, but for convenience, as I did with the Dick Holloway example, I will use the name in connection with how you think of him.

[5] Dennett (1982, 54–8) uses a case of mistaken identity ('The Ballad of Shakey's Pizza') to attack the whole idea of *de re* belief, on the grounds of implausible duplication of beliefs in such cases. However, he finds this implausible only because he overlooks the role of modes of presentation in *de re* beliefs, and thus he supposes that their contents could only be singular propositions. It is easy to object to that. Also, Dennett thinks that the very idea of such a duplication of beliefs presupposes a 'theory that atomizes psychological processes into successive moments with certain characteristics' (1982, 58). However, our notion of merging files assumes nothing of the sort.

handed.' Your prior amazement over Tim's development of a left-handed tennis game quickly gives way to embarrassment over your ignorance. You abandon your identity belief and with it all the new memory-based beliefs you formed about Tim. But you retain all the perception-based beliefs you have formed about Tom, and add to them the belief that he is Tim's twin brother.

To alter the example again, now suppose you later think you recall (you have not been told of Tom) that your old acquaintance Tim once beat Glickstein left-handed, but you no longer remember seeing the match. Who is this memory-based belief about: Tim, Tom, or both? Even though it resulted from watching Tom's match with Glickstein, I say it is about Tim—not because of your present identity belief that it was Tim you remember but because of who your memory image is of. To be sure, your original perception-based beliefs about Tom, though no longer retained, did play a role here, but the role they played, with the support of your *original* identity belief, was to lead to the memory-based belief (about Tim) that you have retained.

2. COMMUNICATION-BASED *DE RE* THOUGHTS

Objects of perception-based thoughts are represented by percepts, and objects of memory-based thoughts by images or concepts derived from percepts, but either way the object is something encountered by the thinker himself. Can one also have *de re* thoughts about things one has not encountered but has merely been informed of? It might seem that you can think of such a thing only descriptively, even if you hear of it from someone who has encountered it, for if it's not there to point to, what more can the speaker enable you to do than think of it under a description? In referring to it, whether he provides you with a description under which to think of it or refers to it in some other way, surely he cannot put you into a position comparable to that of having encountered it yourself. *He* may be in a *de re* relation to it, but how can he put *you* in such a relation? You can think of the referent as the individual that he has encountered and is now telling you of, but that is to think of it under a description.

This objection to the very possibility of communication-based *de re* thought may seem plausible, but it rests on a mistake. It implicitly assumes that reference to something not present and not familiar to the hearer must be *identifying* reference.[6] That is, to succeed in referring the speaker must enable the hearer to determine what he is talking about, and the objection is that under the circumstances the hearer can do so only by description. The speaker is thinking of the referent in a certain *de re* way, but he cannot provide the hearer with that or any other *de re* way to think of it. He can express how he is thinking of it and the hearer can identify how, but that is to think of it only descriptively, as the object the speaker is thinking of in that way: the object of the hearer's thought is determined satisfactionally, not relationally.

What this objection overlooks is that a speaker can not just express but can actually *display* his *de re* way of thinking of the object and thereby enable the hearer to think of it in the same way. To do this the speaker must use either a proper name or some other singular term 'as a name', as Russell (1919, 175) described using a term 'merely to indicate what we are speaking about' (for convenience I will use the word 'name' for any singular term so used). Now if the speaker is thinking of something by name, he is entertaining a mental token of the name; when he refers to it by name, he produces a physical token of that name; and the audience, upon hearing that token, forms a mental token of the same name, which he can then retain in memory. Since the hearer's mental token of the name 'inherits' the same object as the speaker's, the object of the hearer's thought is determined relationally, not satisfactionally.

The reason the object is not determined satisfactionally is that the meaning of the name (even a description used as a name) does not enter into the content of the hearer's thought, hence not into the determination of the object being thought of by that name. A token of a name can function as a *de re* mode of presentation because its reference is determined not by its meaning but by its ancestry. It plays this role by being of a certain form (sound or shape), generally the same as the one to which it is linked.[7] When

---

[6] This is Strawson's phrase, and it was he who insisted that non-demonstrative reference can only be descriptive (1959, 7 ff.). Moreover, he maintained that the only not purely descriptive way to think of an object not in one's presence is to think of it in terms of a spatio-temporal relation to objects that are present. In effect, then, he denied the possibility of both memory- and communication-based *de re* thought.

[7] The form is not the same when indexicals are involved, and adjustments must be made for person or place, e.g. 'your' for 'my' and 'there' for 'here'. Also, when a

the meaning of the token does not matter, its referent cannot be determined satisfactionally. Indeed, that only its form matters is what constitutes its being used as a name. And that is what enables one to form *de re* thoughts about an unfamiliar object referred to by that name. Since the token of a name represents in virtue of its form, not its meaning, its representational features can be perceived by the hearer, who can then and thereafter use mental tokens of the same name to think of (or refer to) the same object.

Singular terms of any kind can function as mental names and as means for enabling others to have *de re* thoughts about unfamiliar things. However, proper names are the only singular terms made to order for these roles. The reason is simple: individuals *have* names. Pronouns and descriptions can and often do play these roles within a given context of thought or utterance, but they are ill-suited to work as *de re* modes of presentation or identification of the same individual on diverse occasions. There is simply no way for a pronoun to inherit its reference from a use of the same pronoun on a previous occasion. And generally there are too many descriptions, often idiosyncratic, which people form of things they remember or have heard of, and too many things of which different people form the same description. However, descriptions can become proper names and thereby function as such. Good examples of descriptive names are 'The Sultan of Swat', a name of Babe Ruth, and 'The Chairman of the Boards', a name of Moses Malone. A descriptive name can work as a *de re* mode of identification (in reference) and as a *de re* mode of presentation (in thought) of the same object on various occasions. Also, a description can be conjoined to a proper name, especially a name belonging to more than one individual, to yield a hybrid singular term that functions as a name. There is 'Aristotle the shipping magnate', for example, which distinguishes Onassis from Aristotle the philosopher.[8] Finally, it seems we each use descriptive and hybrid names privately, for people and things we can no longer visualize and whose proper names we don't know.

How can a name function as a *de re* mode of presentation of the same individual on various occasions? Names play this role, I

---

proper name is misremembered, the name confused with it can still function as a mental name of the same object.

[8] Notice, however, that the hybrid 'Aristotle the shipping magnate' is not itself a proper name, unlike 'Jack the Ripper', which is.

suggest, by serving as labels, so to speak, on the mental files we have on individuals. The files so labelled include not only acquaintances but also individuals no longer remembered and even those we have never encountered.[9] Further, I suggest that to think of an individual by name just *is* to call up a file on that individual. Of course, we should not take the term 'file' too literally, but it suggests that information about an individual thought of by name is all stored together (I mean functionally, not necessarily spatially). If so, that would explain the apparent phenomenon, to which my experience attests, that one cannot think of a familiar individual by name without further thoughts about that individual occurring spontaneously. For example, when Fritz Kreisler's name occurs to me I cannot help but think that he was a great violinist but a mediocre composer. The file model offers a much more natural explanation of the fact that many bits of information about an individual tend to get called up together than do sentential or so-called propositional models, which suggest that each item of information is stored separately. Also, in order to explain the fact that one takes them all to be about the same individual, sentential models require a combinatorily explosive hypothesis about the number of identity beliefs involved here, assuming they are individually represented.[10]

The role of names in language is quite different from their role in thought. The semantics of a linguistic name, considered independently of which mental name it is being used to express, consists in its contribution to the meanings of the sentences in which it occurs. In Chapter 7 I will defend the view, the 'Nominal Description Theory' (NDT), that a name 'N' makes the same contribution as the metalinguistic description 'the bearer of "N" '. To suppose otherwise leads to the absurd position that a name with many bearers (and most names are shared) is semantically

---

9 The idea of names as labels on files on individuals goes beyond the Millian view of names as tags on the individuals themselves. Interestingly, modern proponents of the Millian view, such as Kripke (1980) and Devitt (1980), do not seem concerned about how information on an individual thought of by name gets stored. And their formulations of the causal theory of reference, which is commonly incorporated into the Millian view, emphasize interpersonal, communicative links in the chain of reference and neglect the intrapersonal role of memory.

10 Such considerations support the notion of frames and similiar notions in Artificial Intelligence, which I discuss in Bach (1984). One can think of files (on individuals) as a special case of frames.

ambiguous in as many ways as its number of bearers.[11] I will argue that NDT does not have this consequence[12] and is immune to Kripke's (1980) various objections to description theories generally. NDT does not have the false implication that *linguistic* understanding of a sentence containing a name, say 'Veracruz Fettucini is bald', requires knowing whose name it is. Kripke's own theory does seem to imply that you do not understand the sentence unless you know who Veracruz Fettucini is, as if that is a piece of linguistic information. Further, his view suggests that if you asked 'Who is Veracruz Fettucini?' you would not understand your own question, and that the sentence would not even be meaningful if there were no such person (there is!).

Since NDT applies only to proper name types in language, it does not commit me to a description theory of mental tokens of names. The reference of a mental token of a name, and derivatively that of a physical token used to express it, is determined relationally, not satisfactionally, as the object of the percept token to which it is ultimately linked. Since the relation *being linked to* (as well as the relation *being a percept of*) is a causal relation, I am thereby endorsing for mental names a causal theory of reference, according to which they function as rigid designators. Because a name's reference, if any, is fixed by that of the original percept and not by a linguistic meaning, it refers to the same object in any possible world in which it refers at all. If the original percept to which the name is linked had no object (or if there were no original percept, as with fictional names), the name would not have one either.

Mental names, unlike linguistic names, can and generally do represent particular individuals (the psychological role of mental names is quite unlike the semantic role of linguistic names). When a mental name 'N' occurs to you, you do not start using the concept 'the bearer of "N" '. Rather, its occurrence calls up the file it labels, thereby causing you to think of the subject of that file. This is why I suggest that thinking of an individual by a name just *is* to call up a mental file on that individual which is labelled with that

[11] No less absurd is Kripke's (1980, 8) and Evans's (1982, 384) suggestion of distinct but homonymous words (each with its own phantom subscript, no doubt). See Chapter 7.

[12] If 'N' has many bearers, then 'the bearer of "N" ' is not a *complete* definite description, in the sense of applying to one thing uniquely. However, this presents no problem for NDT, just as incomplete descriptions in general do not present a problem for Russell's theory of descriptions. See Chapter 5.

name.[13] Mental names play this role in communication as well. When you hear a name that labels an existing file, that file immediately gets called up. But if there are several individuals with that name, on each of whom you have files (distinctly labelled, like 'Aristotle the philosopher'), the sorts of things being said should, in the context, lead to just one file being called up. And if the speaker cannot plausibly be taken to be talking about the subject of any such file, a new file must be created. That also happens, of course, when you hear an unfamiliar name and do not take it to belong to anyone on whom you already have a file (of course with a different label). Either way, the speaker has put you in a position to use that name to have *de re* thoughts about the referent, not just in the context of utterance but thereafter, provided you retain the new file or the new label on the old file. New information can be added whenever the file is reopened, and that can happen either spontaneously or when you identify or others refer you to someone you take to be the same individual. And of course *you* can use the name to refer others to that individual, thereby causing either an existing file of theirs to be called up or a new one to be created.

So mental names are used to create new files on individuals and to call up old ones for additions, alterations, or just inspection. Files labelled with names (proper names or descriptions used as names) are relatively permanent ones, stored in long-term memory, but we have temporary files as well. Their natural labels are pronouns, which work on a short-term basis. Demonstratives and indexicals often serve to create temporary files, and personal and relative pronouns serve to keep them open—or to keep open recently reopened permanent files.

---

[13] Schiffer maintains that thinking of an individual by name, e.g. 'Richard Feynman', requires using a metalinguistic description like 'the person such that (*a*) that person is named "Richard Feynman", and that (*b*) my familiarity with the name, as the name of a physicist, derives from my having encountered references to that person by that name' (1978, 198). Schiffer has no doubt that he has knowledge of Feynman under that description, but most people who think of individuals by name are surely not as conceptually sophisticated as Schiffer. He astutely observes that when we know of someone by name only, we could not have thoughts expressed by sentences containing the name if we did not have the name, and perhaps this *is* 'nicely accounted for on the hypothesis that my only knowledge of Feynman is under a description which mentions his name' (1978, 199). However, Schiffer has not shown that *thinking* of Feynman by name involves the use of any description, much less such an elaborate one, and what I am suggesting seems much more realistic psychologically.

Nothing I have said should be taken to suggest that a file, temporary or permanent, must actually be on someone. You can have a file on a figment of your imagination or a fiction of someone else's. If you take one person for another (mistaken identity) or simply confuse two people (as with identical twins), you will have a file containing information derived from both and thus not determinately on either. For that matter, you can have two files on the same individual, perhaps on your friendly neighbour and a notorious war criminal. Here, if you come to believe that they were one and the same, the two files would become merged.

Another Case of Mistaken Identity. A good illustration of mistaken identity (and of the role played by identity beliefs in connection with communication-based *de re* beliefs) is Kripke's story of Gödel the impostor. As Kripke tells it, Gödel betrayed his friend Schmidt, the real discoverer of the incompleteness of arithmetic, by murdering him and taking credit for that discovery himself. Since our concern is not with the reference of the name 'Gödel', let us alter the story slightly and suppose that the discoverer of incompleteness was named 'Gödel' but that his murderer assumed the name (perhaps he was his brother and it really was his name). To avoid confusion I will use 'Gödel' to refer only to the discoverer of incompleteness. Suppose you were never acquainted with either man, but you do have a 'Gödel' file, the file 'labelled' with that name. This is the file containing the beliefs that you would express when using the name 'Gödel'. You believe such things as that the subject of your 'Gödel' file discovered incompleteness, spent his later years at the Institute for Advanced Study, and died a few years ago. Now let us ask which man your 'Gödel'-beliefs are about. Are some about Gödel and some about the impostor, or are they all about the same man, in which case who? If their original sources are all people acquainted only with the impostor, it seems, as Kripke says, that they are all about the same man, the impostor.[14]

Now suppose that your 'Gödel'-beliefs had several sources, one the author of a logic book written prior to the impostor's dastardly deeds, the other an acquaintance of the impostor on the IAS

[14] Even if it turned out that Kripke's story were really true and you, accepting the story, wondered who your belief concerning the discoverer of incompleteness was about, you would have to say it was about the man known at the Institute as 'Gödel'. You would realize that your identity belief that the man known at the Institute as 'Gödel' was the discoverer of incompleteness was false.

campus. Some of these beliefs came from one source and some from the other, with some coming from one having been 'confirmed' by the other. They are all in the same file, but who is each about? The source of the ones about the incompleteness proof, the device of Gödel numbers, and so on is the author of the logic book, and the source of the ones about appearance, manner, and personality is the man from the IAS. So it might seem that the first ones are about Gödel and the second about the impostor. You may believe them all to be about the same man, but this does not mean they are, for at least some of your beliefs about the identity of the object of some of your 'Gödel'-beliefs are false. Yet if they are all stored in the same file, how could some be about Gödel and some about the impostor?

It might be suggested that while your identity beliefs explain why your 'Gödel'-beliefs all go into one file, they also imply that you believe of both Gödel *and* of the impostor (though under different modes of presentation, of course) that he was born in Vienna, discovered incompleteness, worked at the IAS, and had a quiet manner. It is not being suggested that each 'Gödel'-belief is unwittingly about both men—that would not make sense—but that each 'Gödel'-belief about one man has a counterpart about the other. If one is about Gödel, its counterpart about the impostor results from an inference from it and the identity belief that involves both men's respective modes of presentation. And, after all, this was the situation in the Gullikson case, which showed that there is nothing implausible in positing a duplication of beliefs—once we distinguish the modes of presentation operative in the two sets of beliefs.

The trouble with this suggestion in the present case, unlike in the Gullikson case, is that two different modes of presentation are not involved here. Thus, it is not the case that each *de re* belief about one man has a counterpart about the other. Your 'Gödel' file is simply labelled 'Gödel', and that name is the only *de re* mode of presentation available. Not being attached to two different files, it cannot be a mode of presentation of two different individuals. Since there is no reason to say that it is a mode of presentation of one man rather than the other, we must conclude that it cannot be a mode of presentation of either. So your 'Gödel'-beliefs are about neither.[15]

---

[15] Strictly speaking, this point applies only to 'Gödel'-beliefs that have been filed.

A variant of this last version of Kripke's story provides a final illustration of how identity beliefs can work. This time suppose that when you first heard of Gödel, you were told about the murderous impostor. So you were careful about your sources of 'Gödel' information and kept two files, one on Gödel and one on the impostor. However, the story was only a story. As a result, the beliefs in your 'Gödel's impostor' file turn out really to be about Gödel. However, thanks to your belief that they are about someone else, they do not get put into your 'Gödel' file and you do not make the inferences that would be made by someone who took them to be about Gödel.

3. THINKING OF AND IDENTIFYING: A COMPARISON WITH EVANS

I agree with Evans (1982) that thoughts about particular objects can be based on perception, memory, or communication. However, the requirement he imposes on what it is to think of an object, in any of the three ways, is far stronger than anything I have suggested. This is the requirement that one be able to identify the object of thought. It may seem plausible, but it must be rejected as too strong. In order to explain why, I will mention a few basic points about reference which are borrowed from Strawson and will be developed in the next chapter. I will also make some brief points concerning Strawson's (1950) notions of identification and reidentification. These points will help explain why there is a fundamental disanalogy between referring to something and thinking of something.

Following Strawson (1950), I hold that reference is ultimately not a two-place relation between a word and an object but a four-place relation between a speaker, a word, an audience, and an object. That is, a speaker uses a word (or other expression) to refer an audience to an object. DENOTATION is a relation between a word and

If one of your sources uses the name 'Gödel' in an utterance about the object of his 'Gödel'-beliefs (here I am assuming that the first source's beliefs are about Gödel and the second source's about the impostor), whatever 'Gödel'-thought you entertain *then*, prior to filing (which is tantamount to taking the token of 'Gödel' you heard of as of the same type as that which labels your 'Gödel' file), is about the same man. However, without being filed it cannot be integrated inferentially with your 'Gödel'-beliefs, but once it is filed and thus integrated it no longer has a determinate object. When that happens, it can have only what Dennett calls a 'notional object' (1982, 38).

an object, but a speaker can use a word that denotes one thing to refer to something else or use a word that does not denote to refer to something anyway. So when we speak of an expression referring, we are speaking elliptically for its being used to refer someone to some object.

Understood as something speakers do, referring must be explained in terms of the notion of thinking of an object. For referring to an object just *is* a component of the communicative act of expressing an attitude about something one is thinking of. A speaker's intention in using a referring expression is fulfilled only if his audience forms an attitude about the same thing and takes it to be the same. This is not by magic: the utterance, perhaps accompanied by gestures or glances, must enable the audience to infer, in the context of utterance, what the speaker is talking about.

Since thinking of something is necessary for referring to that thing, we cannot expect to understand it on the model of referring. In order to think of something, unlike referring someone else to it, obviously you do not have to refer yourself to it. Whereas there is something for an audience to aim at, to get right or get wrong (namely to think of what you are thinking of), there is nothing for you to aim at, to get right or wrong, when you are thinking of the object already. But you can do something else: wonder about its identity, about who or what it is. Thinking of it in one way, you can ask yourself whether it is the same individual as one you are thinking of in some other way. Is this my long-lost cousin, is that my umbrella, is this politician the actor I saw on the Late Show the other night? But you do not have to know who they are to think of them in the first place.

Plain as it is, this point is not always appreciated. For example, Strawson's 'descriptive metaphysics' (1959, ch. 1), which is meant to capture the essential features of how we conceptualize the basic features of the world and its occupants, is built around the notion of 'identifying reference', as if thinking of an object were a matter of being able to refer to it. At any rate, Strawson does not suggest this when he discusses reidentification, which he does not construe as an interpersonal phenomenon. Reidentification for him seems to be a matter of thinking of an object as the same as a certain one encountered previously. Unfortunately, Strawson does not explicitly draw the distinction between thinking again of an object and the further achievement of thinking that the object is the same one. The ability to reidentify, together with possessing the underlying concept of reidentifiable, persisting objects, may be necessary for maintaining a coherent conception of the world over time, but it does not seem necessary merely for thinking of the objects.

These points all pertain to Evans. Developing an acccount of what he calls 'information-based particular-thought' (IPT), he contends that thinking of an object requires identifying it, or at least being able to identify it. He endorses what he calls 'Russell's Principle', that 'in order to have a thought about a particular object, you must *know which* object it is about which you are thinking' (1982, 74).[16] Although Evans and I agree that the thoughts in question can be based directly on perception or derivatively on memory or communication, where I speak of modes of presentation he speaks of 'modes of identification', which sometimes he calls 'Ideas'.

IPTs yield information about objects by way of causal links with their objects. Evans and I agree about the ways, but the difference between us is that for him IPTs are 'Russellian', in the sense that like sentences containing logically proper names, if they lack reference they lack content. But whereas Russell held, as required by his restrictive doctrine of acquaintance, that particular thoughts can only be about sense data (and perhaps oneself), IPTs can be about external objects. However, the Ideas that enter into IPTs are not like Russellian proper names, in that the sense of an Idea is not exhausted by its object. For ideas are ways of identifying an object, and there can be various ways of identifying the same one: different Ideas of an object can enter into different IPTs that ascribe the same property to the same thing.

An Idea is of the object to which it is 'informationally linked', but, being 'a discriminating conception' of an object, an Idea can be 'adequate' only if it satisfies Russell's Principle. It must enable one 'to distinguish the object of his judgment from all other things', so that one can 'know which' object it is. So if a thought does not have the object one thinks it has, because it has some other object or even none at all, one can fail to have the thought one thinks one has. Indeed, Russell's Principle not only implies that the identity of a thought depends on the identity of its object, as understood by Evans it has the controversial consequence that the

16 Hereafter all references to Evans are to Evans (1982).

very *existence* of the thought depends on the existence of its object.

For Evans there are three kinds of IPTs. A perceptual demonstrative thought contains an Idea consisting in the ability to locate an object in 'egocentric space' (that is, objective space from an ecocentric frame of reference) on the basis of current perception (143–51). Since this requires the maintenance of a *continuing* information link to the object (146), such an Idea is adequate only so long as it enables one to maintain a conception of the object as the same one. Similarly, a demonstrative thought based on memory requires a 'recognitional capacity' to identify the object (267–71). Here Evans makes allowances both for the possibility of duplicates—a capacity is relativized to contextually relevant objects (278–84)—and for the possibility of an object changing beyond recognition—one need merely be able to think of it as the same object as what *was* recognizably such-and-such (272–3). Now an IPT based on communication contains a name of the object, and here (373 ff.) Evans appeals to the notion of a practice of using a name 'N' to refer to an object x. Such a practice depends on there being (or having been) 'producers' of the name who originally identified x demonstratively. Then a 'consumer', having acquired the name from a producer, or a producer who is no longer identifying x demonstratively, can use 'N' to think of and to refer to x and thereby have an adequate Idea of x.

Evans maintains that thinking of an individual requires, in each case, knowing which individual it is. That may involve thinking of it in some other way as well, but for Evans this is not necessary. For surely you can have an Idea I_1 of an object without also having another Idea I_2 of it and thinking that the object I_1 is of = the object I_2 is of. However, although Evans *says* that having a single Idea of something suffices for knowing which thing it is, it is quite unclear what he *means*. An Idea is a 'discriminating capacity', but being able to discriminate something does not entail knowing which thing it is, at least not in any familiar sense of 'knowing which'. So what could Evans mean? One clue is that sometimes he seems to use 'discriminate' and 'identify' interchangeably. He says, for example, that possessing an Idea of an object is to have a capacity for discriminating it and that using an Idea of an object is to identify it. He seems to equate identifying something with merely individuating it.

Let me explain what I mean. 'Identifying an object' here does not mean referring to it, that is identifying it for an audience so that they can think of it. Nor does it mean characterizing the object in some interest-relative way (what Boer and Lycan (1975) call 'knowing what' or 'knowing who'), for example identifying your neighbour as a certain murder suspect. As I understand Evans, what it does mean, depending on the case, can be either of two things: (*a*) reidentifying an object or (*b*) thinking of an object so as to be able to reidentify it.

(*a*) Reidentification is taking an object you are presently thinking of under one mode of presentation to be a certain object about which you already have beliefs and which you think of under some other mode of presentation. The latter functions as a mode of identification in the first way. For example, you might take the umbrella you are looking at as the one you remember losing (your percept matches your memory). Or you might take the man introduced to you as Richard Holloway as your boyhood chum Dick Holloway. Reidentifying an object (correctly) enables you to connect your new beliefs about it to the ones in your file on it. Being about the object under one mode of presentation 'm_1', it cannot be inferentially integrated with your other beliefs about the same object but under another mode of presentation 'm_2' unless accompanied by the identity belief that this is the same object, i.e. that $m_1 = m_2$. For the beliefs under 'm_2' make up your existing file on the object, and unless a belief that m_1 is F is accompanied by the belief that $m_1 = m_2$, that m_2 is F will not be added to that file. The belief that m_1 is F may be retained, but only in a new file labelled 'm_1', since you have failed to identify m_1 as m_2.[17]

(*b*) The second kind of identification is thinking of an object in such a way as to be *able* to reidentify it later. Say a card-sharp shows you three playing cards, an ace and two tens, and places them face-down. They look alike but you think of the ace as the one on the right. He then interchanges them, but so long as you keep your attention on the ace, you can continue to think of it under a certain percept, which then qualifies as a mode of identification of the ace. A memory also can so qualify. If you notice that unlike either of the tens the ace has a bent corner, you may not have to keep your attention on it to be able later to identify it (it will be the one with the bent corner). Your memory of the ace

---

[17] You could *later* identify an object as m_1 (it could *then* function as a mode of identification), but at the time the belief that the object presented by 'm_1' is F was formed you have not identified the object at all.

will enable you to recognize it, in which case the memory counts as a mode of identification.[18] But if the sharper's sleight of hand should keep you from recognizing the ace, its mode of presentation (the memory or, as above, the percept) does not qualify a mode of identification of the ace.

One can think of something without knowing which thing it is. The trouble with Evans's view, whichever way we construe modes of identification, is that what he regards as necessary conditions for using an Idea to think about an object are too strong and are, in fact, necessary conditions for something more. As many of our examples have suggested, one can think of an object without being able to identify it, that is, without knowing which object it is (in any useful sense of 'knowing which'). You can think of a perceptual object merely by attending to it. If you look away and then turn back, you needn't be able perceptually to pick it out of a crown, even in the midst of look-alikes. Similarly, you can think of an object you have perceived before merely by remembering it. That you remember something, hence your ability to think of *it*, does not require that how you remember it distinguishes it from other things. All that matters is that it caused the percept that resulted in the memory. And if someone refers you to something by name, you can think of it simply by name. Of course, if you know of several individuals with that name, you may not know which one he is talking about, if any, but this does not prevent you from thinking of it. Rather, this prevents you from calling up the file you have on that individual and from combining the new information the speaker gives you with the information you already have on that individual.[19] In all three cases, then, you can think of an individual without knowing which one. Of course if its mode of presentation does not enable you to know which individual it is and

[18] Of course, your ability to reidentify the ace (your recognitional capacity) is, as Evans points out, relative to the context. If the three cards were returned to the deck containing other cards with bent corners and the deck were shuffled, you would no longer be able to reidentify that ace. On the other hand, if the ace were lying facedown by itself, you would not have to notice its bent corner to locate it in relation to other things in order to be able to reidentify it.

[19] In your own thinking, having files on several individuals with the same name does not present a comparable problem. There is no problem for you as to which individual you are thinking of by that name. For as we saw earlier, each file must have a distinct label, such as 'Aristotle the philosopher', and since each file's history determines who it is on, once you have opened a file you are *ipso facto* thinking of its subject. You do not have to ask yourself who you are thinking of, in this case the philosopher or the shipping magnate.

you cannot identify it otherwise, your new beliefs about it cannot be integrated inferentially with any old ones you might have. But all this means is that its mode of presentation does not qualify as a mode of identification.[20]

[20] This chapter would not have been the same without the invaluable advice and encouragement of Mike Harnish, notwithstanding the outside chance that he might, just possibly, not agree with every single word of it.

PART TWO

SINGULAR REFERENCE

3

Varieties of Reference

In this chapter and the next, I will merely sketch my general views on meaning and reference. They will be elaborated and defended in later chapters, as they are applied to definite descriptions, to proper names, and to pronouns. In the course of sketching them here, I will also present the theoretical framework within which I will be working.

As drawn in the Introduction, the distinction between speaker reference and linguistic reference is substantive, not just verbal. It captures the fact of linguistic usage that we can just as well say that a speaker uses a term to refer as that the term itself refers, but more importantly, as we saw, it raises some fundamental but often neglected questions. How are the two kinds of referring related, both to each other and to other linguistic and speech phenomena? Is one kind of referring to be explained in terms of the other? How is speaker reference related to speaker meaning (communication) and linguistic reference to linguistic meaning? Before we take up these questions, we should get clear on the two kinds of referring themselves. What it is for a speaker to refer and what constitutes a referring expression?

1. WHAT IS SPEAKER REFERENCE?

Later on I will argue that speaker reference is a more fundamental notion than linguistic reference; referring is ultimately not something that words do but something that speakers use words to do. But just what is speaker reference? I will try to answer this question in a general way, one that does not depend on the kind of singular term being used to refer. A good way to zero in on what referring is is to get clear on what it is not, or not merely.

To refer to something is not merely to talk about it. For example, we could be talking about chess without ever referring to it. We might refer to Anatoly Karpov and Gary Kasparov or to the Ruy Lopez and the Sicilian Defence, making remarks like 'Karpov plays the Ruy with an iron grip' and 'Kasparov always counter-attacks when he plays the Sicilian.' We could be talking at great lengths about chess but never refer to chess itself. Thus, something can be a topic of conversation without ever being referred to.

Nor is referring to something merely having it in mind—even when one is using an expression that denotes it. Of course the notion of having something in mind is notoriously vague, but that is not the problem here (see Chapter 1). Suppose a Hollywood gossip columnist writes, 'The only undivorced nominee for best actress at the 1989 Academy Awards will win the Oscar.' Even if the columnist has Brooke Shields in mind and even if she is the only undivorced nominee, he might not be referring to her. Perhaps the nominations have yet to be made and columnist cannot expect the audience to have any idea who the nominees will be. Then it would be incidental to the columnist's referential intention that the audience think of Brooke Shields. The columnist may be predicting merely that the winner will be the only undivorced nominee (we can imagine a scenario in which, say, having been married to members of the Academy reduces one's chances), who may or may not turn out to be Brooke Shields.

Finally, it is sometimes supposed (by Strawson 1959, Searle 1969, and Evans 1982, among others) that to refer to something is to identify it (verbally). Identifying it is nice but not necessary. A speaker can refer to something, by means of a personal pronoun ('she'), for example, and not even attempt to provide the information needed by the hearer to determine the intended referent. Or he could use an incomplete definite description[1] ('the visitor') or even an indefinite description ('a visitor') to refer to some specific individual without specifying which one. It may be true that referring to something requires being able to identify it, but this is not the same as actually identifying it. Also, *successful* reference requires that the *hearer* identify the referent, but this is not verbal identification. Besides, the hearer may be able to identify the referent without the benefit of any identification on the part of the speaker. Here the hearer relies (and the speaker intends him to rely) on contextually available information rather than on information provided by the speaker, but this is not a case of the

---

[1] By 'incomplete' I mean a definite description that does not apply uniquely to anything. Most of the descriptions we commonly use are incomplete, like 'the store' and 'the girl'.

speaker identifying the referent *for* the hearer. A referring expression such as 'she' serves merely to suggest the sort of information the hearer is to look for and to rely on. 'She' does not itself carry the information needed to single out a salient female.

In order to understand what speaker reference is or, more precisely, what it is for a speaker to use an expression to refer an audience to something, we should first appreciate that referring never occurs by itself. Referring is always part and parcel of performing a larger, illocutionary act. In short, one cannot *just* refer to something. It might seem that one can, for a coherent utterance can be made with just a singular term. But the question is whether a speaker could use it merely to refer. Uttering the name 'Haile Selassie' could be a coherent utterance, but only as more than just an act of reference, say as an answer to the question 'Who was the emperor of Ethiopia?' Without making it fully explicit, a speaker would be answering that Haile Selassie was the emperor of Ethiopia. On the other hand, if a speaker uttered the name in the course of a Rastafarian incantation, he might conjure up in himself and anyone within the earshot the thought of Haile Selassie, but he would not be referring to him, much less be performing some illocutionary act.

Here I should explain what I take illocutionary acts to be. For Harnish and me a (communicative) ILLOCUTIONARY ACT (there are also conventional ones, such as christening and appointing—see Bach and Harnish 1979, ch. 5) is the act, in a certain specific sense, of expressing an attitude. We define EXPRESSING an attitude as uttering a sentence with the intention for the hearer to take one's utterance as reason to think one has that attitude.[2] Succeeding in communicating the attitude to the hearer does not require that he adopt it (or, for that matter, form some correlative attitude, such as intending to do what the speaker wants him to do); it is enough for the hearer to identify which attitude the speaker is expressing. If the illocutionary act is a statement, for example, *perlocutionary* success requires being believed, but *communicative* (illocutionary) success merely requires being understood. As Harnish and I like to

---

[2] We call such intentions reflexive or R-intentions, which are subtly different from Gricean intentions. R-intentions have the distinctive feature that 'their fulfillment consists in their recognition' (Bach and Harnish 1979, 15). In this book I will omit the 'R'- and for convenience just use 'intention' to mean R-intention, the sort of intention essential to communication.

characterize communicative intentions, 'their fulfillment consists in their recognition' (Bach and Harnish 1979, 15).

How are referential intentions related to communicative ones? Since referring to something is always part and parcel of performing an illocutionary act (the act of expressing an attitude) and that in turn is performed with a communicative intention, a referential intention is simply a component of a communicative intention. Of course not every communicative intention includes a referential intention. It includes one only if the attitude being expressed in the utterance has (or purports to have) an object. Then, clearly, the referential intention is the component of the communicative intention that is directed specifically at this object.

This obvious point suggests a provisional definition of referring: to refer to something is simply to express an attitude about it. The idea is that not every attitude is (or even purports to be) an attitude about an individual, but whenever a speaker does express such an attitude, he has a referential intention which is directed at that individual. This definition is too simple, however, for one can express an attitude about something without there being any specific expression in the utterance that is intended to indicate the object of the attitude. For example, suppose someone asks me what I think of Cyndi Lauper and I respond, 'I don't like rock stars with orange hair.' Even though I would be expressing an attitude about her, I would not be referring to her. To exclude such cases, our definition should require that the utterance contain a singular term that is being used specifically to indicate (though, for reasons given earlier, not necessarily identify) to one's audience the object of the attitude being expressed. Accordingly, in the singular case

> To refer to something is to use a singular term
> with the intention (part of one's communicative
> intention) of indicating to one's audience the object
> of the attitude one is expressing. (REF)

Notice that (REF) defines referring as a four-place relation between speaker, expression, audience, and object. We should keep this point in mind when later we discuss the connection between speaker reference and linguistic reference, for the latter is a two-place relation between expression and object.[3]

---

[3] Some have claimed that linguistic reference can be context-relative, as in the case of indexicals, and thus have proposed that it is really a three-place relations between expression, context, and object. I will argue against this view in Chapter 9.

(REF) is not meant to distinguish successful from unsuccessful reference, but since referring is part of communicating, the condition of its success is part of the condition on successful communication itself. Now a communicative act is successful just in case one's audience identifies the attitude one is expressing. So if the attitude is about a certain individual and one is using a singular term to indicate its object, the act of reference is successful only if the audience identifies the object of that attitude. However, this cannot be done in just any way, for it is not enough that the audience identify the correct object. Since identifying the object is part of identifying the attitude being expressed, successful reference requires that the audience identify the object of the attitude being expressed in accordance with how the speaker intends him to identify the attitude as a whole.

I will not discuss in detail the manner in which we schematize the form of inference whereby a hearer is to identify the attitude being expressed by a speaker (Bach and Harnish 1979, chs. 1 and 4). Suffice it to say that the 'Speech Act Schema', which is presented below, is so formulated as to represent the kinds of information available to the hearer as he infers the speaker's communicative intent. The SAS incorporates linguistic meaning, the contextual information shared by speaker and hearer (MUTUAL CONTEXTUAL BELIEFS or MCBs), and mutual beliefs, or presumptions, common to speech situations generally. The latter include the LINGUISTIC PRESUMPTION, that the speaker and the hearer share the language of the utterance, the PRESUMPTION OF LITERALNESS, that the utterance is literal unless there is reason to suppose otherwise, and the COMMUNICATIVE PRESUMPTION, that the utterance is being made with a recognizable communicative intention. In its general form, the SAS covers not only literal and direct utterances but non-literal and indirect ones as well.

THE SPEECH ACT SCHEMA

The SAS covers non-literal and indirect, as well as literal and direct illocutionary acts. S is F-ing that P if in the presence of some H, S utters a sentence e (in some language L) in mood * intending, and expecting (pursuant to the LP, the CP, and the PL) H to recognize that he intends, H to infer (from the fact that S means . . . by e and the fact that S is thereby saying that *(. . . p . . .)) that S is F-ing that P. On occasion S may be also F'-ing that Q. That is, S intends, and expects H to recognize that S intends, H to reason thus:

		Basis
L1.	S is uttering e.	hearing S utter e
L2.	S means . . . by e.	L1, LP, MCBs
L3.	S is saying that *(. . . p . . .).	L2, LP, MCBs
L4.	S, if speaking literally, is F^*-ing that p.	L3, CP, MCBs

Either (*direct literal*),

L5.	S could be F^*-ing that p.	L4, MCBs
L6.	S is F^*-ing that p.	L5, PL

And possibly (*literally based indirect*),

L7.	S could not be merely F^*-ing that p.	L6, MCBs
L8.	There is some F-ing that P connected in a way identifiable under the circumstances to F^*-ing that p, such that in F^*-ing that p, S could also be F-ing that P.	L7, CP
L9.	S is F^*-ing that p and thereby F-ing that P.	L8, MCBs

Or (*direct non-literal*),

L5'.	S could not (under the circumstances) be F^*-ing that p.	L4, MCBs
L6'.	Under the circumstances there is a certain recognizable relation between saying that p and some F-ing that P, such that S could be F-ing that P.	L3, L5', CP
L7'.	S is F-ing that P.	L6', MCBs

And possibly (*non-literally based indirect*).

L8'.	S could not merely be F-ing that P.	L7', MCBs

L9′.   There is some F'-ing that Q
connected in a way identi-
fiable under the circum-
stances to F-ing that P,
such that in F-ing that P, S
could also be F'-ing that Q.   L8′, CP

L10. S is F-ing that P and
thereby F'-ing that Q.   L9′, MCBs

As merely a definition, (REF) leaves open many questions about the nature of reference and its success. Consider the general question, which SAS does not itself address, of the manner in which the audience must identify an expressed attitude in order to be said to understand the speaker. How exactly must he identify it, and by precisely what inferential route? Harnish and I (1979, 85–9) take up this general question, but one aspect of it concerns reference in particular. For just as there are various ways of identifying an attitude, so there are various ways of identifying the individual the attitude is about. The speaker may be thinking of the referent in a certain way, but what if the hearer comes to think of this individual, the right one, but in a somewhat different way? Does referential success, as a part of communicative success, require the audience to think of the referent in just the same way, or is something weaker sufficient? Perhaps it depends on the case. Indeed, perhaps there are cases in which the speaker has no specific intention as to how his audience is to think of the referent. We will distinguish these cases later, in the course of examining the uses of different kinds of referring expression. As we will see, there are various ways in which the speaker, who himself can be thinking of the referent in one way or another, can intend the hearer to think of the referent.

2. REFERRING EXPRESSIONS

We have been considering referring as something that speakers do, but ordinary usage suggests that referring is also something that expressions do. Not surprisingly, the phrase REFERRING EXPRESSION is often applied to singular terms—proper names, definite descriptions, and pronouns—which are, after all, commonly used to refer to individuals. Although I much prefer using the word 'denote', for now I will play along with the double use of 'refer' both for what these expressions do and for what speakers use them to do.[4]

Whatever we call them, we should not suppose that referring expressions always refer. A referring expression can fail to refer because no single individual is its referent, as in (1),

> Let George do it.   (1)

which contains a name with many bearers as well as a pronoun, or (2),

> The car is out of gas.   (2)

which contains an incomplete definite description. A referring expression can fail to refer also because what it purports to refer to does not exist, as in (3) and (4),

> Kilroy was here.   (3)
> The tooth fairy is rich.   (4)

which contain, respectively, a vacuous name and an unsatisfied description. In due course we will take up the problems raised by singular terms which for either reason fail to refer.

There are also contexts in which so-called referring expressions do not even purport to refer, and these raise different problems. Familiar examples of such contexts include existence and belief sentences. In (5), for example,

> Neptune exists.   (5)

most would agree that the name 'Neptune' does not refer, even though it is the name of Neptune. The usual reason for denying that it refers here is that referring, as in the context of a subject-predicate sentence, presupposes the existence of the referent. If that were so with (5), an existence sentence, then (5) would be redundant

---

[4] Notice that there are two ways of taking the phrase 'use an expression to refer', depending on whether it is the user of the expression or the expression itself that is doing the referring. To see the difference, just compare the likely ways in which the phrases 'use a pencil to calculate' and 'use a computer to calculate' would be taken. I have a sneaking suspicion, which I am unable to confirm empirically, that conflating the two uses of 'use an expression to refer' aids and abets the common tendency to equate linguistic reference (especially by tokens of expressions) with speaker reference. This conflation can make it seem that the difference between an expression being used to refer and the expression itself referring is a distinction without a difference.

(at best), since it *says* that Neptune exists. The situation would be worse with (6),

Neptune does not exist. (6)

the negation of (5), since it would be implicitly self-contradictory, denying what it presupposes, the existence of Neptune.

As for belief sentences, it is commonly said that in the context of the 'that'-clause in a sentence like (7),

Tycho believed that the moon of Earth is elliptical. (7)

a description, in this case 'the moon of Earth', does not refer[5] (in Quine's familiar jargon, its occurrence is referentially 'opaque', not 'transparent') even if, as in this case, it applies to something uniquely. The reason is that the 'that'-clause in which it occurs gives the content of Tycho's belief, which would be the same even if Earth had no moon. In (7) 'the moon of Earth' plays a role comparable to that of 'the moon of Venus' in (8),

Tycho believed that the moon of Venus is round. (8)

(8) could be true even though Venus has no moon. Whereas in (9),

The moon of Venus is round. (9)

'the moon of Venus' at least purports to refer, in (8) it does not even do that. By parity of reasoning, neither does 'the moon of Earth' in (7).

So there appears to be a consensus among philosophers, notwithstanding theoretical differences, that certain terms are referring expressions despite the fact that they do not always refer or even purport to refer. In certain sentential contexts, they do not function as referring expressions. This fact, at least if it is assumed to be significant semantically, raises a serious dilemma for any account (there have been many) of the non-referring function of referring expressions in existence and in belief contexts. Any account which makes this assumption presupposes that the semantic function of an expression, in this case a referring expression, *can* depend on the sentential context in which it occurs. If a referring expression functions referringly in some contexts and not in others and that fact is semantically significant, then the expression's semantic contribution to the sentence in which it

---

[5] In Frege's (1892) view it does refer, but not to the moon of Earth. He would have said that instead of having its 'customary reference', in this context 'the moon of Earth' refers to its 'customary sense'.

occurs would have to depend on its sentential context. But this suggests that its very meaning, which presumably determines its semantic contribution, depends on its sentential context. The only way to concede that, and this is one horn of the dilemma, would be to abandon the Principle of Compositionality. According to this well-entrenched principle, almost universally accepted by students of language (regardless of theoretical orientation) from Frege to Chomsky,[6] the semantic properties of a sentence are a function of the semantic properties of its constituents, where the function in question is determined by the structure of the sentence. The cost of giving up this principle is, as is well known, to be confronted with the seemingly impossible task of explaining the learnability of languages whose grammars cannot be specified recursively.

Giving up the Principle of Compositionality is one horn of the dilemma I am claiming for any account which implies that the semantic function of a referring expression depends on the sentential context in which it occurs. The other horn of the dilemma is to accept the dubious implication that referring expressions are systematically ambiguous. So, for example, the definite description 'the moon of Venus' would have one meaning in (9), another in (8), and still another in (10),

The moon of Venus does not exist.   (10)

Yet intuitively it seems that 'the moon of Venus' is not ambiguous, hence that something is wrong with any theory which implies that it is.

There is only one way to escape the dilemma of either giving up the Principle of Compositionality or multiplying meanings beyond necessity. We must take the dilemma by its horns and reject the supposition that the semantic role of a referring expression can depend on the sentential context in which it occurs—even though whether it functions referringly depends on the context. But notice what follows from that: an expression's referring function, when it has one, is simply not part of its semantic contribution to the sentence! This way of escaping the dilemma commits us to denying that when 'the moon of Venus' functions referringly (not that it succeeds in referring, of course), as in the subject-predicate sentence (9) as opposed to (8) or (10), this function is part of its

---

[6] A recent exception is Cresswell (1985, 15), whose account of belief sentences as systematically ambiguous explicitly violates what he calls Frege's principle (138).

semantic role. It makes the same semantic contribution to (9) as it does to (8) and to (10), even though only in the case of (9) does the truth of the sentence require that the moon of Venus exist.

3. RUSSELL AND REFERENCE

Russell may not have explicitly recognized the importance of staying free of the dilemma presented above, but he did recognize the equal importance of something else. What Russell saw, indeed what motivated his theory of descriptions (and its extension to ordinary proper names), was that the meaning of a description, hence that of any sentence in which it occurs, cannot depend on whether or not it is satisfied. The meaning of 'the moon of Venus', for example, cannot depend on whether or not Venus has a moon. Thus Russell proposed (1905) that definite descriptions should not be taken at face value as 'denoting phrases', but should be regarded as 'incomplete symbols'. By this he meant that a description does not denote a constituent of a proposition but, in the context of a sentence, semantically contributes quantifiers and a predicate which combine with the rest of the sentence to express a complete proposition. Thus not only does the meaning of a description not depend on whether or not it is satisfied, its meaning does not depend on the kind of sentence in which it occurs. In the case of (8), (9), and (10), for example, which all contain 'the moon of Venus', their logical forms differ in important ways, but these differences are not due to any ambiguity in the description.

Russell's famous (or is it infamous?) theory of descriptions exhibits how a definite description, as an incomplete symbol, does not denote a constituent of a proposition but semantically contributes a quantificational structure which combines with the rest of the sentence to express a complete proposition. This proposition is not a singular but a general proposition. In the case of description sentences of simple subject-predicate grammatical form,

> The F is G. (11)

one of the English paraphrases given by Russell is (12),

> Something is F, nothing else is F, and it is G. (12)

which clearly expresses a general proposition. The most perspicuous way to represent the logical form of (11) is with the logical formula (13),

$$(Ex)(Fx \& (y)(\text{if } Fy \text{ then } y = x) \& Gx).^7 \tag{13}$$

Because (13) does not contain a referring expression corresponding to 'the F' but contains quantificational apparatus instead, it makes explicit that (11) expresses a general proposition. Thus Russell's theory implies that (11), being of subject-predicate grammatical form, is misleading as to its logical form. (13) makes explicit why the semantic role of 'the F' in (11) has nothing to do with the fact that it purports to refer. Similarly, although I will not go into the details now, the application of Russell's theory to the occurrence of descriptions in existence or belief sentences makes explicit why their semantic role has nothing to do with the fact that they do *not* purport to refer.

Russell (1918) extended his theory of descriptions to ordinary proper names (as opposed to what he called logically proper names). Names may indeed be referring expressions *par excellence*, but Russell held that their semantic contributions to the sentences in which they occur can be characterized without mention of their referring (denoting) role. Whereas logically proper names, such as individual constants in logic, play the semantic role of contributing their referents to the propositions expressed by the sentences in which they occur, ordinary names do not. For Russell they are disguised or 'truncated' descriptions, and their semantic contribution is like that of overt definite descriptions.

Later I will defend Russell's theory of descriptions and a version of his claim that ordinary proper names are semantically equivalent to descriptions. For now suffice it to say that if Russell was right (or at least on the right track), then the sometime referring function of ordinary referring expressions is never part of their semantic role. If we are prepared to accept this conclusion, we will escape the dilemma that faces theories which imply that the semantic role of a referring expression depends on the sentential context in which it occurs. Current theories, both about names and about descriptions, are subject to this dilemma. Rather than abandon the

---

[7] There are various alternatives to (9), which is not Russell's own formulation. I avoid that because of his idiosyncratic metalinguistic treatment of the quantifiers. In his analysis of the existential and the universal quantifier, respectively, he employed the metalinguistic predicates 'is sometimes true' and 'is always true' and applied them to open sentences.

Principle of Compositionality, generally they regard referring expressions as systematically ambiguous. Some theories take this course enthusiastically, some reluctantly, and some unwittingly.

Despite their fame, Russell's theories have seemed implausible to most philosophers. I believe this has been partly the fault of Russell's own ways of formulating and defending his views, which did not bother to distinguish sentences from utterances (or even sentences from propositions). Also, he did not have the benefit of the concepts belonging to pragmatics, the theory of language use. Separating these concepts from those belonging to semantics will play a key role in my effort to vindicate Russell. I will avoid the above dilemma by taking the position that the study of reference belongs not to semantics but to pragmatics. Of the two main notions of reference, I will argue that speaker reference is the primary notion and linguistic reference the secondary one. Ironically, this was a point urged long ago by Russell's best-known critic Strawson, in 'On referring' (1950). Whereas Strawson used it against Russell, I will use it to defend him. Now Strawson goes so far as to say that ' "mentioning", or "referring", is not something an expression does; it is something that someone can use an expression to do' (1950, 180). I agree with the spirit of this remark,[8] but I disagree with Strawson when he goes on to charge Russell with confusing meaning and mentioning. However, I do applaud Strawson when, after observing that different expressions can vary in the degree to which their referring uses can depend on the circumstance of utterance (pronouns are on one end of the scale and definite descriptions on the other), he refuses to call any of them referring expressions.

I will use a traditional term for what so-called referring expressions do when their doing it does not depend on the speaker's intentions. I will say that an expression DENOTES if by virtue of its meaning it picks out an object uniquely. Denoting expressions include complete definite descriptions, like 'the author of *Waverley*' (as opposed to incomplete ones like 'the author'), and proper names with only one bearer, such as (so far as I know) 'Bertrand Arthur William Russell' (as opposed to ones like 'Russell'). For reasons to be explained later, I will not say that an

---

[8] Even though I do say (guardedly) that an expression can refer, since I regard linguistic reference as derivative and speaker reference as primary I am in effect agreeing with Strawson on this point.

expression denotes if the object it picks out can vary with the context of utterance. I will speak of any expression that can be used to refer to an individual, whether or not it denotes, as a SINGULAR TERM, and, following Strawson, I will generally say not of expressions but of people that they REFER.

4. MEANING AND REFERENCE

It is a platitude that words, though loaded with meaning, are intrinsically just sounds and shapes.[9] We are reminded of this whenever we hear an utterly alien tongue. When that occurs, what is it that we do not know? Roughly, knowing a language is knowing the meanings of its words, a solid core of them anyway, and being able to understand sentences constructed out of these words in accordance with the syntax of the language.[10] This systematic pairing of sounds/shapes with meanings is in a certain way arbitrary. There is nothing about the sound or shape of 'rot', as opposed to 'fot', in virtue of which it had to mean anything, and certainly it did not have to mean decay in English and red in German. An obvious extension of the above platitude expresses this arbitrariness: words have the meanings they do as a matter of convention.

Platitude though it is, it should be kept in mind when we consider such fundamental questions as (*a*) how is language related to the world?, and (*b*) how does language express our thoughts? It is obvious to many, though not to some, that the second question is the more fundamental, for it seems difficult to deny that 'semantics

[9] Here it is useful to distinguish types and tokens. Word types are patterns of sound (specified phonologically) and shape (specified orthographically). A token of a given word type is either an uttered noise of the specified sound pattern or a written (or printed) sequence of letters of the specified sort. In practice, allowances must be made for tokens that do not quite fit the type intended by the speaker/writer.

[10] In this section and occasionally elsewhere, it may appear that I am illicitly trafficking in the notions of meaning and synonymy and am ignoring Quine's (1956) well-known attacks on these notions. The same may be said for my occasional use of the notion of proposition, another Quinean target. Whether or not Quine can be answered in his own terms, I must confess my inclination to stick with these notions come what may. I share Cresswell's view, for example, that 'the problem about propositional semantics is not a problem about any particular view of what propositions are' (1985, 74), and feel something like a mathematician who does not wish to go on furlough until philosophers determine the nature of mathematical objects.

reduces to propositional attitude psychology',[11] if I may quote Schiffer (1978, 175). Yet there is a tradition according to which the relation between words and the world is deemed direct rather than mediated by the thoughts these words are used to express. This tradition is a residue of behaviourist philosophy of language and still flourishes in philosophy of logic and in extensionalist versions of formal semantics, which, to borrow more of Schiffer's words, have 'ignored the connection between semantics and psychology'. To appreciate this consider an example like (1),

White dwarfs are dense. (1)

'White dwarfs' means stars of a certain sort (it also means diminutive Caucasians, but never mind that), 'are' is a copula connecting subject and predicate, and 'dense' means having a high ratio of mass to volume (it also means being slow-witted, but never mind that either). An extensionalist would say something (just what would depend on his theory) to the effect that the sentence as a whole represents the world as being such that anything which is a white dwarf is dense, so that the sentence is true just in case that it is so. But from this we do not really have an answer to the question, posed by (*a*) above, of how the sentence is related to the world. For that we need to know not only the meaning of the sentence, as given, say, by its truth conditions, but also its truth value. And that requires knowing whether or not white dwarfs are dense. In other words, knowing the meaning of the sentence does not constitute knowing its relation to the world but only how it represents the world as being. But how it represents the world as being is independent of how the world is. Only its truth or falsity depends on how the world actually is. So if the sentence is correlated with anything, it is not with any *specific* state of affairs in the world but with the thought (or proposition) that white dwarfs are dense (I am not denying that thoughts or propositions can be individuated by state of affairs *types*). This correlation obtains regardless of how the world is, given that the sentence, as used literally in English, expresses that thought. So it would seem that the sentence has the

---

[11] To be sure, it has been argued that people think in their native language, but mere arguments cannot establish such a strong empirical claim. I find these arguments (see Harman 1973, 56–9, and Devitt 1980, 75–80, for example) far from persuasive. Without reviewing them or my objections to them, I can express my main worry: whereas they seem to assume that the sentences we utter generally express complete thoughts, I believe that most of our utterances do not make our thoughts fully explicit (see Chapter 4).

meaning it has because of the thought it is used to express, when used literally. Its truth condition, therefore, is not intrinsic to it but derives from the truth condition of that thought. And if this is correct, then question (*a*) in the form posed above has no direct answer. But that is all right, for we must revert to question (*b*) anyway: how words are related to the world depends on what thoughts those words can be used literally to express. Here arises a further question, or rather a logically prior question, (*c*) how is thought related to the world? This is question (*a*) asked about thought, not language. It is a question not in linguistic semantics but in what is sometimes called PSYCHOSEMANTICS. So Schiffer's point can be put by saying that linguistic semantics reduces to psychosemantics: the theory of meaning for sentences reduces to the theory of content for thoughts.

Even though the platitude above on the conventionality of linguistic meaning makes this claim, I do not pretend to have established it, and thus can adopt it only as a working hypothesis. However, I must register an objection to at least one argument against it, put forth by Cresswell (1985, 56–7): 'For semantics the invoking of internal representations is idle. If the meaning is now a property of representations, why not cut out the middleman and apply this property directly to the sentence itself?' Although the target of this argument is the view that thought involves mental representations, my quarrel with it does not depend on that. Cresswell's question may be rhetorical but it could still use a good answer. He must *show* that sentences have semantic properties intrinsically, not merely derivatively as determined by the thoughts they are used literally to express.

Although the connection between words and thoughts is more direct than that between words and things, there is certainly no one-to-one correlation between words and thoughts. Obviously the same thought can be expressed by different sentences, even in the same language. I will not dwell on this familiar fact, that different sentences can be semantically equivalent, for it is the other direction of the many–many correlation that is relevant here. The fact is that the same sentence can be used to express different thoughts, and there are many reasons for this. First, sentences are often ambiguous, having several literal meanings. The ambiguity of a sentence usually stems from the ambiguity of one or more of its constituents, as in (1),

White dwarfs are dense. (1)

but sometimes the ambiguity is not lexical but structural, as in (2),

Teaching students can be frustrating. (2)

Second, a sentence can be used to express a thought that does not correspond to its linguistic meaning (or, if it is ambiguous, to any of its meanings); it can be used non-literally. If, after a meal at the Greasy Spoon, I utter (3),

I've never had a better hamburger. (3)

chances are I am expressing my opinion, in ironic (non-literal) terms, of how awful the hamburger is. Third, even if a sentence is unambiguous and is being used literally, it can still be used to express different thoughts on different occasions. For it may contain some indexical elements, as in (4),

I wonder who's kissing her now. (4)

which contains three. The sentence itself is univocal, but the statement a speaker makes in using it depends on who he is using 'her' to refer to. Despite being indicative, the sentence (as a type) has no truth condition, although any statement made in using it does, assuming the indexicals have determinate referents (*not* denotations, since the referents are not determined, even relative to the context, solely by the meanings of the words).[12]

In these three ways, then, a sentence can be used to express diverse thoughts. The existence of each is enough to undermine the view that meaning determines reference, a vulgar misinterpretation of Frege's doctrine that sense determines reference.[13] Which

---

[12] Notice that nothing is gained by speaking of the sentence as having merely a context-relative truth condition, for that is but a misleading way of saying that the statement made in using the sentence in that context has a truth condition. Worse, it falsely suggests that values of contextual variables determine what the truth condition is. This is true for 'I' (and perhaps for 'now') but surely not for 'her'. So whereas 'I' can be used only to refer to oneself, the speaker, and 'now' only to the present time, the use of 'her' to refer is not similarly restricted. It can be used to refer to any contextually identifiable female or, for that matter, to such things as a boat or a country. Whatever the referent in a particular case, it is determined by the speaker's intention, not merely by the context of utterance. The contribution of context is insufficient to determine the reference; at most, it can enable the hearer, in considering what the speaker might reasonably be taken to be intending (in that context), to identify the referent. All these points will be spelled out in Chapter 9.

[13] This misinterpretation, possible only if one has not read 'The thought' (Frege 1918), has been exposed by Burge (1979a), who points out that although Frege may have overworked the term 'sense', linguistic meaning was not one of the things he meant by it.

thought an utterance of a sentence expresses depends not only on the meaning(s) of the sentence but also on the speaker's communicative intention. If the sentence is ambiguous, the speaker's intention determines which of its meanings is operative (Bach and Harnish 1979, 20–3). If the sentence is not being used literally, that is because of the speaker's intention. In this case he must intend the hearer to recognize a certain connection between what the sentence means and what he means in order for the hearer to identify the latter (Bach and Harnish 1979, 65–70). And if the sentence contains an indexical, its meaning underdetermines what the speaker means (even if the sentence is unambiguous and is being used literally), and how the gap is to be filled depends on the speaker's referential intention. The form of inference whereby the hearer is to bridge these and other gaps between what a sentence means and what its utterer means is captured, at least in general terms, by the Speech Act Schema presented above.

5. TYPES OF REFERRING

The distinction between linguistic and speaker reference should not blind us to more specific distinctions within the category of speaker reference itself. For there are various kinds of referring and various ways of doing it. It will be useful to draw now a number of distinctions that will prove useful later. I will not justify them here but will merely sketch them and give them labels.

First there is what I call OBJECTUAL as opposed to DESCRIPTIVE reference. Roughly the distinction is this: a speaker refers to an individual objectually if it is not part of his referential intention how the hearer is to identify the referent; he intends only that the hearer identify the individual he has in mind and take it to be the one that he is talking about. The speaker refers descriptively if he intends to be talking about whatever uniquely satisfies the individual concept that the hearer is to recognize (even if the speaker is not using a definite description to express it) as determining the referent. If this distinction sounds familiar, that is because it is intended as a generalization of Donnellan's (1966) well-known distinction between referential and attributive uses of definite descriptions, to be taken up in Chapter 6.

Discussions of reference are usually restricted to SINGULAR reference, where the speaker is referring to just one individual, but there is no reason why a speaker cannot refer to more than one. PLURAL reference can be achieved either with a conjunction of singular terms, such as 'Bach, Beethoven, and Brahms', or with a plural term of one sort or another. This might be a plural noun like 'sharks', a quantifier phrase like 'every hustler in town', or a plural definite description like 'the best poker players in Las Vegas'. Notice that the objectual/descriptive distinction drawn above can be extended in an obvious way to plural reference. When several individuals are being referred to, each can be referred to either objectually or descriptively.[14]

In regard to plural reference, we can distinguish COLLECTIVE from DISTRIBUTIVE reference. Compare the likely uses of 'Homer and Jethro' in (1) and (2),

Together, Homer and Jethro weighed 500 pounds. (1)
Homer and Jethro each weighed 500 pounds. (2)

which is collective in (1) and distributive in (2). Of course the speaker does not always have to make explicit whether the reference is collective or distributive, since this may be obvious from the context or from the background information. Compare, for example, likely uses of 'the fugitives' in (3) and (4),

The fugitives wanted a car. (3)
The fugitives wanted a meal. (4)

which undoubtedly would be used to refer collectively in (3) and distributively in (4). Obviously this is not a linguistic fact.

There are different ways in which a speaker can refer to something, depending on the relationship between the words he uses to refer and the way in which the referent is to be identified by the hearer. The following categories all apply to plural reference, but for clarity the discussion will be limited to cases of singular reference. Reference is explicit when the speaker identifies the referent uniquely. One can do this verbally, either with a proper name belonging to but one individual or with a complete definite

---

[14] There is no requirement that the references being made in a given utterance all be objectual or all be descriptive. In practice this generally happens, but there are plenty of mixed cases, e.g. 'The first person to guess the weight of this horse wins $100'.

description.[15] One can refer explicitly also by using either a pronoun or a demonstrative description (like 'that table') and by pointing to the referent. Then the reference is DEMONSTRATIVE. Pronouns can be used not only for demonstrative but also for ANAPHORIC reference, reference to something previously mentioned. In (5), for example,

> Michele told only her lawyer, for he was the only man
> she could trust.   (5)

'her' and 'she' presumably are being used to refer anaphorically to Michele, and 'he' to Michele's lawyer.

Reference can also be INEXPLICIT or even NON-LITERAL. In the first case, the referring expression does not pick out the referent uniquely, but some elaboration of it does. For example, in a suitable context a speaker might use 'the table' as if it meant 'the table in the living room of my house' and thereby refer inexplicitly to the table in the living room of his house. His reference would be not just inexplicit but non-literal if he used 'the table' to refer to the large wooden box in front of his living room sofa.

A different kind of distinction is that between direct and INDIRECT reference. Something is referred to indirectly just in case it is referred to by way of referring to something else.[16] Typical examples of phrases used to refer indirectly are 'Henny Youngman's wife', 'all the tea in China', and 'the house that Jack built'. There is no limit on the number of links in a chain of reference, as illustrated by the ever longer chains in 'The House that Jack Built'.[17] A special case of indirect (and non-literal) reference is what Nunberg (1979) calls DEFERRED reference. For example, a waitress might use 'the hamburger' to refer to the diner who ordered a hamburger.

[15] Explicit reference can be either descriptive or objectual, provided that the expression used applies to the referent uniquely.

[16] Both Schiffer (1981, 73) and Wettstein (1981, 252) have discussed indirect reference.

[17] These are not to be confused with the quite different phenomenon of anaphoric chains discussed by Chastain (1975).

4

Semantics, Pragmatics, and Reference

For both singular terms and sentences containing them, we should take care not to confuse the theory of their meaning with the theory of their use. We should avoid trying to explain their pragmatic properties semantically. Grammar is complex enough without letting it be further complicated by phenomena which can be explained independently with the help of general pragmatic principles. For example, when an expression has two uses, if we can explain one use in terms of the other pragmatically, we can regard just the one use as literal and avoid taking the expression to be (semantically) ambiguous.[1] With this strategy we can avoid what Kripke calls 'the lazy man's approach in philosophy to posit ambiguities when in trouble' (1977, 269). He himself avoids this approach in connection with the distinction between referential and attributive uses of definite descriptions, and I will try to do likewise here, on that and other points. We should keep the semantics of sentences containing singular terms separate from the pragmatics of their use.

In this chapter I will draw certain distinctions, terminological and otherwise, to help us keep them separate. Then I will explain more fully the rationale of keeping them separate. We will find that the various distinctions to be drawn here will not only sharpen the boundary between semantics and pragmatics but also enable us to understand the connections between them.

1. BEYOND LITERALITY: GRADES OF INEXPLICITNESS

There is an undeniable connection between meaning and use, in that the meaning of a sentence determines its literal use. But what is

---

[1] For me 'semantic ambiguity' is a redundancy, since there is no other kind. In particular, I take 'pragmatic ambiguity' to be a misnomer, as when Donnellan (1966, 298) uses it to describe the referential/attributive distinction (the phrase is used also by Cresswell 1985, 155). At best it is a misleading label for an expression that is standardly used in more than one way. Genuine ambiguity is usually lexical, as with 'sty', but sometimes is structural, as illustrated by Chomsky's famous 'Flying airplanes can be dangerous.'

it to use a sentence literally? Katz has suggested that the literal meaning of a sentence is what a speaker would mean if he used it in an 'informationally impoverished context' (1977, 14 ff.). In this, which Katz also calls the 'null context', there is no information available to the hearer, apart from what the sentence means, to enable him to infer what the speaker means. However, as Harnish and I have argued (Bach and Harnish 1982), Katz's null context is really an artificial idealization in which the hearer cannot know what to think the speaker means. Even literal utterances cannot be understood in the null context, for in such an informationally impoverished context the hearer has no basis for supposing that the speaker means anything at all in his utterance, never mind whether he means what the sentence means or something else. We regard the literal meaning of a sentence not as what it is used to mean in the null context, where the speaker might not mean anything, but as determining the 'default value' (Bach 1984, 39) of its utterance in any context: what a speaker can be presumed to mean in the absence of any reason to the contrary. A speaker can always mean something else or something more, but his audience cannot infer this without relying on information beyond the meaning of the sentence uttered. Also, if the speaker does mean something else or something more (if he is performing a non-literal or an indirect illocutionary act), still it is the literal meaning of the sentence that provides the linguistic portion of the hearer's basis for inferring what the speaker means. Everything else that goes into inferring that involves interpersonal and common social knowledge, not linguistic.

Utterances can be literal or non-literal but sentences cannot. Sentences can be used literally or non-literally, but they cannot have non-literal as well as literal meanings. So it is redundant to speak of sentences as having literal meanings. Notice here that meanings are properties of sentence *types*. The meaning of a sentence does not change just because a speaker does not mean what it means, but then there is more to understanding an utterance of a sentence type (the production of a token of that type) than merely understanding the sentence uttered. Whether or not the speaker means what the sentence means, the meaning of the sentence provides the hearer's linguistic basis for inferring what the speaker means.

As a first approximation, to use a sentence literally is to mean what the sentence means, and to use it non-literally is to mean something else. Matters are more complex than that, since non-literal illocutionary acts must be distinguished, as in Bach and Harnish (1979), from indirect as well as from direct and literal illocutionary acts. In performing a non-literal act, as in using a metaphor, the speaker does not mean what the sentence means but means something else instead, whereas in performing an indirect one he means both what it means and something else as well. For example, if a child says to his mother, 'I am getting hungry', he is not only directly (and literally) telling her that he is getting hungry, he is indirectly asking her for something to eat. We could say that in performing an indirect illocutionary act beyond the direct one, the speaker is using his sentence both literally and non-literally.

Matters are even more complex than Harnish and I recognized. First of all, there are really two kinds of non-literality. One kind is familiar, the non-literal use of some specific word or phrase in a sentence, as in (1),

> My grandmother was a saint. (1)

where 'saint' is being used non-literally (metaphorically) to mean a kind and selfless person. Call this constituent- or C-NON-LITERALITY. Even without using any of the constituents of a sentence non-literally, one can use the sentence as a whole non-literally, as in irony. Call this S-NON-LITERALITY. If I uttered (2),

> Josef Mengele was a saint. (2)

I would mean quite the opposite of what I said. I would be using the entire sentence non-literally, not the word 'saint' in particular, for I would be asserting the negation of the sentence.

The phenomenon of *s*-non-literality will prove important to our discussion (in later chapters) of singular terms and their use. It should be noted here that when an utterance of a sentence is *s*-non-literal, typically there is some lexical material that the speaker could have inserted into the sentence to make fully explicit what he meant. For example, if Michael uttered (3),

> I don't like Mary. (3)

and followed it with 'I love her', he would mean that he does not merely like Mary. If he had said what he meant, he would have inserted the word 'merely' between 'not' and 'like' in his utterance of (3).

With the help of the various distinctions drawn thus far, we can classify utterances by the degrees to which they are more or less literal and explicit. I will first enumerate them and then give examples of each:

- (*a*) *literal and explicit*: the uttered sentence is unambiguous and what the speaker means corresponds to its meaning;
- (*b*) *literal but not explicit*: the uttered sentence is ambiguous and what the speaker means corresponds to one of its meanings;
- (*c*) c-*literal but not* s-*literal* (hence not fully explicit): what the speaker means corresponds to the meaning of some expansion of the sentence uttered;
- (*d*) c-*non-literal but* s-*literal*: what the speaker means corresponds to the meaning of the sentence resulting from replacing some expression in the sentence uttered with another expression;
- (*e*) c-*non-literal and* s-*non-literal*: what the speaker means corresponds to the meaning of the sentence resulting from replacing some expression in the sentence uttered with another expression *and* expanding the result.

Case (*a*) is illustrated by a literal utterance of the univocal sentence (4),

> Dogs are bigger than cats. (4)

and case (*b*) by an utterance of the ambiguous sentence (5),

> Dogs are dearer than cats. (5)

In uttering (5) the speaker means not that dogs are more expensive than cats but perhaps that dogs are more cherished than cats. We have already seen two examples of (*c*), namely (2) and (3),

> Josef Mengele was a saint. (2)
>
> I don't like Mary. (3)

whose utterances, in the ways indicated earlier, are c-literal but not s-literal. Case (*d*) is illustrated by (1), whose utterance is not c-literal.

> My grandmother was a saint. (1)

And case (*e*), combining (*c*) and (*d*), is illustrated by (6),

> Zsa Zsa doesn't like rocks. (6)

followed by 'She loves them', where the speaker means that Zsa Zsa doesn't merely like diamonds.

Despite their differences, (*a*) to (*e*) are all case of direct illocutionary acts, since the speaker means only one thing in uttering the sentence, even if he is not speaking literally and fully explicitly. There is also the case of indirect illocutionary acts:

(*f*)   *indirect*: not only is the speaker using the sentence, whether literally or non-literally, to mean one thing, he means something else as well.

For example, if a child says to his mother,

I am getting hungry.   (7)

he is not only directly (and literally) telling her that he is getting hungry, he is indirectly asking her for something to eat. If he had said,

I am starving.   (8)

he would have been directly but non-literally telling his mother that he is hungry, as well as indirectly asking her for something to eat.

A Terminological Point. The notion of utterances that are not fully explicit but are otherwise literal will prove to be of great importance when we later take up incomplete descriptions and names that have many bearers. Since it might seem that 'elliptical' is the word to use to describe such utterances, perhaps I should explain why I do not use it. For example, when Michael says 'I don't like Mary, I love her', is he speaking elliptically? He is not saying but he does mean that he does not merely like Mary, and to say this explicitly he would have included 'merely' in his utterance. Does that make his utterance elliptical? I avoid that term because of its narrower uses. One such use applies to utterances of a sentence fragment, such as (9),

Mary doesn't want to.   (9)

where it is evident in the context how the sentence is to be completed. Perhaps Michael means that Mary doesn't want to get married. There is an obvious difference between 'I don't like Mary' and (9): (9) is not a complete sentence.

Another kind of ellipticality is very important in linguistics. It involves sentences which, despite being complete, contain elements that are not phonologically realized. In (10), for example,

Mary is taller than Michael (is).   (10)

although 'is' is not uttered, it is said to be present in the deep structure of the sentence. Without dwelling on the linguistic issues here, such as the current theoretical status of the notion of deep structure, suffice it to say that in order to account for the ambiguity of sentences like (11),

Mary knows a taller man than Michael (is/knows). (11)

a grammar must attribute a phonologically unrealized constituent to (11). Otherwise, there is no way to account for the reading with an implicit 'is' as opposed to that with an implicit 'knows', as well as for the fact that no other verb can implicitly fill that slot.

2. SEMANTIC INDETERMINACY AND AMBIGUITY

Earlier I suggested that an utterance of a sentence is literal (and fully explicit, if the sentence is unambiguous) if the speaker means what the sentence means and nothing more. However, this way of characterizing literal utterances is not quite right and must now be qualified. It turns out that there are many sentences such that the speaker cannot mean merely what the sentence means.

The obvious case is that of a sentence containing an indexical, such as (1),

She is a fine actress. (1)

To use (1) literally one must mean that a certain female is a fine actress, but one must also be referring to some particular female, and which one that is is not determined by the meaning of the sentence. (1) is not semantically equivalent to (2),

A certain female is a fine actress. (2)

for 'she' does not *mean* 'a certain female'. As I will explain when we take up indexicals later, the way to give the meaning of 'she' or any other indexical is not to provide some synonymous phrase but to specify the rule of its use. The rule for 'she' is to use it to refer to a certain female. Successful communication with an utterance of (1) requires that the intended referent be identified by the hearer in the context of utterance. Although the meaning of the sentence does not determine the speaker's intended referent, we should not conclude that the sentence is semantically ambiguous. Rather, the sentence is REFERENTIALLY INDETERMINATE. All sentences containing indexicals (included here are demonstratives and demonstrative descriptions, such as 'this' and 'that car') are referentially indeterminate. So are tensed sentences, whose use involves an implicit temporal reference.

Thus there are sentences which, because of referential indeterminacy, can be used literally despite the fact that a speaker does not (and cannot) mean just what the sentence means. There is another way in which this can happen that is important but not widely recognized: a sentence can be SEMANTICALLY INDETERMINATE. This notion is important—and not widely recognized—because it is easily confused with ambiguity. If someone uttered (3), for example,

Pepsi is better. (3)

he would probably mean that Pepsi is better than Coca-Cola, but that is not what the sentence means. (3) is not an elliptical form of (4),

Pepsi is better than Coca-Cola. (4)

for (3) could just as well be used to mean that Pepsi is better than 7-Up or Budweiser, and surely it is not ambiguous in as many ways as the countless number of things with which Pepsi can be compared. Nor is (3) an elliptical form of (5),

Pepsi is better than x. (5)

where 'x' is a variable whose value is to be determined in the context of utterance, or of (6),

Pepsi is better than it. (6)

where what 'it' is being used to refer to is to be determined in the context of utterance. (3) could be used not only to mean that Pepsi is better than some one other soft drink (or some one other beverage) but also that it is better than any other soft drink (or any other beverage). Finally, (3) might be thought to be an elliptical form of (7),

Pepsi is better than [NP]. (7)

where [NP] is a slot unfilled by a lexical item. To this I would have no objection, since it implicitly concedes that (3) is semantically indeterminate.

Later we will see the importance of semantic indeterminacy to the theory of reference. The point here, to qualify what I said earlier about literality, is that a speaker cannot use a semantically (or referentially) indeterminate sentence to mean merely what the sentence means. This is not to say that such a sentence cannot be used literally, for surely any sentence can be used literally, but that its utterance cannot make fully explicit what the speaker means. If a sentence is semantically indeterminate, it cannot encode a complete thought content because it contains a semantic 'hole', so to speak. Its utterance expresses only a partial thought content, so that even if a speaker uses it literally to express a thought he must intend the hearer to rely on contextual information to infer what fills the hole and thereby completes the content. In contrast, if a hearer is to understand a literal utterance of an ambiguous sentence, he must disambiguate it, taking one of its meanings as the operative one. Clearly that involves a different sort of inference than the one required for completing the content of the utterance of a semantically (or referentially) indeterminate sentence.

Now it might be objected that the difference between ambiguity and indeterminacy is terminological at best. One might wonder how there could be a substantive difference between a sentence's having one underspecific meaning that can be filled out in any one of several ways and its having several meanings. We can address this issue by considering (3) or, to vary the example, (8),

> The King will attend. (8)

Presumably a user of (8) would mean that the King will attend a certain event, even though there is no mention of it in the sentence. Since the speaker means that the King will attend it, he intends his audience to infer which event this is. But what does the sentence itself mean? Attending is something one does (or does not do) with respect to some event, but (8) does not specify any event. It might be thought that the meaning of (8) can be represented by (9),

> There is some event that the King will attend. (9)

but this will not do. (9) is much too weak, implying that (8) is true just in case the King should later attend some event or another, and no other way of giving a truth condition for (8) works either. The fact is that although (8) is grammatical, it has no determinate truth condition. As a school grammar book might have said, it does not express a 'complete thought'. One might suppose that (8) contains a hidden indexical, which is being 'used' to refer to the relevant event,[2] but there is no basis for this suggestion beyond a dogged

---

[2] I am not objecting to the idea of an abstract pronominal element (defined as in Chomsky 1981) to reflect the syntactic fact that 'attend' is a transitive verb, but it would be absurd to say that this element is being *used* to refer.

insistence that non-indexical sentences have determinate truth conditions. The natural alternative is to allow that sentences can fail to have determinate truth conditions even if they do not contain indexicals. They can still have definite meanings, but their meanings are conceptually incomplete. And for this reason, a speaker cannot use a semantically indeterminate sentence (or a referentially indeterminate one) to mean merely what the sentence means.

3. OCKHAM'S SEMANTIC RAZOR

Another phenomenon often confused with ambiguity is what I call 'standardized non-literality'. This confusion illustrates the all-too-common tendency of mechanically invoking ambiguity to explain puzzling linguistic phenomena. I grant that on occasion what Kripke calls the lazy man's approach is warranted, but wholesale pleas of ambiguity generally yield cheap explanations. The value of such pleas is no greater than the false assumption behind them: different uses, different meanings. This assumption has been forcefully repudiated by Grice (1975), who appeals to certain pragmatic principles or 'maxims' of conversation to show how multiple uses can arise from single meanings.

One common case of standardized non-literality involves disjunction.[3] As Grice explains, there is no need to posit an exclusive as well as an inclusive senses of 'or'. If someone utters (1),

Either George is in London or he is in Paris.   (1)

he is likely to mean one or the other but not both. However, explaining this does not require positing an exclusive sense of 'or', since what the speaker means can be explained by the fact that he is relying on the common knowledge that a person cannot be in two places at once. Here the speaker, knowing that he can be presumed to be saying no more than is necessary, is exploiting Grice's 'maximum of quantity'.

---

[3] Although Grice regards this as a case of 'conversational implicature', in fact it illustrates standardized non-literality. Harnish and I argue (1979, 165–70) that implicature is a kind of indirect statement, in that the speaker means one thing by way of meaning another. However, in the present example (and in the ones to follow), the speaker does not mean literally what he is saying but something else *instead*—he is speaking non-literally, not indirectly.

Logical connectives are but one of many cases in which appeal to ambiguity is tempting but unwarranted. Where one standard use of a sentence can be explained, with the help of conversational principles, by another standard use which uncontroversially corresponds to a literal meaning, the first is a standardized non-literal use. An utterance of (2), for example,

I have two rackets.   (2)

is true if the speaker has at least two rackets, but he could well have meant exactly two. Just compare the following two uses of (2): as a response to your tennis partner's admission 'I forgot my racket', and as an answer to the question 'How many tennis rackets do you own?' Ordinarily, only the second use would be meant as and be taken as implying 'exactly two'. However, that (2) has two uses hardly justifies deeming it ambiguous, with an 'exactly' as well as an 'at least' sense. It is better regarded as univocal, possessing only the logically weaker 'at least' sense. That a speaker can mean 'exactly' without saying it does not begin to show that (2) has an 'exactly' sense as well. Surely no one would argue that since there are many kinds of rackets, the term 'racket' (as well as (2) itself) is ambiguous in as many ways; a user of (2) can mean that he has two tennis rackets without using the word 'tennis'. No better would be to argue for the ambiguity of (2) by appealing to (3),

I don't have two rackets, I have three.   (3)

which contains the negation of (2). Here the dubious argument is that although (3) can be used to state something true, if (2) had only an 'at least' sense (3) would be inconsistent. The trouble with this argument is its false assumption that the utterance is literal. Of course (3) can be used to state something true, but the question is whether, in being so used, it is being used literally. Consider an utterance of (4),

I don't believe Moriarty did it, I know he did it.   (4)

Believe it or not, at least one philosopher has appealed to uses of sentences like (4) to argue that, contrary to popular philosophical opinion, knowledge does not imply belief. But surely the saner course is to say that anyone who uses (4) is likely to have suppressed the word 'merely' before 'believe'. Once it is recognized that the utterance is a case of standardized non-literality, the above argument collapses. Similarly, the explanation for the fact that (3) is being used to state something true is that the speaker has suppressed 'merely' before 'two', and so was not speaking quite literally.

As we will discover later, only by wielding Ockham's semantic razor can we clear the stubble off the face of the theory of reference.

4. INEXPLICITNESS AND STANDARDIZED NON-LITERALITY

There is the wide range of expressions, including a variety of singular terms, which are standardly used non-literally. Or, to be precise, the sentences in which they occur are standardly used *s*-non-literally (the non-literality is not attributable specifically to the expression in question). There are even cases in which not just *a* but *the* standard use is non-literal. In suggesting here that a standard (or the standard) use of an expression can be non-literal, I am implying that literality is not a statistical notion. Identifying the most common use of an expression can be relevant to determining its literal meaning, but statistical considerations can be overridden by explanatory ones. Unless we recognize this, we run the risk of multiplying meanings beyond necessity or, even worse, of rendering the theory of their meaning needlessly convoluted. As we will see, this has happened more than once in the theory of reference.

The kind of explanatory considerations I speak of are evident from such examples as the following. Each is an utterance whose *standard* use illustrates that people often say something without making fully explicit what they mean. Suppose you meet a friend at 8 p.m. and utter the interrogative,

Have you eaten?   (1)

Obviously you are asking him whether he has had dinner that evening, not whether he has ever had anything to eat. Of course, you could have asked him that by uttering (2),

Have you ever eaten?   (2)

a reasonable question to ask if he had a reputation for never consuming solids. And you could have made your question explicit by uttering (3),

Have you eaten dinner this evening?   (3)

but that is unnecessary, since your intended question is the standard use of (1), at least at night. Nevertheless, that is surely not its literal use (there is no linguistic basis for supposing that a counterpart of 'this evening' occurs in the sentence itself). If this is not patently clear, consider what question you would be asking by uttering (4),

Have you eaten caviar?   (4)

Surely you are not asking your friend whether he had eaten caviar that evening but whether he had ever eaten caviar. Moreover, you are using (4) literally in asking him that, even though your utterance does not contain the word 'ever'. A perfectly good answer to (4) would be 'Yes, just the other day', but if that were your friend's answer to (1), he would be either taking you literally or just trying to be cute. The literal use of (1) is not its standard use, and its standard use is not literal.

Now suppose that prior to a dinner party a fashion-conscious woman complains to her husband by uttering (5),

I have nothing to wear.   (5)

Presumably she means not that she will have to go naked but that she has nothing appropriate to wear. But this is not what she said—she is not using (5) literally. And although she could have made explicit what she meant by uttering (6),

I having nothing suitable to wear to tonight's party.   (6)

that would have been quite unnecessary. Her husband is to reason that under the circumstances she could not reasonably be taken to mean just what she said and therefore must have meant something more, which he ascertains by reading something inexplicit into the utterance. In different circumstances, say at a nudist colony, she might have used (5) literally, to mean no clothes at all. Notice that this literal use of (5) is not its standard use. In contrast, the literal use of (7)

I have nothing to read tonight.   (7)

is its standard use.

I have claimed that the standard uses of (1) and of (5) are not their literal uses. However, I am not suggesting that in their standard uses any of the words they contain are being used non-literally. It would be futile to try to pin down the non-literality of these standard uses to particular words. It might seem that in (5) 'nothing' is being used non-literally for 'nothing suitable' and 'wear' for 'wear to tonight's party', for if what was meant had been made explicit, with an utterance of (6), 'I have nothing *suitable* to wear *to tonight's party*', the inserted words (italicized) would have been syntactically closest, so to speak, to 'nothing' and to 'wear', respectively. However, even though the speaker meant (6) by (5) as a whole, there is no reason to suppose that she meant 'nothing suitable' specifically by 'nothing' and 'wear to tonight's party' by 'wear'. She could just as well have been using 'wear' literally and have meant 'nothing suitable for tonight's party' by 'nothing'. Rather than try to ascribe non-literality to specific expressions in such utterances, we should realize that there is no requirement that just because a sentence is being used non-literally, any of its constituents are being used non-literally; we are dealing not with c-but with s-non-literality.

We can now suggest a test for standardized non-literality. Suppose that an expression e has two commonly accepted uses,[4] a common use M and an uncommon use L. Then e is semantically unambiguous, L is its literal use, and M is a non-literal use if:

- (*a*) on the supposition that L is e's literal use, use M can be explained pragmatically (i.e. by the SAS) in terms of L;
- (*b*) on the supposition that M is e's literal use, use L cannot be explained pragmatically in terms of M; and
- (*c*) there is some other expression with analogous uses but whose standard use corresponds to L and is uncontroversially its literal use.

This test applies neatly to (1) and to (5). For (1) L is given by (2) and M is given by (3). As we saw, the use of (1) to mean (3) can be explained pragmatically by its use to mean (2) but not conversely. (5) has uses analogous to those of (1). Clearly its standard use, corresponding not to (2) but to (3), is not its literal use, and can be explained pragmatically.

The theory of reference, as part of the theory of speech acts, must reckon with the fact that people often say something without making fully explicit what they mean, leaving it up to the hearer to figure out the rest. Many of the claims to be made later about the various kinds of singular terms and their use to refer will take this

---

[4] If there are more such uses, matters are complicated, since several of these uses may be literal—e may be genuinely ambiguous.

fact into account. These claims will illustrate why the theory of their meaning is but one element of the theory of singular reference. Not only are there many questions in the theory of reference that the semantics of singular terms does not address, there are many distinctions to be drawn in the theory of reference that do not correspond to semantic distinctions among types of singular terms. As we will see, the limited role of semantics in the theory of reference is explained, given that their semantics is concerned only with their literal meanings, by the fact that many of their standard uses to refer are not literal uses. It is because of these standard but non-literal uses that I contend that certain prevalent views about the semantics of singular terms are misplaced. They capture facts about standard uses of these terms, not about their meanings. However, when these facts are recognized for what they are, the views in question are no longer controversial—they are innocuous.

5. SINGULAR TERMS AND STANDARDIZED NON-LITERALITY

The notion of standardized non-literality is important to the theory of reference, as we can see if we apply our test for it to occurrences of singular terms. Although separate chapters will be devoted to definite descriptions and to proper names, I would like to illustrate this point now by applying the test to incomplete descriptions and to names with more than one bearer. In so doing I will rebut a certain intuitively plausible but dubious view about their semantics, according to which these terms function semantically as indexicals.

A definite description 'the F' is INCOMPLETE if there are many Fs. In (1), for example,

   The door is open.   (1)

there occurs the incomplete description 'the door'. In my view the only literal use of (1) is to mean that the only door there is is open, though of course no one would ever mean that. If you were to utter (1), probably you would mean that the main door of the room (or perhaps the front door of the house) you are in is open, even though you have not indicated which door that is. I claim that you would not be using (1) literally, not that you are using 'the door' (in particular) non-literally to mean 'the door in this room' (your utterance is s-non-literal). 'Door' means door and nothing more, and although the determiner 'the' implies uniqueness, unlike (1) as a whole *it* does not seem to be used non-literally.

Uniqueness is implied by proper names as well. For this reason, I claim, the literal use of (2), for example,

> Bill Russell was a better shot blocker than Wilt
> Chamberlain.   (2)

would be to mean that the only bearer of the name 'Bill Russell' was a better shot blocker than Wilt Chamberlain. However, if you uttered (2) you would not mean that, since you know that the name is a SHARED NAME (that it has more than one bearer). Presumably you would be referring to the famous basketball player and not to anyone else of the same name, such as the recent Dodger shortstop. But since uniqueness is implied and it does not seem that you are using 'Bill Russell' non-literally, your use of (2) as a whole is not *s*-literal.

In both cases you are not making fully explicit what you mean or what you are referring to (what attitude you are expressing about what individual). In suggesting that these uses of (1) and (2) are not literal, just as in the examples of the previous section, I am resisting the view that the singular terms they contain function semantically as indexicals. On that view (1) means something like 'This/that door is open' (or 'The contextually relevant door/The door I have in mind is open'), and has no absolute truth condition (even modulo tense) but is true or false only relative to a context of utterance. It is true or false depending on whether or not the door being referred to is open. No one would deny that this is the (context-relative) truth condition of a statement made in using (1), but the question is whether the sentence itself has this context-relative truth condition. In short, is 'the door' a disguised indexical? Kripke (1977, 255 and 271) has suggested as much, and recently Wettstein (1981) has defended this suggestion. Neither, however, takes into account the distinction between a sentence such as (1) and the statements it can be used to make. Instead, they just assume that a description like 'the door' has variable reference because it can be used to refer to various things. From this they argue that the sentence is not amenable to Russell's analysis, according to which it has an absolute truth condition (at least modulo tense), and is true just in case there exists exactly one door and it is open.

Kripke and Wettstein overlook the possibility that Russell's analysis might be correct as an account of the meaning of the sentence but that the speaker does not mean what the sentence means. Of course no speaker in his right mind would mean that there exists exactly one door and that it is open, but it hardly follows that the sentence means something else. The natural alternative is that the speaker is not making fully explicit what he means in uttering (1). He intends the hearer to infer that he is talking about a certain door, which is to be identified in the context as the one he can reasonably be taken to be talking about. There is no good reason to assume, as Kripke and Wettstein appear to do, that the standard use of a sentence must be literal. It seems to me that in (1) 'door' means door and the determiner 'the' implies uniqueness, thereby making the standard use of (1) not *s*-literal.

There are two further considerations to support the view that incomplete descriptions and shared names are not disguised indexicals, even though it requires claiming that the sentences in which they occur are standardly not used *s*-literally. Consider complete definite descriptions and proper names having only one bearer. No one would suggest that they are indexicals—and no one has. If they are not, however, then the indexical view has a consequence that seems theoretically arbitrary: whether or not a description is complete affects the semantics of any sentence it occurs in. Surely the semantics of such a sentence cannot depend on the answer to that factual question. The same point applies to names: whether a name is shared or has but one bearer should not make a difference to the semantic analysis of the sentences in which it occurs. Answers to such factual questions cannot determine whether or not a given singular belongs to the grammatical category of indexicals.

Secondly, there is a basic difference between incomplete descriptions or shared names and genuine indexicals, such as personal pronouns. If a speaker utters a sentence containing an indexical, even though the speaker does not mean what the sentence means, his utterance is literal. The point is that in this case the speaker *cannot* mean just what the sentence means. That is due to the very nature of indexicals—sentences containing them are referentially indeterminate. But in uttering a sentence containing an incomplete definite description or a proper name with more than one bearer, a speaker *can* mean what the sentence means (that is, at least on my account, according to which uniqueness is implied). Someone who utters (1) or (2) might believe (or believe the hearer believes), however ignorantly, that the description is satisfied uniquely or that the name has but one bearer.

These points will be developed in later chapters. I have made them now just to illustrate the theoretical advantage of giving pragmatic explanations, when they are feasible, of seemingly semantic phenomena. In this case we can wield Ockham's semantic razor by appealing to the notion of standardized non-literality. If this appeal should seem counter-intuitive, keep in mind that we are speaking of *s*-non-literality. I am not claiming here that incomplete descriptions and shared names are themselves standardly used non-literally. I am claiming this of the sentences in which they occur. That they function semantically as indexicals is simply not the conclusion to draw from the fact that a hearer cannot infer the speaker's referential intention merely from the singular term he uses.

6. AGAINST TOKEN SEMANTICS

The point just made, that sentences containing incomplete descriptions or shared names are standardly used non-literally, is relevant to our earlier discussion of the distinction between speaker and linguistic reference. Although I agreed with the spirit of Strawson's insistence that speakers refer, not expressions, I was willing to go along with common practice and allow that expressions refer. But speaker reference is the more fundamental notion. For one thing, most so-called referring expressions—indexicals as well as incomplete descriptions and shared names—do not denote. A singular term denotes only if in virtue of its semantics it picks out an object uniquely. Moreover, I argued that the semantic role of a description or a name does not depend on whether it actually denotes anything or, for that matter, on the kind of linguistic context in which it occurs—it plays the same semantic role in existential and belief contexts as in simple subject–predicate sentences. For these reasons I concluded that linguistic reference, in-so-far as it is semantic at all (is denotation), is a derivative notion as far as the theory of meaning is concerned.

Now I wish to make a further point in order to sharpen the line I have drawn between semantics and pragmatics. Semantics, as part of grammar, concerns linguistic types, not tokens. Accordingly, when linguistic reference is semantic, it is a property of the expression type, and when it merely is a property of a token of a type (as when we say that an expression refers to something 'in a context'), it is not a semantic property at all. Rather, the expression (token) refers *only* in the sense that it is being used to refer. Token reference without type reference is a thoroughly derivative notion: a token refers to an object just in case it is being used to refer an audience to that object. The reference of a token is derivative also, though in a less flimsy sense, if it is a token of a type that denotes; in that case, the token inherits its reference from the type. Notice, however, that if the type is being used non-literally, for example 'the king of France' to refer to the president of France, then it is the speaker's reference that determines the token reference.

In my view the notion of token reference has no more than a parasitical role to play in both the semantics and the pragmatics of reference. Semantics has a place only for the notion of type reference, or denotation. As for pragmatics, the operative notion is speaker reference. Reference by a linguistic token is always inherited either from the denotation of its linguistic type or from the speaker's intended reference. Token reference is never autonomous. To describe tokens as referring misleadingly suggests that they somehow have referring powers of their own. A token 'refers' either because it is of a type that denotes or because it is being used to refer. Tokens do not refer in their own right. Indeed, they have no autonomous semantic properties at all. Every seemingly semantic property of a token is either inherited from its type or is really a pragmatic property of the act of producing it. In particular, a token of an (indicative) sentence containing a singular term does not have an autonomous truth condition. Even though the statement made in uttering such a sentence token has a truth condition (it expresses a belief with a truth condition), the token itself does not have an autonomous truth condition.

It might seem that, in insisting that except as types tokens of singular terms do not refer but are used to refer,[5] I am making an

---

[5] Notice the ambiguity in saying that a term is 'used to refer': what is being said to refer can be either an unspecified speaker or the term itself. I will always mean the former, but one could mean the latter. In my view only the former serves any positive theoretical purpose and the latter alludes to a relation of referring that is either non-existent or at best Pickwickian. I suspect that failing to distinguish the two may have contributed to the common practice of speaking of tokens of singular

issue out of a mere terminological point. However, more than terminology is a stake here. As we will see, some recent theories of reference implicitly assume that semantics is concerned with linguistic tokens. It is implicit, for example, in Kaplan's (1979) claim that indexicals refer as a function of context. However, I argue in Chapter 9 that this claim could qualify as semantic only if the function in question were well defined, which it is not (except in the case of 'I'). Devitt is a rare token semanticist who is explicit about his conception of semantics, as when he says, after distinguishing types from tokens, that tokens designate objects and that this is a semantic relationship (1980, 11 and 129). However, linguistic knowledge concerns expression types, not tokens. 'What every speaker [of a language] knows', as we say, is knowledge that people, as speakers and as hearers, apply to communication situations. If tokens of expressions had autonomous semantic properties, a hearer would have to discover them in order to understand an utterance, and a speaker would have to predict them correctly in order to produce an understandable utterance. In fact, however, it is by applying antecedent linguistic knowledge (along with general presumptions and specific mutual contextual beliefs), that speakers can produce understandable utterances and hearers can understand them.

Linguistic knowledge is knowledge about the properties of linguistic types. In-so-far as tokens have linguistic properties, these are wholly derived from the properties of their types. The physical properties of tokens, sounds of spoken ones and shapes of written ones, determine the types they belong to. Otherwise, their physical properties can only have pragmatic import. Tokens have no semantic properties of their own, and there is no more to understanding a token than using one's linguistic knowledge to identify and understand its type. The semantics of a type constrains the pragmatic properties of its utterance, but an utterance is an act of producing a token, not a linguistic item itself. So-called semantic properties of tokens are epiphenomena, wholly derived from (i.e. reducible to) semantic properties of types and pragmatic properties of utterances. They play no explanatory role in the theory of communication.

terms as referring (autonomously). If not that, it may at least have led people to think that the difference between speaker reference and token reference is merely terminological.

Once we get the explanatory order straight, we can see that the 'semantic' properties of tokens are epiphenomenal at best. Beyond appealing to the properties of the expression type being used, an explanation of an act of communication and its success is a matter of social psychology, adverting to information available in the context of utterance, the intention of the speaker, and the inference by the hearer. This type of explanation, along the lines of the SAS, is quite different from an appeal to semantics. As we will see when we examine various ostensibly semantic claims about various singular terms, often what is in question is the very domain of semantics.

PART THREE

SINGULAR TERMS

5

Definite Descriptions I: Vindicating Russell

Even though Russell's theory of descriptions has long been out of favour, it has remained remarkably influential. Maybe its influence has been due to the absence of a generally accepted alternative, or perhaps to the fact that it was Russell's. At any rate, I will rely on the strategy of the previous chapter to defend his theory against some familiar and seemingly forceful objections. I will argue that each objection is based on a misconstrual of Russell's theory and thereby imposes unreasonable demands on it. I view it merely as a semantic account of definite descriptions, and as such it should not be expected to explain pragmatic phenomena not within its province. The trouble with these objections is that they expect it to do what it does not even purport to do.

1. RUSSELL'S THEORY

As Frege's work made clear, the subject–predicate distinction of grammar had played an unduly prominent role in classical, Aristotelian logic. Before Frege the form of proposition expressed by sentences like (1) and (2)

| Some lawyers are honest. | (1) |
| All philosophers are wise. | (2) |

was thought to be directly reflected in their grammatical form. It would have seemed that in (1) honesty is predicated of some lawyers and in (2) wisdom is predicated of all philosophers. Moreover, the propositions expressed by these sentences were thought to have constituents expressed by the corresponding constituents of those sentences. So the properties being predicated, honesty and wisdom, are expressed by the grammatic predicates 'are honest' and 'are wise', and what they are predicated of, some lawyers and all philosophers, is expressed by the grammatical subjects 'some lawyers' and 'all philosophers'.

Grammatical appearances can be deceiving. This seems clear with (1) as soon as we ask which lawyers are the ones of which honesty is being predicated. (1) is true if there is at least one honest lawyer, but it does not matter which one. Also, if we make the natural assumption that a proposition is about its subject (at least if it has one), then the proposition expressed by (1) is about some lawyers. But which ones is it about? Only the honest ones? Then if (1) were false, the proposition that some lawyers are honest would not be about anyone. On the other hand, if the proposition were about all lawyers but not all lawyers are honest, then the subject expression of (1) would not express what the proportion is about.

Recognizing these and other difficulties, Frege took the radical step of denying that sentences like (1) and (2), despite being of subject–predicate grammatical form, are of subject–predicate logical form. He introduced the ingenious apparatus of quantification to represent them as having the quite different forms (3) and (4),

$(Ex)(x$ is a lawyer & x is honest). (3)

$(x)(if x is a philosopher, x is wise). (4)

Of course these formulas, with their quantifiers and variables, do not have exact counterparts in English (or German), but, as everyone knows, what (3) says is that there exists something that is both a lawyer and is honest, and (4) says that anything that is a philosopher is wise. Their English translations contain the words 'something' and 'anything', which, as nouns grammatically, are misleading logically. Only formulas like (3) and (4) perspicuously capture Frege's idea of eliminating grammatical subject expressions like 'some lawyers' and 'all philosophers' in favor of quantifiers, variables, predicates, and connectives. (3) and (4) make explicit that the propositions expressed by (1) and (2) are not of subject–predicate form, contrary to grammatical appearances.

Philosophers do not seem to appreciate that Frege's approach to 'all' and to 'some' sentences is no less radical than Russell's (1905) treatment of DESCRIPTION SENTENCES, as I call sentences of the form 'The F is G.' The only difference is that while Frege's approach has long since become orthodox, Russell's theory of descriptions has always been controversial, especially since Strawson's (1950) critique of it. We will take up that and other objections, but first we should be clear about what Russell's theory says.

Russell, like Frege, held that the grammatical form of a sentence can be misleading as to its logical form.[1] But whereas it has not been tempting, at least not for over a century, to regard the grammatical subjects of (1) and (2) as logical subject expressions, people are still tempted to regard description sentences as being of subject–predicate logical form. This temptation is understandable. Whereas no one with even minimal ontological sensibilities would suppose there to be an entity that 'some lawyers' denotes (surely not the 'disjunctive lawyer'), it is natural to suppose in the case of a description sentence like (5),

> The composer of *Turandot* was Italian. (5)

that 'the composer of *Turandot*' denotes the composer of *Turandot*. Russell does not suppose otherwise,[2] but he also supposes that definite descriptions, like quantifier phrases, are 'incomplete symbols'. An incomplete symbol is meaningless in isolation, says Russell, because its semantic contribution to sentences in which it occurs is not its denotation but its quantificational structure. For example, under analysis the logical form of (5) can be represented as (6),[3]

> $(Ex)(Cx$ & (y)(if Cy, then $y = x$) & x was Italian). (6)

where 'C' is shorthand for 'composed *Turandot*'. Using the inverted iota symbol, (6) can be abbreviated as (7),

> $\imath xCx$ was Italian. (7)

If '$\imath xCx$' were a logical singular term, then (7), hence (5), would indeed be of subject–predicate logical form, but for Russell it is not, as (6) indicates. (6) represents the proposition expressed by (5) as a kind of existential proposition to the effect that there exists

---

[1] It was actually Strawson (1952, 51) who coined this phrase. See Bach and Harnish (1979, 144-8) for further discussion.

[2] Indeed, Russell's (1905) list of denoting phrases includes quantifier phrases and indefinite descriptions as well. The fact that they are eliminated in favour of the apparatus of quantification makes clear that Russell does not regard denoting, in his broad sense of the term, as of fundamental semantic importance. All denoting phrases turn out to be 'incomplete symbols'.

[3] Again I am avoiding Russell's own formulation because of his idiosyncratic account of the universal and existential quantifiers in terms of an open sentence's being 'always true' or 'sometimes true'. Indeed, he seems implicitly to recognize how idiosyncratic it is when he translates it 'into ordinary language' (1919, 177) and produces something that sounds much more like a translation of (6) than of his own formulation. I will stick to the more straightforward apparatus of modern logical theory.

(timelessly) one and only one composer of *Turandot* and that he was Italian. Contrary to grammatical appearances, (5) expresses not a singular, subject–predicate proposition but a general one, specifically what may be called a UNIQUENESS PROPOSITION.

The rationale of Russell's theory of descriptions is nearly as familiar as the theory itself. Even if the theory seems implausible at first glance (description sentences do not *appear* to have anything like the form that (6) displays), it does offer neat solutions to four notorious puzzles. Indeed, as we will see later on (Chapter 8), since the same puzzles arise for sentences containing proper names as for description sentences, Russell subscribed to a description theory of ordinary proper names, according to which they function logically not as proper names but rather as disguised or, as he called them, 'truncated' descriptions. Here let us see how Russell's theory solves the traditional puzzles as they arise for description sentences.

First, the meaningfulness of a sentence like (5) does not depend on there being anything which satisfies the description it contains. If *Turandot* had no composer (or had more than one), (5) would be false but not meaningless. To appreciate this point one must realize that for Russell a subject–predicate proposition is expressible only by a sentence of the form '*a* is F',[4] where '*a*' is a logically proper name. The constituent contributed by the subject term '*a*' to the proposition expressed by the sentence is the individual it denotes. This is what the name means. Accordingly, if the name fails to denote, any sentence in which it occurs does not express a proposition and is therefore not (fully) meaningful. However, as (6) makes clear, a sentence containing a definite description is meaningful and expresses a proposition even if nothing satisfies the description. What the description contributes to the proposition expressed by the sentence is not the individual (if any) that satisfies the description but the concept expressed by the predicate it contains ('composer of *Turandot*'), as incorporated into Russell's quantificational apparatus. And because the proposition expressed by (5) has the form of (6), it is not singular but general. It is a uniqueness proposition.

Second, Russell's theory neutralizes the puzzles posed by existential sentences containing definite descriptions in subject position. Since Kant, most philosophers have thought that 'exists',

---

[4] Here and throughout I will limit discussion to sentences containing monadic predicates. The discussion can be extended straightforwardly to cover sentences with polyadic predicates.

though grammatically a predicate, does not function logically as one. Just as Frege's quantificational symbolism expresses this fact, so Russell's theory of descriptions reflects the fact that descriptions in grammatical subject position in existence sentences, such as (8) and (9),

The abominable snowman exists. (8)

The largest prime does not exist. (9)

cannot function as logical subject expressions. Russell's theory represents the form of (8) as (10),

$$(Ex)(Sx \,\&\, (y)(\text{if } Sy \text{ then } y = x)). \qquad (10)$$

where the predicate 'abominable snowman' is abbreviated as 'S'. A negative existential like (9) has the form of the negation of (10). Notice that the meaningfulness of (8) and (9), the first of which happens to be false, does not require that the descriptions denote anything. If it did, then no positive existence sentence could be false without being meaningless and no negative one could be true.

Then there is the case of identity sentences involving definite descriptions, as illustrated by (11),

The 1982 Wimbledon champion is the same as the 1974
Wimbledon champion. (11)

Here the problem is how (11), if true, can be informative. On the view that the semantic contribution of the descriptions is what they denote, namely Jimmy Connors, the semantic content of (11) is that Jimmy Connors is identical to Jimmy Connors. But surely that is not what (11) says.[5] Rather, what it says, according to Russell's theory, is represented by (12), where 'W' symbolizes '1982 Wimbledon champion' and 'C' '1974 Wimbledon champion'.

$$(Ex)(Wx \,\&\, (y)(\text{if } Wy \text{ then } y = x) \,\&\, Cx \,\&\, (z)(\text{if } Cz$$
$$\text{then } z = x)). \qquad (12)$$

(12) represents the form of (11) as a complex existential proposition, to the effect that there is an individual who was both a 1982 Wimbledon champion and a 1974 Wimbledon champion and that there was no other 1982 or 1974 Wimbledon champion.[6] A

---

[5] I suppose it could be argued that this is what (11) says but not what a speaker would mean in using it, just as someone who utters 'Boys will be boys' does not mean merely that. The problem is that if this view were correct, then (11) would not even be meaningful if there were no 1982 and 1974 Wimbledon champions.

[6] Obviously it would be incorrect to put the simpler (i),

$$(Ex)(Wx \text{ and } Cx \text{ and } (y)(\text{if } Wy \text{ and } Cy, \text{ then } y = x). \qquad (i)$$

in place of (12). (i) does not exclude the case in which, in addition to the one noteworthy consequence of Russell's approach is that a sentence like (13),

> The 1982 Wimbledon champion is identical to the
> 1974 Wimbledon champion. (13)

is not trivially true. For by replacing 'C' in (12) with 'W' and simplifying, we can represent (13) by the existential (14),

> $(Ex)(Wx \& (y) (\text{if } Wy \text{ then } y = x))$. (14)

As we can see from (10), (14) represents not only (13) but also (15),

> The 1982 Wimbledon champion exists. (15)

and that is anything but trivial.[7]

Finally, there is the case of belief sentences, such as (16) and (17),

> Giacomo believed that the composer of *Turandot* was
> Italian. (16)
>
> Bjorn believes that the 1982 Wimbledon champion is
> the same as the 1974 Wimbledon champion. (17)

To get the logical form in each case, we simply substitute the Russellian analyses of the 'that'-clauses, representing what Giacomo believed as the uniqueness proposition (6) and what Bjorn believes as (12). Since these are not singular but general propositions, (16) and (17) can be true whether or not the descriptions they contain denote anything. Once again, we see that on Russell's theory sentences containing definite descriptions can be meaningful without the descriptions having to denote. Descriptions make their semantic contributions with or without denotations.

As we will now see, these four virtues of Russell's theory have not made it immune from criticism. To the contrary, it has met with severe attacks. In the remainder of this chapter we will take up the three most influential ones.

2. STRAWSON'S OBJECTION

Strawson's paper 'On referring' (1950) poses what is still an influential objection to Russell's theory of descriptions. Strawson

individual who was both 1982 and 1974 Wimbledon champion, there were two other individuals, one of whom was 1982 and one 1974 champion. In fact, there were: Martina Navratilova and Chris Evert.

[7] I suppose it might be objected that since the two sentences (13) and (15) are syntactically so different, something must be wrong with Russell's theory if it has (14) representing both. But syntactic difference does not entail semantic difference, and (14) is not meant to capture the syntactic difference.

bases his objection on certain distinctions that Russell neglected. There is an irony here: as I will argue, these are just the distinctions Russell could have used to defend his theory against Strawson's objection. Strawson insists that

'Referring' is not something an expression does; it is something that someone can use an expression to do. Mentioning, or referring to, something is a characteristic of a *use* of an expression, just as 'being about' something, and truth-or-falsity, are characteristics of a *use* of a sentence. (1950, 80)

These distinctions are music to my ears. Yes, people refer, expressions are used to refer. Yes, assertions are true or false, sentences are used to make true or false assertions.[8] Nevertheless, these distinctions fail to undermine Russell's theory.

First notice how Strawson represents, or rather misrepresents, Russell's position. 'According to Russell, anyone who *asserted* S ["The king of France is wise"] would be *asserting*' that there is one and only one king of France and whoever is king of France is wise (1950, 178; my emphasis). If this is what Russell held (or an implication of it), Strawson's objection would have merit. However, Russell talks not about assertions but about sentences and about propositions, which he takes to be the meanings of sentences. He does not speak of asserting sentences, and his theory concerns the meanings of description sentences, not assertions made in using them. Granted, it would have been helpful if Russell had explicitly distinguished between sentences and the assertions made in using sentences, but nothing Russell does say implies that his claims about sentences were to apply to assertions they are used to make.

In Strawson's view, when a speaker uses a description sentence to make an assertion, not only does the speaker not assert what Russell supposedly says he asserts, the speaker does not assert something that has to be either true or false. If there is no king of France, according to Strawson the assertion of S is neither true nor false. As he says, the truth or falsity of the assertion 'does not arise', and the speaker is not asserting that there is a king of France

---

[8] Actually, I would not deny that some expressions (namely complete definite descriptions and proper names with only one bearer) refer in the sense of denoting, but with descriptions denoting is a derivative semantic property, since, as Russell showed, it drops out upon analysis. Also, I would grant that some sentences are true or false, namely what Quine (1960, 193) calls 'eternal sentences'.

but is merely 'implying' it. He can successfully use 'the king of France' to refer only if there is a (unique) king of France. As Strawson would later (1952) put it, the sentence (not merely the speaker) *presupposes* the existence (and uniqueness) of a king of France. By this Strawson could not mean that the *sentence* is true or false only if its presupposition holds, for in his view the truth or falsity of sentences does not arise. Rather, it is the assertion made in using the sentence that is true or false, but only if the presupposition holds. However, this only goes to show that presupposition is not a (semantic) property of sentences.

The trouble with Strawson's objection is that the claims on which it relies pertain not to description sentences but to assertions made in using them. Russell's theory of descriptions does not concern such assertions but rather the meanings of the sentences themselves. It was meant to exhibit the form of proposition expressed by description sentences, not a theory of their use. The Russellian analysis of, for example, (5) in terms of (6) gives the form of a proposition, not the content of an assertion. A proposition can be true or false, of course, but on Russell's theory (6) is true if the composer of *Turandot* was Italian and false otherwise. Nothing that Strawson says shows that this proposition, and not just an assertion of it, could be neither true nor false. And even though Strawson defines presupposition as a property of sentences, it is so only derivatively. This property is not a semantic property and a sentence possesses it only by virtue of a property of assertions made in using the sentence. To be relevant to Russell's theory, it would have to be a semantic property, not merely a pragmatic one.[9]

3. DONNELLAN'S OBJECTION

Donnellan's well-known distinction between REFERENTIAL and ATTRIBUTIVE uses of definite descriptions, though interesting and important in its own right (see the next chapter), was presented originally as posing a fundamental problem for Russell's unitary

---

[9] In Bach and Harnish (1979, 155–65) it is argued that there is no legitimate notion of semantic presupposition (as a property of sentences). And it turns out that there are several distinct kinds of pragmatic presupposition, each of which is a property of utterances.

theory of descriptions.[10] Donnellan suggested that there are two different sorts of assertion a speaker can make in using a description sentence, depending on which way he is using the description.

A speaker who uses a definite description attributively in an assertion[11] states something about whoever or whatever is the so-and-so. A speaker who uses a definite description referentially in an assertion, on the other hand, uses the description to enable his audience to pick out whom or what he is talking about and states something about that person or thing. (1966, 285)

Curiously enough, Russell himself formulated a similar distinction in contrasting two uses of names. When a name is used 'as a name', it is used 'merely to indicate what we are speaking about' (1919, 175), just as when a definite description is used referentially.[12] In both cases it is the referent, not the way in which it is referred to, that enters into what is asserted, yielding a singular proposition.[13] But when for Russell a name is used 'as a description' or for Donnellan a description is used attributively, the way in which the reference is made, not the referent itself, enters into what is asserted. Here 'we introduce an element of generality', as Donnellan (1966, 303) puts it, and are referring only 'in a very weak sense'. That is because what is being asserted is not a singular but a general (uniqueness) proposition.

The referential/attributive (R/A) distinction will be clarified in the next chapter, but we can consider here whether the distinction

[10] Actually, there is a wrinkle in Russell's theory making it not quite unitary, though in a way irrelevant here. He complicates his account (1919, 179) by distinguishing primary and secondary occurrences of descriptions in sentences like (i),

> The present king of France is not bald. (i)

'This is ambiguous', he says, because of a scope ambiguity. Negation can apply either to the predicate alone (primary), in which case, because there is no king of France, (i) expresses a false proposition, or to the entire sentence (secondary), in which case (i) expresses a true proposition. However, in consideration of a convincing argument due to Atlas (1977) that this is not a genuine ambiguity, I will persist in calling Russell's theory unitary.

[11] As Donnellan notes, the distinction applies to speech acts generally, but for ease of exposition he focuses on assertions (or statements). We will do likewise.

[12] Indeed, Russell (1918, 246) himself even suggested that descriptions can be used as names, that is 'merely to indicate what we are speaking about', i.e. referentially!

[13] As a matter of terminological preference, beginning with the next chapter I will call what is asserted here a SINGULAR STATEMENT. As I will explain there, my reason for not calling it a proposition is that it is not a complete thought content.

really does pose a problem for Russell's theory. Donnellan claims that Russell neglected the referential use and that while Russell's theory works fine for attributive uses, it is inapplicable to referential uses (1966, 283).[14] However, as many writers have since recognized,[15] Donnellan's distinction poses a problem for Russell only if it is semantically significant, with description sentences regarded as ambiguous and Russell's theory applying only to the attributive case. If the R/A distinction applies only to how descriptions and description sentences are *used*, it is simply irrelevant to Russell's theory.

Even Donnellan himself doubts that description sentences are ambiguous, and holds that 'whether or not a definite description is used referentially or attributively is a function of the speaker's intentions in a particular case' (1966, 297).[16] Nevertheless, he thinks that the R/A distinction indicates that Russell's view

that sentences can be divided up into predicates, logical operators, and referring expressions is not generally true. In the case of definite descriptions one cannot always assign the referential function in isolation from a particular occasion on which it is used. (1966, 297)

There is a fallacy in this argument, however. Donnellan is implicitly assuming that if a description sentence is unambiguous but has two uses (its meaning underdetermines how the description is being used), then both uses are strictly literal. He says nothing that might defend this assumption, which I believe to be false in any case, for reasons given by Kripke (1977). In brief, Kripke argues that even if Russell's theory of descriptions were incorrect for English, we can imagine a hypothetical language, call it Russell English, to which the theory applies. Moreover, we can imagine that users of Russell English operate perfectly well with the R/A distinction. Then we can conclude that the existence of the R/A distinction in and of

[14] He says just the opposite about Strawson's view, claiming that Strawson's doctrine of presupposition applies only to referential uses and that Strawson overlooked attributive uses.

[15] They include Kripke (1979), Bertolet (1980), Wettstein (1981), Devitt (1981), and Salmon (1982).

[16] For this reason Donnellan suggests that we might call description sentences 'pragmatically ambiguous'. However, inasmuch as he explicitly contrasts this with syntactic and semantic ambiguity, it is clear that he does not view this as ambiguity in the relevant (grammatical) sense, that is such that an ambiguous sentence has more than one reading. To me his phrase is an oxymoron.

itself does not refute Russell's theory for English. The burden is still on Russell's critics to refute Russell's theory.[17]

Donnellan's argument against Russell's theory fails to allow for the possibility of an account of the R/A distinction on which only the attributive use counts as strictly literal: a speaker who uses a description sentence in a strictly literal way is using the description attributively and is asserting a uniqueness proposition. The assertion is about whatever fits (uniquely) the description used, and the speaker is referring to that individual, though only in Donnellan's 'very weak sense'. In contrasting this with the referential use, Donnellan overlooks the possibility that the referential use is not strictly literal, and gives no reason to rule that out. In my view, which I will defend in the next chapter, the referential use involves the attributive and is not strictly literal because indirect. That is, when a speaker uses a description referentially, thereby to assert a singular proposition about the individual he is referring to (in the strong sense), he is also asserting the general, uniqueness proposition associated with an attributive use.

One possible basis for the argument needed by Donnellan appeals to his observation that in using a description referentially, a speaker can refer to something and make a true statement about it even if it fails to satisfy the description. Donnellan gives the now famous example of a certain Jones on trial for the murder of Smith. Jones is behaving rather strangely there in the defendant's box, and Brown, assuming the innocent Jones to be Smith's murderer, utters (1),

Smith's murderer is insane.   (1)

Clearly Brown is referring to Jones, not to the real murderer (as he would be if he were using 'Smith's murderer' attributively), and yet Jones does not fit the description.[18] Surely Brown is asserting a

---

[17] Devitt, who defends the semantic significance of the R/A distinction, gives several arguments against Kripke, including one directed at Kripke's appeal to Russell English. Devitt appeals to what he calls a 'referential convention for definite descriptions' (1981, 516), but he makes no effort to show that such a convention exists or that the referential use of descriptions requires its existence. In addition, he gives the argument from incomplete descriptions, which we will take up in the next section. Devitt is rightly dubious about Kripke's account of the difference between referential and attributive intentions, but Kripke's account can be improved upon.

[18] Although Donnellan uses such examples to motivate the R/A distinction, Wettstein (1981) thinks they are inessential to it and to its semantic significance. However, in arguing for its semantic significance, Wettstein fails to distinguish, as Salmon (1982) has pointed out, what the speaker asserts from the semantic content

singular proposition about Jones (that he is insane). However, does the fact that Jones did not murder Smith show that Brown is not also (indeed literally and directly) asserting the uniqueness proposition that the murderer of Smith is insane? Not in the least. All it shows is that this proposition could be false while the singular proposition about Jones is true. Of course Brown, taking Jones to be the murderer, has implicitly ruled out this possibility, and so Donnellan might object that Brown did not mean and did not assert that whoever murdered Smith is insane. For suppose that after uttering (1) Brown is told, and believes, that Jones is not guilty. Brown is still prepared to assert of Jones, on the basis of his behaviour, that he is insane. Accordingly Brown says, 'I didn't mean that Smith's murderer is insane but that Jones, the man on trial for Smith's murder, is insane.' But Brown's willingness to take back (1)—he would not continue to use (1) to assert of Jones that he is insane[19]—does not show that when he uttered (1) he did not mean that whoever murdered Smith is insane. Quite the contrary, he is now taking back (1) because he *did* mean that.

So the fact that definite descriptions can be used referentially as well as attributively does not refute Russell's theory of descriptions. That would require an argument that establishes the semantic significance of the R/A distinction. Unless such an argument is forthcoming, Russell's theory can allow for the referential as well as the attributive use. When a speaker uses a description attributively in uttering a description sentence, he is asserting a uniqueness proposition. When using the description referentially, as I will argue, he is also asserting a singular proposition about the individual he takes (or takes the audience to take, as in the last footnote) to satisfy the description. In this case, the speaker must be thinking of the referent in some other way than under the description he is using, and he must intend the hearer also to think of the referent in some other way. As we will see when this account of referential uses is developed in the next chapter, it is not necessary that the hearer's way of thinking of the referent be the same as the speaker's. This is because the speaker is asserting a

of the sentence used. As a result, Wettstein mistakenly classifies the former as semantic.

[19] There is a ,variant of this situation in which he would continue to use (1) to assert this, namely if his audience is unaware of Jones's innocence and he does not wish to enlighten them. He would still be stating (1), for he would be expressing the belief that (1), a belief that he does not have.

singular proposition (over and above the uniqueness proposition expressed by the sentence containing the description being used), so that it does not matter precisely how either party thinks of the object that proposition is about, provided that they are both thinking of the same object.

4. THE INCOMPLETE DESCRIPTION OBJECTION

So far we have considered only sentences with complete definite descriptions. As we have seen, Russell's theory is not threatened by the fact that when a speaker utters such a sentence,

The discoverer of X-rays was bald. (1)

he can use the description referentially. But some philosophers have thought that a more serious threat to Russell's theory is posed by incomplete definite descriptions.[20] Considering how much more common they are than complete ones, it would certainly be a lame defence of Russell to say that his theory is meant to apply only to sentences containing complete descriptions. On the other hand, it would be an equally lame objection to Russell's theory to claim that it is refuted by descriptions like 'the table' and 'the man', as in the case of a sentence like (2),

The table is covered with dust. (2)

simply because no one who uttered (2) would mean it. In my view, sentences like (2) are standardly used *s*-non-literally. Russell's theory may imply (2) is true just in case there is exactly one table and it is covered with dust, but the theory does not imply that anyone who utters (2) would mean what it means. Russell's theory is concerned with the meaning of such sentences, not their use, and surely it is not a *semantic* fact that there is more than one table in the universe. Nor, in regard to the description in (3),

The man who has crossed continents walking backwards
wears glasses equipped with rear-view mirrors. (3)

is it a semantic fact that there is only one man who has crossed continents walking backwards. To suppose that 'the table' and 'the

---

[20] There is no uniform label for them. They have been variously called 'improper', 'imperfect', and even 'indefinite definite descriptions', but I prefer 'incomplete', if only by default.

man who has crossed continents walking backwards' make different kinds of semantic contributions to sentences in which they occur would have the following absurd consequence. If, perchance, there existed but one table and many men, not just Pleni Wingo, who crossed continents walking backwards, the two descriptions would then receive reverse semantic treatment.[21] For this reason alone, I believe that incomplete definite descriptions deserve the same semantic treatment as complete ones—the difference between them is not semantic.[22]

Yet it might be objected that something must be wrong with any semantic account of a sentence which predicts (together with common knowledge) that we never use the sentence literally. Surely, it would be insisted, every sentence must have a literal use. But the Russellian account does not deny this of (2). Of course every sentence *can* be used literally, but as we saw in the previous chapter, there are many sentences which are standardly used (*s-*) non-literally. A sentence whose utterance, if taken at face value, is conspicuously false, uninformative, or irrelevant is likely to be used non-literally (if used at all). This often happens when lexical material is absent from an obviously false sentence but where the speaker intends the hearer to fill it in. For example, a spectator might say at the finish line of a race, 'Sebastian doesn't look tired, he is tired.' Since Sebastian obviously looks tired, the speaker would likely be intending a suppressed 'merely' before 'look', and the hearer would infer this because the speaker could not reasonably be taken to be stating that Sebastian does not look tired but is tired (anyway). Non-literal utterances like this are common. We much prefer not to make fully explicit what we mean when that can easily be inferred, and, indeed, speech is stilted when words that can easily be filled in are not suppressed.

Using an incomplete definite description in place of a complete but more elaborate one is just one case of this widespread phenomenon. So if a speaker were to utter (2), surely he would not be asserting that the one and only table in the universe is covered

[21] These possibilities are exceptions to Salmon's suggestion that what makes some descriptions incomplete is how 'little descriptive content is found in the wording' (1982, 44).

[22] There are, to be sure, definite descriptions that are complete in virtue of their meanings (they might be called 'semantically complete'), such as 'the smallest prime number' and 'the first president of Zimbabwe', but in general, whether or not a description is complete is not a semantic question.

with dust. He is likely to be using 'the table' as short for some complete description like 'the table nearby', 'the table previously mentioned', 'the table I am pointing to',[23] or something of the form 'the table which is G'. Whenever a description 'the F' is used as short for a complete description 'the F_c', I will refer to the latter as its COMPLETION, which the hearer is intended to identify as such. So if a speaker utters (2) but is implicitly asserting what could be made explicit by (4),

The table I am pointing to is covered with dust.   (4)

(2) can still be given a Russellian analysis, which after all concerns only the meaning of (2), not its every use.[24]

Now Kripke thinks that incomplete descriptions pose a problem for Russell's theory because he doubts 'that such descriptions can always be regarded as elliptical with some uniquely specifying conditions added' and he finds it 'tempting to assimilate such descriptions to the corresponding demonstratives (for example, "that table")' (1977, 255 and 271). Kripke is assuming here that 'the Russellian picture' requires supposing that a speaker who utters an incomplete description is using it as 'elliptical' for some complete one. Kripke's worry, and his reason for wanting to assimilate incomplete descriptions to the corresponding demonstratives, is that they are not always used as short for some completion. However, this worry is based on the false assumption that Russell's theory requires that they must always be so used. His assumption would be true if incomplete descriptions had to be used attributively, for then there would always have to be some specific completion that the speaker intends, but they do not have to be so used.

Incomplete definite descriptions are often used referentially, as when used anaphorically or demonstratively. If a certain table is being discussed, it might be referred to as 'the table' (or, for that matter, as 'it'). If a certain table is the only one present, again it

---

[23] Strictly speaking, these descriptions, as well as Russell's famous 'the present king of France', are not complete because they contain indexicals. Indeed, they should not be called definite but 'indexical descriptions'.

[24] Occasionally I have heard Russell's theory defended against the incomplete description objection as follows: the quantifiers are restricted, so that the variables range only some narrow, contextually determined domain. However, there is no clear sense in which context does determine the range of variables and thereby restrict quantifiers. Context is not fixed independently of the utterances made in it (see Chapter 9).

might be referred to as 'the table'. There may or may not be some completion of 'the table' that the speaker intends the hearer to figure out, but if he has a certain table in mind and intends to be making a statement about it regardless of how the hearer may think of it, his use of 'the table' is referential and no unique intended completion is required for the success of his referential intention. He is referring to a certain table objectually, not descriptively. So Kripke is right to doubt that an incomplete description must always be used elliptically (i.e. as short) for some completion of it, but he is wrong to think that this poses a problem for Russell's theory. Nor should he find it 'tempting to assimilate such descriptions to the corresponding demonstratives', because the fact that certain uses of 'the table' are the same as certain uses of 'that table' does make the two phrases synonymous. After all, 'the table' does have an attributive use. It might be suggested that it has two senses, one of which is the same as that of 'that table', but here, as always, we should remember Kripke's own caution against 'the lazy man's approach in philosophy to posit ambiguities when in trouble' (1977, 268).

Wettstein (1981) produces a more subtle objection in connection with incomplete definite descriptions. He is aware of the point made above but claims that there are *attributive* uses of incomplete descriptions where the speaker has no single completion in mind. Wettstein borrows an example from Donnellan, sentence (5).

The next president will be a dove on Vietnam.   (5)

We are to suppose that the speaker has no idea who the next president will be and is thus using the description attributively. Wettstein suggests, quite plausibly, that there is no reason to think that the context will supply an implicit 'of the United States' rather than 'of our country' (1981, 256). So the problem is to specify just what uniqueness proposition the user of (5) is asserting.

There are two distinct questions here. One is whether the speaker's intention regarding how the description is to be completed is identifiable. The other is whether he has such an intention. The former question is relatively unimportant, for if the speaker has such an intention but it is not identifiable, all this means is that he is communicating with less than full success. If the speaker was using 'the next president' as short for 'the next president of my country' but it was taken as short for 'the next president of the United States', and speaker and hearer mutually believed both completions to denote the same individual, for all practical purposes the speaker would have communicated successfully. This would be an example of the sort of minor discrepancy (discussed by Bach and Harnish 1979, 87–9) between the speaker's intention and what the hearer takes it to be that is insufficient to vitiate communication. In the example, communicative success might not be achieved if the speaker was not American but the hearer took him to be.

The important question is whether a speaker, in using an incomplete definite description attributively, must have a certain completion in mind. Suppose that two musicians are speculating on the hazards of performing the world première of the newly discovered fifth symphony of Charles Ives. His fourth symphony, experience has established, demands more than one conductor for a coherent performance. The two musicians know that the Hartford Symphony is scheduled to perform the Fifth that evening, but they have no idea who the conductor will be. After studying the score one of the musicians utters (6),

> Before he's through, the conductor won't be able to see
> straight, much less stay on his feet. (6)

Is there some completion of 'the conductor' that he intends the other musician to identify? Suppose there are many complete descriptions that the speaker believed to be true of the conductor he is talking about, such as 'tonight's conductor of the Hartford Symphony', 'the conductor of the world première of Ives's Fifth', 'today's most foolhardy conductor', and 'the conductor soon to be most in need of psychiatric treatment'. There may be more such descriptions, but even if only the first two are good candidates for the intended completion, the problem is that there is no reason for us to think (or for the speaker to expect) the hearer to opt for one rather than the other. But why not both? Then he would take the intended completion to be 'the conductor who tonight will lead the Hartford Symphony in the world première of Ives's Fifth'. The same thing is likely in the example involving 'the next president'. Given that it is mutually believed that the speaker and the hearer's country is the United States, the speaker could intend, and reasonably expect to be taken to be intending, the hearer to take the completion to be 'the next president of our country, the United States'.

Thus we need not abandon the position that attributive uses of incomplete definite descriptions must have intended completions. The two problem cases show that there does not have to be a simple and unique completion (unique at least up to synonymy) which the hearer must identify if communication is to be successful. In one case the speaker may intend the hearer to identify a specific completion but the circumstances of utterance do not suffice to enable the hearer to identify it rather than some other one (mutually believed to be true) of the same individual. In this case the hearer may pick a different one but still, for all practical purposes, understand the speaker. In the other case the speaker's intention combines the several coextensive descriptions that are equally salient under the circumstances. The hearer understands him if he identifies this complex completion.

Each of the three objections to Russell's theory relies on pragmatic considerations to make a semantic point. Strawson's appeal to presupposition rests on intuitions about assertions, not about sentences used to make them. Donnellan, though correct to note that Russell's theory does not take the referential/attributive distinction into account, is wrong to think that it should. He himself presents the distinction as between two *uses* of definite descriptions and explicitly doubts that it generates any semantic ambiguity. And Kripke's and Wettstein's objection that Russell's theory fails for incomplete descriptions wrongly assumes that the completeness or incompleteness of a description is semantically significant. The existence of incomplete descriptions only goes to show that in using an incomplete description to refer to some specific individual, one is not quite speaking literally. In sum, all three objections cite irrelevant facts about use to draw conclusions about meaning.

6

Definite Descriptions II:
The Referential/Attributive Distinction

If Russell's theory of descriptions concerned their use and not just their meaning, it could account only for attributive uses of complete definite descriptions, where what is asserted[1] is a uniqueness proposition. But it is not a theory of their use, contrary to what the various objections to it implicitly assume. In the course of defending it against these objections, I sketched how it could be supplemented with a pragmatic account of referential uses. Now I will develop that account in detail, but not before examining how Donnellan formulated the referential/attributive distinction originally.

1. DONNELLAN'S ACCOUNT

Donnellan contrasts referential and attributive uses in a number of ways. Sometimes he emphasizes the role of the description in determining the object being talked about. Sometimes he focuses on the contribution of the description to the statement made in using a sentence containing it. Often he stresses how the speaker is thinking of the object being talked about. In fact, there are at least five different ways in which Donnellan attempts to clarify the R/A distinction, and I will discuss them in turn. None does full justice to the distinction, but they will head us in the right direction as well as point to several other distinctions that will prove useful later.

For the moment, let us assume that the descriptions under consideration are complete. According to Donnellan's initial formulation,

A speaker who uses a definite description attributively in an assertion states something about whoever or whatever is the so-and-so. A speaker who uses a definite description referentially in an assertion, on the other hand, uses

---

[1] Again it should be noted that the R/A distinction is not restricted to statements and assertions, though it is convenient to focus on those cases.

the description to enable his audience to pick out whom or what he is talking about and states something about that person or thing. (1966, 285)

When used attributively the description determines which individual is being talked about, namely the one (if there is a unique one) that fits it. When a speaker uses a description referentially, 'to enable his audience to pick out whom or what he is talking about', he does not intend his audience simply to determine what fits the description. A description used referentially can enable the audience to pick out the referent even without applying to it. But how is this accomplished? A proper formulation of the R/A distinction should explain how. Unfortunately, the various glosses that Donnellan gives on the distinction tend more to cloud than to clarify it.

(*a*) When a description is used attributively the statement is about whatever uniquely satisfies the description. In the case of (1),

> Smith's murderer is insane.   (1)

the statement is about whoever murdered Smith, regardless of who the speaker may believe that to be. So if the speaker is mistaken about that, his statement is not about who he thinks it is about. But if 'Smith's murderer' is being used referentially, then according to Donnellan the statement is about whoever the speaker 'has in mind', even if that individual, say the man in the dock, is not Smith's murderer.

Intuitively there does seem to be a distinction here, but the notion of having someone (or something) in mind is not all that helpful. A speaker who uses 'Smith's murderer' attributively and has no beliefs about who Smith's murderer is could still be said to have Smith's murderer in mind, though only under the description 'Smith's murderer'. If thinking of Smith's murderer under the description 'the man in the dock' qualifies as having him in mind, then thinking of him under the description 'Smith's murderer' should qualify as well. It seems that Donnellan should have said that if a description is being used attributively, it determines what the speaker is talking about regardless of who he has in mind, whereas if it is being used referentially, there is a certain individual he intends to be talking about even if that individual does not fit the description and someone else does. Notice that for this to be possible the speaker must be thinking of that individual in some other way than under the description used. Otherwise he could not believe a certain individual to satisfy that description, in which case he would be in no position to intend to talk about that individual.

So the difference between having and not having an individual in mind does not help clarify the R/A distinction. More to the point is a different distinction, that between intending to be talking about a certain individual, who may or may not satisfy the description used, and intending to be talking about whichever individual satisfies that description. But then the question arises of what it is to intend to be talking about a certain individual.

(*b*) Sometimes Donnellan seems to be suggesting that with a referential use the speaker is expressing a *de re* belief about some individual, whereas with an attributive use he is expressing a *de dicto* belief, which is about whatever (uniquely) fits the description.[2] Donnellan is not explicit on this point but suggests it with his contrast between believing something about 'someone in particular' and 'someone or other' (1966, 299). The situation is not clarified by his occasional reliance on the difference between 'believes of' and 'believes that' forms of belief ascription. Here the trouble is that both sentences of the form 'S believes of the F that it is G' and those of the form 'S believes that the F is G' can be used to ascribe either *de re* or *de dicto* beliefs about the F.[3] S could intend to be talking about someone in particular without having a *de re* belief about him, or intend to be talking about whoever is the F while having a *de re* belief about the F.

An analogous problem arises when Donnellan appeals to the distinction between saying of and saying that. He says that in using a description referentially a speaker expresses a belief about, or says something of, a certain individual. But if Donnellan means that the belief expressed must be *de re*, his requirement is too strong. One can use a description referentially to talk about an

---

[2] David Kaplan goes so far as to suggest that description sentences exhibit 'a kind of *de dicto–de re* ambiguity . . . [in which] there is no question of an analysis in terms of scope, since there is no operator' (1979, 395). The content of an utterance of a description sentence can be either a general, uniqueness proposition or a singular proposition. Unfortunately, Kaplan gives no reason for claiming ambiguity or for denying that the singular proposition being asserted is a matter of the speaker's intention rather than of the content of the utterance. Although Kaplan is often careful to distinguish utterances from sentence types, when he suggests ambiguity he seems to be slipping from sentence type to utterance.

[3] Also, recall that treatments of the *de re/de dicto* distinction have been clouded by the ambiguity of the phrase '*de re* (or *de dicto*) belief ascription'. '*De re*' (and '*de dicto*') can modify either 'belief' or 'ascription'. Moreover, the type of belief ascription does not determine the type of belief being ascribed.

individual one is thinking of not in a *de re* way but only under a description (in a *de dicto* way). What matters is not how the speaker is thinking of the referent but only that he be thinking of it in some other way than under the description he is using. He need not be thinking of it in a *de re* way but merely under some FALL-BACK DESCRIPTION. If he uses 'the F' but intends to be talking about the G, presumably believing the G to be the F, should it turn out that the G is not the F, he could stil have successfully used 'the F' referentially to talk about the G. His intention to be referring to the G is controlling.

(*c*) Sometimes Donnellan says that only descriptions used attributively 'occur essentially' in an utterance. Evidently, his point is that, in using 'the F' attributively in 'The F is G', a speaker intends to be asserting the uniqueness proposition that the F is G. The trouble is that the speaker could state that the F is G without using 'The F is G' to state that. He could use some other description that expresses the same individual concept as 'the F', in which case the description does not occur essentially in the utterance. All that is essential is the individual concept the description expresses.[4]

(*d*) Contrasting attributive and referential uses, Donnellan remarks, 'In the first, if nothing is the [F] then nothing has been said to be [G]. In the second, the fact that nothing is the [F] does not have this consequence.' (1966, 287) The trouble is that a description can be used attributively even if nothing is the F. Surely one can use a description non-literally and yet use it attributively, as in (2),

The next turkey to buy a used car from us may not
live to regret it.   (2)

It might be objected that Donnellan was talking only about literal uses, but he himself gives examples of descriptions used non-literally, though referentially. One can ask 'Is the king in his countinghouse?' (1966, 291) and use 'the king' to refer to a usurper, where the speaker does not think, and does not think his audience thinks, this person to be king. Donnellan overlooks that this very description could be used attributively, yet non-literally, to talk about whoever happens to be the pretender to the throne. The same point applies to a non-literal but attributive use of 'the

---

[4] This point is made by Loar (1976), who suggests further, without giving a full explanation, that attributive uses are 'generalizing' while referential uses are 'identifying'.

man drinking a martini'. Suppose that the Company prohibits drinking on the job and that a spy is ordered by his boss to go to a certain bar and deliver an envelope to the man drinking a martini. Not knowing who this man is (it could be anyone the Company sent), the spy could still use the description attributively, believing and intending his audience to believe that this man, whoever he is, will be drinking water in a martini glass.

Even if we restrict our attention to descriptions used referentially but otherwise literally,[5] still it is not true that if nothing is the F something must have been said to be G. For example, suppose a courtroom observer looks at the man in the dock, who is waving his arms wildly, and utters (1),

> Smith's murderer is insane.   (1)

He mistakenly thinks this man to be Smith's murderer and uses 'Smith's murderer' to refer to him. I certainly agree with Donnellan that the speaker does not merely intend to be but really is referring to the man in the dock, and I agree that the speaker is not referring to whoever Smith's murderer may be, someone other than the innocent man in the dock. Even so, the courtroom observer is not *saying* that the man in the dock is insane but that Smith's murderer is insane. However, he is *asserting* that the man in the dock is insane, for that is who he is referring to.

Here I have not really contradicted Donnellan, for he does distinguish saying that from saying of. In the case of (1) his claim is that the speaker is not saying *that* the man in the dock is insane but rather is saying *of* the man in the dock that he is insane. I am willing to grant that the speaker is stating of the man in the dock that he is insane, for that is the man he is referring to. But stating is an illocutionary act, and referring is a component of illocutionary acts. Saying is a locutionary act and does not include the speaker's act of referring. At that level expressions refer, i.e. denote, and in the case of (1) 'Smith's murderer' refers to (denotes) the individual who murdered Smith.

It could be objected here that Donnellan did not have a rigorous locutionary/illocutionary distinction in mind when he made the point I am quarrelling with. In that case I have no objection, except

---

[5] Strictly speaking, no referential use is literal, as I have suggested already and will argue for shortly. However, examples like the one discussed in this paragraph do not have features like the obviously non-literal cases mentioned above, since the speaker is using the description to refer to an individual he takes to satisfy it.

that the point does not help illuminate the R/A distinction. It is just another way of indicating that a description, if used referentially, can be used to refer to something that does not satisfy it. What we need to know is how that can be done and whether it has any semantic significance, for example for Russell's theory. So if Donnellan's point is meant to apply at the locutionary level, it would be semantically significant. It would imply that a sentence like (1) is ambiguous and that there are two distinct things that a speaker could be saying in uttering it. If he is using the description attributively, what he is saying is a uniqueness proposition (that Smith's murderer is insane); if he is using it referentially, what he is saying is a singular proposition, of the man in the dock that he is insane. However, Donnellan has given no reason to think that description sentences are ambiguous and can be used to say (in the strict, locutionary sense) two different things.

(*e*) Finally, Donnellan explains the R/A distinction in terms of the kind of proposition being asserted by the speaker. As noted in the previous chapter, Donnellan remarks that with an attributive use (the only use, he thinks, allowed by Russell's theory), 'we introduce an element of generality which ought to be absent if what we are doing is referring to some particular thing' (1966, 303). We assert only general, uniqueness propositions and are referring only 'in a very weak sense'. In other words, the identity of the individual (weakly) referred to does not contribute to the identity of the (uniqueness) proposition asserted. With a referential use, we really are 'referring to some particular thing' and are asserting a singular proposition whose identity does depend on that of the referent.

It should be clear that I have no quarrel with this way of formulating the R/A distinction. The problem is to clarify the formulation. As I have suggested, that will require characterizing the contents of the intentions associated with both types of use. What matters here is not how the speaker is thinking of the individual to which he is weakly or strongly referring but how he intends the hearer to think of that individual. Moreover, as we have seen, the R/A distinction is independent of that between thinking of an individual under a description or thinking of an individual in some non-descriptive way. The importance of distinguishing these distinctions, if not evident already, will become clear as we take up Searle's account, which is very much on the right track but gets derailed because he slights these distinctions.

2. SEARLE'S ACCOUNT

Recently Searle (1979) has debunked the R/A distinction but not by claiming it to be illusory. Rather, he tries to assimilate it to a general distinction in the theory of speech acts and denies that it has any independent significance. I agree that it can be so assimilated but claim that it is still significant in its own right. I share with Searle the view that sentences containing descriptions used referentially are used to perform indirect illocutionary acts, but this does not mean there is nothing more to the R/A distinction than that. Doing justice to the several distinctions mentioned in the previous paragraph shows that there is.

Searle agrees that a (complete) definite description used attributively determines, given the way the world is, the object being talked about, namely the object that fits it uniquely. When one uses a description referentially, however, according to Searle (1979, 146–50) there are two aspects under which the object referred to is being thought of. The description being used expresses the 'secondary aspect', but the speaker is prepared to 'fall back' on some 'primary aspect'. The description need not be true of the referent, and the speaker need not believe it to be. Expressing only the secondary aspect, its purpose is not to determine but merely to enable the audience to identify the referent. The referent is determined by the primary aspect, for that is the aspect under which the speaker is thinking of the referent. For the speaker's statement to be true, the object satisfying the primary aspect must have the property being ascribed. Contrary to Donnellan, who claims that to use a description attributively is to refer 'in a very weak sense' at best, Searle maintains that there is the same kind of reference in both uses. The difference between the two consists in whether or not the description being used expresses the primary aspect under which the reference is being made.

Searle is surely on the right track, but there are three difficulties or unclarities with his formulation of the R/A distinction. First, he is unclear about the role of the primary aspect, under which the speaker is supposed to think of the object. Most of Searle's discussion suggests that when a speaker uses a description referentially, he need not intend the hearer to think of the referent under that aspect. Even when he gets down to details and says that in the referential use of definite descriptions one performs the act of referring to an object as satisfying the primary aspect by way of performing an act of reference expressing a secondary aspect,

and adds that

one's communication intentions will succeed if one's hearer grasps the primary intention on the basis of hearing the expression which expresses the secondary intention. (1979, 147)

Searle does not state explicitly that grasping the speaker's primary intention requires identifying the primary aspect under which the speaker is thinking of the object or that this intention contains such a requirement—but he does not deny it either. In any case, such a requirement would reduce a referential use of one description to an attributive but non-literal 'use' of another. That is, the speaker would be using one to mean another. However, what distinguishes referential uses is not that the speaker intends the hearer to identify the primary aspect under which he is thinking of the object but that he intends the hearer to identify the object itself. The account to be developed in the next section will spell out what such an intention involves.

The second shortcoming of Searle's formulation stems from his neglect of incomplete descriptions. In saying that in attributive cases 'the expression uttered expresses the primary aspect under which reference is made' and that 'speaker meaning and sentence meaning are the same' (1979, 148), he cannot be talking about incomplete descriptions, which too can be used attributively (by way of being used as short for their intended completions). At any rate, what Searle says can be easily corrected: when one utters a sentence with an incomplete description used attributively, its intended completion expresses the primary aspect, and what the speaker means is the same as the meaning of the sentence yielded by replacing the incomplete description used with its intended completion.

The third difficulty, again easily remedied, is an apparent inconsistency. Despite holding that referential uses involve two acts of referring, one under the secondary aspect and one under the primary, Searle seems to deny that two statements are being made, one associated with each act of referring. This is evident when he says that 'The content of the statement cannot be expressed by "Smith's murderer is insane" for the statement can be true even though there is no Smith's murderer', and he describes the primary aspect as 'that aspect under which reference is made that actually counts in the truth conditions of the statement' (1979, 147). He thereby implies that the speaker is making but one statement and that the description used does not express a part of its content. Searle is being faithful to Donnellan's picture, but his formulation seems to involve an inconsistency. For how can there be two acts of referring but only one statement? This is possible only if one of those acts, the one under the secondary aspect, is not associated with any statement. Searle should explain how an isolated act of referring is possible.[6] However, I see no reason why he should commit himself to this view. As Donnellan emphasized, a speaker using a description referentially can make a true statement even if the description does not apply to the object being referred to, but this is not a good reason for denying that the speaker is making a (uniqueness) statement involving the secondary aspect, since that is not the statement that would be true. So Searle should say that it is precisely by using 'The F is G' to state directly that the F is G that a speaker can state (indirectly) that the object he is thinking of under some unexpressed primary aspect is G. Since Searle allows two acts of referring anyway, he might as well acknowledge that a statement is being made directly under the secondary aspect expressed by the description being used.[7] And that would explain why a speaker would withdraw his original statement if that description does apply to the intended referent.

3. REFERENTIAL USES

In uttering a sentence of the form 'The F is G', a speaker is saying that the F is G. He may not be stating that, however, for he might not take 'the F' to be complete[8] or he might be using it

---

[6] Indeed, in *Speech Acts* Searle seems to deny that this is possible, as when he says that 'one cannot *just* refer and predicate without making an assertion or asking a question or performing some other illocutionary act' (1969, 25).

[7] If it were objected that this secondary act of referring is associated not with a direct act of stating but merely with the act of *saying* that the F is G, I would reply that if 'the F' is incomplete, some intended completion of it expresses the secondary aspect. For this reason the secondary act of referring cannot be associated merely with an act of saying.

[8] So far I have paid little heed to the distinction between actual and believed completeness. It should be clear that since the speaker's intention determines the

non-literally. If the speaker believes that it is complete and is using it (and 'is G') literally, he is stating that the F is G. But if he is using 'the F' referentially, he must, I claim, be thinking of the individual he is talking about in some other way than merely as the F. Only then could he be in a position to make a statement about that individual even if it is not F. This does not mean, however, that he is not literally and directly making a uniqueness statement. Indeed, it is by so doing that he is indirectly making a primary statement about that individual. We now need to ask what is the content of that statement and how the hearer is to identify it.

Since the speaker is using 'the F' referentially, he must be thinking of the referent in some other way that just as the F. He could be thinking of it under some other description, in some non-descriptive way, or, mixing the two, under an indexical description. Let us abbreviate this other way of thinking of the putative F with a singular term '*d*', of unspecified type. Presumably the speaker believes that *d* is the F.[9] However, he need not be expressing the belief (stating) that *d* is the F, for that requires intending the hearer to think of the referent as *d* and the speaker may have no such intention. In using 'the F' referentially, he is making an objectual reference. His referential intention is to be expressing a belief about the object that he presumably takes to be the F, but it does not specify how the hearer is to think of that object. It is satisfied if the hearer does think of that object in some way or another (perhaps under some other description), taking that object to be the one the speaker is expressing a belief about.[10]

type and content of the illocutionary act being performed, what matters is not whether the description being used is complete but whether the speaker believes (or believes the hearer to believe, or at least believes the hearer to believe him to believe) it to be complete. In practice, of course, these subtleties are inconsequential, since people generally know whether or not a description is complete.

[9] I say 'presumably' because he might believe only that the audience believes that *d* is the F or even merely that the audience believes that he believes that *d* is the F. Ordinarily it will be mutually believed by speaker and audience that *d* is the F. Donnellan's emphasis on extraordinary cases creates the false impression that the speaker is not asserting (directly and literally) a uniqueness proposition even in ordinary cases.

[10] This leaves open the possibility that the hearer is thinking of the object in no other way than as the one the speaker is expressing a belief about. That is a case of what I call UNSPECIFIED reference, in which the object the hearer actually thinks of depends on the object the speaker is thinking of and intends him to be thinking of.

Thus if the speaker utters 'The F is G' and is speaking literally except for using 'the F' referentially, he is not making merely a uniqueness statement that the F is G but also a singular statement of the object he is referring to as the F that it is G. Even if he is thinking of this object as d, he is not thereby stating *that d* is G, at least not if 'd' is essential to his statement. For if it were essential, the hearer could not understand the statement unless he too thought of the object as d and thereby took the speaker to be stating that d is G. Rather, the speaker is stating *of d* that it is G. Accordingly, the hearer understands this statement if he takes it to be the expression of a belief about d that it is G. But again, the hearer need not think of d as d. Neither how the speaker thinks of d (i.e. as d) nor how the hearer thinks of d enter into the identity of the statement being made. What does enter is the object itself.[11]

This point has a curious consequence. When a speaker uses a description referentially, the referent itself, not how it is thought of or referred to, is essential to the identity of the (singular) statement that the speaker is making. Therefore, he can be making a determinate statement, and the hearer can understand him fully,

---

[11] Evans (1982), though not concerned specifically with referential uses of descriptions, rejects this view. He agrees that the hearer must identify the referent but he insists that how the hearer thinks of the referent matters to the success of the speaker's communication. That is, the speaker must intend the hearer to think of the referent in a certain way, or at least in a certain kind of way (e.g. visually). To the objection that 'this puts an additional burden upon the speaker, requiring him to indicate not only which object he wishes the hearer to think of, but, in addition, *how* he wishes him to think of it', Evans replies, 'Understanding the remarks we are concerned with requires not just that the hearer think of the referent, but that he think of it in the *right way*. But we recognize the primacy of the referent by recognizing that the hearer always confronts just one question, "Which object does the speaker mean?"—not two questions, "Which object does the speaker mean?" and "How am I intended to think of it?" The second question is answered in passing; for if he understands the remark, he will *know* which object is meant; and in the normal course of events . . . he will *know* which object is meant only if he thinks of it in the particular way intended by the speaker.' (1982, 315–16) However, these remarks actually vindicate the notion of objectual reference. Since a referential intention, as part of a communicative intention, must be recognizable to be reasonable, an utterance with a recognizable referential intention must, in the context, provide the hearer with the means for identifying the referent. After all, the hearer must identify the referent on the basis of the utterance together with mutual contextual beliefs, and not just any way of thinking of the referent will come to mind on that basis. Evans is right that a particular way, or at least kind of way, is required for identifying the referent, but this is explained not by the specific content of the speaker's referential intention but by the general conditions on rational, i.e. recognizable, communicative intentions. Evans in effect concedes this when remarking that the hearer is faced with one question, not two.

only if the intended referent exists. If the speaker does not succeed in referring to anything, there is nothing for his statement to be true or false of and nothing for the hearer correctly to think of as the object he is making his statement about.

This point does not rest on any metaphysically weighty thesis about the status of non-existent entities, for it pertains only to a speaker's referential intention and its recognition. Of course, the hearer can recognize *that* the speaker has an objectual referential intention, but there is no way for the hearer to fulfil this intention since there is nothing that the speaker intends to be talking about. Nothing the hearer takes him to be talking about can be the individual he is talking about, for there is none. So for example, he could use 'the man in the moon' referentially ('*d*' might be 'the astronaut Neil Armstrong left behind'), but he could succeed only if there were a man in the moon or at least someone left behind by Neil Armstrong. Otherwise, nothing could count as the hearer's thinking of the same individual as the one the speaker intends him to be thinking of.

As I urged while examining Searle's view, when a speaker uses a complete description referentially he is making a uniqueness statement directly (that the F is G) and a singular statement indirectly (about the putative F that it is G).[12] It seemed to me that if, as Searle maintains, two acts of referring are being performed, he has no reason to deny that two statements are being made, even though the direct one is secondary to the speaker's communicative intent. A concrete example will make this clear by enabling us to see what is involved in the speaker's referential intention and the hearer's recognition of it. What does it take for the hearer to figure out that the speaker is making not merely a uniqueness statement (about whatever satisfies the description) but a singular statement about a certain individual? And when is it reasonable for the speaker to intend to make such a statement?

In general, when a speaker performs an illocutionary act indirectly he intends the hearer to reason that he (the speaker) could

[12] Concerning Donnellan's observation that a true statement can be made even if the referent is not F, I pointed out that this does not show that a false statement is not being made as well. Also, I noted that Searle's secondary act of referring cannot be associated merely with the locutionary act of saying but is part of the illocutionary act of stating. That is because 'the F' might be incomplete, in which case, although the speaker is still saying that the F is G, his secondary act of referring is not under the aspect of 'the F' but of some completion of 'the F'.

not, under the circumstances, be expressing merely the attitude being expressed directly (Bach and Harnish 1979, 70–6). Classic examples are utterances of 'It's getting cold in here' used to request the hearer to close the windows and 'Do you have the time?' used to ask what time it is. The situation is a bit more subtle with uses of description sentences to make singular statements. The indirect act is of the same type as the direct one, typically a statement,[13] and their contents are very closely related. In this case how can one reasonably expect one's audience to take one to be making not merely a uniqueness statement directly but a singular statement indirectly?

Suppose the speaker utters 'Smith's murderer is insane', thereby saying and stating directly that the murderer of Smith is insane. He is making this statement in a courtroom in which a crazed-looking defendant, who is flailing his arms wildly, is being tried for the murder of Smith, and no one doubts that the man in the dock is the murderer. In such circumstances the speaker can reasonably intend the hearer to take, and the hearer would take, the speaker to be expressing a belief (i.e. to be stating) of the man in the dock that he is insane. The hearer may not be thinking of him as the man in the dock but maybe as the defendant or as the man flailing his arms wildly. This does not matter so long as he takes the speaker to be talking about that man. Moreover, the hearer has no reason to think that the speaker is talking about whoever Smith's murderer might be. Under the circumstances, where the behaviour of the man in the dock is evident to one and all, the hearer can reasonably infer, and the speaker cannot but expect him to infer, that this behaviour is the evidence on which the speaker's remark is based. It is evidence for the insanity of the man in the dock, not for the insanity of whoever might have murdered Smith, and the hearer operates on the presumption that the speaker asserts that for which he has evidence.[14]

What if the man in the dock were *not* Smith's murderer? Given that the speaker and the hearer mutually believe that he is, I have maintained that the speaker is making a uniqueness statement as well as a singular statement. Since the man in the dock is not

[13] It could be an act of another sort, e.g. a request, as in an utterance of 'Please examine Smith's murderer for insanity.'

[14] This is an example of what we call a presumption of quality (Bach and Harnish 1979, 63). Because it figures in the hearer's inference we prefer the term 'presumption' to Grice's (1975) term 'maxim'.

Smith's murderer, it follows that the two statements are not about the same individual. If the man in the dock's demeanour and behaviour are any indication, the singular statement is true, while the uniqueness statement, about the real culprit, whoever he may be, may very well be false. But the speaker has made both statements, and both he and the hearer take both to be about the same individual, the man in the dock. That both statements have been made is suggested by what the original speaker might say if the jury returned with a verdict of acquittal: 'I guess I was wrong about the defendant, but I still think he's crazy!' He would thus be taking back the original statement (made in using 'Smith's murderer is insane' literally) that Smith's murderer is insane, while sticking with his (indirect) statement that the defendant is insane. Surely he would not withdraw the statement that Smith's murderer is insane (he now has no idea who Smith's murderer is) unless he had made it in the first place. It could be objected that the speaker might go on to *say*, 'I didn't mean that Smith's murderer (whoever he is) is insane, but that the defendant is insane', but he did mean both. After all, he was not using 'the murderer' non-literally (say to mean 'the accused murderer'). The fact that he took the defendant to be Smith's murderer suggests that he did mean that Smith's murderer was insane, for if he had not believed the defendant to be Smith's murderer, not only would he have not meant that Smith's murderer was insane, he would not have said that.

Donnellan's emphasis on cases where the description is not satisfied by the referent has caused considerable confusion about just what a speaker is stating when using a description referentially. As Wettstein (1981) has rightly pointed out, such cases are not central to the R/A distinction but merely a nice way to illustrate it. Ordinarily the speaker does believe and does expect the hearer to believe that the referent satisfies the description. However, suppose the hearer did take the defendant to be innocent but believes that the speaker takes him to be Smith's murderer. The hearer's inference about the speaker's intention will be the same, but now he will realize that the direct, literal statement being made (the uniqueness statement) is not about who the speaker thinks it is about. To vary the example again, suppose that the speaker takes the defendant to be innocent but takes the hearer to believe him guilty. This time something devious is going on, for the speaker is making a literal statement he believes to be false. Yet his communicative intention is the same, as is the inference by which the hearer is to identify that intention. A similar point can be made about the further variant in which the speaker believes the defendant innocent and takes the hearer to believe this but takes the hearer to believe that he, the speaker, believes the defendant guilty. In all these cases the speaker is making both a uniqueness statement about Smith's murderer and a singular statement about the man in the dock. Only in the case where the speaker and the hearer mutually believe the man in the dock to be innocent is the speaker not making the uniqueness statement. Only in that case is he not using 'Smith's murderer' literally. In this case, unlike the others, the referential use does *not* involve a direct statement of a uniqueness proposition. In this respect it is like the referential use of an incomplete description which, as we will see in the next section, is ordinarily not used literally.

Not to be overlooked here is the case in which the speaker, even though he thinks of the referent in other ways than under the description being used (he has many beliefs of the form '*d* is the F'), is using it attributively. For these beliefs may play no part in his referential intention ('the F' may, in Searle's terminology, express the primary aspect under which reference is being made). As Donnellan puts it, a description can 'be used attributively even though the speaker (and his audience) believes that a certain person or thing [in particular] fits the description' (1966, 290), that is, they think of the individual they take to be the F in other ways as well. In such a case the speaker's belief about the identity of the F has no bearing on what he is stating. He is making merely a direct uniqueness statement, and should he be mistaken that *d* is the F, his statement would be about some other individual than the one he thought he was talking about. So for example, someone might utter 'The next president of the United States will raise taxes' and be making merely a uniqueness statement even if he happens to believe that Ted Kennedy will be the next president. The hearer might even take the speaker to believe this and yet, at least if the belief is not mutual,[15] not take him to be making a statement about Ted Kennedy. The description used determines what the statement is about, regardless of what the speaker happens to believe fits the

---

[15] Of course, if the belief were mutual, the speaker could not but expect, since the hearer could not but suppose the speaker intends, the hearer to take the statement to be about Ted Kennedy. If he were reasonable, that would be his intention.

description. Moreover, he intends the hearer to take the description as determining what his statement is about.

In contrast, in the referential case there is a sense in which it is false that the speaker 'uses the description to enable the audience to pick out whom or what he is talking about', as Donnellan (1966, 285) put it originally. For here the description does not determine what the singular statement is about. It may apply uniquely to what the statement is about, but if the hearer thinks the speaker intends to be talking about whatever individual happens to fit the description, he has not fully identified the speaker's referential intention. That is why a necessary condition for a successful referential use is that the hearer think of the F in some other way than as the F and take the speaker to be expressing a belief about that individual. For this is what the speaker intends him to do. In the referential case, then, we might say that when the speaker believes that *d* is the F, '*d*' has PRIORITY over 'the F' in determining what the speaker's primary statement is about. In the attributive case 'the F' has priority, regardless of what the speaker takes to be the F. It must be mutually believed of a certain individual that the speaker takes it to be the F. Indeed, when such a mutual belief prevails, the referential use is virtually unavoidable.[16]

4. INCOMPLETE DEFINITE DESCRIPTIONS

Our account of referential uses has so far been limited to complete definite descriptions, which are relatively infrequent, but it can easily be extended to incomplete ones. In this regard recall several

[16] We should note certain cases in which the speaker does not believe the intended referent to be the F, cases which require some Gricean word-play to be described. If the speaker does not believe the referent to be the F but believes the hearer to believe that, both still have the higher-order beliefs required for mutual belief (S believes that H believes, H believes that S believes, S believes that H believes that S believes, and H believes that S believes that H believes). If neither one believes the intended referent to be the F but the speaker believes the hearer to believe that and the hearer does not believe the speaker not to believe that, they both still have these higher-order beliefs. Finally, there is the case in which not only do both believe the intended referent not to be the F but the speaker believes that the hearer believes it not to be the F and yet believes the hearer to believe that he the speaker believes it to be the F. Here the speaker has only the third-order belief required for mutual belief, but, with the hearer still having the required second- and third-order beliefs, the speaker can still successfully use the description referentially.

of the points made in the previous chapter in reply to the incomplete description objection. First, since incompleteness is not a semantic property of descriptions, incomplete descriptions make the same sort of semantic contribution to sentences in which they occur as do complete ones. That is, a description sentence of the form 'The F is G' expresses a uniqueness proposition whether or not the description it contains is complete. However, and this is the second point, if 'the F' is incomplete and the speaker takes it to be so, then he is unlikely to be asserting that the F is G—even if he is using 'the F' attributively. In that case he is not using it literally but as short for 'the F_c' (an intended completion of 'the F') and is asserting the uniqueness proposition that the F_c is G. Third, if he is using the incomplete 'the F' referentially, he need not be using it as short for any intended completion. As we saw, this does not threaten Russell's theory of descriptions, but it does suggest, as we will see now, a difference between referential uses of incomplete descriptions and of complete ones.

When a speaker uses a complete description referentially (and literally), he is making two statements, a singular one about the individual he takes to be the F and a uniqueness statement about the F. But if 'the F' is incomplete (or if he takes it to be or takes the hearer to take it to be), he does not have to intend the hearer to identify some completion of it in order to identify the referent. Instead, he might intend the hearer to figure out that he is talking about a certain F concerning whose identity he is not expressing a belief at all, not even in an abbreviated fashion. In that case he is not making any uniqueness statement, literally or in some abbreviated way, but is directly, though not literally, making a singular statement about a certain F (or what he takes to be F).

Is this feature of referential uses of incomplete descriptions at all inconsistent with our account of (literal) referential uses of complete descriptions? Incomplete descriptions can be used to make singular statements non-literally but directly, whereas complete ones are used to make singular statement indirectly, by way of making uniqueness statements directly. There is no inconsistency here. Indeed, the difference between the two cases stems not from any semantic difference between the two sorts of descriptions but from the difference in what the speaker believes, and can reasonably expect the hearer to believe, about the description he is using. If he believes the description to be incomplete and assumes the hearer to believe likewise,[17] he cannot expect to be taken literally when he utters 'The F is G'. Rather, he intends and can reasonably expect the hearer to take him to be talking about a certain F that is identifiable in the context of utterance. However, in the case of referential uses of descriptions that are complete (or mutually believed to be), the speaker has no reason not to expect to be taken to be talking about the unique F (if he does he would not, as we saw, be using the description literally). In this case he does intend and can reasonably expect to be taken to be talking about the individual he believes to be F, even if it turns out that something else is the unique F instead.

So the difference between referential uses of (believed) complete and incomplete descriptions is really a matter of what the speaker can reasonably expect and intend the hearer to infer from his utterance. This is reflected in the fact that speakers normally use only complete descriptions literally and thereby make uniqueness statements directly while making singular statements indirectly. There is no semantic difference between the two kinds of descriptions, and, as noted in the previous chapter, there is good reason not to regard incomplete descriptions as a kind of indexical, as equivalent to demonstrative descriptions—their incompleteness is a matter not of meaning but of how the world is. What they have in common with indexicals is that they can be used to make objectual reference, but this does mean that they should be assimilated to indexicals semantically.

5. LOOSE ENDS: NEAR MISSES, MISFITS, AND FALL-BACKS

Our investigation of the R/A distinction would not be complete without touching on three topics mentioned by Donnellan. First there is the case of attributive 'near misses' he mentions when observing that referential uses can succeed even when the description does not fit the referent (1968, 209). Once again suppose someone utters 'Smith's murderer is insane', this time at the scene of the discovery of Smith's mutilated body. He is using the description 'Smith's murderer' literally and attributively,

---

[17] It is convenient but not necessary to ascribe metalinguistic beliefs here. Strictly speaking, we could say that the speaker believes and assumes the hearer to believe there to be more than one F, and avoid mention of beliefs about the completeness of a description.

having no idea who the culprit might be. The speaker is unaware that Smith died from heart failure, not from the vicious assault on his dead body—'Smith's murderer' does not apply to anyone. So it would seem that a uniqueness statement had been made, and that it was not true. But Donnellan suggests that a true statement was made. He observes that the speaker was prepared to fall back on a description like 'Smith's attacker', close in meaning to the description used (hence 'near miss'), and yet 'Smith's murderer' was not used referentially. As Donnellan puts it, the speaker was aiming not at a 'particular target' but at 'some target or other'. Whatever that means, I take Donnellan's point to be that the speaker had no one in particular in mind but rather some property, which the description used did not quite express. So if a true statement was made with 'Smith's murderer is insane', it was not made literally. However, it seems that no true statement was made at all. Unaware of how Smith actually died, the speaker made a false statement. Apprised of the facts he might say, 'What I meant was that Smith's attacker is insane', but *that* would not be literally true. He meant what he said, given his ignorance. Had he known how Smith died, he would have said—and meant—that Smith's attacker was insane.

I have agreed with Donnellan that referential uses can succeed even when the description does not fit the referent. So if a speaker utters 'The F is G', he can make a true statement about a certain individual, which he must be thinking of in some way '*d*' other than as the F, that it is G. However, I have argued that if 'the F' is complete, the speaker is saying and thereby directly stating that the F is G. This is so even if he does not believe that *d* is the F and even if *d* is not in fact the F. In the first case he may be exploiting what he takes to be the hearer's false belief of *d* that it is the F, but in either case his direct statement is false, for all he knows (it might be fortuitously true of the real F). But despite the misfit of 'the F' with *d*, he can still make an indirect statement about *d* that it is G, and it can be true even if the direct one is not. I have tried to explain how and why this should be, but a fundamental question remains. Suppose there is no unique '*d*' but various ways in which the speaker thinks of the object he is referring to. If it turns out that they do not all apply to the same object, what determines which one he is prepared to fall back on, hence which object (if any) he is talking about?

A speaker may think of the individual he is referring to with 'the F' in many different ways, any one of which he is prepared to fall back on if that individual is not in fact (the) F. There may be no unique 'd' under which he thinks of it and yet all of the 'd_1' through to 'd_n' might get priority over 'the F' in his primary statement. So he believes that $d_1 = \ldots = d_n$ even if he is prepared to give up all his beliefs that $d_1 (\ldots d_n) = $ the F. But what if it is false that $d_1 = \ldots d_n$? Now the problem is that not only does the speaker not know what he is talking about, he may not even know what he is thinking about! If different 'd_i' apply to different individuals, then it would seem that his referential intention can have a determinate object only if a certain 'd_i' constitutes his primary way, in some sense, of thinking about that putative individual. [18]

There remains one loose end to be tied up in regard to referential uses of descriptions. It is a question that often gets overlooked: what is the rationale for using descriptions referentially rather than always making explicit how we are thinking of the object we are talking about? There are several reasons. For one thing, we may be thinking of the object primarily in a non-descriptive, *de re* way rather than under some description, in which case it is difficult to make explicit (and often impossible to display) how we are thinking of it. For another, we may be thinking of the object indifferently under several descriptions, all of which we take to be satisfied by the same object. However, as Donnellan observed originally, the main reason for using descriptions referentially is that in trying to communicate we need to find a practical means of enabling the hearer to pick out the object we are speaking of. Just how does not matter so long as it works. If we are thinking of an object in a *de re* way or under various descriptions and believe it to be (or to seem to the hearer to be) the F (or the F_c), we will use 'the F' to refer to it because even though 'the F' (or 'the F_c') is not our primary way of thinking about the object, it is easier for the hearer to identify the object by means of 'the F'. For the object might be visibly or otherwise obviously the F (or the F_c). Our own ways of thinking of the object may have priority for us but be too cumbersome to express or not readily available to the hearer. In any case, notwithstanding Donnellan's emphasis on the fact that a description used

---

[18] Realistically, no one of the 'd_i' is likely to be primary, but if several of them jointly constitute one's primary way of thinking of the putative object, they must all apply to the same object.

referentially need not apply to the referent, the main reason a speaker uses it that way is not to have something else to fall back on but simply to enable the hearer to identify what he is referring to.

Of course there are other singular terms besides definite descriptions with which we can refer to objects, but descriptions are indispensable. Most objects do not have names, and pronouns are often insufficiently informative to secure reference. However, as I will suggest in succeeding chapters, the basic features of objectual reference are the same as those of referential uses of definite descriptions: the speaker is making a singular statement whose precise content depends on the identity of the referent. Regardless of the type of singular term being used, in order for the speaker's referential intention to be fulfilled the hearer must think of the same object in some way or another and take it to be the one the speaker is talking about.

7

Proper Names I: The Nominal Description Theory

No doctrines in twentieth-century philosophy have met with more unwarranted abuse than Russell's theory of descriptions and his description theory of ordinary proper names. In Chapter 5 I tried to answer the main objections to his view that definite descriptions, despite grammatical appearances, function semantically not as logical subject expressions but as (disguised) quantifier phrases. I argued that the underlying problem with these objections is their systematic confusion of pragmatics with semantics: in so far as Russell's theory is understood to concern only the meaning of sentences containing descriptions, it is immune to these objections. Now we will take up his view that proper names are disguised or 'truncated' descriptions. I will not defend his version of the description theory, which suffers from some serious problems exposed by Kripke. Instead, I will develop a different version, which Russell hints at but never actually endorses. I will defend it against Kripke's objections.

I am well aware that a major obstacle to the general acceptance of any description theory is the widespread appeal of Kripke's thesis that names are rigid designators. It is an offshoot of Mill's idea that names denote directly rather than by way of having senses, that they lack descriptive contents. In Kripke's terms, the thesis is that a name designates the same individual in all possible worlds (in which it designates at all). Speaking of 'Aristotle' and Aristotle, for example, Kripke says,

> Not only is it true *of* the man Aristotle that he might not have gone into pedagogy; it is also true that we use the term 'Aristotle' [unlike 'the teacher of Alexander', for example] in such a way that, in thinking of a counterfactual situation in which Aristotle didn't go into any of the fields and do any of the achievements we commonly attribute to him, still we would say that was a situation in which *Aristotle* did not do these things. (1980, 62; Kripke's emphasis)

What gives RDT its intuitive appeal is Kripke's method of comparing the ways in which simple modal sentences containing descriptions and those containing names are evaluated. With a description we go to a possible world and find the individual that satisfies the description. With a name we find the individual that bears the name and then go to a possible world. As a result, it seems patently clear that names are rigid and descriptions are not.

Despite my recognition of RDT's immense appeal, I will proceed full steam ahead with a defence of my version of the description theory. I do not doubt for a moment that in order to make it convincing I must answer Kripke. I do believe that the intuition of rigidity can be explained away and that Kripke's arguments against description theories can be answered, but for expository reasons I will save the task of meeting these challenges for the next chapter.

1. RUSSELL ON NAMES

Unlike a definite description, a genuine or 'logically proper' name serves 'merely to indicate what we are speaking about' (1919, 175). For Russell only a logically proper name can occur as subject of a sentence that is not merely grammatically but genuinely of subject–predicate form. Such a sentence expresses what we have been calling a singular proposition, in contrast to the general, uniqueness proposition expressed by a description sentence. A singular proposition has as one of its constituents not an individual concept but the individual denoted by the name. Such a proposition literally contains that individual. Whereas a description sentence is fully meaningful (expresses a proposition) even if the description it contains does not apply to anything, a sentence containing an empty name is not. This stark contrast reflects the essential difference, according to Russell, between definite descriptions and genuine proper names.

Now Russell construed propositions not merely as meanings of sentences but as contents of thoughts. This set him apart from those formal semanticists of today who regard propositions as set- or model-theoretic constructs.[1] Furthermore, Russell held that the constituents of propositions, as contents of thoughts, must be objects of direct acquaintance. Here was the rub. How could his conception of names as introducing individuals into propositions be squared with the fact that, in Russell's restrictive sense of

[1] These are not the likeliest candidates for thought contents, but most formal semanticists seem unconcerned with the relations between language and thought.

'acquaintance',[2] we cannot be acquainted with the individuals bearing ordinary names like 'Jack Kemp' and 'Polaris'? Russell's answer was that these names do not qualify as genuine names, since ordinary individuals like Jack Kemp and Polaris, not being objects of direct acquaintance, cannot be constituents of propositions.[3]

Russell held that the only particulars that can be objects of direct acquaintance are sense data and perhaps oneself (on this he was never certain). Russell supposed these objects could be named only by such terms as 'this', 'that', and (perhaps) 'I'. He held that only these terms qualify as genuine names. The latter claim is puzzling to say the least, for obviously 'this', 'that', and 'I' are not names at all but pronouns; perhaps it should be written off as an aberration. Even given Russell's reasons (they are based on his controversial doctrine of acquaintance, which I will not take up here) for denying that ordinary names are logically proper and for claiming that only sense data and possibly oneself can be constituents of propositions, one is hard put to explain why Russell insisted on calling these pronouns logically proper *names*. After all, he did recognize the difference between a proposition and its 'verbal expression' (1918, 251–2), as well as the difference between the meaning of a term and its use, and he allows that expressions do not have to be names in order to be 'used as names' (e.g. 1919, 175), that is 'merely to indicate what we are speaking about'. Thus, in order to give verbal expression to a singular proposition, a speaker can use any sort of singular term to mention the particular that is the subject of that proposition. Unfortunately, Russell sometimes disregarded distinctions he recognized. In particular, since a sentence containing a pronoun can be used to express different singular propositions in different contexts, Russell had no reason to regard 'this', 'that', and 'I' as logically proper names, not even by default. What they are used to refer to may vary from context to context, but their meanings do not.

Strawson may have had this in mind when he gave the following diagnosis of why Russell endorsed what has generally been viewed as an unduly restrictive conception of proper names.

---

[2] I cannot go into Russell's doctrine of acquaintance, which can be said to be to Russell's semantics what foundationalism is to traditional epistemology.

[3] For Russell they cannot be constituents of thoughts because, to use modern technical terminology, they are not in the head.

Because Russell confused meaning with mentioning, he thought that if there were any expressions having a uniquely referring use, which were what they seemed (i.e. logical subjects) and not something else in disguise, their meaning must *be* the particular object which they were used to refer to. Hence the troublesome mythology of the logically proper name. (1950, 181–2)

But Strawson's diagnosis is incomplete, for he fails to mention that Russell assumes that there *are* logically proper names. Had Russell not made this assumption, he could have reached the truly Russellian conclusion that in ordinary language there simply are no logically proper names (at least for particulars). Russell could—and I believe should—have concluded that every singular term either is a definite description, is semantically equivalent to a description, or is an indexical. Then instead of developing his own mythology of pronouns as the only logically proper names, he could have exposed the mythology of names—that they denote directly—which Mill (1872) had fathered long before and which Kripke has lately resuscitated. According to this view, a name does not denote by expressing an individual concept but somehow denotes directly, in the manner of an individual constant in logic (it is given an interpretation just by being assigned an individual). Even though Russell denies that ordinary names are logically proper names, it is important here to realize that Russell's *conception* of a logically proper name is essentially the same as Mill's and Kripke's. He may be applying an impossibly high standard of what qualifies as a genuine name, but despite what Strawson says, his is not an unreasonably high standard. For that blame logic, not Russell.

At any rate, having made these observations and disclaimers about the letter of Russell's view of names, I will defend it at least in spirit. I too deny that ordinary names are logically proper names and will defend a version of the description theory, though one that Russell only hints at.

2. NDT AND THE DESCRIPTIVE CONTENTS OF NAMES

Because the semantic contribution of a definite description to the sentences in which it occurs is not an individual but an individual concept,[4] the famous four puzzles for proper names do not arise

---

[4] I put it this way to make clear that one can grant the following points without having to accept the quantificational apparatus of Russell's theory of descriptions.

for descriptions: a description does not have to denote anything to be meaningful, and it retains its usual meaning in existence, identity, and belief sentences. Now Russell realized that these four puzzles can arise for proper names only on the supposition that their semantic contributions to the sentences in which they occur *are* the individuals they denote. But if, as Russell maintained, proper names are semantically equivalent to definite descriptions or, as he put it, are 'truncated' or disguised descriptions, these puzzles do not arise for names, at least not for ordinary ones.

Avoiding these puzzles is the theoretical motivation underlying any description theory of names. Of course, not only must a theory be well motivated, it must work, and it has seemed that description theories cannot work. They have the well-known problem of finding the right description, the one that is semantically equivalent to a particular proper name. For any given proper name, it can easily seem that no description will do the trick. Take the stock examples. Does 'Aristotle' *mean* 'the teacher of Alexander', 'Walter Scott' 'the author of *Waverley*', or 'George Gödel' 'the man who proved the incompleteness of arithmetic'? No, because Aristotle might not have taught Alexander, Scott might not have written *Waverley*, and Gödel might not have proved incompleteness.

Now these examples do not refute description theories once and for all, and perhaps more judicious choices would give better results. The trouble seems to be, however, that regardless of the choice the result would be the same: the individual named might not satisfy the individual concept expressed by the chosen description. Searle (1958) and Strawson (1959, ch. 6) both acknowledge this problem for simple descriptions but suggest that complex descriptions expressing cluster concepts will do the trick. A cluster concept expresses a family of properties, a majority (or a weighted majority) of which an individual must possess in order to satisfy that concept. Kripke (1980) discusses the cluster description theory in detail and shows that it fares no better than simpler versions. A little imagination is all it takes to see that there is no cluster concept that an individual not only happens but has to satisfy, hence no complex description semantically equivalent to the name of the individual. Kripke concludes, prematurely in my opinion, that description theories are doomed to failure. Before taking up Kripke's reasons for this sweeping conclusion, I will present one particular version of the description theory of names which, I will argue, escapes that conclusion.

This version of the description theory has received little attention and even less appreciation. I suspect that it strikes most philosophers as too absurd to take seriously, but I hope to remedy that. It was first mentioned by Russell (1919, 174) in passing and has lately been revived, though discussed only briefly, by Loar (1976). On this version of the description theory, a name 'N' is semantically equivalent to the description 'the bearer of "N" '.[5] The distinctive feature of this version is that the description mentions the name to which it is semantically equivalent. It does not require that the individual denoted by the name possess any property except for that of bearing the name. Thus I dub it the NOMINAL DESCRIPTION THEORY, or NDT.

Two virtues of NDT are immediately apparent. First, it can readily explain, unlike other description theories, the fact that a name can be used literally to refer only to something that bears the name. Second, NDT does justice to the widespread intuition which underlies the view that names denote directly rather than by way of their senses. This is the intuition that names lack descriptive contents. NDT does justice to this intuition, I claim, because as far as this intuition is concerned the property of bearing a certain name does not count as an element of descriptive content, unlike such properties as writing a certain book or proving a certain theorem. After all, no one who has this intuition, not even Mill or Kripke,[6] would deny that a name at least conveys the information that its bearer bears it. Otherwise it would make no sense to speak of non-literal uses of names, as would happen if one used the name 'Elvis' to refer to Melvin, a local performer of old rock-and-roll songs.

---

[5] This is my wording, which I prefer to the usual 'the individual called "N" '. The latter is unfortunate because 'is called' suggests not only 'is named' but 'is referred to by', thereby provoking the charge, to be answered below, that description theories cannot avoid being viciously circular.

[6] Indeed, Kripke remarks that 'the linguistic function of a proper name is completely exhausted by the fact that it names its bearer' (1979, 240), though he does not indicate how his own theory can account for this. And Mill, whom Kripke credits with the view that names denote directly (according to Mill proper names lack 'connotations'), remarks that proper names 'do not indicate or imply any attributes as belonging to . . . the individuals who are called by them. . . . [W]hen we say, pointing to a man, this is Brown or Smith, . . . we do not, merely by so doing, convey . . . any information about them *except that those are their names*' (1872, 20–2; my emphasis).

This fact does not seem explicable on the view that names denote directly and convey no information at all.

Kripke, who briefly takes up NDT, is dissatisfied with how it explains why it is trifling, for example, that Socrates is called 'Socrates'. Kripke observes that it is no less trifling to be told that in English horses are called 'horses' and sages are called 'sages' (1980, 69), but NDT is surely not posing as a special case of a general theory of meaning. Of course, a 'nominal theory' of meaning in general would be ludicrous, but that does not show, as claimed by Kripke, that there is no more reason 'to suppose that being so-called is part of the meaning of a name than of any other word'. In fact, there *is* a reason: there is nothing else for a name to mean! Whereas horses are called 'horses' because they each have the property of being a horse—it is another matter that this property is expressed by the word 'horse'—Socrates is called 'Socrates' because he has the property of bearing the name 'Socrates'. He is called 'Socrates' because that is his name. It is a semantic fact that a name can be used literally to refer only to an individual that bears the name, and NDT can account for this fact. Moreover, as mentioned already, names can be used non-literally, of which a further example is using the name 'Napoleon' to refer to a diminutive megalomaniac of some other name. Only a theory on which 'being so-called is part of the meaning of a name' can explain the difference between literal and non-literal uses of names.

Still, it might be objected that NDT goes too far. How could a name 'N' be semantically equivalent to 'the bearer of "N" ' when, as is all too common, more than one individual bears 'N'? Surely 'George Smith' cannot mean the same as 'the bearer of "George Smith" ' if there are many people with that name, as indeed there are. However, SHARED NAMES pose no problem for NDT. Just as it is no problem for Russell's theory of descriptions that there are incomplete descriptions, such as 'the man', so it is no problem for NDT that there are many bearers of names like 'George Smith'. When a name has many bearers, its nominal descriptive equivalent is predictably incomplete and can be treated accordingly. As we saw when we took up the incomplete description objection to Russell's theory in Chapter 5, one must distinguish what an expression means from its use, especially when it is commonly used as short for (not: synonymous with) a more elaborate expression.

By applying our treatment of incomplete definite descriptions to NDT, we avoid what seems to be the absurd result that a shared name is semantically ambiguous in as many ways as it has bearers. Evidently it is not widely recognized that this is a consequence of the view that names denote directly,[7] but if a name means what it denotes[8] then it has as many meanings as things it denotes. A sentence like (1)

George Smith is bald. (1)

would be ambiguous in as many ways as there are people named 'George Smith', and that strikes me as absurd.[9] If the name's having many bearers were a semantic fact, then understanding (1) fully, as a sentence type in all its supposed senses, would require knowing that it has all these bearers (and understanding an utterance of (1) would involve disambiguating the name). Surely linguistic competence with the name does not require that. NDT allows us to treat (1) as univocal semantically, expressing the

[7] In fact, a literal-minded version of NDT would have the same consequence, saying that if a name 'N' has many bearers, it is ambiguous in as many ways. Its nominal descriptive equivalent, 'the bearer of "N" ', would be equally ambiguous, but would be complete in each sense. However, this literalistic version of NDT is not only unmotivated theoretically, it is ultimately circular. If it is to be intelligible that a given individual is the unique bearer of 'N' in a given sense of 'N', that sense of 'N' must be specifiable without having to specify the relevant bearer of 'N'. But there is no way to do that, since these would-be senses of 'N' are individuated by the bearers of 'N'.

[8] Actually, there are two alternatives, on the view that names denote directly, to the claim that names mean what they denote (note that this claim has the unwelcome implication that codesignative names are synonymous). (a) Their senses could be identified with causal chains leading back to what they denote. Then names like 'Cicero' and 'Tully' would not be synonymous and the fact that the statement that Tully is Cicero is informative could be explained. The trouble with this view, however, is that understanding expressions is to grasp their senses, but surely people do not grasp causal chains. (b) The senses of names could be individual concepts involving essential or necessary properties of individuals. The problem here is to find suitable candidates for the necessary properties. Is being identical to Cicero a necessary property of Cicero? If so, then so would being identical to Tully, in which case 'Cicero' and 'Tully' would again be synonymous. Moreover, it is not at all obvious what the property of being identical to Cicero is. Part of the problem is verbally to specify that property. The Roman orator was not the only person named 'Cicero', and presumably the others do not have the same essential property as he. But then how is the property of being Cicero to be specified? And if the property is ineffable, then grasping it would not be required for understanding the name 'Cicero'—the sense would have to consist in something else.

[9] That is not how it strikes Evans (1982) or Devitt (1980), who do not hesitate to call shared names 'ambiguous'. Neither did Russell, but he used the word loosely, even calling indefinite descriptions 'ambiguous' (1919, 167).

uniqueness proposition that the unique bearer of 'George Smith' is bald, not that anyone would mean this in uttering (1). As illustrated by a sentence like (2),

The man is bald. (2)

which is uncontroversially unambiguous, the truth condition of a statement does not have to be the same as that of the sentence used (*s*-non-literally) to make it. So even though NDT explains the fact that a name has no descriptive content beyond implying that what it is used to refer to should bear the name, it avoids the suggestion that a shared name is semantically ambiguous. It does this by applying our account of incomplete definite descriptions to the nominal descriptive equivalents of names.

3. EXPLAINING LITERAL USES OF NAMES: ALTERNATIVES TO NDT

There are several alternatives to NDT which, unlike other description theories, do face up to the problem of explaining the fact that a name used literally must be used with the intention of referring to something that bears it.

Kripke recognizes this problem, and, indeed, he is aware that because of shared names it leads to a further problem: a name can be used literally to refer to any individual that it belongs to, but it also implies uniqueness. However, Kripke's way around this problem is rather implausible. He simply denies that names ever do have more than one bearer! He can deny this only by proposing (as does Evans 1982, 384) that we individuate names in a way

according to which uses of phonetically the same sounds to name distinct objects count as distinct names. This terminology certainly does not agree with the most common usage, but I think it may have a great deal to recommend it for theoretical purposes. (1980, 8)

The trouble with this proposal is that parity of reasoning would require construing clearly univocal expressions, such as 'the man' and 'it', as actually comprising a myriad of homonyms, and that has little to recommend it. Or do names have phantom subscripts?

There is another approach to proper names which also has the virtue of explaining, while avoiding ambiguity, the fact that a name used literally is used to refer to something bearing it. The idea is that names are implicitly indexicals. So just as a sentence like (3)

He is bald.   (3)

does not have a context-independent truth condition, neither does
(1). To specify the meaning of such a sentence is not to specify its
truth condition but only how it contributes to the truth conditions
of statements made in using it literally. Two versions of this
approach have appeared. Burge (1973) treats names as predicates
which, when they occur in sentences like (1), have implicit indexical
prefixes. Thus (1) is to be read as (4),

This George Smith is bald.   (4)

Burge observes that proper names are often used in other ways than
to make singular reference, as in sentences like (5) and (6),

There are few Cohens in Baghdad.   (5)

A B + is not good enough for a Zimmerman.[10]   (6)

Burge offers some interesting arguments for his proposal, but Boer
(1975) seems to me to have refuted them. I will mention just one.
Burge rightly urges that despite the difference between these
predicative uses of names and ordinary referential uses, an account
of them should, if possible, avoid the consequence that names are
ambiguous. Moreover, Burge claims that his theory enables us to
explain the ordinary referential use of names in terms of the
predicative use. However, Boer insists that Burge must show also
that the predicative use cannot be explained in terms of the
ordinary referential use. In particular, Boer notes that Burge says
nothing to rule out the possibility that the uses of names in
sentences like (5) and (6) are cases of what he calls 'conventional
ellipsis', in which a name 'N' is elliptical for the phrase 'person
named "N" '.

Burge is of course correct that proper names can be used like
common nouns, as when they are pluralized or are preceded by the
indefinite article 'a', but it does not follow that names are like
common nouns syntactically (of course they are unlike common
nouns morphologically). If they were, they could be preceded by
the definite article 'the' to form definite descriptions. But this is not
possible—a sentence like 'The Tyler Burge is a philosopher of
language' is simply not grammatical. Besides, in the case where a
proper name 'N' is used as though it were a common noun, it is
used, as Boer points out, as if it meant 'bearer of "N" '.

[10] This was the caption of an old cartoon I recall from *The New Yorker*, in which
a boy shows his father a report card indicating straight As but for one B + .

The other indexical approach is closer to NDT in that it treats a name 'N' as semantically equivalent to the demonstrative description 'this [that] bearer of "N" '.[11] It too has the virtue of implying that a name can be used literally to refer only to something bearing the name. Although a sentence like (1) has no context-independent truth condition, its semantics determines that a statement made in uttering it is true just in case the speaker is referring to someone who bears the name 'George Smith' and that person is bald. However, the fact that 'George Smith' can be used to refer to a certain person bearing it does not show that it should be given a demonstrative reading. An incomplete description 'the F' can be used to refer demonstratively to a certain F, but, as argued in Chapter 4, this does not make the description a demonstrative semantically. After all, the reference to a certain F need not be made demonstratively. The same goes for the use of a name like 'George Smith' to refer to a certain bearer of the name. In both cases, the fact that the sense of the expression does not determine the specific individual being referred to shows not that the expression has a demonstrative reading but merely that its use does not make the speaker's referential intention fully explicit. Thus, like the other two alternatives to NDT, this way of explaining literal uses of names does not succeed.

4. OBJECTIONS TO NDT

In my experience, NDT has met with less than wholehearted enthusiasm. Many resist it simply because it conflicts with their 'intuitions'. It happens that these are the very intuitions that are used in support of the view that names denote directly or, in Kripke's view, that they are 'rigid designators'. Yet even in the unlikely event that these intuitions are untainted by theory, they would pose a problem for NDT only if, from the standpoint of NDT, they could not be successfully explained away. Naturally, if the theory they support were tenable in its own right, then NDT would have a problem anyway. At any rate, since these intuitions

---

[11] Burge repudiates this version because there is no need to 'claim that a proper name abbreviates *another* predicate, even a roughly coextensive predicate such as "is an entity called 'PN' ". A proper name is a predicate in its own right' (1973, 428), or so he claims.

do not constitute an objection to NDT by themselves, I will not take them up until I examine their theoretical background in the next chapter. There I will take up Kripke's thesis on names and his arguments against description theories, and only then try to explain these intuitions away. Their strength, I will argue, depends on a conflation of speaker reference and linguistic reference. Here I will try to answer what strike me as the most compelling substantive objections to NDT. I fear that to anyone already given to the intuitions just noted, my replies to these objections will seem to beg the question in favour of NDT; but if they can at least serve to clarify NDT, perhaps the question will be allowed to remain open until the end of the next chapter.

Lehrer's objection. Keith Lehrer[12] has argued that NDT has the following absurd implication.

A sentence of the form 'The bearer of "N" is F' implies that the name 'N' exists—it cannot be true otherwise. However, a sentence of the form 'N is F' carries no such implication. It can be true even if there is no such name as 'N'. Therefore, 'N is F' is not semantically equivalent to 'The bearer of "N" is F'.

This objection can easily be misunderstood. Suppose that Mt. Etna first blew its top one million years ago. Then one million years ago it would have been true that Mt. Etna was blowing its top. And it might seem that one million years ago it was false that the bearer of 'Mt. Etna' was blowing its top, inasmuch as the name 'Mt. Etna' didn't exist then. One might as well argue that Pope John Paul II was not born in Poland because at the time he was born he did not bear the name 'Pope John Paul II'. This is not Lehrer's objection.

The objection is that if (1) is semantically equivalent to (2),

> Mt. Etna erupted. (1)
> The bearer of 'Mt. Etna' erupted. (2)

as NDT says, then both sentences express the same proposition. However, so the objection goes, whereas (2) expresses a metalinguistic proposition implying the existence of the name 'Mt. Etna', (1) does not. (1) expresses a proposition about Mt. Etna, a proposition that has nothing to do with what Mt. Etna is called and does not imply the existence of any name.

---

[12] Lehrer raised this objection at a colloquium at the University of Arizona on 21 October 1982. The misunderstanding mentioned in the text, as well as several others, came up during the discussion on that occasion.

The trouble with this objection is its assumption, false in my view, that a sentence of the form 'N is F' expresses a proposition about N. This assumes that what a name contributes semantically to the sentences in which it occurs is its bearer, and implies that such a sentence expresses a proposition only if what it names exists. (1), for example, can express a proposition about Mt. Etna only if Mt. Etna exists. Also, as we have seen, that assumption has the dubious implication that a name which has many bearers is *ipso facto* ambiguous (and also, of course, there are the problems of existence, identity, and belief sentences). If we give up this assumption, we must deny that (1), 'Mt. Etna erupted', is about a certain particular mountain, and can say instead that what is about that mountain is the statement made in using that sentence. But once we realize that, it is no objection to NDT that (1), if equivalent to (2), would imply the existence of the name 'Mt. Etna'. Rather, this is an immediate and welcome consequence of NDT. The objection fails because 'Mt. Etna erupted', *qua* sentence, cannot express a singular proposition but only a general proposition, the same uniqueness proposition as the one expressed by (2). The objection seems plausible only if the statement made in using (1) is not distinguished from (1) itself.

Brand's objection. Myles Brand[13] has offered a translation argument against NDT. Consider the German sentence (3) and its English translation (4),

Johann ist unbehaart.   (3)

John is bald.   (4)

According to NDT, the nominal descriptive equivalent of (4) is (5),

The bearer of 'John' is bald.   (5)

Yet, so Brand's objection goes, surely (5) is not semantically equivalent to (3), since the name mentioned in it ('John') is not the name ('Johann') used in (3). Accordingly, if any English sentence is semantically equivalent to (3), it is (6),

The bearer of 'Johann' is bald.   (6)

in which the name occurring in (3) is mentioned. So the objection is that since names occurring in nominal descriptions are not used but mentioned and so do not get translated, NDT is forced to regard (5), not (6), as semantically equivalent to (3).

<hr />

[13] He raised this objection at a colloquium at the University of Illinois at Chicago, 1 April 1981.

In reply to this objection, I must reject its presupposition that proper names get translated at all. It seems to me that (7),

Johann is bald. (7)

is a perfectly legitimate English version of (3). Perhaps (4) is an acceptable version of (3) as well,[14] but even if it is, 'John' does not *mean* in English what 'Johann' means in German. That is, 'John' is not a translation or synonym of 'Johann' but is merely the orthographic and phonological counterpart of 'Johann'. If the two were synonyms, so that (4) would be the English translation of (3), the man named 'Johann' (in German) would also have to be named 'John' (in English). Indeed, he would have to have as many names as there are languages into which his name could be 'translated', and that seems absurd; he does not have different names in different languages. Furthermore, he can be referred to as 'Johann' in any language, whether or not that language contains a counterpart of 'Johann' (and many do not).

Underlying my reply to this objection is that, strictly speaking, names do not belong to particular languages at all. Numerals obviously do not, even though they can occur in (written) sentences. At the very least, we should not regard proper names as belonging to the lexicon of a language—they are not vocabulary items or dictionary entries. Besides, new ones can be freely invented. Names do not belong to a language, but are merely marked as names, that is, as belonging to a distinctive syntactic type.

This is the syntactic type whose semantic role is determined in the general, systematic way which NDT encapsulates. Any name can occur in any noun phrase position in a sentence, but 'John' can just as well occur in a German sentence as 'Johann' in an English one. Proper names may seem to belong to particular languages but that is only because they are usually spelled and pronounced in accordance with the same rules as words in particular languages. Indeed, some names are derived from or even morphologically identical to words belonging to specific languages. However, there is nothing to prevent a Dutch, Hungarian, or Japanese name from occurring in an English sentence, even when the name does have an English counterpart. A name of any sort can be used in an English

[14] This is debatable, but assuming that one could use 'John' to refer to a German man named 'Johann', it would not follow that the man has thereby acquired the name 'John'. He would have to anglicize his name.

sentence, but that does not add the name to the lexicon of English. If it did, speakers of English would have to be familiar with a name in order to understand sentences in which it occurred. In fact, recognizing it as a name is sufficient. NDT predicts, in a thoroughly general way, how a name, any name, contributes semantically to the sentences in which it occurs.

Because names are not really lexical items in a language, I prefer to put NDT as saying not that a name 'N' means the same as but that it is semantically equivalent to the description 'the bearer of "N" '. So, for example, strictly speaking I would not say that 'John' means in English the same as 'the bearer of "John" '. This point may seem to be a mere nicety, but in fact it suggests at least one respect in which, just as many opponents of description theories have long maintained, names really are meaningless. Consider the innumerable proper names whose histories suggest a certain descriptive content, such as 'Johnson', 'Lefty', and 'Oakland'. Such names can be used *literally* even if, as is generally the case, their bearers do not fit these descriptive contents.

The wide scope objection. It is often suggested that whereas definite descriptions can take either wide or narrow scope[15] with respect to modal operators and psychological verbs, proper names can take only wide scope, as in the case of (8),

Spiro Agnew might have been president. (8)

So a natural objection to NDT is that it cannot account for this fact, assuming it is a fact. The idea is that nominal descriptions, like other descriptions, can take narrow as well as wide scope, as in (9),

The bearer of 'Spiro Agnew' might have been
president. (9)

but proper names, which according to NDT are semantically equivalent to them, can take only wide scope.

For the sake of replying to this objection, I will assume that the scope of an expression in a given sentential context is a real, syntactic property. That is, it must be represented at some level of linguistic description and not be a mere artefact of how sentences are represented formally in logical notation.[16] If so, what does the

---

15 As Kripke notes (1977, 259), descriptions can also take intermediate scope.
16 For in that notation, as opposed to natural language, scope relations are represented by order of occurrence. A sentence like 'Everybody loves somebody' is

distinction between wide and narrow scope amount to, specifically in the case of a sentence containing a singular term and a modal operator, such as (8) or (9)? Intuitively, the distinction corresponds to two different ways of evaluating the sentence. We treat an occurrence of a singular term as wide if we fix its referent and then consider a counterfactual situation; we treat the occurrence as narrow if we first consider a counterfactual situation and then determine the term's reference with respect to that situation.[17] In this sense names obviously can take narrow scope, so below we will take the claim that names always take wide scope more precisely as the claim that for names narrow scope has the same semantic effect as wide.

The objection is that NDT conflicts with the apparent fact that names always take wide scope. A short reply is to deny the conflict. For there is an obvious syntactic difference between names and descriptions: names are syntactically simple, whereas descriptions are structured. This difference does not *explain* why they should behave differently in respect of scope (assuming they do), but its existence shows that NDT, as merely a semantic thesis, does not imply that they should behave similarly. NDT simply leaves that question open. Indeed, it is precisely because nominal descriptions and the names they mention are not *syntactically* equivalent that I have been careful to describe NDT as the thesis that they are *semantically* equivalent.

In any case, I do not concede that names do always take wide scope. I grant (still assuming that scope has a truly syntactic basis) that they standardly take wide scope,[18] but as the word 'standardly'

often said to have a scope ambiguity, with the wide scope reading (of 'everybody' relative to 'somebody') '$(x)(Ey)Lxy$' and the narrow scope reading '$(Ey)(x)Lxy$', but for this ambiguity to be genuine the sentence must have two distinct syntactic representations. Be that as it may, in Chapter 10 I argue that in the case of attitude sentences with 'that-clauses' scope is a mere artefact, and that the so-called scope ambiguity is really semantic indeterminacy.

[17] Where quantifiers are involved, scope distinctions correspond to the order in which the ranges of the relevant variables are considered (see note 16). Notice that if we regard possible worlds as counterfactual situations, then we can construe modal operators as quantifiers over possible worlds, e.g. 'necessarily' as 'for all possible worlds'.

[18] In fact, this is true also of many descriptions. Only those which are obviously complete readily take narrow scope. I have in mind ordinal and superlative descriptions, such as 'the first man on the moon' and 'the oldest man on earth', as well as descriptions like 'the inventor of Silly Putty' and 'the editor of *Mind*'. The reason that only they can be readily so used is that only they express a property

suggests, I take this to be a pragmatic fact, not a semantic or a syntactic one. I will explain why, but first let me suggest why this has seemed to some to be a grammatical fact about names. When people consider a typical example of a modal sentence, such as (8),

Spiro Agnew might have been president.   (8)

it is evident from how they discuss the example that they assume the referent of the name to have been fixed already. This assumption is natural enough, but it illicitly presupposes that the semantic role of a name is to introduce its bearer into the proposition expressed by the sentence. And, as I argued earlier, this presupposition wrongly implies that shared names are semantically ambiguous. Even so, it is incumbent upon me to explain how, in a sentence like (8), a name can be used as if it had narrow scope.

In order to see how the name 'Spiro Agnew' can be used with narrow scope in (8), consider what it is for the nominal description ('the bearer of "Spiro Agnew" ') in (9)

The bearer of 'Spiro Agnew' might have been
president.   (9)

to be so used. When that happens, (9) is true just in case (in possible worlds parlance) there is a possible world in which the bearer of 'Spiro Agnew' (at that world) is president. The question is whether (8) can be construed in a like manner, for it seems that (8) is true only if there is a possible world in which the actual Spiro Agnew is president. (8) does not seem to have the desired interpretation because it does not seem to mention a property, such as being the unique bearer of 'Spiro Agnew', by which an individual in a possible world could be picked out. But consider an utterance of (10)

Aaron Aardvark might have been president.   (10)

made under the following circumstances. The electoral process is under attack, and it is proposed, in light of recent results, that alphabetical order would be a better method of selection than the

---

which is likely to belong to only one individual with respect to a given possible world and to different individuals at different worlds. Descriptions which are obviously incomplete, such as 'the front table' and 'the girl with a curl', cannot readily be used with narrow scope because the property being expressed is likely to be widely possessed at any given possible world. As observed in the previous chapter, they tend to be used to make objectual reference, and in this respect they are like proper names, which are often shared.

present one. Someone supposes that 'Aaron Aardvark' might be the winning name and says, 'If that procedure had been instituted, Ronald Reagan would still be doing TV commercials, and [(10)] Aaron Aardvark might have been president.' Who Aaron Aardvark is, if anyone, has no bearing on the statement being made with (10), and indeed the speaker may not believe that anyone possesses this name, much less intend his audience to believe that. His statement is true if there is a possible world in which whoever possesses that name is president (presumably as the result of the hypothetical voting procedure). So as used here 'Aaron Aardvark' has narrow scope with respect to 'might'.

'Spiro Agnew' can also be so used. Suppose that someone is contemplating a procedure whereby the president is selected on the basis of alphabetical order from a list of state governors. He has never heard of Nixon's first vice-president but he imagines, for the sake of discussion, that 'Spiro Agnew' is the name of a state governor. If he uttered (8) under these circumstances, he would be using 'Spiro Agnew' as having narrow scope—who actually bears the name would be irrelevant to his statement.

The reason that 'Spiro Agnew', unlike 'Aaron Aardvark', cannot *readily* be used in this way is merely pragmatic. When we consider a typical use of 'Spiro Agnew', we implicitly assume that the speaker and his audience mutually believe it to be the name of a certain person, namely Nixon's first vice-president. This is true not only if hearing the name calls up an old file labelled with that name (to recall an idea from Chapter 2) but even if it causes a new file to be created.[19] Either way, since the speaker is expressing an attitude about a certain person, he cannot reasonably intend his use of 'Spiro Agnew' not to have wide scope. The reason that a nominal description, in this case the one in (9), more readily lends itself to narrow scope use is that it makes explicit the property, that of bearing a certain name ('Spiro Agnew'), which is germane to his utterance, and thus the speaker can reasonably expect the hearer to take it as such. No special circumstances must be imagined for the narrow use of the nominal description, except that the name should

---

[19] Either way, the hearer is to take the speaker as expressing an attitude about a certain individual, and this attitude is not made fully explicit by the sentence being uttered. For whereas that sentence expresses only a uniqueness proposition, the speaker is making a singular statement about a certain bearer of the name.

be unusual and therefore not likely to be shared at a given possible world (see note 18).

Notice that this pragmatic difference between a name and its descriptive counterpart is compatible with the fact that they are semantically equivalent. Consider another example of the same phenomenon, this time involving 'standardized indirection' (Bach and Harnish 1979, 192–8). The two interrogatives 'Can you pass the salt?' and 'Are you able to pass the salt?' are semantically equivalent, and yet only the first is standardly used to make a request.

Finally, it should be pointed out that proper names can take narrow scope relative not only to modal operators but also to psychological verbs. I grant that here too they generally take wide scope, but the reason is again pragmatic. For example, a likely use of (11)

> George thinks that Spiro Agnew is a shipping
> magnate.   (11)

would be to ascribe to George a belief about Spiro Agnew. However, there is also a narrow scope use, in which the property of bearing the name is germane to the utterance, namely, to ascribe to George a belief about who bears the name 'Spiro Agnew'. These are two different beliefs, although that can be obscured by the fact that in both cases (11) might be described casually as saying that George does not know who Spiro Agnew is. The difference is clear: the second belief could have been about Aristotle Onassis.

So far I have tried to explain and defend the thesis that proper names are semantically equivalent to nominal descriptions, and I have answered some objections to it. However, I know it can gain credence only in so far as it can be defended from Kripke's well-known arguments against description theories generally. In the next chapter we will take up these arguments. I will try to show that NDT is immune to them, and why. Understanding why will, I hope, lead to a greater appreciation of the merits of this deceptively simple thesis. Indeed, it is because of its simplicity as a semantic thesis and nothing more that NDT leaves room for relying on general pragmatic considerations to explain away the illusion of rigidity.

8

Proper Names II: Answering Kripke

When applied to NDT, how effective are Kripke's celebrated arguments against description theories of names? Equally celebrated, of course, is Kripke's version of Mill's view that proper names denote directly. This is the semantic thesis that names are rigid designators (RDT), that a name designates the same individual in all possible worlds in which it designates at all. Unlike all description theories save NDT, RDT attempts to do justice to Mill's observation that names seem to have no descriptive content and function simply as labels or tags.[1] Accepting Mill's observation, most philosophers have found RDT to be intuitively appealing, especially in light of the difficulties that Kripke has found with description theories. Kripke does recognize that the motivation behind description theories is to avoid for names the notorious problems (existence, identity, and belief sentences) that Russell's theory avoids for descriptions. He also recognizes that his theory of names cannot avail itself of Russell's method of avoiding these problems, and later we consider whether RDT can avoid them at all. But first we will examine Kripke's two main arguments against description theories, the modal argument and the argument from ignorance and error. I will contend that even if they refute description theories generally, they are ineffective against NDT. Then I will answer Kripke's objection to NDT in particular, that it is viciously circular. To complete my defense of NDT, I will try to explain pragmatically what I call the illusion of rigidity.

1. KRIPKE'S FIRST OBJECTION: THE MODAL ARGUMENT

Kripke offers the following modal argument, as neatly schematized by Loar (1976, 373):

---

[1] Does this indicate that names have *no* meaning? Mill denied that they have 'connotations', but that does not show that they mean nothing at all, for it could be said that names mean what they denote. Kripke prefers not to commit himself on this issue, which seems merely terminological in any case.

(*a*) If 'N' meant 'the F', then 'N might not have been the F' would be false.

But

(*b*) 'N might not have been the F' is true.

Therefore,

(*c*) 'N' does not mean 'the F'.

Assume here that 'N' has but one bearer, that N is the actual F, and that 'the F' is the description which, according to the description theory in question, is synonymous with 'N'. This pattern of argument is formally valid, Loar points out, provided that 'N' (in 'N might not have been the F') takes the same scope in (*b*) relative to 'might' as it does in (*a*). However, Loar suggests that the argument trades on an illicit shift of scope. 'Names are normally read as having wider scope than modal operators', and although (*b*) is true on the wide scope reading, (*a*) is false (Loar 1976, 373), for 'N might not have been the F' is true no matter what 'N' is supposed to mean. After all, even 'The F might not have been the F' is true on the wide scope reading.

In order for (*a*) to be true, 'N' must take narrow scope relative to the modal operator. So the question (which Loar did not ask) is whether (*b*) is true on *its* narrow scope reading. Now how we assess it depends on what, according to the description theory in question, particular instances of 'N' are supposed to mean. We can accept (*b*) only if we have independent reason to reject that theory; otherwise, we are just begging the question. For example, *if* 'Aristotle' meant 'the teacher of Alexander', then 'Aristotle might not have been the teacher of Alexander', read narrowly, *would* be false, since there is no counterfactual situation with respect to which the teacher of Alexander (in that situation) is not the teacher of Alexander. Of course we do accept (*b*), but we do not have to rely on the modal argument to know that 'Aristotle' does not mean 'the teacher of Alexander'. We have independent reason to reject any description theory according to which 'Aristotle' means *that*.

So let us try applying the modal argument to NDT. Replacing 'the F' with 'the bearer of "N" ', we have:

(a_n) If '*N*' meant 'the bearer of "N"'', then 'N might not have been the bearer of "N"'' would be false.

But

(b_n) 'N might not have been the bearer of "N" ' is true.

Therefore,

(c_n) 'N' does not mean 'the bearer of "N" '.

As with (*a*) above, (a_n) is true only on the narrow scope reading. Then the question is whether (b_n) is true on that reading (note well that (b_n) is about a sentence, not about its utterance).

The truth of (b_n) cannot be ruled out simply on the grounds that with narrow scope we first consider a counterfactual situation and then determine reference with respect to that situation. For it might be that where names are involved, the effect of narrow scope is the same as that of wide scope, that is, that scope makes no difference. Along these lines it could be argued against NDT and in support of (b_n) that NDT mistakenly identifies the referent of 'N' *with respect to* a counterfactual situation with the bearer of 'N' *in* that situation. Even though 'N' takes narrow scope rather than wide, its referent relative to that situation is the actual N (this is, of course, just what RDT says). But the referent of 'the bearer of "N" ' relative to that situation is not the actual N. So (b_n) is true, even on the narrow scope reading, and 'N' does not mean 'the bearer of "N" '.

However plausible this defence of (b_n) may be, it does not have adverse consequences for NDT as a semantic thesis about sentences containing names. To the extent that the referent of a name, even when it has narrow scope, is constant across counterfactual situations, this is not the semantic fact that RDT says it is. I contend that it really describes merely a pragmatic phenomenon involving *uses* of names, and that it seems significant semantically, as in the context of Kripke's appeal to intuition, only because of a certain method he adopts for individuating uses of names. I will argue that this seemingly innocuous method has no semantic basis.

The method of individuating uses appears, for example, in a passage where Kripke is explaining rigidity.

When I say that a designator is rigid, and designates the same thing in all possible worlds, I mean that, as used in *our* language, it stands for that thing, when *we* talk about counterfactual situations. (1980, 77)

Kripke does not mean that we can talk only about counterfactual situations in which the designator stands for that thing; rather, he wishes to take into account the boring fact that a designator, like any other expression, might have been used differently from how it is actually used. Such a restriction is needed to keep RDT from being falsified trivially (just as it would be absurd to claim that the number nine might have been red, had 'red' been used to mean odd, so it would be absurd to reject RDT on the grounds that a name might have been used differently). However, Kripke goes too far. As is evident from the words 'as used in our language it stands for that thing', Kripke is *stipulating* that utterances of a name count as instances of the same use only if the reference is the same. The stipulation is repeated when he goes on to say, 'in describing that world, we use *English* with *our* meanings and *our* references' (1980, 77; his emphases).

Is there any semantic basis for individuating uses of names by references as well as by meanings? With descriptions there is clearly no such basis. Only meanings matter. If, when talking about a counterfactual situation, we use 'the F' to refer to an individual other than the actual F, semantically this does not count as a different use (no ambiguity is involved). If someone talked about a counterfactual situation with respect to which he used 'the fortieth president of the US' to refer to Walter Mondale, semantically this would not count as a different use from its use, with respect to the actual world, to refer to Ronald Reagan. Yet if Kripke is right, matters are different with names. Suppose that Ronald Reagan's parents had intended to name their first son 'Ronald', so that if Ronald Reagan had had an older brother, the brother would have been named 'Ronald'. We would not conclude that Ronald Reagan might have been the older brother of the fortieth US president, for in considering the relevant counterfactual situation, we still use 'Ronald Reagan' to refer to the actual fortieth US president; we would refer to his brother in some other way, even though in that situation his brother would bear the name. We are imagining 'Ronald Reagan' being used to refer to the brother, but that is not how *we* use it. We could so use it, but then we would be using it differently.

This is what Kripke would say, and it does seem plausible, but the question is whether the two uses count as different *semantically*. The two analogous uses of 'the bearer of "Ronald Reagan" ' do not involve different meanings of the description. If someone said 'the bearer of "Ronald Reagan" might have been the older brother of the fortieth US president', he could be referring either to the actual Ronald Reagan in some counterfactual situation or to whoever bears that name in some counterfactual situation. Which reference he is taken as making depends on the context, but the meaning of the nominal description is the same either way.

I suggest that similar points apply to the name itself. If someone said, 'Ronald Reagan might have been the older brother of the fortieth US president', he could be referring either to Ronald Reagan with respect to some counterfactual situation or to whoever bears that name in some counterfactual situation. He could mean that there is a possible situation in which (the actual) Ronald Reagan is the older brother of the president or that there is a possible situation in which the older brother of the president bears the name 'Ronald Reagan'. Even though the first use is a narrow scope use that does not differ materially from a wide scope use, the second is a narrow scope use, like those uncommon uses discussed in the previous chapter, that does make a difference. And the fact that the name can be used either way does not make it semantically ambiguous (recall that we found no reason to regard shared names as ambiguous). Uses of the second sort may be less common, but we saw that there are pragmatic reasons for this. In any event, the possibility of the second use is enough to falsify (b_n) in the modal argument against NDT.

What, then, of Kripke's powerful appeal to our intuitions, as in the following passage (presumably he would say of the description 'the bearer of "Nixon" ' what he says of 'the winner')?

Well, of course, the winner of the election *might have been someone else.* The actual winner, had the course of the campaign been different, might have been the loser, and someone else the winner; or there might have been no election at all. So such terms as 'the winner' and 'the loser' don't designate the same objects in all possible worlds. On the other hand, the term 'Nixon' is just a *name* of *this man.* When you ask whether it is necessary or contingent that *Nixon* won the election, you are asking the intuitive question whether in some counterfactual situation, *this man* would in fact have lost the election. (1980, 41)

Of course 'Nixon' is being used to refer to a certain man, but when Kripke says that 'the term "Nixon" is just a name of this man', he is begging the question, at least if the question concerns the semantics of names (it must do this if it is to be relevant to the truth of (b_n) in the modal argument). He has not shown that uses of 'Nixon' to refer to other individuals count for semantic purposes as different uses.

So far, while assessing this argument, we have been pretending that a given name has only one bearer. In fact, it is false that ' "Nixon" is just a name of this man'; rather, in the context of utterance it is being used as a name of just this man. It is the name of many men and could have been used as the name of still others. In order to take into account the fact that names can have many bearers, perhaps rigidity should be relativized to particular uses, as Ackerman does with the following definition.

A singular term 'T' (as used in a particular way) is a rigid designator of entity *x* iff 'T' (in that use) designates *x* in every possible world where *x* exists, and there is no possible world where 'T' (in that use) designates an entity distinct from *x*. (1979, 61)

With rigidity so defined, RDT no longer even appears significant semantically. It is true all right, indeed trivially true, only because Ackerman is individuating uses of a name by each thing the name is used to refer to. By this method, a name has as many uses as it has bearers. No wonder that a name, as used in a particular way, rigidly designates! If this is Ackerman's way of individuating uses—nothing she says suggests otherwise—it renders RDT so trivial as to apply even to descriptions. For example, 'the first man on the moon' would rigidly designate Neil Armstrong, since if Armstrong had not been the first man on the moon and Buzz Aldrin had been instead, the use of 'the first man on the moon' to refer to Aldrin would count as a different use. Of course, no one would dream of individuating uses of descriptions in this way, but semantically there is no basis for individuating uses of names in this way either. Doing that would beg the question in favour of RDT, by presupposing that names lack sense and cannot be semantically equivalent to definite descriptions.

When Kripke briefly takes up shared names, he makes a proposal similar to Ackerman's. In regard to the example of (1),

Aristotle was fond of dogs.   (1)

he recognizes that there have been other people called 'Aristotle' besides the great Greek philosopher.

When I spoke of 'the truth conditions' of (1), I perforce assumed *a particular reading* for (1). (So, of course, does the classical description theorist; this is not an issue between us. Classical description theorists, too, tended to speak for simplicity as if names had unique references.) In practice it is usual to suppose that what is meant in a particular use of a sentence is understood from the context. (1980, 8–9; my emphasis)

To assume 'a particular reading for (1)' is to assume that (1) is semantically ambiguous. To say that description theorists have assumed the same thing is not to justify the assumption. And the assumption is not justified by the observation that 'what is meant in a particular use of a sentence' varies with the context, for nothing follows about the sentence itself.

Using the notions of meaning and ambiguity rather loosely, Kripke assumes that the use of 'Aristotle' in (1) is for the great philosopher.

Then, *given* this fixed understanding of (1), the question of rigidity is: Is the correctness of (1), *thus understood*, determined with respect to each counterfactual situation by whether a certain single person would have liked dogs (had that situation obtained)? I answer the question affirmatively. But Russell seems to be committed to the opposite view, even when what (1) expresses is fixed by the context. . . . This question is entirely unaffected by the presence or absence in the language of other readings of (1). For each such particular reading separately, we can ask whether what is expressed would be true of a counterfactual situation if and only if some fixed individual has the appropriate property. *This* is the question of rigidity. (1980, 9; his emphasis)

In fact, Russell is not committed to the view that what (1) expresses, as 'fixed' (whatever that means) by the context, is not a singular proposition, for he allows that ordinary names, and definite descriptions as well, can be used 'merely to indicate what we are speaking about' (1919, 175). Russell was not especially cognizant of the distinction between a sentence and statements it can be used to make, but he was certainly not committed to the view that a sentence like (1) is semantically ambiguous, with different 'readings'. Kripke is committed to such a view, for which he should offer an argument.

Kripke says that 'to speak of "the truth conditions" of a sentence such as (1), it must be taken to express a *single* proposition—otherwise its truth conditions . . . are indeterminate', and for this purpose 'it must be fixed whether "Aristotle" names the philosopher or the shipping magnate. Only *given* such a reading can Russell propose [his] analysis.' However, Kripke does not consider the possibility that (1) is univocal and that the single proposition it expresses is a uniqueness proposition, where 'Aristotle' is replaced by its nominal descriptive equivalent. So understood (1) would ordinarily be used (*s*-) non-literally, whether to make a uniqueness or a singular statement. If the latter, the statement could be about the philosopher, the shipping magnate, or someone else named 'Aristotle', but it would hardly follow that the name is rigid. So it takes considerable credulity to accept Kripke's remark 'that we have a direct intuition of the rigidity of names, exhibited in our understanding of the truth conditions of particular sentences' (1980, 14).

Once RDT is relativized to uses of names, it becomes not only trivial but misdirected. For if we individuate uses by bearers while recognizing that shared names are not thereby ambiguous, we must acknowledge that RDT thus relativized is no longer a thesis about the semantics of names but one about uses of names to refer.[2] Nothing about the semantics of a name tells us which of its bearers it is being used to refer to on a given occasion. That is a question for the theory of speech acts. The semantics of a name tells us only that if it is used literally to refer it must be used to refer to something whose name it is. NDT accounts for this semantic content; the relativized version of RDT, not being semantic, is not even a rival to NDT.

---

[2] This objection applies also to Evans's suggestion that uses of names be individuated not by their referents but by the practices of using them. Generally there is a distinct practice of using a name for each of its bearers, but this is not always so. Evans imagines a case in which 'the name "Jack Jones" was bestowed upon two individuals who happened to look alike, with the consequence that they were regularly confused. Instead of two separate name-using practices, it may be that information from both men has become merged, so that there is a single name-using practice with no one referent. In this community, I would maintain that the name "Jack Jones" does not have a referent.' (1982, 374) The truth in this, it seems to me, is simply that users of the name often do not have a definite person in mind and thus have no fully determinate referential intention. Sometimes they do, as when they refer to one of the men in his presence, or simply address him. In any case, since Evans grants that both men bear the name, his question of whether the name has a referent can be nothing more than the question of whether users of the name have definite referential intentions. It is true that sometimes they do not and that they have one 'Jack Jones' file when they should have two, but nothing is added to this by the claim that there is one rather than two practices of using the name. The notion of a practice bears no real weight here.

2. KRIPKE'S SECOND OBJECTION: THE ARGUMENT FROM IGNORANCE AND ERROR

This argument is designed to show that for any description thought to be semantically equivalent to a given proper name, a speaker can be ignorant or even mistaken about who satisfies the description but still use the name to refer to the appropriate individual. If so, this description cannot determine the reference of the name.

Kripke devises the case of Schmidt, Gödel's murderous impostor. Assume for the sake of argument (the choice of description is not supposed to matter anyway) that the name 'Gödel' means 'the man who proved the incompleteness of arithmetic' ('the PIA', for short). Then what if, unbeknownst to everyone but Gödel, the real PIA was a man named 'Schmidt' whom Gödel had murdered and whose work Gödel took credit for? The description theory implies that 'when our ordinary man uses the name "Gödel", he really means to refer to Schmidt, because Schmidt is the unique person satisfying the description ["the PIA"]' (1980, 84). However, Kripke insists that a user of the name, despite the murderous fraud, would still intend to refer, and indeed would be referring, to Gödel rather than Schmidt. After all, we do not use 'Gödel' to mean 'the man, whoever he is, who proved the incompleteness of arithmetic'.

Like the modal argument, the argument from ignorance and error is not supposed to depend on the choice of descriptions, and Kripke (1980, 87–90) shows how it works if the description is varied. Unfortunately, he does not consider whether it works for nominal descriptions (he does object to NDT on other grounds, as we will see in the next section, claiming it to be viciously circular). A description like 'the PIA' does not mention the name whose meaning is under consideration, and thus a description theory relying on that sort of description is in no position to explain the fact that to use a name literally to refer one must intend to refer to something whose name it is. So we must use the nominal description 'the bearer of "Gödel" ' as the candidate for being the descriptive equivalent of 'Gödel' and see how well it fares against Kripke's argument.

To do this we must modify Kripke's story somewhat. This time suppose that the man who proved the incompleteness of arithmetic was in fact named 'Gödel' but that he was murdered by a man who has since managed to pass himself off as the PIA and as named 'Gödel'. A speaker ignorant of all this would use the name to refer to the murderous impostor rather than to the real Gödel. This is supposed to show, according to Kripke's argument, that the name 'Gödel' does not mean 'the bearer of "Gödel" ', but does it show this? True, the speaker would not be referring unwittingly to the real Gödel, but he would still be using 'Gödel' to mean 'the bearer of "Gödel" '. Unfortunately, both for the real Gödel and for Kripke's argument, the speaker would be referring to the man he mistakenly believes to be the bearer of 'Gödel'.[3] In this version of Kripke's story, the speaker has used the name 'Gödel' in the manner of a referential use of a definite description. Indeed, if NDT is right, that is precisely what he has done. He has used 'Gödel', the semantic equivalent of 'the bearer of "Gödel" ', to refer to someone whom he falsely believes to satisfy that description. NDT explains just how this is possible: because the name is semantically equivalent to the nominal description that mentions it, one can use the name to refer to something one thinks bears it.[4] As I will explain later, the reason that names have seemed to be rigid designators is that their standard use is referential. And the reason for that is that we almost always think of the bearer of a name in some other way than as the bearer of the name. This is not surprising, considering how uninformative names are about their bearers.

Now Kripke does anticipate the suggestion 'that a name is associated with a referential use of a description', but he summarily rejects it.

A referential definite description, such as 'the man drinking champagne', is typically withdrawn when the speaker realizes that it does not apply to its object. If a Gödelian fraud were exposed, Gödel would no longer be called 'the author of the incompleteness theorem' but he would still be called 'Gödel'. The name, therefore, does not abbreviate the description. (1980, 87)

However, consider the result of applying this argument to nominal descriptions: if the fraud about the man referred to with 'Gödel'

---

[3] I have been assuming, in fairness to Kripke, that the impostor has not come to bear the name 'Gödel' even though he is passing himself off under that name. Of course it could come to be his name, even legally.

[4] Even when a speaker uses a name to refer to something he privately believes does not bear the name, he still intends the hearer to rely on this semantic equivalence in order to identify the referent.

were exposed, this man would no longer be called 'the bearer of "Gödel"' but, according to the argument, he would still be called 'Gödel'. In this case its conclusion is patently false, precisely because the name *does* abbreviate the description.

As for the argument from ignorance and error itself, we can resist it further by considering some further variations of my version of the impostor story. Suppose the speaker is aware that the man passing himself off as Gödel is an impostor. If he believes that the hearer is unaware of this, he can use the name 'Gödel' to refer to this man anyway. That he is aware of the hoax does not mean that he is not using the name literally.[5] If anything, he is relying on its semantic equivalence to 'the bearer of "Gödel"' to enable the hearer, with his false belief, to identify the referent. But if the speaker believes the hearer to be aware of the hoax and to realize that he the speaker is aware of it, he would then be using the name non-literally, as if it meant 'the individual posing as Gödel', and would expect the hearer to take him to be so using it. Then the hearer would identify the impostor as the referent.

These variations provide further reason for rejecting the assumption central to Kripke's argument, that if a name is semantically equivalent to a definite description, it must be used (if used literally) to refer to whatever satisfies that description, even if the satisfier of the description is not the individual the speaker intends to be referring to. As we have seen, however, a speaker can use a name literally not only to refer to what does not (and what he believes does not) bear the name but also, by relying on its semantic equivalence to the nominal description that mentions it, succeed in referring to the intended individual. NDT recognizes these possibilities, and, as the last version of our story shows, it can even make intelligible non-literal uses of names, something that Kripke's conception of names seems unable to do.

3. KRIPKE'S OBJECTION TO NDT: THE CIRCULARITY ARGUMENT

However effective they may be against description theories in general, the modal argument and the argument from ignorance and

[5] Just as if he were using a definite description referentially (recall our discussion in Chapter 6), so here the speaker is literally and directly asserting a uniqueness proposition, which in the present case he does not believe, but he is also indirectly making a singular statement.

error do not undermine the nominal description theory. Perhaps Kripke is aware of this, for he offers an additional argument directed specifically at NDT, which charges it with being viciously circular. To support this charge against NDT Kripke lays down what he calls the non-circularity condition, which prohibits a theory of names from using any 'notion of reference in a way that is ultimately impossible to eliminate' (1980, 68). I will argue that NDT does not violate this condition, and seems to only if one conflates the meaning of a name with its use to refer.

If a speaker is to use the name 'Socrates', 'how are we supposed to know to whom he refers?' asks Kripke. He represents NDT's answer to be, 'by using the description which gives the sense of it, . . . "the individual called 'Socrates' " ' (I prefer 'the bearer of "Socrates" '[6]). Kripke charges that this 'tells us nothing at all, . . . it seems to be no theory of reference at all. We ask to whom does he refer by "Socrates" and then the answer is given as, well he refers to the man to whom he refers.' (1980, 70).

How serious is this charge? To say that NDT is 'no theory of reference at all' is simply irrelevant. NDT is a theory of the meaning of names, not a theory of their use to refer. For that we need the help of speech act theory, which Kripke himself (1977) recognizes that we need in the case of referential uses of definite descriptions. Moreover, he seems to imply that if NDT were correct, then someone who utters 'Socrates drank hemlock' is stating nothing more than that the man he is referring to drank hemlock. But NDT allows that the speaker is doing more than that. After all, there is information on which the speaker expects the hearer to rely in order to identify the individual being referred to. If the sentence is semantically equivalent to 'The bearer of "Socrates" drank hemlock', as NDT claims, the hearer can infer the name of the intended referent (it is mutually believed that the relevant bearer of this name is an ancient Greek philosopher). Thus the speaker intends, and can reasonably expect the hearer to infer that he intends, to be stating that the ancient Greek philosopher bearing the name 'Socrates' drank hemlock. Of course not all the relevant

---

[6] As noted earlier, 'the bearer of "Socrates" ', unlike 'the individual called "Socrates" ', does not even suggest circularity. Bearing a name does not imply being referred to by that name. There was an ancient Hebrew stricture against referring to God by a certain name, but this did not prevent him from bearing that name. Luckily, transmitting this stricture from generation to generation required only mentioning the name, not using it.

information is built into the meaning of the name, but NDT does not require that it should be.

Thus, Kripke's charge of circularity against NDT is unfounded. His non-circularity condition stipulates that a theory of names should not employ an ineliminable notion of reference, but NDT is not guilty of that since it does not even purport to be a theory of reference. It is nothing more than a modest theory of the modest meaning of names. How they are used to refer is not explained by their meaning alone, especially when, as is common, there are many bearers of the name. Moreover, bearing a name, like bearing a Social Security number, does not imply ever being referred to by it. People could bear names even if they were referred by to their Social Security numbers instead.

Even if NDT is not circular, one might object that it is viciously regressive. For surely not everyone who has ever referred to Socrates by name could have relied on the semantic equivalence claimed by NDT. The original sources of the use of 'Socrates' to refer to the man we refer to by 'Socrates' had to be in a position to think of Socrates in some other way than as the, or even a, bearer of 'Socrates', and surely his parents, not to mention his fellow Athenians, were in that position. Devitt (1980) has charged that NDT is viciously regressive in this way, but Loar (1980, 86–7) has a neat reply. For he observes that NDT, just like RDT, is entitled to 'help itself' to the notion of 'referential dependence on sources'. I would put Loar's point this way. Like the charge of circularity, the charge of vicious regressiveness is predicated on the false assumption that for a name to be used to refer to its bearer, its bearer must have been previously referred to by that name. But this is absurd. After all, for an individual to have acquired the name in the first place, it had to be referred to in some other way than by name, or at least in some other way than by that name. Otherwise, *it* could not have been given that name. However, once it has acquired the name (thereby coming to have the property of bearing the name), people other than the original sources used it to refer to. That is why Loar can say, 'The description theory of names [i.e. NDT], as it treats those cases involve reference to others' references, is the causal theory made self-conscious' (1980, 86), provided, of course, that the causal theory is conscious of the difference between the meaning of a name and its use to refer.

4. FOUR FAMILIAR PROBLEMS FOR RDT

So far I have defended NDT against objections both to it and to description theories in general. Now we should take up the familiar problems raised by vacuous names and by existence, identity, and belief sentences containing proper names. Supporters of RDT recognize that while description theories can handle these cases with ease, these cases do pose serious problems for RDT.[7]

Vacuous names. Names without bearers pose no problem for description theories, since the semantic contribution of a name to the sentences in which it occurs is the same whether or not it denotes. Its contribution is not the individual it denotes (if any) but the individual concept it expresses (as given by the description it abbreviates). However, on RDT, according to which a sentence containing a name expresses a singular proposition about the individual the name denotes, the semantic contribution of the name is that individual.[8] So the problem for RDT is to explain how a sentence containing a vacuous name can be fully meaningful. I know of no well-developed attempt to solve this problem.[9] Moreover, it would seem that a theory should treat names uniformly. Description theories do this, of course, but it is difficult to see how RDT can avoid giving vacuous names separate treatment.

Peacocke acknowledges that on his version of RDT 'a general uniformity of treatment of both denoting and non-denoting names . . . is impossible' (1975, 129). For him a name is a 'genuine'

---

[7] This has not abated the enthusiasm for RDT, whose advocates are well aware of its failure so far to solve these four problems, which they seem to regard as minor nuisances. Although they regard (what they take to be) legitimate objections to description theories as casting doubt on these theories, it is a curious sociological fact that they are not similarly moved by what they recognize to be legitimate objections to RDT. See Searle (1983, 239).

[8] One theoretical possibility is that its contribution is a causal chain, which may or may not originate in an actual object. This approach distinguishes Devitt's (1980) version of RDT. However, even though he claims to be doing semantics, Devitt is explicitly concerned with tokens of names, not types, and is therefore not offering an account of the meaningfulness of sentence types containing (vacuous) names.

[9] Donnellan (1974) presents the suggestion of a solution, his theory of 'blocks'. However, he is not very confident of it and acknowledges that vacuous names (as well as negative existential sentences) do present a serious difficulty for RDT (here Donnellan assumes an historical (causal) theory of reference). Recognizing the considerable refinement his theory needs to handle vacuous names, Donnellan readily concedes that description theories can handle them straightforwardly, in the fashion of Russell.

singular term only if it denotes. The occurrence of a genuine singular term in subject position licenses existential generalization, but clearly the occurrence of a vacuous name cannot. Peacocke cheerfully concludes from this that the logical form of a sentence containing a name depends on whether or not the name denotes. Instead of regarding this as a problem for his position, he asks rhetorically, 'Why should we not say that there are some sentences such that only when we know whether the names in them denote do we know their logical form?' (1975, 130) This means that the logical form of (1)

Neptune exists.   (1)

was unknown prior to the discovery of Neptune.[10] I wish Peacocke had answered his rhetorical question, for if knowing whether a name denotes is necessary for knowing the logical form of sentences containing it and if the logical form of a sentence is a semantic property, then one cannot know the meaning of such a sentence unless and until one knows whether or not the name it contains denotes. But surely, lacking such knowledge is no more of a deficiency in linguistic competence than is not knowing who all the bearers of a name are. One does not need such knowledge to understand a sentence containing the name.

Existence sentences. The problem with existence sentences containing proper names is to explain how they can be meaningful. As above, description theories have no trouble here. On NDT in particular, a sentence like (1) is equivalent to (2),

The bearer of 'Neptune' exists.   (2)

which is then given a Russellian analysis. When couched in the notation of predicate logic, such an analysis contains no individual constants but only variables. However, since RDT does liken proper names to individual constants, it represents (1) with (3),

$(Ex)(x = n)$.   (3)

where 'n' abbreviates 'Neptune'. The problem for RDT is to explain the meaning of 'n' in (3). Ordinarily the way to interpret an individual constant is to assign it an individual to denote, but if that is done here then (3) is meaningful only if it is true (and its

10 Since he claims that a sentence like (1), if it contains a denoting name, is a 'first level predication of an object', it is no wonder that he laments the absence of an adequate account of negative or positive existential sentences containing non-denoting (vacuous) names.

negation, representing the negation of (1), is meaningful only if it is false). Tautologies might have this property, but (3) is hardly a tautology. Indeed, a sentence like (4),

Vulcan exists. (4)

though false, is perfectly meaningful. Furthermore, RDT is in no position to explain the fact that the negation of (4) is not only meaningful but true.[11]

Identity sentences. Whereas the problem of existence sentences containing names is how they can be meaningful, the problem with identity sentences is how they can be informative. Frege's (1892) distinction between sense and reference provides a familiar solution to this problem, but of course that solution is unavailable to anyone who denies that this distinction applies to proper names. Take a sentence like (5),

Scott is Sir Walter. (5)

On the view that names denote directly, the semantic contributions of 'Scott' and of 'Sir Walter' to (5) are their denotations, in which case, since (5) is true so that these names have the same denotations, all (5) can say is that this individual is identical to himself. But then (5) would have the same content as (6),

Scott is Scott. (6)

Now surely (5) is more informative than that. What (5) says is not that Scott is identical to himself but, as Russell puts it (along the lines of NDT), that 'the person called "Scott" is the person called "Sir Walter" ' (1918, 246). For 'if one thing has two names, you make exactly the same assertion whichever of the two names you use, provided they are really names and not truncated descriptions' (Russell 1918, 245). Of course Russell does not regard ordinary names as genuine names.

It is well known that Kripke (1980) holds that a sentence like (5) is, if true, necessarily true, just as (6) is. The difference, he says, is that (6) can be known a priori, whereas (5) cannot. This claim is a corollary of RDT. Even if RDT were correct, however, the problem

---

[11] The argument of this paragraph comes from Russell. Assuming that Romulus did not exist, Russell says, 'It is obviously a perfectly significant statement, whether true or false, to say that Romulus existed. If Romulus himself entered into our statement, it would be plain that the statement that he did not exist would be nonsense, because you cannot have a constituent of a proposition which is nothing at all.' (1918, 242)

raised above would still arise. For an account is needed of the difference in meaning between (5) and (6), and RDT does not provide it.

Belief sentences. Unlike the other problems, this is one that Kripke (1979) addresses at length. He calls it 'a puzzle about belief'. Kripke imagines one Peter who, having learned 'Paderewski' as the name of a famous pianist, assents to sentence (7),

Paderewski had musical talent. (7)

Later Peter learns 'Paderewski' as the name of a Polish statesman and, thinking politicians unmusical, assents to sentence (8),

Paderewski had no musical talent. (8)

Peter does not realize that in (8) 'Paderewski' also refers to the pianist. Kripke's puzzle is whether we should conclude, by the seemingly innocuous 'disquotational principle', not only (9),

Peter believes that Paderewski had musical talent. (9)

but also (10),

Peter believes that Paderewski had no musical talent. (10)

The disquotational principle seems to licence inferring both (9) and (10), since Peter assents to both sentences (7) and (8). Kripke is thus faced with a dilemma. If both (9) and (10) are true, he seems to have no way to account for the fact that Peter is not guilty of a contradiction but is merely the victim of ignorance. For there seems to be no way (consistent with his view of names) to express what Peter is ignorant of. It surely won't do to represent Peter as ignorant that Paderewski = Paderewski, but Kripke seems to have no better way to represent Peter's ignorance. In particular, he cannot do it by associating different descriptions with the two occurrences of 'Paderewski', for that would be to revert to a description theory. The only alternative for Kripke, the other horn of the dilemma, is to abandon or somehow modify the disquotational principle, but he sees no clear way to do that.

Kripke should have considered how Schiffer (1977) treats this problem (in a paper appearing in the same volume as Kripke 1977). Schiffer points out that sentences like (9) and (10) do not fully specify the contents of the beliefs being ascribed. In each case what is missing is a specification of the mode of presentation under which Peter is thinking of Paderewski. These modes of presentation under which Peter is thinking of Paderewski are expressed by two different descriptions. With them we can state the obvious, that what Peter is ignorant of is that Paderewski the pianist = Paderewski the statesman. Now Kripke does *seem* to consider this obvious solution in discussing the suggestion that a believer associates two distinct 'uniquely identifying properties' with the names he uses, but these, according to Kripke, 'description theorists have regarded as "defining" proper names' (1979, 261). However, Schiffer, who endorses Kripke's view of names, nowhere says that the *meaning* of a name is the individual concept, as expressed by a definite description, under which one thinks of what the name names,[12] and there is no reason to assume that the linguistic meaning of a belief sentence with a proper name in the content clause, as illustrated by (9) and (10), gives the full content of the belief the sentence is being used to ascribe.[13]

Unfortunately, Schiffer's move does not ultimately help RDT, because it does not satisfactorily explain the semantic role of names in belief contexts. Schiffer seems to assume that they have their usual denoting role, so that the ascribed belief is about what the name denotes, but this cannot be true in cases like (11) and (12),

> George believes that Spiro Agnew is a shipping
> magnate. (11)
> Carl believes that Vulcan is round. (12)

As I am imagining it, George's belief is not about Agnew, whose name George has managed to confuse with someone else's, say Aristotle Onassis's. And Carl's belief cannot be about Vulcan, since it does not exist.

Belief contexts pose no problem for NDT, on which a name 'N' means 'the bearer of "N" '. When 'N' has many bearers, this description is incomplete, so that a full specification of the content of a belief involving 'N' would be of the form (13),

> S believes that the bearer of 'N' who/which
> is F is G. (13)

---

[12] Not only does Schiffer distinguish the description under which one thinks of an object from the meaning of the name one uses to refer to it, he claims that one can think of an object only under a description. I argued against this reductive, description theory of *de re* thought in Chapter 1.

[13] By the same token, as we have seen, there is no reason to assume that the linguistic meaning of a simple sentence containing a name, such as (7) and (8), fully captures the belief it is used to express.

Peter's two beliefs are that the bearer of 'Paderewski' who was a pianist had musical talent and that the bearer of 'Paderewski' who was a statesman had no musical talent. In short, Peter believes that Paderewski the pianist had musical talent and that Paderewski the statesman did not.[14] And, of course, he did not believe that they were one and the same. In this way NDT can treat only 'the bearer of "N" ' as semantically equivalent to 'N' while construing other descriptions under which one has beliefs (or makes statements) about a certain bearer of 'N' merely as cognitively (or contextually) associated with particular uses of 'N'. This is how NDT can distinguish Peter's two beliefs without assuming anything about how many bearers 'Paderewski' has. NDT can also handle (11) and (12) without difficulty. George believes that the man with the name of 'Spiro Agnew' is a shipping magnate, and Carl believes that the planet named 'Vulcan' is round. In (12), the 'that'-clause does not express the full content of the belief being ascribed, but this is generally true when proper names are involved.

5. THE ILLUSION OF RIGIDITY

Despite the popularity of RDT, most philosophers who accept it still recognize the trouble it has with the four familiar problems rehearsed above. This recognition makes it puzzling why RDT should have such widespread appeal. I cannot solve that puzzle, but at least, having argued already that NDT escapes the usual objections to description theories, I can try to explain away the intuitions that give RDT its popular support. For this purpose we should keep in mind that since NDT is a semantic thesis only, it leaves room for an independent account of the pragmatics of names. It may be simple but it is not simplistic. As a semantic thesis, NDT does not pose as a theory of how names are used to refer. Silent on their pragmatics, it also leaves room for an account of how names, without change of meaning, can be used *without* referring, as with vacuous names and with utterances of belief or

---

[14] I have been supposing that the name is part of the contents of Peter's beliefs (it obviously is in the cases of (11) and (12) above), but this is not essential, since not every element of a 'that'-clause in a belief sentence needs to be used to express an element of content in the belief being ascribed. Kripke's puzzle about belief can still arise, and NDT can still solve it.

existential sentences. The way to do this, I suggest, is to extend our pragmatic account of uses of definite descriptions and thereby assimilate referring uses of names to referential uses of descriptions.[15] First I will try to diagnose the illusion of rigidity, which I believe has three distinct though related sources.

(*a*) Kripke's appeal to our intuitions about names may be compelling, but I believe these intuitions have been misdescribed as semantic and are properly understood as implicitly pragmatic. Their reputed semantic significance can be explained away if we realize that whenever Kripke presents an example (recall the ones involving Nixon and Aristotle, for example), the intention being imputed to the speaker fixes the reference. Then Kripke makes his appeal to intuition. The name, as a linguistic type, does not carry the information that it is being used to refer to some particular individual. There is nothing in (1), for example,

> Aristotle was fond of dogs.   (1)

to indicate who 'Aristotle' is being used to refer to. However, before putting our intuitions to the test, Kripke builds into the example that 'Aristotle' is being used to refer to the philosopher rather than to the tycoon. To be sure, Kripke thinks this is innocuous, as when he acknowledges that he previously 'spoke for simplicity as if each name had a unique bearer' and denies, 'as far as the issue of rigidity is concerned, that this is a major over-simplification' (1980, 7). In fact it is major, for, as we saw early in this chapter, it commits Kripke to the implausible view that a shared name is ambiguous in as many ways as its number of bearers. We saw that what Kripke describes as 'various readings of (1)' are really various ways of using it, and that relativizing RDT to uses of a name serves only to trivialize it. When Kripke states that he will defend RDT by arguing that 'although the man (Nixon) might not have been the President, it is not the case that he might not have been Nixon', I can only say 'Of course!' But this is not a fact about 'Nixon' but about the man being referred to, whether by 'Nixon' or by 'the President'. Yes, *that* man could not have been someone other than Nixon; he had to be identical to himself.

In light of these points, it does not seem unfair to suggest that in a sentence like (2),

---

[15] We have seen also how NDT, combined with a Russellian account of definite descriptions, incomplete as well as complete, can assimilate shared names to incomplete descriptions.

Aristotle might not have been a philosopher. (2)

the name 'Aristotle' seems rigid only because its use to refer to a certain individual is fixed before the question of its rigidity is raised. I do not mean that Kripke is doing the fixing; rather, it is the imagined speaker. What renders the use fixed—and helps explain away the intuition of rigidity—is the imputed intention to refer (objectually) to a certain bearer of the name (this is what Kripke often calls (1980, e.g. 57) 'using the description to fix the referent'). It is the imputed intention that makes it the case that the name (i.e. the speaker's use of it) refers to the same individual in all possible worlds. The name itself simply does not carry the information needed to determine the referent.[16] NDT does not require that it should, since this determination is a matter of the speaker's intention.

(*b*) Another source of the impression of rigidity is the platitude that names do not describe. As Kripke puts it, 'the function of names is simply to refer, and not to describe the objects so named by such properties as "being the inventor of bifocals" ' (1971, 141). And when he remarks that 'unlike a definite description, a name does not describe its bearer as possessing any *special* identifying properties' (1979, 240; my emphasis), he neglects to mention the fact that a name used literally to refer *does* implicitly describe the referent as bearing the name. Of course there is generally nothing 'special' about bearing a certain name,[17] since anyone or anything can bear virtually any name, but there is more to being the referent than bearing the name. From the hearer's standpoint, it is not very helpful, in order to identify a referent one does not know of by name, simply to hear him being referred to by name. And if the name has many bearers, knowing the name will not, by itself, enable one to identify the relevant bearer. Yet it does not follow that the name does not describe at all.

If a name is used literally to refer to someone, he is implicitly being described as bearing the name, but, contrary to what Kripke

[16] It could do that if it contained a subscript, but it does not. In saying this I am not being facetious, for I seriously believe that the appeal of RDT stems partly from the tendency in philosophy to liken natural languages to formal ones, e.g. the language of standard first-order logic with its convention that individual constants denote one individual apiece and its practice of using subscripts when one runs out of letters. In natural languages, however, a name can have one, many, or no bearers and neither its sound, its shape, nor any other linguistic feature indicates which.

[17] Certain *names* are special, by being highly unusual or richly descriptive, but such a name may not tell us anything special about its bearer.

apparently assumes, a description theory like NDT is not committed to the view that the meaning of a name determines which individual it is being used to refer to on a particular occasion. Precisely because a name provides so little information about the referent, a speaker who uses a name is likely to have some further information in mind on which his audience is to rely, information which is not part of the meaning of the name. Unless you know of an individual only by name, when you refer to him by name you are likely to be thinking of him in some other way, a way that does not entail his bearing the name. Indeed, it is because you are thinking of him in some other way, whether descriptively or in some *de re* way, that you are in a position to think of *him* as bearing the name. And you intend your audience to rely on more than just the name to identify who you are talking about.[18]

(*c*) There is a rather different way in which the platitude that names lack descriptive content might contribute to the illusion of rigidity. Recall that Kripke's appeal to intuition involves a comparison between the ways in which modal sentences containing descriptions and those containing names are evaluated. With a description we go to a possible world and find the individual that satisfies the description. With a name we find the individual that bears the name and then go to a possible world. Instead of concluding that names are rigid and descriptions are not, however, we can interpret these intuitions in a different way. This interpretation does not concern the difference in the semantics of names and descriptions but rather the difference in how they acquire their connections to objects. The difference is simply this: things fit descriptions, whereas names are given to things. Whereas there is something that an individual has to be, namely F, in order to be the F, there is nothing that an individual has to be in order to be given a name. We might say that an individual has to qualify in order to fit a description, but there is no qualification that an individual has to meet in order to be given a name. Thus there is a difference in the direction of connection between expression and object.

This difference helps us to account not only for the intuition that names but not descriptions are rigid but also for the fact that it is

18 Ordinarily the referent bears (and is believed to bear) the name, but not necessarily, just as when one uses a description to refer to something that does not satisfy it. In the context of Kripke's story, for example, one can use the name 'Gödel' to refer to Schmidt.

illusory. Because this difference is not semantic, the intuition is not semantic either. Indeed, at the semantic level there is no difference in direction of connection. Just as the description 'the F' applies to an individual because that individual has the property of being F, so the name 'N' applies to an individual because that individual has the property of bearing the name 'N'—because it was given the name. Just as having invented bifocals makes it the case that a certain man is the inventor of bifocals, so having been given the name "Benjamin Franklin" makes it the case that a certain man is Benjamin Franklin. The difference is not in the semantics of the description and the name but in how the description and the name came to apply to the man in the first place. What I have been calling the difference in the direction of connection consists simply in the fact that this man had the property expressed by the description independently of fitting the description but had the property expressed by the name in virtue of a fact involving the name itself, the fact that he was named 'Benjamin Franklin'.[19]

Each of the foregoing considerations helps explain away the illusion of rigidity. As for the data that fuel this illusion, our strategy is simply to extend our account of referential uses of definite descriptions (especially incomplete ones) to referring uses of names. Recall that when a description is used referentially, its meaning does not determine the referent. Instead, the identity of the referent is fixed by the governing way in which the speaker is thinking of the intended referent. These points are especially evident when the description being used referentially is incomplete. If I utter (3), for example,

> The radio is on too loud. (3)

my reference to a certain radio (or perhaps to what I mistakenly take to be a radio) cannot possibly be fixed by the meaning of the

[19] Since the difference in direction of connection is not a semantic difference between names and descriptions, I do not accept Devitt's characterization of 'the semantical problem for proper names [as] that of explaining the nature of the link between name and object in virtue of which the former designates the latter' (1980, 6). For although it is the link (the connection) between name and object that explains the semantic relation between the former and the latter, the latter relation is no different in kind—or direction—than that between description and object. Just as 'the F' denotes an object if it (alone) has the property of being F, so 'N' denotes an object if it (alone) has the property of bearing 'N'. In the latter case, of course, the object has that property because it was given the name, not because it 'fits' the name.

incomplete description 'the radio'. An analogous point applies to an utterance of (4),

John is talking too loud. (4)

where again the referring expression carries far too little information to fix the referent. The speaker must exploit mutual contextual beliefs to make the intended referent identifiable, and the hearer, presuming the speaker to be doing this, must rely on such information in order to have a basis for identifying what the speaker is using 'the table' or 'John' to refer to.

The reason we can assimilate referring uses of names to referential uses of definite descriptions, incomplete ones in particular, is that in general names are used to refer objectually. And the reason for this is that the property of bearing a name is hardly ever the primary aspect (to borrow Searle's phrase) under which one thinks of an individual or uses the name to refer to him. You do not refer to someone by name unless you know him by name and suppose your audience to know him by name; but knowing someone by name involves thinking of him in some other way than as the bearer of the name. To be sure, you could use a name to refer to an individual even if you were thinking of him only by name, but then you would be referring descriptively. This use of a name would be like an attributive use of a definite description. For example, if you noticed the name 'Pierre Perrier' in the phone book and said 'Pierre Perrier must be French', you would be using the name to refer, but the reference would be descriptive—to whoever Pierre Perrier happens to be. In general, however, we use names to refer objectually because we do think of their bearers in other ways than by name.

Curiously, Kripke does consider, though all too briefly, the suggestion that 'a name is associated with a "referential" use of a description', but he argues that such a description

is typically withdrawn when the speaker realizes that it does not apply to its object. If a Godelian fraud were exposed, Godel would no longer be called 'the author of the incompleteness theorem' but he would still be called 'Godel'. The name, therefore, does not abbreviate the description. (1980, 87)

But suppose, in accordance with NDT, that the description in question is 'the bearer of "Gödel"'. If *that* description did not apply to the individual one is referring to by 'Gödel', that individual would not be called 'Gödel' and one would withdraw the name when one realized that.[20] So Kripke has failed to show that a name does not abbreviate the nominal description that mentions it.

In order further to understand the use of names to refer objectually, let us look at the situation from the hearer's point of view. What happens when someone mentions by name a person you are not familiar with? You might not even be familiar with the name, but even then you can understand the speaker. You can think of the individual being referred to as the bearer of the name who the speaker has in mind. Indeed, you could proceed to use the name yourself, and intend to be talking about whoever your source of the name had referred to. In fact, chains of reference are commonly forged in this manner, link by link, as in Kripke's causal–historical picture. As he says, 'When the name is "passed from link to link", the receiver of the name must, I think, intend when he learns it to use it with the same reference as the man from whom he heard it.' (1980, 96) We can acknowledge that this picture is perfectly compatible with NDT ('the causal theory made self-conscious', as Loar (1980, 86) aptly describes NDT) provided we distinguish the meaning of a name from a particular use of it to refer. This was implicit in my application, back in Chapter 1, of the causal–historical picture to my theory of *de re* thought. Grafting this picture on to NDT yields an account of the use of names as well as of their meaning. Kripke is right, but for the wrong reasons, that the description giving the meaning of a name generally does not determine what the name is being used to refer to. The right reason is that a speaker almost always thinks of, and intends his audience to think of, the referent in some other way than simply as the bearer of the name. Indeed, Kripke's main arguments against description theories of names are not so much wrong as misdirected. Their proper target is description theories of *de re* thought, as illustrated by our versions of Kripke's Gödel/Schmidt example. These arguments are relevant to the theory of linguistic reference only indirectly, and then only in so far as names (or other expressions) are used to refer objectually in the course of expressing *de re* thoughts.

[20] Along with Kripke I am assuming that ordinarily the speaker does believe the intended referent to fit the description. That is why he would withdraw it if he were corrected. As we saw in Chapter 6, there are other cases, e.g. where the speaker does not believe the referent to fit the description but exploits the audience's belief that it does.

As we have seen in the last two chapters, RDT is committed to the implausible view that shared names are semantically ambiguous. Indeed, it seems mistakenly to presuppose that names are lexical items in particular languages. Further, it does not provide for the literal/non-literal distinction as to uses of sentences containing names or for the extension to names of either the referential/attributive distinction or the narrow scope/wide scope distinction. And finally, it does not provide a unitary account of names on which both meaningful failures to refer with names and non-referring uses of names can be explained.

As for NDT, as a semantic thesis it is immune to the objections against description theories generally, is not guilty of circularity, and avoids wanton proliferation of readings for shared names and for sentences containing them. Also, by providing for the difference between understanding the use of a name to refer and understanding the name itself, NDT leaves room for a pragmatic account according to which uses of names to refer can be assimilated to referential uses of definite descriptions. Then it is clear why reference is not determined by linguistic meaning, why reference failure does not lead to loss of meaning, and why the meaning of a singular term does not change when it is not used to refer, as in utterances of existence and belief sentences.

In sum, as a linguistic item a name is equivalent semantically to the nominal definite description that mentions it. Although names do not belong to particular languages, each language provides for this semantic equivalence in the general way given by NDT. When a name is used, generally the speaker's referential intention is not determined by this equivalence, for he is likely to have a particular bearer of the name in mind, which he intends the hearer to think of. As we observed in Chapter 2, the speaker intends the hearing of the name either to call up an old file or to create a new file labelled with the name. Either way, the hearer is to take the speaker as expressing an attitude about a certain individual, and this attitude is not made fully explicit by the sentence being uttered. For whereas that sentence expresses only a uniqueness proposition (assuming NDT together with Russell's theory of descriptions), the speaker is making a singular statement about a certain bearer of the name.

9

Reference and Pronouns

As I have tried to show concerning descriptions and names, it may seem to be a semantic fact that they are referring expressions, but their referring function can and should be explained in strictly pragmatic terms. In contrast, it is undeniable that the referring function of pronouns is inseparable from their semantics.[1] They do not denote in the strict (context-independent) sense, of course, and sentences containing them do not have absolute truth conditions. Yet the fact that they are characteristically used to refer does seem to demand a semantic explanation. Indeed, it might even be suggested that even though the reference of a pronoun is fixed only *relative* to the context of utterance, still it is fixed semantically, hence that the meaning of a sentence containing a pronoun determines a truth condition relative to the context.

One virtue of this suggestion is that it accounts for the fact that the meaning of a given pronoun remains constant even though it can be used literally to refer to various individuals. However, the suggestion also has a serious difficulty. I will argue that the speaker's intention always (except in the case of 'I') plays an essential role in determining reference and, further, that for semantic purposes this intention cannot count as an element of context. Nevertheless, I will gladly concede that the referring function of indexicals is part and parcel of their semantics. Indeed, I will explain in detail how pronouns and other indexicals can be distinguished semantically from one another in terms of their respective constraints on how they can be used literally to refer. Finally, I will point out that they can be used to refer descriptively as well as objectually.

---

[1] Incidentally, there has been some terminological confusion here due to the fact that indexical semantics has been called 'pragmatics', primarily by formal semanticists. Along with most linguists, I have been using that term for the theory of language use. In the various places where I have contrasted pragmatics with semantics (i.e. the theory of use with the theory of meaning), it should have been clear that I was using 'pragmatics' in this way.

1. REFERENCE AND CONTEXT

Let us take up the suggestion that pronouns refer semantically, though relative to a given context of utterance, and its corollary, that a sentence containing a pronoun has a context-relative truth condition. What is being suggested here is not the trivial point that a pronoun refers in the sense that it refers to whatever it is used to refer to, and that a sentence containing it is true (relative to the context) in the sense that the speaker is using it to make a true statement. If the suggestion is to be genuinely semantic, the context-relative determination of the referent and the truth condition cannot involve the speaker's intention. If the speaker's intention were a factor, the suggestion would lose its semantic import. Or so I will argue.

The suggestion does apply to the special case of 'I'. One must use 'I' to refer to oneself, and that is a fact about its meaning. Moreover, who is using it is a fact about its context of utterance. And notice that there seems to be no description, not even an indexical one, capable of giving the meaning of 'I'. For example, 'the utterer of these words' will not do as a definition, since I could use that description to refer to the person I am presently quoting. The semantics of the word 'I' seems to come to no more and no less than the fact that to use it literally is to refer to oneself: the meaning of the word type is a rule for using a token of that type to refer—to oneself.

Could it be that the semantics of every other indexical also consists in such a rule, a rule specifying how reference is a function of the context of utterance, hence that a sentence containing an indexical has a semantically determined, though context-dependent, truth condition? Take the case of 'now'. (1), for example,

I am ready to go now. (1)

obviously has no absolute truth condition but does seem to have a relative truth condition varying with context. Corresponding to the indexicals in (1) are the contextual parameters of speaker and time of utterance.[2] Accordingly, (1) is true, relative to a given context of

---

[2] In fact, one can use 'now' to refer to other times than the time of utterance, as in a narrative.

utterance, just in case, in that context, the speaker is ready to go at the time of utterance.

This suggestion seems plausible enough, and Kaplan (1979) has turned it into an influential theory. Kaplan thinks of the meaning, what he calls the character, of indexicals and of sentences containing them, as a function from context to content.[3] This conception is plausible, but it can succeed only if for each indexical there is a well-defined function of a well-defined set of contextual parameters. The trouble is that there is not, as shown by (2),

He was ready to go then. (2)

which is structurally like (1) but contains different indexicals (and is in the past tense). In fact, notice that one speaker can use (2) to say at one time what another speaker could have used (1) to say at another, earlier time. Yet they differ considerably in how the relevant referents are determined. Whereas the referents of 'I' and 'now' in (1) are clear-cut functions of context (who uttered (1) and when he uttered it), that is not the case with the referents of 'he' and 'then' in (2). Their referents depend on the speaker's intentions, not on the context of utterance. In a given context a speaker could use 'he' to refer to any male other than himself[4] and 'then' to refer to any earlier time. So it seems that the meanings of these indexicals are not functions from context to content. Depending on the speaker's intentions, the same utterance in the same context can have different contents.

To avoid this result it could be suggested that speaker intention is part of context. Unfortunately, such a suggestion would effectively dilute the notion of context to the point where anything other than linguistic meaning is included. This would trivialize the theory that meaning is a function from context to content. Even worse than trivializing it, to include intention in context would undermine the

---

[3] For Kaplan content is intension, not extension. Working in the framework of possible-worlds semantics, he takes intensions of sentences to be not truth conditions but functions from possible worlds (or, more generally, indices) to extensions. In the case of indexicals (as well as of proper names) these are constant functions. Thus he thinks of indexicals as 'words and phrases whose *in*tension is determined by the contexts of their use' (1979, 401). For present purposes these niceties can be safely ignored.

[4] In fact, it is possible to use 'he' to refer to oneself, though only if one does not realize (or believes that the hearer does not realize) that the referent is oneself. For example, one might utter 'He sure has a funny voice' and be using 'he' to refer to someone whose taped lecture is being broadcast. That person might be oneself.

very point of the theory. For according to the theory, associated with each indexical is some determinate function which is given *independently* of the context. Since the meaning of an indexical is supposed to specify the contextual parameters that constrain the referential intentions with which the indexical can be used (literally), the theory cannot allow the speaker's intention to count as a separate parameter of context. If it did allow this, it could not explain how that intention is constrained by the meaning. Instead, it would self-defeatingly treat that intention as just another contextual parameter, an independent variable on which meaning operates.

Thus Kaplan's theory cannot coherently include speaker intention in context. But with intention excluded from context, for any indexical other than 'I' and 'now' meaning does not determine reference as a function of context (even assuming the speaker is being literal). It might be thought that Kaplan's proposal works at least for 'you'. We could say that just as the context specifies the speaker, so it specifies the addressee, but there is a problem with that. What if a number of people are present when (3) is uttered?

You may go now. (3)

If one person in particular is being addressed, his identity cannot be a matter of context, at least not according to the way of specifying contextual parameters required for an indexical semantics, as in (4),

'You may go now' is true in $C(t,s,a)$ iff a may (is permitted by s to) go at t. (4)

where '$C(t,s,a)$' represents the context as a function of the time of the utterance, the speaker, and the addressee.[5] The idea is that once the value of $C(t,s,a)$ is fixed, an utterance of (3) in that context has the truth condition specified by (4) with the designated values of the contextual parameters filled in. But how is the value of 'a' to be determined? The problem is not merely that the identity of an

---

[5] As Lycan makes clear in his survey of various alternatives to Kaplan's proposal, with other indexicals the contextual parameters seem to multiply beyond limit. Finding it 'disturbing that an n-tuple of this type has no definite number of members' (1984, 50), Lycan offers a formulation of his own which contains a single, catch-all contextual parameter 'C' (1984, 54). This may simplify the notation but it does not begin to address the question of the role of the speaker's intention. Even though Lycan admits that it is a pragmatic matter how the value of this parameter is determined, he claims to have established a 'context-relative notion of truth' which, because it applies to sentences, is supposed to be semantic.

addressee is not a straightforward physical fact in the way that the identities of the time of utterance and of the speaker are, but that an utterance like (3) might be directed at one particular person among several present. Moreover, the speaker may intend the others to recognize this. Thus we need to draw a distinction between the audience as a whole and those to whom specific remarks are directed, in which case we are no longer dealing merely with 'contextual factors which help us interpret the actual physical utterance as having a certain content' (Kaplan 1979, 389).

The view that meaning does determine reference as a function of context is not only false but misleading, in that it misrepresents the role of context in determining reference. For what context does, together with the meaning of the expression, is to provide the hearer with the information, in the form of mutual contextual beliefs (Bach and Harnish 1979, 5–6), needed for determining what the speaker intends him, in that context, to identify as the referent. Since the speaker's referential intention is part of his communicative intention, what he can reasonably intend to be referring to in the context is what he can reasonably be taken, in that context, to be referring to. Thus, the role of context is not to provide the parameters on which an alleged meaning function operates but to provide information on the basis of which the speaker can reasonably form a referential intention and on which the hearer can reasonably identify that intention. The meaning of an indexical constrains the reference but hardly determines it, even as a function of context.[6]

2. REFERRING AND SAYING

Here I anticipate a certain objection to my claim that what a pronoun can be used (literally) to refer to is not determined by context, and that the meaning of a pronoun cannot be construed as a function from contexts to contents because of the essential role of

---

[6] Thus I cannot accept the claim of Barwise and Perry's 'situation semantics', on which 'the interpretation of an expression must be a product of . . . the linguistic meaning of the expression [and] its context of use' (1983, 32). Barwise and Perry consistently avoid using the notion of speaker intention, which would turn interpretation into a pragmatic notion, but the aspect of context which for them plays a comparable role, what they call 'speaker connection', is far too indeterminate to fix reference, except in the case of 'I' and 'now'.

the speaker's intention in determining the referent. This objection appeals to the notion of *what is said* when an utterance is made.

In speech act theory there is a basic distinction between LOCUTIONARY and ILLOCUTIONARY ACTS.[7] When a speaker utters a sentence, the content of his locutionary act (what he says as opposed to what he is doing in saying it) is determined by the meaning of the sentence, not by any intention on the part of the speaker.[8] Thus we should take the claim that meaning is a function from context to content as applying to the content of locutionary acts. However, my argument against this claim appealed to the role of the speaker's intention in determining reference. So the objection is that the speaker's referential intention, as part of his total communicative intention, contributes to the content of the utterance not at the level of the locutionary but only at the level of the illocutionary act. And, so the objection concludes, once we distinguish these levels of content, we can see that my appeal to intention is simply irrelevant to the claim.

It is true that a speaker's referential intention is part of his illocutionary intention, but the objection mistakenly assumes that there must be reference at the level of the locutionary act. How could 'he' refer in a context where there are many males around, unless the speaker intends (as part of his illocutionary intention) to refer to a certain male in particular? For instance, suppose a latter-day French monarchist is in the habit of standing on a soap-box in Hyde Park extolling the virtues of royalty. A park gardener, who is familiar with this man, known fondly as the 'king of France', utters (1),

<blockquote>He is defending the throne again.   (1)</blockquote>

The gardener is stating that the so-called king of France is defending the throne again, but he cannot be *saying* this, since that

---

[7] Searle (1968), observing that every sentence has some illocutionary force potential built into its meaning, has argued that speech act theory should reject the locutionary level of description. However, there are two important reasons for retaining it, as Bach and Harnish (1979, 288) have pointed out. First, a speaker can make a meaningful utterance (he can say something) without performing *any* illocutionary act. Second, he can speak non-literally, in which case he is saying one thing while meaning another.

[8] This is not quite right, because the sentence might be ambiguous. In that case, what is said is determined by the 'operative meaning' of the sentence (Bach and Harnish 1979, 20–3). Which meaning is operative in a given utterance is, of course, a matter of the speaker's intention.

is not determined by the meaning of (1), not even in the context (there are many males around). Then what is he saying? Surely he is performing some locutionary act, and its content must be determined by the meaning of (1), but what is that content? I suggest that his locutionary act is properly described by (2),

> The gardener is saying that a certain male is
> defending the throne again.   (2)

In using (2) to describe the gardener's locutionary act, we are implying nothing about the identity or even the existence of any male. Nor are we implying that the gardener is referring to a certain male, as we would be if we described his illocutionary act of assertion, with (3),

> The gardener is asserting of the 'king of France'
> that he is defending the throne again.   (3)

In contrast, (2) merely suggests that a reference to a certain male is in the offing (provided that the utterance of (1) is serious and 'he' is being used literally); (2) does not specify that reference or even indicate how that reference is to be determined. All it does is restrict any literal reference being made to some male.[9]

If (2) is the way to describe the gardener's locutionary act, then (4)

> A certain male is defending the throne again.   (4)

is the way to specify its content. But like 'he' as used by the gardener, 'a certain male' does not denote anyone, not even relative to the context. 'A certain male' is equivalent neither to the definite description 'the male' nor to the indefinite description 'a male' (being more indefinite than the first and more definite than the second, it might be called a 'definite indefinite description'). At any rate, the meaning of the sentence containing it, (4), does not fix a truth condition, even relative to a given context of utterance, since the speaker's intention plays an essential role in determining reference. In this way (4) paraphrases (1).

However, what is said (the content of the locutionary act), as opposed to what is asserted, in uttering (1) or (4) *is* determined solely by meaning, indeed independently of context. Anyone who

---

[9] In denying that there is speaker reference at the locutionary level, as in (2) or in (1) with the description being used non-literally, I am modifying the conception of locutionary acts in Bach and Harnish (1979, ch. 2). We accepted Austin's (1962) view of them as involving reference as well as sense.

utters (1) at any place and at any time says the same thing, that a certain male is defending the throne again. There is no specification of who that is at the locutionary level; there is determinate reference, but only at the illocutionary level, where the speaker's referential intention plays an essential role. Thus we must reject the claim that the meaning of sentences containing pronouns is a function from context to content, where now the claim concerns the content of what is said. This claim is undermined not by the fact that the referential intention contributes to content, for that contribution is only at the illocutionary level, but by the fact that at the level of what is said context plays no role at all in determining content.

In the section after next I will sketch an account of the meaning of pronouns as rules for using them to refer. We will see that for each pronoun there is a referential constraint on what it can be used literally to refer to. But first I will take up one last defence of the suggestion that the reference of a pronoun does not depend on the speaker's intention.

3. INTENDING AND DEMONSTRATING

A clever example devised by Kaplan suggests a different reason for supposing that reference occurs at the level of what is said, independently of the speaker's intentions. Before I can explain how Kaplan exploits this example, I should briefly mention a key aspect of his view on demonstrative reference.

According to our Russellian approach to the semantics of definite descriptions and of proper names, sentences containing descriptions or names in grammatical subject position actually express not singular but general, uniqueness propositions. This is true even when these terms are being used referentially, although then the primary proposition being *asserted* is singular. Now although Kaplan accepts the Russellian approach 'for a large portion of language behavior, in particular, communication by means of general propositions', he claims that when a singular proposition is being asserted,

some or all of the denoting phrases used in an utterance should not be considered part of the content of what is *said* but should rather be thought of as contextual factors which help us interpret the actual physical utterance as having a certain content. (1979, 389; my emphasis)

This sounds very much like our conception of referential uses of definite descriptions and, more generally, of objectual as opposed to descriptive reference. However, Kaplan is talking not about what is asserted but about what is said. True, he does not pay much attention to this distinction, but if his point is to be significant semantically, it must apply at the level of the locutionary act. Accordingly, that is how I am going to interpret his example. The example is supposed to show that something can be demonstrated in fact even if it is not what the speaker intended to demonstrate and thereby to refer to. If Kaplan is correct, 'a person can fail to say what he intended to say'[10] (1979, 396), in which case there are at least some instances of reference with pronouns (other than 'pure' indexicals like 'I' and 'now') which do not depend on the speaker's intention and do occur at the locutionary level.

Kaplan supposes that on the wall behind him is a place which has long been occupied by a picture of Rudolf Carnap. Pointing to that spot but without turning or looking, Kaplan utters (1),

Dthat [he points as above] is a picture of one of the
greater philosophers of the twentieth century.　　　　(1)

'Dthat' is Kaplan's reference-fixing demonstrative, but the ordinary 'that' would do. However, unbeknownst to him at the time of his utterance, someone has replaced the picture of Carnap with one of Spiro Agnew. Obviously Kaplan did not intend to point to Agnew's picture, but he did. The question is, what has he referred to and what has he said? According to Kaplan, he has 'said of a picture of Spiro Agnew that it pictures one of the greatest philosophers of the twentieth century', though that is not what he intended to say. Kaplan has nothing against intentions, for he allows in cases like this that we may 'succeed in communicating what we intended to say in spite of our failure to say it' (in the example, his audience might realize that Carnap's picture had previously been there on the wall). And he recognizes that in demonstrating something we often point in the direction of other things as well and only roughly in its direction, so that our intention can be essential to determining which particular thing we

[10] He adds the necessary qualification, 'and the failure is not a linguistic error (such as using the wrong word) but a factual one'.

are talking about. However, Kaplan's example is not a case of a vague demonstration that needs sharpening by the speaker's intention. Here, Kaplan plausibly suggests, intending to refer to Carnap's picture does not keep Agnew's from being the referent.

But has he really, contrary to his intention, referred to a picture of Spiro Agnew? True, he has inadvertently pointed to that picture, and clearly his 'speech and demonstration suggest no other natural interpretation to the linguistically competent public observer', but it does not follow that he has referred to Agnew's picture. My first reaction, no doubt clouded by theory, was that he has not succeeded in referring to anything: he intended to refer to Carnap's picture and is merely being taken to be referring to Agnew's. There is no further question of what he actually referred to. He did not say anything of Agnew's picture, even if he was taken as so doing. The mistake in Kaplan's interpretation of the example, or so I thought, is to assume that the object actually demonstrated, even though it is not what the speaker had in mind, is automatically the actual referent.

I now reject the theory-laden intuition of the preceding paragraph. Perhaps Kaplan is right to claim that he has unwittingly referred to Agnew's picture. Still, I would argue, this does not show that the reference is just a matter of context and not of intention. To see why, let us consider just what Kaplan's intentions are in uttering (1) and which ones are essential to his act of referring and which ones are not.

Kaplan is pointing to the picture behind him of Spiro Agnew, but that is not exactly his intention. He intends to be pointing to the picture behind him, but he does not intend to be pointing to a picture of Spiro Agnew. He intends to be pointing to a picture of Carnap. Similarly, he intends to be referring to the picture behind him, but he does not intend to be referring to a picture of Agnew. He intends to be referring to a picture of Carnap. What is the intention that is part of his communicative intention? It would seem that when he utters 'Dthat is a picture of one of the greatest philosophers of the twentieth century', he intends and expects to be taken to be talking about the picture behind him. As is common with uses of demonstratives, he intends the hearer to rely on the predicative content of his utterance to figure out what he is using 'Dthat' to refer to. Thus if he had uttered 'Dthat is the wall on which a picture of . . . used to hang' (or 'Dthat is the flowerpot that is filling the spot where a picture of . . . used to hang'), he would intend and expect the hearer to take him to be talking about the wall (or the flowerpot). In the actual example, he intends the hearer to take him to be talking about a picture behind him, which unbeknownst to him is a picture of Agnew. If there were more than one picture hanging on the wall right behind him, then the hearer would rely (and assume he is intended to rely) on what they depict to determine which one Kaplan is talking about. For example, if one picture were of Agnew and the other of a melon, presumably the hearer would take Kaplan to be talking about the picture of the felon.

The point is that not all the speaker's (Kaplan's) intentions and beliefs are relevant to his referential intention. Although he is not using it, the operative description in his referential intention, the one on which he communicatively intends the hearer to rely, is 'the picture behind me'. It is under this description that he believes the picture to be of Carnap, and it has priority (in the sense of our account in Chapter 6 of referential uses of descriptions) with respect to his *statement*, though of course not with respect to his belief, over the description 'my picture of Carnap'. The fact that both descriptions have equal priority in his belief (he believes the picture behind him to be of Carnap and he believes the picture of Carnap to be the picture behind him) has nothing to do with their relative priority in his statement. For he has no reason to expect, hence no basis for intending, 'my picture of Carnap' to play a role in the hearer's identification of the referent. In short, it is not part of his referential intention to be referring to Carnap's picture. That intention is simply to refer to the picture behind him.

So the example does show that a speaker can fail to refer demonstratively to what he thinks he is referring to and can refer to something he thinks he is not referring to. However, it fails to show that the speaker's referential intention does not play its usual role in determining the referent. This is clear once we ascertain just what the decisive intention is, the one that is part of the speaker's illocutionary (communicative) intention. Thus Kaplan's example does not support the view that reference is determined, given the meaning of the referring expression, by the context and not by the speaker's intention.

Now it might be objected that I have rigged the discussion of the example by invoking the speaker's referential intention and then relying on the fact that this intention is part of his illocutionary intention. After all, we are supposed to be interpreting the example at the level of the locutionary act. So the question is whether Kaplan, in uttering (1), really did say something that was, just because of the context, about Agnew's picture. It may seem that he did, but consider the following variants of Kaplan's example. Suppose Carnap's picture had been removed and nothing had been put up in its place. Would Kaplan have said of the wall that it was a picture of one of the greatest philosophers of the twentieth century? Would he have said this of the portion of the wall previously covered by the picture? Suppose a potted plant had been put up in place of Carnap's picture. Would Kaplan have said the same thing of the potted plant? And what if a picture of a melon had replaced Carnap's picture? Even then it seems that what Kaplan said would not have been about anything. These variants of the example show that demonstrating an object and thereby saying something about it is, in a given context, not merely a matter of pointing to it while making an utterance.

4. THE SEMANTICS OF INDEXICALS: REFERENTIAL CONSTRAINTS

We have seen why it is a mistake to take the meanings of indexicals (other than 'I') as functions from context to reference. And the meanings of INDEXICAL SENTENCES (as I will call sentences containing indexicals) do not fix truth conditions, even relative to a given context of utterance, since the speaker's intention plays an essential role in determining reference. However, we also saw that what is said (the content of the locutionary act), as opposed to what is asserted (or the content of whatever is the illocutionary act), in using such a sentence *is* determined by meaning, indeed independently of context. If the indexical sentence is of the form 'He is G', what is said is given by a sentence of the form of (1),

A certain male is G.   (1)

Anyone who utters (1) at any place and at any time is saying the same thing, that a certain male is G. That is because at the locutionary level the male being referred to is not determined. Reference occurs only at the illocutionary level, where the speaker's referential intention plays an essential role. So it might be suggested that 'he' is semantically equivalent to 'a certain male'. Generalized, the idea is that the meaning of an indexical is given by what I earlier called a definite indefinite description, of the form 'a certain F'.

This suggestion is more plausible than the view that meaning is a function from context to reference, but still it is not correct. 'He' is literally used to refer to a certain male, which one a matter of the speaker's intention; but it does not follow that 'he' *means* 'a certain male'. This phrase is simply not intersubstitutable with 'he', as shown by a comparison of (2) with (3),

> John thought he was hungry but he couldn't eat.   (2)
> John thought a certain male was hungry but a certain
> male couldn't eat.   (3)

of (4) with (5),

> A doctor arrived but he was too late.   (4)
> A doctor arrived but a certain male was too late.   (5)

and of (6) with (7),

> When he arrived, the doctor could do nothing.   (6)
> When a certain male arrived, the doctor could do
> nothing.   (7)

More importantly, the suggested paraphrase does not capture the fact that indexicals are, as Reichenbach so aptly called them, *token reflexives*. In general, when a speaker refers to a certain individual, he intends his audience to identify that individual as the object of the attitude he is expressing. But when he is using an indexical to refer, he intends his audience to identify that individual by way of ascertaining a certain relation that it bears to the very token of the indexical he is using to refer to it. The relation depends on the indexical, and our survey of indexicals will indicate just what these relations are. As token reflexives, indexicals are made to order as referring expressions, and their semantics should reflect this. Giving their meanings with paraphrases like 'a certain male', although it gives their contribution to what is said in uttering sentences containing them, does not capture the fact that when used literally they are used to refer, and do so by way of certain semantically specified relations to their tokenings. After all, it is part of a competent speaker's linguistic knowledge to be able to use indexicals to refer and to recognize their use to refer.

The relevant relation varies with the indexical, and it includes what I call a REFERENTIAL CONSTRAINT on the sort of individual the indexical can be used to refer to. It should be understood, of course, that these constraints apply only to literal uses. Let us begin with personal pronouns.

The referential constraint on 'he' is that the speaker utter a token of it with a certain male in mind. For 'she' the constraint is that the speaker have a certain female in mind, and for 'it' any other individual.[11] A speaker utters a token of 'we' having in mind a certain group to which the speaker belongs, 'you' having in mind one or more of those he is addressing, and 'they' any other plurality of individuals. Of all the personal pronouns, only 'I' has a meaning that determines reference as a function of context. One can use 'I' literally to refer only to oneself.[12] It might seem that 'you' is analogous to 'I' in this respect, that is that it does not matter which individual the speaker has in mind and that it is literally used to refer to all of those, whether one or many, he is addressing. However, there are cases in which 'you' is used to refer only to the target of one's illocutionary act. One might be giving an order or making a promise, for example, to some specific member of one's audience (of course by 'audience' I do not mean all of those within earshot but only those one is addressing). So unless it is one in number, one is not constrained to use 'you' to refer to one's entire audience.

It might seem that certain of the temporal adverbs, such as 'now', are analogous to 'I'. For example, 'now' is standardly used to refer to the time of its tokening, 'today' to the day of its tokening, and similarly for 'yesterday', 'tomorrow', 'last week', 'next month', 'ten years ago', and so on. However, as we saw just now with 'you' and in the previous section with the demonstrative 'that' (or 'this'), so with these temporal indexicals meaning does not determine reference as a function of context. In fact, they too are demonstratives, as are the adverbs 'then', 'later', and 'earlier'. To see why let us consider these latter ones first.

---

[11] Actually, this is not quite right, since 'it' is often used to refer to animals and babies, especially when the sex is not known. I hope I can safely ignore this complication. A different complication occurs in those languages, like German and French, in which nouns have genders that often have nothing to do with sex.

[12] It might seem that 'I' cannot be used non-literally, but it can, as when one pretends to be someone else.

The adverbs 'then', 'later', and 'earlier' can be paraphrased with prepositional phrases containing the demonstrative adjectives 'this' or 'that'. 'Then' means 'at that time', 'later' means 'after that (this) time', and 'earlier' means 'prior to that (this) time'. Which time that (this) time is is a matter of the intention of the speaker producing the token of the adverb. It could be the time the token is produced, the time just mentioned, or a certain time to be recognized as salient in the context. Compare utterances of (8) and (9), for example,

I can meet you later. (8)

I have a meeting at six, but I can meet you later. (9)

In uttering (8) the speaker is referring to a certain time after the tokening of 'later' but in (9) to a certain time after the time of the meeting.[13] 'Now', 'tomorrow', and the other temporal adverbs function analogously. For example, 'now' does not have to be used to refer to the time of its tokening but, for example, to the current time in a narrative, as in (10),

Caesar knew it was now time to cross the Rubicon. (10)

Similarly with the temporal adverb 'tomorrow' in (11),

He was convinced that tomorrow would be too late. (11)

It seems, then, that 'now' means 'at this (the present) time', 'tomorrow' the day after this (the present) day', and so on. What counts as the present time may be, but need not be, the time at which the token is uttered.

Analogous points apply to the spatial adverbs 'here' and 'there'. 'Here' can but need not be used to refer to the place of its tokening. It can be paraphrased with 'at (in, to) this place', but this place could just as well be a place the speaker of the token has in mind, say the place of some event just described. Similarly, 'there' can but need not be used to refer to a place in the vicinity of the place of its tokening. It means 'at (in, to) that place', and that could be anywhere. Which place it is depends on the intention of the speaker of the token, and whatever restriction there is on that place is really a restriction on the rationality of the speaker's intention. Being part of his communicative intention, it is rational in the context to the extent that he can reasonably expect it to be recognized.

---

[13] A noteworthy complication here is that if the time is not definite, 'later' functions not as an adverb but as a restricted quantifier, paraphrasable as 'at some subsequent time' (after the time of the meeting).

What about the demonstrative pronouns 'this' and 'that', as well
as their occurrence as adjectives in demonstrative descriptions of
the form 'this F' and 'that F'? Taking the latter pair first, it seems
that they both can be used literally to refer to some contextually
identifiable F. Which F that is may be indicated by a demonstrative
gesture, or it may be evident from the direction the speaker is
looking. However, the relevant F might not be present at all.
Instead, it might be an F already mentioned or, for that matter, the
only F relevant to the conversation. The difference between 'this'
and 'that' (as pronouns or as adjectives) seems to be a matter of
relative proximity, either literal or figurative, to the time and place
of their tokenings. Typically, one uses 'this F' to refer to a nearby
(and identifiable) F and 'that F' to refer to one that is at a
distance (also identifiable). This contrast is obviously vague.
The difference between 'this F' and 'that F' is clearer when both are
used in the same sentence (or in a short stretch of discourse), as in
(12),

> This horse is faster than that one [horse].   (12)

If both horses are present, the speaker would use 'this horse' to
refer to the nearer one. If he wanted to say that the further one
were faster, in uttering (12) he would be misusing these
demonstrative descriptions, even if he pointed first to the further
horse and then to the nearby one. Indeed, it would be a misuse to
utter (13)

> This horse is very fast.   (13)

if he pointed to the further horse while there was another horse
nearby. The same points apply when 'this' and 'that' modify
different nouns, as in (14),

> This horse is faster than that car.   (14)

If you were standing next to the car and the horse were running out
on a track, you would interchange 'this' and 'that'.

Spatial proximity is not the only dimension on which the
difference between 'this' and 'that' operates. It could be temporal
proximity, for example. If two tennis buffs are comparing, at the
end of the match, Jimmy Connors's performance in the 1982
Transamerica final, where he lost badly to John McEnroe, with his
performance against McEnroe in the Wimbledon final three
months earlier, one might utter (15),

Connors played far better in that match than in
this one. (15)

Clearly 'this match' would be used to refer to the more recent
match. And there may be other dimensions of contrast between
'this F' and 'that F'.

As demonstrative pronouns, 'this' and 'that' by themselves are
quite uninformative (beyond their semantic difference in respect to
proximity). Each is characteristically used to refer to a contextually
identifiable individual, but neither provides much information for
the hearer to use in identifying the individual being referred to.
Each can be used anaphorically, to refer to something previously
mentioned,[14] but their fundamental use is demonstrative. When
'this' or 'that' is used demonstratively, what it is being used to refer
is often pointed at. However, from a purely physical standpoint
pointing is merely extending a finger or arm in the approximate
direction of the intended referent, and since there may be many
objects in that direction, not to mention their parts, surfaces,
shapes, and colours (etc.), the act of pointing does not by itself
enable the hearer to identify the referent. In fact, the decisive
source of information, with or without pointing, may be the
predicative content of the sentence being uttered. For each of the
following sentences, one can easily imagine circumstances under
which only its predicative content would make evident what 'this'
or 'that' were being used to refer to:

That looks just like Ariel Sharon. (16)
This is the record you wanted to hear. (17)
This must be the itchy part of your back. (18)
That is a lovely shade of red. (19)

In uttering (19), for example, the speaker might be pointing to a
certain object, but he would obviously be talking not about it but
about its colour.

Incidentally, just what is the difference between demonstrative
pronouns (or adjectives) and personal pronouns? It seems that
demonstratives are used to call the hearer's attention to the
referent, whereas personal pronouns are used to refer to something
to which the speaker and hearer are, indeed mutually believe they
are, already attending. In using a demonstrative to call the hearer's

---

[14] This something is often a fact or a proposition, as in 'That is why cigarettes are
hazardous to your health' and 'I wouldn't believe that for a moment.'

attention to something, one often accompanies it with a gesture or a glance to enable him to identify the referent. However, we can also use a demonstrative to refer to one among several objects just mentioned. For example, when two have been mentioned we use 'this' to refer to the more proximate one and 'that' to refer to the less proximate one.

Personal pronouns are generally used to refer to something to which the speaker and hearer are already attending (that fact is likely to be mutually believed). This occurs most frequently when the intended referent is already a topic of conversation. For example, 'she' is generally used to refer to a female mentioned shortly before, either in the same utterance or in an earlier one. There is no definite limit on how recent the previous mention must be, but we generally use a pronoun only when it is clear what we are referring to. We refer to the individual by name or by description if the interval seems too long or if there is another plausible candidate. Even when it is clear what the referent is, as when one individual is the current topic of conversation, for stylistic reasons we use a name or a description every so often rather than keep using a pronoun. On the other hand, even when several individuals of the same gender have been mentioned, often we can safely use a pronoun to refer to one of them, as in (20),

> Addie likes Betty and Cindy, but she dislikes Daisy
> and Effy. (20)

A personal pronoun can be used even if the referent has not been mentioned but is readily inferable. For example, if when asked when Jack wants to get married one replies with (21),

> Jack wants the wedding to be in June, but she would
> rather wait until August. (21)

presumably one would be using 'she' to refer to Jack's fiancée. Or the clue might be provided by the perceptual context rather than the linguistic one. You hear an annoying racket coming from the next apartment and say to your room-mate, 'I wonder what she's doing', using 'she' to refer your room-mate to your notoriously noisy neighbour. These examples show that personal pronouns can be used demonstratively, even though they are not demonstratives like 'this' and 'that'.

5. OBJECTUAL AND DESCRIPTIVE REFERENCE WITH INDEXICALS

The referential constraints indicate how each indexical is used to refer in virtue of being a token reflexive. Which object a speaker is using a given indexical to refer to is the one that is appropriately related to the token he utters. The fact that a relation to a token is involved suggests, by analogy with the relational character of *de re* thought, that indexical reference is inherently objectual. Indeed, this suggestion is reflected in several tempting views about indexicals: that they occur only with wide scope, that their occurrence is always referentially transparent, and that they are always used as rigid designators. These views are rarely stated explicitly but often seem to underlie comparisons of proper names to pronouns. For example, Wettstein observes that 'like Millian proper names, [indexicals are] used simply to make certain items subjects of discourse', and suggests that 'whatever information content is possessed by an indexical does not figure in what someone asserts by its use' (1979, 98). And when Kripke remarks that 'demonstratives can be used as rigid designators' (1980, 49), he too may be thinking that demonstratives are used primarily to refer objectually (his statement is difficult to take literally, since rigidity is a matter of meaning, not use). In any case, we should not accept the above suggestion, for it is clear that indexicals and demonstratives can both be used to refer descriptively as well as objectually.

Let us begin with demonstrative descriptions. A hunter who utters (1),

That fox must be hungry. (1)

might be referring objectually to a nearby canine beast, one that may or may not be a fox, which is baring its teeth. On the other hand, a farmer, noticing the nightly depletion of poultry stock, might utter (1) to refer descriptively to whichever fox is raiding his chicken coop every night.

Even though it is not as informative as a demonstrative description, a pure demonstrative can be used also to refer descriptively. If the doorbell rings and one utters (2),

That must be a salesman. (2)

one could be using 'that' to refer descriptively to whoever rang the doorbell. Indexicals can be used similarly. If someone says 'The heaviest man in the world weights 900 pounds', and in reply you utter (3),

> I bet he has a gargantuan appetite. (3)

you would be using 'he' to refer descriptively to the heaviest man in the world. Notice that a descriptive use of an indexical does not require the prior use of a definite description.[15] Suppose a detective spots a footprint eighteen inches long and utters (4),

> He must be a giant. (4)

Here the detective is using 'he' to refer descriptively to whoever left the huge footprint. Under the circumstances he can reasonably expect his audience to identify this individual concept as what he is using 'he' to express. Descriptive reference can also be made with a temporal adverb. A teacher, having told his students to remain seated until the bell rings, might go on to utter (5),

> Then you can go home. (5)

using 'then' to refer descriptively to the time the bell rings.

In so far as it makes any sense to talk about the wide scope, referential transparency, or rigidity of *uses* of terms, the above examples and similar ones show that indexicals can be used with narrow scope, can be referentially opaque, and need not be used rigidly. For example, in reply to the remark that the richest man in the world is an American oil-man, one might reply with (6),

> I think he is an Arabian sheikh. (6)

Here 'he' is obviously being used with narrow scope and is not being used rigidly. A referentially opaque occurrence of 'he' is illustrated by (7),

> Still believing in Santa Claus, Virginia thinks he
> ate the milk and cookies. (7)

So indexicals and demonstratives can be used to refer descriptively as well as objectually—or not to refer at all.

---

[15] Even when a description has been used, the indexical need not be used to refer to what the description was used to refer to, as in the following discourse:
A: The best restaurant in Northern California is in San Francisco.
B: No, it's in Berkeley.

10

Singular Terms in Belief and in Fictional Contexts

One of the themes of this book is that the notion of denotation is tangential to the semantics of singular terms. I have tried to support this thesis by defending Russell's theory of descriptions, by developing a version of the description theory of names (it implies that their meanings are neither given by their denotations nor dependent on their having denotations), and by arguing that pronouns do not denote, not even relatively to contexts of utterance. As I will now suggest, occurrences of singular terms in belief (or other attitude[1]) contexts do not pose for my approach the problems that arise for those views that rely on the notion of denotation. So my account of the occurrence of singular terms in such contexts will be rather straightforward. That will not prevent it from being controversial, however, for the distinction between referentially transparent and opaque occurrences will be interpreted pragmatically. The theoretical benefit of drawing this distinction at the level of speaker intention rather than of sentence grammar is that, contrary to popular opinion, belief sentences are not systematically ambiguous.[2] As for occurrences of singular terms in fictional contexts, in the final section a pragmatic account will be given of them as well.

1. DESCRIPTIONS IN BELIEF CONTEXTS

Suppose Russell was wrong and that definite descriptions did generally function semantically as singular terms rather than as (disguised) quantifier phrases. Even then it might seem that descriptions could not function as singular terms in belief

---

[1] We will restrict ourselves to belief contexts, but the points to be made about them apply equally to other attitude contexts.

[2] Indeed, this opinion is the main theme of Cresswell (1985).

contexts,[3] that is in subject position of 'that'-clauses in belief sentences. Indeed, it is widely held that in (1), for example,

> Bertie believes that <u>the king of Belgium</u> is bald. (1)

the position (underlined) in which the description occurs is REFERENTIALLY OPAQUE (Quine 1960, 144–51).[4] Two things follow from that. First, (1) does not imply that the king of Belgium is such that Bertie believes him to be bald, because Bertie could believe that the king of Belgium is bald even if there is no such king. Indeed, (1) does not imply that there is anyone whom Bertie believes to be bald. So to treat the description as a singular term requires explaining why existential generalization is invalid here and why exportation of the description from, and 'quantifying in' to, the that-clause is prohibited. Second, assume that Belgium does have a king and that he composed the ballet *Les Sordides*. (1) could be true even if Bertie does not believe that the composer of *Les Sordides* is bald, for he might be unaware of the fact that the king of Belgium was the composer of *Les Sordides*. An opaque context, then, does not freely allow existential generalization or substitution of co-referential expressions.[5]

Neither Quine nor anyone else suggests that *all* belief contexts produce referentially opaque positions. Here it is usual to contrast a 'believes-that' sentence like (1) with a 'believes-of' sentence like (2),

> Bertie believes of <u>the king of Belgium</u> that he is
> bald. (2)

Whereas (1) can be true even if Belgium has no king, (2) can be true only if it does. Moreover, it does not matter how the king of Belgium is mentioned. If (2) is true and if, unbeknownst to Bertie,

---

[3] Another important context of this sort, though not of concern here, is their occurrence within the scope of modal operators.

[4] As Quine points out, the transparent/opaque distinction can be extended in a straightforward way to occurrences of predicates. Consider (i), for example,

> Zippy believes that taco sauce is <u>the colour of</u>
> <u>chlorophyll.</u> (i)

where what might be meant is not that Zippy believes taco sauce to be green but that he takes it to be red, which he thinks is the colour of chlorophyll.

[5] An interesting question here, though hardly ever addressed, is whether either generalizability or substitutivity is possible without the other. If so, we would say that some contexts are existentially opaque but substitutionally transparent or substitutionally opaque but existentially transparent. An example of the latter is 'Bertie knows that <u>the king of Belgium</u> is bald.'

the king of Belgium is the composer of *Les Sordides*, then Bertie believes of the composer of *Les Sordides* that he is bald, though of course Bertie does not think of him in those terms. The occurrence of 'the king of Belgium' in (2) is said to be REFERENTIALLY TRANSPARENT. In this position both existential generalization and substitution of co-referential expressions are permitted.

The transparent/opaque distinction, as illustrated by the difference in the occurrences of 'the king of Belgium' in (1) and (2), suggests to some a further difference between such sentences. In their literal uses (1) and (2) supposedly ascribe two different kinds of belief, 'notional' and 'relational' (Quine 1956), or, as they are often called today, *DE DICTO* and *DE RE* belief. The suggestion is that in (1) 'believes' expresses a two-term relation between Bertie and what he believes, whereas in (2) it expresses a three-term relation between Bertie, the king of Belgium (the object of his belief), and what Bertie believes of him. Because it ascribes a relational belief, a sentence like (2) allows 'quantifying in'. (1) does not, in that there might not be someone whom Bertie believes to be bald.

Thus according to common opinion there is a general distinction between referentially opaque and transparent contexts: with belief sentences it is exemplified by the difference between 'believes-that' and 'believes-of' constructions, and that difference corresponds to the difference between *de dicto* and *de re* belief. Not surprisingly, though, matters are more complex than common opinion would suggest. For one thing, applying the transparent/opaque distinction to the different occurrences of 'the king of Belgium' in (1) and (2) is not as clear-cut as suggested above. Implicit in the suggestion is that while a speaker uttering (2) would be using 'the king of Belgium' to refer (he could be speaking truly only if Belgium had a king), he could not so use it in uttering (1). But in fact he could. Suppose that visiting a certain house of ill repute in Luxemburg is a man wearing a funny wig. Bertie mutters to himself 'The man wearing a funny wig is bald.' Overhearing this, the royal Belgian police chief utters (1) to the royal Belgian executioner. Now the fact that the man wearing the wig is the king is a secret between the king, the police chief, and the royal executioner. In uttering (1) the chief is referring to the king of Belgium but is not implying that this is the way in which Bertie is thinking of the man. That would be evident if the chief had expanded his utterance of (1) into (3),

Bertie believes that the king of Belgium is bald, but of course
he has no idea the man wearing a wig is the king.   (3)

Here the chief would be using 'the king of Belgium' to refer; and he
would not be using it, contrary to how we assumed it was being
used in (1), to express how Bertie thinks of the man he believes to
be bald. And there is no reason why 'the king of Belgium', as it
occurs in (1), could not similarly be used to refer, though as we saw
initially it need not be so used.

Moreover, a speaker could use (2) without referring to the king
of Belgium or implying that Belgium has a king. Suppose that
Belgium has no king but that Bertie believes that it does, as
indicated by his derogatory remarks about the (imagined) king. He
takes up the subject of the king's funny wig and makes insinuations
about why the king wears it. Later one of his listeners reports,
'Bertie has a fantasy about there being a king of Belgium. Although
Queen Victoria wore a funny wig Bertie did not believe of her that
she was bald. Yet [(2)] Bertie believes of the king of Belgium that
he is bald.' It seems to me that this is a perfectly literal use of (2)
and that it is being used to make a perfectly true statement, even
though there is no implication that Belgium has a king. I grant that
(2) more strongly suggests that Belgium has a king, but I would
deny that it implies this.

Moreover, as noted in Chapter 1, there is no reason to suppose
that, philosophical tradition notwithstanding, 'believes-of' sentences must be used to ascribe *de re* beliefs or that 'believes-that'
sentences must be used to ascribe *de dicto* beliefs. A worse mistake,
also noted in Chapter 1, is to suppose, because the difference
between ascriptions is marked by the terms '*de re*' and '*de dicto*',
that there is no *de re/de dicto* distinction to be drawn between
beliefs themselves—that the latter distinction can be reduced to the
former. Perhaps this reductive view is due to a simple syntactic
oversight. For the phrases '*de re* belief ascription' and '*de dicto*
belief ascription' are syntactically ambiguous in just the way that
'French wine lovers' and 'little bird watchers' are ambiguous. That
is, '*de re*' and '*de dicto*' can each modify either 'belief' or
'ascription'.

The fact that 'believes-of' and 'believes-that' constructions can
both be used to ascribe either *de re* or *de dicto* beliefs suggests that
the difference between ascriptions of *de re* and *de dicto* beliefs is

not marked at the level of sentence grammar.[6] In my view neither is the transparent/opaque distinction. It is commonly taken to be a distinction between occurrences of singular terms or, as Quine puts it, between sentential positions in which singular terms occur. From what was said above, it is clear that this distinction is not marked by the difference between 'believes-of' and 'believes-that' constructions. However, one might take a different tack in trying to defend the grammatical status of the transparent/opaque distinction. One might grant that in the 'believes-that' sentence (1) 'the king of Belgium' may or may not be used referringly, but proceed to argue that 'believes-that' sentences are semantically ambiguous. The suggestion is that (1) means one thing when 'the king of Belgium' occurs opaquely and another when it occurs transparently.

Before being tempted by this appeal to ambiguity, consider the two uses of the description in (1). The use corresponding to the so-called transparent occurrence is to (purport to) refer to the king of Belgium. Corresponding to the opaque occurrence is the ascription to Bertie of a certain (descriptive) way of thinking of some putative individual. Assume that the predicative part ('is bald') of the 'that'-clause is being used to ascribe the predicative content of Bertie's belief.[7] Then with the second use of 'the king of Belgium' a speaker would be ascribing to Bertie belief in a uniqueness proposition and be specifying its full content, whereas with the first use the speaker would be referring to the king of Belgium but not be specifying how Bertie thinks of him. He would be specifying only the predicative content of Bertie's belief. And, as Loar (1972) has observed, there is nothing to prevent a speaker from using a definite description in both ways, to refer to an object *and* to express how the believer thinks of it. Even ignoring this last possibility, once we reduce the opaque/transparent distinction to a distinction in uses by speakers there is no longer any reason to speak of the description's occurrence or position in the *sentence* as

---

[6] Hardly worth mentioning, though it has been made, is the suggestion that there is *de de/de dicto* ambiguity in the word 'believes'.

[7] It need not be so used, since the opaque/transparent distinction can be extended to general terms. Perhaps the content of Bertie's belief is that the king of Belgium has no more hair than Kojak but he also believes that Kojak is not bald (but shaves his head twice daily). Still, if the speaker believes that Kojak is bald, he might use (1) to ascribe Bertie's belief.

being transparent or opaque. For depending on how the description is used, one and the same position in (1) can be transparent or opaque (or both).

Since how 'the king of Belgium' is to be taken in an utterance of (1) does not depend on its position, the suggestion that (1) is ambiguous just seems gratuitous. Since there is obviously no lexical ambiguity in (1), the ambiguity would have to be structural. But what could it consist in and how would it be represented grammatically? Perhaps a suitable proposal could be formulated, but the question is whether one is needed. If there is no reason to multiply meanings beyond necessity, is there any necessity here? Sentences containing several definite descriptions, such as (4),

> Van believes that the most famous American linguist is smarter than the greatest living American philosopher.

certainly multiply the possibilities. Each of the definite descriptions in (4) can 'occur' either opaquely or transparently. (The quotes around 'occur' are meant to suggest that this distinction is not semantic; I will generally omit them from now on.) Indeed, each description can occur either way independently of how the other occurs. So on the ambiguity thesis, (4) would be ambiguous in four ways. In general, it would seem that according to this ambiguity thesis, if the 'that'-clause of a belief sentence contains n singular terms that can occur either way, the entire sentence is ambiguous in 2^n ways. That would make a sentence like (5) ambiguous in thirty-two ways (not that it could be used successfully in all those ways).

> Melvin thought that the lawyer for the plaintiff was more likely to convince the judge than would the lawyer for the defendant.   (5)

At this point we must wield Ockham's semantic razor: none of the descriptions in (5) are ambiguous, and the sentence as a whole surely does not have thirty-two underlying structures.

If the opaque/transparent distinction is construed not as concerning the positions or occurrences of expressions but as a distinction in their uses, the distinction is rendered not only more plausible but more flexible, as shown by a sketch of the different possible uses of the descriptions in (6),

> Van believes that the most famous American linguist admires the greatest living American philosopher.   (6)

which differs from (4) in that it is an iterated attitude sentence. One could use 'the most famous American linguist' and 'the greatest living American philosopher' to express either Van's way or the speaker's own way of thinking of the objects of Van's belief. They would express Van's way if, for example, the speaker is asserting that Van believes that Chomsky admires Quine and thinks of them respectively under these two descriptions. On the other hand, the speaker might not mean that Van thinks of Chomsky and Quine under these two descriptions; rather, he the speaker might be using the descriptions to refer to Quine and Chomsky, thereby to assert that Van believes the one to admire the other. As far as that is concerned, the speaker might be using 'the most famous American linguist' to refer to S. I. Hayakawa and 'the greatest American philosopher' to refer to Jerry Falwell, and be ascribing to Van the belief that Hayakawa admires Falwell. Or he may be ascribing that belief to Van but implying in addition that Van thinks of Hayakawa and Falwell under those descriptions. The situation is further complicated by the fact that the two descriptions need not be used in the same way; one could be used to express Van's way of thinking about one of the individuals while the other is used to express the speaker's way of thinking about the other. For example, the speaker and hearer might mutually believe that Van regards Chomsky as the most famous American linguist but that he does not regard Angela Davis as the greatest living American philosopher. But speaker and hearer might both regard her as such, and the speaker's utterance of (4) might be a response to the hearer's remark that Van thinks that Chomsky admires Davis. Finally, there is the possibility that each description is being used in both ways at once, say if the speaker agrees with Van about who the most famous American linguist and the greatest living American philosopher are.[8]

Despite all the different ways in which an utterance of a sentence like (6) can be taken, a speaker would ordinarily intend it to be taken in one particular way and expect the hearer, under the circumstances of utterance, to take it that way. If there is any

---

[8] I do not know how many different meanings a supporter of ambiguity would be willing to ascribe to (4). He might, for example, appeal to our earlier account of the referential/attributive distinction in order to reduce the number of senses of (4). He could argue that since the speaker can use the descriptions to refer (weakly) without using them referentially and since referential uses are not literal but indirect, referential uses do not have to be counted among the senses of (4).

likelihood of misunderstanding, the speaker can always find a suitable way to qualify his utterance. He need not do that only if he can rely on what he and the hearer mutually believe, namely about who they take and who Van takes to be the most famous American linguist and the greatest living American philosopher.

In denying that a sentence like (6) is multiply ambiguous, I do not mean to suggest that it has a single truth condition.[9] It could not, since each of its uses has a different truth condition, as determined by whether each of the descriptions is being *used* to refer and/or to express Van's ways of thinking of the objects of his belief. Thus I am suggesting that the sentence is SEMANTICALLY INDETERMINATE, in the sense of Chapter 4. That is, even though the sentence does not have a single truth condition, it is not ambiguous; rather, its univocal meaning underdetermines the truth condition of each of its literal uses. I will defend this suggestion later in the chapter, but first we must consider the occurrence in belief contexts of proper names and indexicals.

2. NAMES AND INDEXICALS IN BELIEF CONTEXTS

So far we have dealt with the opaque/transparent distinction as it applies to occurrences of definite descriptions in belief contexts. We have considered sentences like (1) and (2),

> Lee Marvin believes that his former mistress is
> insane. (1)
> Lee Marvin believes of his former mistress that she
> is insane. (2)

---

[9] It would take us too far afield to give iterated attitude sentences all the attention they deserve, but I believe that what has been said here of (6) can be generalized, even to such seemingly puzzling sentences as (i),

> Hob thinks a witch has blighted Bob's mare,
> and Nob wonders whether she (the same witch)
> killed Cob's sow. (i)

which was made famous by Geach (1967, 628). To unravel the different ways in which an utterance of (i) could be taken, we might first distinguish the cases in which the speaker does and does not believe in witches. If he does, he could be imputing one attitude to Hob and another to Nob, while expressing his own belief that both attitudes are about the same witch. If he does not believe in witches, he could still be imputing one attitude to Hob and another to Nob, part of whose content is given by the description 'the witch who blighted Bob's mare'. Needless to say, there are other possibilities.

and although the opaque/transparent distinction is not what it is commonly thought to be, there is at least *some* contrast between (1) and (2). In (1) 'his former mistress' tends to be used to express part of how Lee frames his belief, so that (1) could be true even if he never had a mistress, whereas in (2) the description tends to be used to refer to the object of his belief, regardless of how he thinks of her. He might have forgotten that a certain woman was once his mistress and yet think of that woman that she is insane. But what about occurrences of proper names in the same contexts, as in (3) and (4)?

> Lee Marvin believes that <u>Michele Triola</u> is insane.   (3)
> Lee Marvin believes of <u>Michele Triola</u> that she is insane.   (4)

There seems to be less of a difference between (3) and (4) than between (1) and (2). Of course (4) does not imply (3) any more than (2) implies (1), since Lee might not think of Michele as Michele Triola (he might not know her by that name), but whereas (1) could be true and (2) false, it does seem that (3) implies (4). Yet does the name really occur transparently in (3)? Consider (5) and (6),

> Lee believes that <u>John Wayne</u> was a great actor.   (5)
> Lee does not believe that <u>Marion Morrison</u> was a great actor.   (6)

If Lee does not realize that John Wayne was in fact Marion Morrison, (5) and (6) can both be true.[10] This suggests that names are not substitutionally transparent[11] but at most existentially so. But even that is not true, as illustrated by (7),

> Ronald Reagan believes that <u>Santa Claus</u> is jolly.   (7)

(7) may not be true but it could be true, even in the event that Santa Claus does not exist.

Then there is the case of existential beliefs ascribed with sentences containing proper names as subject of the 'that'- clause,

---

[10] Thus arises Kripke's (1979) 'puzzle about belief', at least for him, because he maintains that names refer directly rather than by way of their senses. If the sole contribution of a name to the sentences in which it occurs is the individual it names, then the two names of John Wayne make the same contribution to the sentences in which they occur; thus Kripke's puzzle.

[11] I say 'suggests' because there is a way of taking (5) so that truth would be preserved if 'Marion Morrison' replaced 'John Wayne': Lee might believe that Marion Morrison was a great actor without thinking of him under that name.

Reagan believes that <u>Santa Claus</u> exists. (8)
Reagan believes that <u>Tip O'Neill</u> exists. (9)

Obviously 'Santa Claus' cannot occur transparently in (8), but it might seem, since Tip O'Neill exists, that 'Tip O'Neill' can occur transparently in (9). A user of (9) might be referring to Tip O'Neill and, without giving the full content of Reagan's existential belief, state that Reagan believes Tip O'Neill to exist. But then by the same token someone who believes in Santa Claus might intend to refer to Santa and use (8) to state that Reagan believes him to exist. Of course, the statement could not be true. These uses of the names may be referring, but they fail to show that the names occur transparently. That is, there is no *sense* of (8) in which the sentence is true only if Santa Claus exists. It would be just plain silly to think that there is a sense of (9) in which that sentence is true only if Tip O'Neill exists, for then (9) would have had one less sense had Tip O'Neill not existed. Reagan may believe that O'Neill had excessive powers, but I doubt that they were semantic.

Similar points apply to the ascription of negative existential beliefs, as in (10),

Marlowe [falsely] believed that <u>Shakespeare</u> did not
exist. (10)

Notice that if the speaker asserts the belief to be false, he thereby implies that Shakespeare did exist. But obviously this implication is carried not by the way 'Shakespeare' occurs but by the total content of the assertion.

Not unpredictably, I propose that we combine the nominal description theory of names with our non-semantic construal of the opaque/transparent distinction for occurrences of definite descriptions in belief sentences. Then we will have no need for any special account of the occurrence of names in belief sentences and can simply apply to names the observations of the previous section about descriptions. After all, the examples considered above do show that names do not invariably occur transparently in belief contexts. Still, there is a need at least to explain why names, unlike descriptions, strongly *tend* to occur transparently in belief contexts. My explanation will rely on one of the observations made in Chapter 8 when we diagnosed the illusion of rigidity. Names generally have many bearers and people generally think of a bearer of a name in other ways than (merely) as the bearer of the name.

Accordingly, in using a sentence in the form of (11)

S believes that N is F.   (11)

to ascribe a belief to someone, one is not likely to be using 'N' to express the primary way in which the person is thinking of N (or a certain bearer of 'N', if there is more than one), but that leaves using 'N' to refer. Names seem to occur transparently in belief contexts only because ascribers are much more likely to use a name to refer to the object of a belief than to express how the believer thinks of the object.

One important exception to this rule is where the thought of something's bearing the name is essential to the content of the belief being ascribed. This can occur in cases of mistaken identity, as in a likely use of (12),

Jerry thinks that <u>Moon Mullins</u> is an astronaut.   (12)

It can also occur when one acquires information, as in reading a newspaper story, about an unfamiliar individual. One is likely to think of that individual primarily as the bearer of the name (or at least as the bearer of the name mentioned by the source of the information). Someone ascribing such a belief would, accordingly, intend the name to figure in the content of the belief being ascribed.

As for indexicals, relatively little attention has been paid to their behaviour in belief contexts. Perhaps this is why no one seems to question the popular opinion that indexicals can occur only transparently in belief contexts. Indexicals are commonly used to refer, but not always. So why should it be supposed that they can only be used transparently in belief contexts, as in an utterance of a sentence like (13)?

Clara believed that <u>he</u> had musical talent.   (13)

The belief being ascribed to Clara is that a certain male had musical talent, and presumably the male in question is the one that 'he' is being used to refer to. In the context of a discussion of the life of the young Brahms, for example, Brahms would be the likely referent. Obviously (13) does not specify how Clara was thinking of Brahms (except as a male), and so it seems that 'he' must be used referringly, i.e. that it 'occurs' transparently. But this is false. Suppose that (13) was used in the discourse (14),

Clara Schumann was under the false impression that
Brahms had a younger brother who was a violinist.

Though doubting that there could be two geniuses in
one family, Clara believed that he had musical talent.   (14)

Here 'he' does not occur transparently, for it is obviously not being
used to refer (to Brahms's non-existent brother). Clara could have
had the belief being ascribed even if Brahms did not have a younger
brother and, indeed, even if there was no one whom Clara believed
to be his younger brother. A belief is being ascribed to her whose
content is that Brahms's younger brother had musical talent, where
'he' is being used to express, in the context, the individual concept
given by the description 'Brahms's younger brother'. Thus 'he'
occurs opaquely here, not transparently.

Even the demonstrative 'this' can occur opaquely in belief
contexts. In (15),

Hallucinating another dagger, Macbeth believed that
this was the one that would do him in.[12]   (15)

clearly the ascriber is not using 'this' to imply the existence of a
certain hallucinatory dagger. Rather, he would intend it to be taken
as shorthand for 'the dagger that Macbeth seemed to be seeing'.

Similar examples can easily be given for other indexicals. The
only exception seems to be 'I'. It cannot occur opaquely in belief
contexts because the ascriber could not reasonably intend not to be
referring to himself. For example, someone who mistakenly
thought he was Julius Caesar and uttered (16),

I believe that I once crossed the Rubicon.   (16)

would still be using the 'I' in the 'that'-clause to refer to himself.

3. SCOPE AND AMBIGUITY

I have maintained that the seemingly semantic distinction between
opaque and transparent *occurrences* of definite descriptions and of

[12] A demonstrative description can occur opaquely in much the same way, as in
(i),

Having another hallucination, Macbeth believed that
this dagger was the one that would do him in.   (i)

A demonstrative description ('this F') can also occur opaquely whenever it is being
implied that the mode of presentation includes the concept of being F, as in a likely
use of (ii),

Unaware that his new butler was Moriarty, Holmes
believed that this mannerly fellow would serve
him well.   (ii)

other singular terms comes to nothing more than a distinction between their *uses*. The distinction is neither structural nor semantic (it is not a distinction at the level of sentence grammar) and it does not generate systematic ambiguities. I have claimed also that so-called opaque occurrences attribute ways of thinking, but to this it could be objected that there are other contexts in which descriptions can occur opaquely, notably modal sentences, in which there is no mention of the contents of anyone's psychological state and which do seem genuinely ambiguous. Accordingly, it would seem that the distinction ought to be explained in more general terms. One plausible suggestion is that this distinction can be given a structural account in terms of *scope ambiguity*. The idea is illustrated by (1),

Necessarily, the number of planets is odd.　　　　(1)

which can be taken in two ways, in only one of which is it true. If it is understood to mean that the number of planets, no matter what that number happens to be, is odd, then the sentence is false. For the number of planets might have been eight rather than nine. (1) is true only if understood to mean that the number which is in fact the number of planets (nine) necessarily is odd. These two ways of taking (1) can be symbolized as (2) and (3),

$$N(Ex)(Px \,\&\, (y)(\text{if } Py \text{ then } y = x) \,\&\, Ox). \qquad (2)$$
$$(Ex)(Px \,\&\, (y)(\text{if } Py \text{ then } y = x) \,\&\, N(Ox)). \qquad (3)$$

where 'N' abbreviates 'necessarily', 'P' 'number of planets', and 'O' odd. In (2) 'N' takes wide scope with respect to the existential quantifier, in (3) narrow scope. Moreover, scope in the two logical forms seems to correspond to syntactic position in the two structural descriptions of sentence (1), if we assume it to be ambiguous. In one 'necessarily' attaches to the sentence node, in the other to the verb phrase node. Indeed, it may seem that only (2) symbolizes (1) and that (3) symbolizes (4),

The number of planets is necessarily odd.　　　　(4)

in which case scope corresponds to word order in the sentence.

Logicians and linguists commonly assume that because a sentence can be represented by a certain logical form, it *has* that logical form. This is a *non sequitur* and, if true, needs to be argued for. However, it does seem that some aspects of logical form do not correspond to elements of syntactic structure. A patent example of this is the discrepancy between sentences containing quantifier phrases and the logical formulas used to represent them. Compare (5) with (6),

All men are mortal.   (5)

(x)(if x is a man, then x is mortal).   (6)

Even if (6) is logically equivalent to (5), it is anything but obvious that (5) has the form of (6). It is even less obvious in the case of definite descriptions, at least if you accept Russell's theory. This consideration alone should make one wary of relying on the notion of scope in logical formulas to elucidate the opaque/transparent distinction in linguistic contexts. The latter distinction must be syntactically grounded if it is to qualify as a distinction between occurrences, not just between uses. There may be some syntactic basis for it in the case of modal expressions, in so far as terms like 'necessarily' and 'possibly' have different import in different sentential positions, but the same cannot be said for psychological verbs like 'believes'. There seems to be no syntactic basis for attributing scope ambiguities to belief sentences.

This problem is especially evident with sentences containing several descriptions in the belief clause, as in (7),

S believes that the point of the rubber knife is
sharp.   (7)

One possible reading of (7) is given by (8),

S believes that $(E!x)(x$ is a rubber knife & $(E!y)(y$ is a point
of x & y is sharp)).   (8)

Of course this is not what a user of (7) is likely to mean, since presumably S would not believe that a rubber knife is sharp. Rather, he is likely to mean (9), though there are other readings as well (assuming (7) is ambiguous).

$(E!x)(x$ is a rubber knife & S believes that $(E!y)(y$ is a point
of x & y is sharp)).   (9)

The trouble is that the representations of different relative scope in (8) and (9) do not correspond in any discernible way to what appears to be a unique syntactic relation between the two definite descriptions in (7). (9), for example, may represent the transparent occurrence of 'the rubber knife', but, lacking syntactic import, it is ill-equipped to explain that occurrence.

Despite finding no syntactic basis for the alleged scope ambiguities in belief sentences, let us pretend there is such a basis in

order to see if the notion of scope *could* explain by means of
logical form, presumably a syntactically based notion, the
opaque/transparent distinction as applied to occurrences of
definite descriptions in belief contexts. For this purpose it does not
matter whether we assume that a sentence of the form (10)

S believes that the F is G.   (10)

is ambiguous, with 'the F' being capable of wide as well as narrow
scope (with respect to 'believes'), or assume that it takes only
narrow scope in (10) but wide scope in (11),

S believes of the F that it is G.   (11)

with 'the F' occurring only transparently in (10) and only opaquely
in (11). It does not matter because now we are concerned only with
whether narrow scope corresponds to opacity and wide scope to
transparency, not with how they might be marked syntactically.
Assuming a Russellian analysis of descriptions, the narrow and
wide scope forms are (12) and (13), respectively:

S believes that $(Ex)(Fx \& (y)$ (if Fy then $y = x$) &
Gx).   (12)

$(Ex)(Fx \& (y)$ (if Fy then $y = x$) & S believes that
Gx).   (13)

If you ascribe a belief with a sentence in the form of (12), clearly
you are not implying the existence either of the F or of anything
that S believes to be the F, and this is just what we would expect if
narrow scope is to explain opaque occurrence in terms of logical
form. And if the ascription is in the form of (13), where wide scope
is meant to reflect transparent occurrence, it implies the F's
existence but not S's belief in it, again as expected.

So far, so good. However, there are some problems with (12) and
(13) as representations of opaque and transparent belief
ascriptions, respectively. The trouble with (12) is that the question
of opacity arises for it in turn. Mere inspection does not tell us
whether some coextensive 'f' can be substituted for 'F' in (12)
itself, much less in (10). Unless we assume that the context after
'believes that' in (12) is opaque, we cannot exclude such
substitution. Of course we can exclude it by stipulation, since we
already know that opacity prohibits substitution, but the point was
to explain opacity in terms of *scope*.

In (13), where the quantifier has wide scope, so that 'x' is bound
from outside, S is represented as believing that Gx. (13) says that

there is something that S believes to be G, but it does not specify how S thinks of that individual. Nevertheless, there must be some way, either descriptive or *de re*, in which S thinks of *x*. Otherwise, we would be hard put to explain the possibility that S might also believe the F not to be G without being guilty of inconsistency. That is, if the content of a belief about *x* were a singular proposition that contained *x* rather than a mode of presentation under which S thinks of *x*, then it would be inconsistent of S to think of *x* also that it is not G. But if the content of the belief ascribed by (13) does include a mode of presentation, then, though not mentioned by (13), that mode of presentation (or at least the existence of one) must be mentioned by the truth condition of (13). That is, (13) is true just in case (14),

$(Ex)(Em)(x =$ the F and *s* believes under *m*
that *x* is G). (14)

where *s*'s way *m* of thinking of *x* can be either descriptive or *de re*. (14) gives the truth condition of (13) but itself contains the 'believes-that' locution. This is just what (12) was supposed to explicate syntactically, and, as we saw above, (12) fails to do that. So (13), by implicitly relying on (12), has not succeeded in explicating the transparent occurrence of 'the F' in (11) (or in (10), assuming it to be ambiguous and both occurrences to be possible).

Thus it appears that logical forms like (12) and (13) do not do justice to the opaque/transparent distinction in belief contexts. This distinction simply lacks the syntactic basis that the claim of scope ambiguity requires. At best, these logical forms serve to represent what speakers can mean in using sentences of the form 'S believes that the F is G.' And I see no reason to regard such sentences as ambiguous. Rather, since there is no basis for assigning either the opaque or the transparent construal of the description to what seems to be its *single* literal meaning, such sentences are semantically indeterminate.

4. THE SEMANTIC INDETERMINACY OF BELIEF SENTENCES

Recall the belief sentence with which we began,

Bertie believes that the king of Belgium is bald. (1)

The orthodox view is that because the description can 'occur' either opaquely or transparently, the sentence is ambiguous. On one supposed reading (1) is true just in case Bertie has just the descriptive belief that the king of Belgium is bald. On the other it is true just in case Bertie believes of the king of Belgium (however he may be thinking of the king) that he is bald. I argued, however, that (1) is unambiguous. It contains no lexical ambiguities. In particular, 'the king of Belgium', whether used to refer or to express part of the content of Bertie's belief, has its usual meaning.[13] As for structural ambiguity, there does not seem to be any way to express this grammatically. The only plausible candidate is difference in scope at the level of logical form, but we found that scope did not do the job.[14] Besides, we saw that sentences like (2),

Van believes that the most famous American linguist
admires the greatest living American philosopher.　　　(2)

and especially (3),

Melvin thought that the lawyer for the plaintiff was
more likely to convince the judge than would the
lawyer for the defendant.　　　(3)

would have far more senses than the ambiguity theorist bargained for. The problem here is not the sheer number of interpretations of utterances of such sentences but rather that their proliferation is not grounded grammatically (they are not the product of any lexical or structural ambiguities). In other words, while additional descriptions or embeddings produce incremental increases in the syntactic complexity of a belief sentence, the number of interpretations increases exponentially.

---

[13] As is well known, Frege held that in this context such a description does not have its usual reference (the king of Belgium) but here refers to its usual sense. Since for Frege sense determines reference, presumably the description does not have its usual sense either. Just what is its sense here has proved to be a vexing question for Frege scholars. One source of trouble is the apparent implication of an endless hierarchy of senses for this one description. No theory should imply this but it seems that Frege's does. A Russellian approach to descriptions obviously avoids such problems, because the question of the reference of descriptions drops out as semantically irrelevant.

[14] As Heny has aptly pointed out, 'it has been increasingly insisted by linguists that syntactic analyses of natural language expressions must be motivated "independently": if there are to be two analyses of an expression, then there must be some rather direct morphological, word order or other overt superficial reflex of these analyses' (1981, xxxvi). Heny recognizes the limitations of scope analyses, that they do not fully capture the apparent ambiguities and that they are not well motivated syntactically, but he never considers the possibility that belief sentences are not ambiguous but semantically indeterminate.

To refuse to multiply senses beyond necessity and instead treat the opaque/transparent distinction as pragmatic (it applies to *uses* of belief sentences) is, in effect, to regard the sentences themselves as semantically indeterminate. Even though the uses of such a sentence have different truth conditions, the sentence itself is univocal—but has no definite truth condition. As I suggested in Chapter 4 when introducing the notion of semantic indeterminacy, in some cases the sentence contains several elements that can be combined in various ways, but whose manner of combination is not indicated syntactically. Of the various possible combinations there is one that constitutes the content of a given utterance of the sentence, which is determined by the speaker's intention. To illustrate this idea in the case of belief sentences, I will use brackets to represent the different possible combinations. For example, the two main ways (there is also the dual use) of using (1) are given by (1*a*) and (1*b*),

Bertie believes that [the king of Belgium is bald].　　　(1*a*)
Bertie believes that the king of Belgium [is bald].　　　(1*b*)

If the user of (1) intends to be giving the full content of the belief he is ascribing to Bertie, his utterance is represented by (1*a*). (1*b*) represents it if, on the other hand, he is using the description to refer and not to express part of the content of Bertie's belief. (2) admits of at least the following possibilities:

Van believes that [the most famous American linguist
admires the greatest living American philosopher].　　　(2*a*)
Van believes that the most famous American linguist
[admires the greatest living American philosopher].　　　(2*b*)
Van believes that [the most famous American linguist
admires] the greatest living American philosopher.　　　(2*c*)
Van believes that the most famous American linguist
[admires] the greatest living American philosopher.　　　(2*d*)
Van believes that [the most famous American linguist
admires [the greatest living American philosopher]].　　　(2*e*)
Van believes that the most famous American linguist
[admires [the greatest living American philosopher]].　　　(2*f*)

I won't spell out the paraphrases of all of these, but each corresponds to one of the ways given earlier of how (2) can be used. The difference between them is the bracketing in the 'that'- clause. Material in single brackets expresses elements of the content of the belief being ascribed to Van. Material bracketed twice expresses how Van takes the most famous American linguist (or whoever he thinks of as such) to represent the object of the latter's admiration. Unbracketed material is 'transparent' and does not express either. It corresponds to elements in the content of the belief that the *user* of (2) is expressing.

Leaving aside the complications of cases like (2) and (3), we have seen that a singular noun phrase in the subject position of the 'that'-clause of a belief sentence like (1) can be used in either of two ways (or both). It can be used to express an element of the content of the belief being ascribed, the element that represents the putative object of the belief, or it can be used to express the speaker's own way of thinking of what he takes to be the object of the belief. There are similar possibilities for singular noun phrases in other positions, such as the embedded description in (4),

> Bertie believes that the king of the dullest country
> in Europe is bald.   (4)

as well as for plural noun phrases, as in (5),

> Bertie believes that the philosophers of France are
> obscure.   (5)

And as we have seen with (2), there are further possibilities for ascriptions within ascriptions.

The semantic indeterminacy of belief sentences reflects the fact that the 'that'-clauses they contain are themselves semantically indeterminate. It is often said that 'that'-clauses are ambiguous, since they sometimes 'refer' to propositions and sometimes to states of affairs. So in (6), for example,

> That 7 is an odd number is necessarily true.   (6)

the 'that'-clause refers to a proposition (states of affairs cannot be true or false), whereas in (7),

> That 7 is the winning number is unfortunate.   (7)

the 'that'-clause refers to a state of affairs. Notice that what resolves the so-called ambiguity is the meaning of the predicate. The same thing can happen with attitude sentences. Ordinary belief sentences like (1) can go either way, whereas sentences like (8) and (9) tend toward the factive interpretation,

> Bill knows/regrets that his number lost.   (8)
> Bill rightly believes that his number lost.   (9)

On the other hand (10),

    Bill mistakenly believes that his number lost.   (10)

leans heavily toward the propositional interpretation.

We could go into much greater detail here, but I mention such examples simply to suggest a further argument for indeterminacy over ambiguity. It seems that even in the examples in which one way of taking the 'that'-clause is preferred, the explanation is not linguistic. Ordinary language just does not discriminate between different ways of taking 'that'-clauses or their constituents. In any case, Ockham's semantic razor provides the main argument for indeterminacy: whereas the syntactic complexity of a belief sentence increases incrementally with additional descriptions or embeddings, the number of possible interpretations of its utterance grows exponentially.

5. FICTIONAL CONTEXTS

In this section we will briefly take up reference in fictional discourse and in discourse about fiction. We will not be concerned with the ontological status, if any, of fictional entities, but only with talk (or writing) about them. From my point of view, at the semantic level the occurrence of proper names in fictional contexts, like their occurrence in belief contexts, raises no special problems. A fictional name is no different semantically from any other name—'Sherlock Holmes' is equivalent semantically to 'the bearer of "Sherlock Holmes" '. Semantics aside, there are some interesting pragmatic questions about what authors do and what we do when writing or talking about their characters and other creations.

By and large, the language of fiction is perfectly ordinary language. Of course there are those authors, such as Anthony Burgess and James Joyce, who invent new language or devise new uses of familiar language, but they are exceptions. No changes of meaning or novelties in the expressions used are necessary for language to be fictional. What is essential to fiction is how its language is used. Walton (1978) describes this use as a kind of 'make-believe'. As Lewis says, 'Storytelling is pretence. The storyteller purports to be telling the truth about matters whereof he has knowledge.' (1983, 266) He is pretending to report a series of events, to describe settings, situations, and characters, and even to quote characters. If this view is correct—one can hardly dispute it—then the storyteller is not performing acts of communication but is merely pretending to, and what appears to be reference in fiction is really feigned reference. He is not even purporting to express attitudes about the world or to refer to particular individuals (except in so far as real people and places occupy the world of the fiction), though he does intend his audience to pretend that he is.

The situation is different from an ordinary conversational situation, where there prevails a communicative presumption (Bach and Harnish 1979, 7). Ordinarily, a speaker takes for granted that his utterance will be taken as being made with a communicative intent which is identifiable under the circumstances of utterance, partly on the supposition that this presumption is in effect. Correlatively, the hearer takes for granted that the speaker is using his words with an identifiable intent and he relies on this presumption (among others) to identify that intent. In fictional discourse this presumption is suspended. That is true even if the setting of a fiction is or includes the actual world. In that case the author can make non-fictional remarks to the reader about the world, but the reader must infer the author's intention to be communicating—he cannot rely on the communicative presumption.

Feigned reference in a fiction is bound to the world of that fiction. Fictional 'reference' is relative to a particular fiction (one story or group of stories, one myth or mythical tradition) or, as Lewis puts it, 'different acts of storytelling, different fictions' (1983, 265)—we do not pretend that all fictional characters occupy some unitary all-encompassing fictional world. However, within the confines of a particular fictional world, feigned reference is somewhat like real reference. Dostoevsky's many acts of feigned reference to Raskolnikov (whether by name, definite description, or pronoun) in the world of *Crime and Punishment* all pretend to be to the same individual. And the reader is to take them as such. Indeed, he is to treat them much as he would treat repeated acts of reference to a real individual. Just as you put everything you hear or read about Nixon into one mental FILE (think of the name 'Nixon' as the label on this file), so you put everything you read about Raskolnikov into one such file, though of course it does not function like a file on a real person. Even so, mistaken identity is possible in fiction, as in real life. The author can intend the reader (or allow a character) to confuse two characters or to be unaware of an assumed identity. That is, one file can be on two characters, and two files can be on one (see Chapter 2).

Although it is reasonable to describe fictional discourse as a kind of make-believe, Searle speaks also of discourse *about* fiction as make-believe or what he calls 'let's pretend' (1969, 78). He suggests that when we use the name 'Sherlock Holmes', like Conan Doyle we too are referring to a 'fictional character', that is, pretending to refer to Sherlock Holmes. This is a natural way to describe what we are doing, but I suggest that there is a better way. When we 'refer' to a fictional character, we are implicitly referring (in the literal sense) to the fiction in which that character occurs and are thereby imputing to that fiction (strictly speaking, to its author) a feigned reference. Our discourse about fiction is not itself make-believe, for we are performing genuine acts of communication and are expressing real propositional attitudes—attitudes about the fiction and what it says or implies, in a sense to be explained below. If I say 'Yossarian feared combat missions', I am expressing the belief that *Catch 22* said (or at least implied) that Yossarian feared combat missions. I am not referring to Yossarian but am merely ascribing to *Catch 22* (or to Joseph Heller) a feigned reference to Yossarian. So, I suggest, discourse about fiction is, just as the phrase indicates, second-order or indirect discourse—we are implicitly talking about what (the author of) the story says or implies. It is the fiction that is make-believe, not our discourse about it.

In order to account for discourse about fiction, some philosophers have proposed special operators on sentences. Lewis suggests taking 'descriptions of fictional characters . . . as abbreviations for longer sentences beginning with an operator "In such-and-such fiction . . . " '. (1983, 262) Devitt has made a similar suggestion (1980, 172). Yet there is really no need to suppose that the *sentence* 'Polonius was an old buffoon' should be read as 'In *Hamlet* Polonius was an old buffoon.' Rather, the sentence is being used non-literally. The sentence is being used to state that in *Hamlet* Polonius was an old buffoon, but no special operator needs to be assigned to the sentence being used non-literally to make that statement. Of course a speaker could always make fully explicit what he means by including 'In *Hamlet*' in his utterance.

The trouble with the operator approach is that it attempts to deal semantically with a phenomenon that is patently pragmatic. A speaker who is talking about fiction (or a producer of fiction, for that matter) is using a normal sentence differently than normal; he is not using a different sentence. One particular remark by Devitt betrays the weakness of the operator approach: 'Acceptance of the idea of an operator on a sentence should not be difficult. It seems that a semantic theory will have to allow such operators to explain, for example, irony and metaphor; perhaps also to distinguish assertions, questions, and commands.' (1980, 174) This suggestion is reminiscent of the thoroughly discredited 'Performative Analysis' once popular in linguistics, according to which most sentences contain a hidden performative prefix, such as 'I state that . . .' or 'I order you to . . .', to explain speech acts like statements and orders. Similarly, it might seem that we need prefixes like 'In *Hamlet* . . .', 'According to myth . . .', or 'Legend has it that . . .' to explain speech acts about fiction. The fundamental error in both cases is seeking to explain the variety of uses of sentences by sentence semantics rather than by a (pragmatic) theory of sentence use.

A pragmatic approach will help clarify the suggestion made above that discourse about fiction can concern what a fiction implies as well as what it says. The point of this suggestion is that there is much in a fiction that is not made explicit. But since a fiction does not purport to tell the truth, what is it for a fiction to imply something? In other words, to borrow a distinction from Lewis, what is the difference between truth *according* to a fiction and truth *in* a fiction?

Lewis plausibly suggests that we 'analyze statements of truth in fiction as counterfactuals' (1983, 269). The idea is to consider what would be true if a story 'were told as known fact rather than fiction' (270). Lewis applies his theory of counterfactuals to formulate several accounts of truth in fiction. On one analysis, we assume the fictional world to be as much like the actual world as possible; on another, we assume the fictional world to be in accordance as much as possible with the generally prevalent beliefs of the community in which the story originates. Lewis seems to prefer the latter to the former, primarily because there can be facts about the actual world which, because they are unknown to the community of origin, could yield implausible evaluations of statements about a given fiction. Several other approaches occur to me besides those that Lewis considers. Perhaps what matters is not the beliefs that actually prevail but what the storyteller takes to be the beliefs that prevail among his intended audience; or maybe what matters are the beliefs of the storyteller himself (compare the case of describing a dream).

Whatever the preferred analysis—there are arguments for each and perhaps none is to be accepted categorically—it must be acknowledged that statements about fiction should not in general be expected to possess definite truth conditions. Once we go beyond what is said explicitly in a story and ask what is implied by it, there may be no determinate answer. There may be too many equally good possibilities, or there may be no determinate set of features about the world in question which are being held fixed for purposes of evaluation. The truth or falsity of many statements about fiction can be as indeterminate as the truth or falsity of statements about people's hopes, dreams, fantasies, and delusions. Even so, it is plausible to say that discourse about a given fictional work is a kind of discourse about discourse, concerning what the work says or implies.

PART FOUR

OTHER KINDS OF REFERENCE

11

Anaphoric Reference: Grammatical or Pragmatic?

Our discussion of pronouns and reference in Chapter 9 did not take up the topic of ANAPHORIC reference. A pronoun is said to (be used to) refer anaphorically if it is used to refer to that which some other referring expression was used to refer to, as in (1),

Sam lost his money. (1)

The 'antecedent' of a pronoun can follow it, as in (2),

Losing his money upset Sam. (2)

a point to which we will return later.

Anaphoric reference has been discussed much more by linguists than by philosophers. It should be addressed by philosophers as well, for it raises some interesting questions about the syntax, semantics, and pragmatics of pronouns. The main question concerns the status of the relation of co-reference between a pronoun and its antecedent: is this a semantic or merely a pragmatic relation? In my view, an answer to that question depends on the answer to a similar question about antecedency, which seems to be a syntactic relation. But is this relation really syntactic? In other words, do pronouns literally have antecedents? If they do, then anaphoric reference would have a syntactic basis and, since it would be explained at the level of sentence grammar, would have to be regarded as a semantic phenomenon. Otherwise, it would have to be explained pragmatically and be understood merely as a special case of indexical reference. Not surprisingly, I will take the latter position, which I can sum up very simply: being mentioned elsewhere in a sentence is just one way of being salient.

Conventional wisdom has it that an anaphoric pronoun refers to whatever its antecedent refers to and that this is a matter not of speaker intention but of sentence grammar. The rationale for this view is that the very possibility of co-reference between a pronoun and a noun phrase is sensitive to syntactic structure. Linguists have marshalled a rich body of data which suggest that there are certain syntactic relationships between pronoun and noun phrase that preclude co-reference. They have made many attempts to formulate a grammatical rule that captures the syntactic feature these relationships have in common, but there is no consensus among linguists on its precise formulation. This disagreement reflects both theoretical differences and divergent intuitions about certain of the data. I cannot survey the diverse theories and the wealth of data, but for our purposes that will not matter. What concerns me is what the linguists seem to agree upon, that co-reference is syntactically based.

As might be expected from my generally pragmatic approach to referential phenomena, I reject the *syntactic thesis*, which says that anaphoric reference should be explained at the level of sentence grammar. I believe this thesis has two serious difficulties. For one thing, it implies that personal pronouns are systematically ambiguous and thus, I argue, it multiplies meanings beyond necessity. For it must give separate semantic accounts of pronouns when used to co-refer with antecedent noun phrases and when used to refer independently (indexically). In addition, there is an in-principle objection to the very possibility of the grammatical rule required by the syntactic thesis (I will ignore the linguists' problem of precisely how to formulate the rule). The difficulty here is how to state the rule at the level of sentence grammar. The rule is supposed to specify the syntactic conditions under which the relation of antecedency between pronoun and noun phrase is possible, but how is that relation itself to be specified? 'Co-reference' is not the proper term, as most linguists seem to recognize, even though they use it. The phrase 'referential dependence', as introduced by Evans, is more appropriate, but the relation of referential dependence must be regarded as pragmatic, I will argue, for it essentially involves the speaker's intentions. In brief, the fundamental issue here is whether using a pronoun to refer to something mentioned elsewhere in a sentence is anything more than a special case of using it to refer to something salient.

1. ANAPHORIC AND OTHER USES OF PERSONAL PRONOUNS

When anaphoric pronouns were first discussed by transformational grammarians, they were thought to be the product of a pronominalization transformation. The idea was that an anaphoric pronoun appears in the surface structure of a sentence as the result of replacing a duplicate occurrence of a noun phrase in the deep structure. This view has long since been abandoned.[1] More recent approaches, such as Chomsky's (1981), employ the device of referential indices to mark co-reference (or non-co-reference), as in the two different 'readings' of (1),

$$\text{Sam}_i \text{ lost his}_i \text{ money.} \tag{1a}$$
$$\text{Sam}_i \text{ lost his}_j \text{ money.} \tag{1b}$$

There are various alternatives to Chomsky's approach, but, details aside, they all assume that when pronouns are used to co-refer with their antecedents they do so as a matter of sentence grammar. This assumption covers not just the special cases of reflexives and reciprocals,[2] which must be so used, but any pronoun whenever it is used to co-refer with a noun phrase.

We can begin to evaluate this assumption by comparing different uses of 'his'. In an utterance of (1), for example,

$$\text{Sam lost his money.} \tag{1}$$

'his' is likely to be used to refer to Sam (not that it must be). A personal pronoun can also be used simply as an indexical, as in (2),

$$\text{The muggers took his money.} \tag{2}$$

to refer to a contextually salient individual, perhaps poor Sam. Finally, a personal pronoun like 'his' can also be used as a 'bound pronoun', as in (3),

$$\text{Every gambler lost his money.} \tag{3}$$

These three uses may seem different enough to suggest that the pronoun itself is ambiguous in three ways and that its semantics should reflect this, but I will argue against this suggestion. I will propose instead that at the level of sentence grammar a unitary treatment of personal pronouns will do, and that their different uses can be explained pragmatically. In particular, anaphoric uses

---

[1] The intuitive idea is that the second occurrence (usually) in a sentence of the same noun phrase gets replaced by a pronoun. For example, (i) becomes (ii),

$$\text{Blinky wanted Blinky's money back.} \tag{i}$$
$$\text{Blinky wanted his money back.} \tag{ii}$$

Difficulties with pronominalization, and with other approaches to anaphoric pronouns, are discussed in Soames and Perlmutter (1979, 323–404).

[2] As a matter of terminology, linguists generally withhold the word 'pronoun' from reflexives and reciprocals, which they call 'anaphors'.

can be assimilated to indexical uses (I will leave to Chapter 12 the more challenging problem of assimilating bound uses to indexical ones). Let us call the competing views the *ambiguity thesis*, which, if construed not as lexical but as structural, is entailed by the syntactic thesis, and the *assimilation thesis*.

Ordinarily, we think of lexical ambiguity, as illustrated by such words as 'bear', 'bank', and 'bore', as a kind of linguistic coincidence. The several meanings of each of these words are unrelated semantically, and there is no etymological reason why any of these words should have several meanings. So consider what is implied by the ambiguity thesis if construed as lexical: the fact that the same word 'he' (or 'she', 'it', or 'they') can be used both indexically and anaphorically would be mere coincidence. So would be the fact that both as an anaphor and as an indexical 'he' has the same possessive and the same accusative forms, 'his' and 'him'.

If the ambiguity thesis is construed as structural, consider the fact that anaphoric uses, which are claimed to be distinct semantically from indexical uses, can occur not only within a sentence, as in (1), but also across sentence boundaries, as in (4),

> Sam is broke. The muggers took his money.   (4)

Note that the second sentence in (4) is (2), where 'his' can only be used as an indexical. There can be no syntactic connection between 'his' and 'Sam' in (4),[3] but we need not assume any such connection to explain the use of 'his' to refer to whoever 'Sam' is being used to refer to. Rather, since the speaker has just mentioned Sam, he can reasonably expect to be taken to be using 'his' to refer to Sam. Notice, moreover, that if this explanation will do for (4), no special explanation is needed for the use of 'his' in (1) to refer to Sam. In particular, there is no need for a syntactic explanation. Besides, 'his' could just as well be used to refer to someone other than Sam, say Sal or Sid, and the explanation for its being used to refer to Sal rather than Sid is no different in kind from the explanation for its being used to refer to Sam rather than Sal. (1) is referentially indeterminate with respect to 'his', and the fact that 'his' can be used to refer to someone mentioned elsewhere in the sentence does

---

[3] That this relation can be syntactic seems to be suggested by Cooper, when he speaks of 'discourse anaphora, i.e. the possibility of having a pronoun in a sentence related to a noun-phrase occurring in an earlier sentence' (1983, 93). However, because constituents of different sentences cannot be syntactically connected at all, its difficult to see how this suggestion, if indeed Cooper is making it (he does speak of 'anaphoric readings' in this context), could be made intelligible, much less plausible.

not show that its semantic contribution is different from when it is used to refer to someone else.

Linguists generally regard sentences like (1) as ambiguous, taking them to have both anaphoric and indexical 'readings'. I have never run across an argument for the ambiguity thesis, however, and can only conjecture why it has such widespread appeal in linguistics. I suspect that it is a relic of the hypothesis, mentioned above, that anaphoric pronouns appear in sentences as the result of the pronominalization transformation. Clearly the ambiguity thesis is implied by that hypothesis, because if the same pronoun in the same sentence can be used indexically as well as anaphorically, then the sentence has two distinct transformational derivations and is syntactically ambiguous. I suspect that this hypothesis, though long discredited, is still influential, and I conjecture that it simply has not occurred to linguists to question the ambiguity thesis. They just take for granted that sentences like (1) are ambiguous and have two readings.

Lasnik (1976) is one linguist who has argued against the ambiguity thesis and has endorsed the assimilation thesis. His argument was implicit in our comparison of (1) and (4), where in both sentences 'his' can but need not be used to refer to Sam; and if its being so used in (4) cannot be registered grammatically and therefore cannot be explained grammatically, there is no reason why its being used anaphorically in (1) should be so explained. As Lasnik points out, we would expect the anaphoric relation to be a matter of sentence grammar only in a case like (5),

Sam lost his own money.   (5)

where the co-reference is marked by the occurrence of 'own'. Lasnik's claim is in effect that unmarked co-reference is not a grammatical phenomenon.[4] As I like to put it, being previously mentioned is just one way of being salient in a context.

2. EVANS VS. LASNIK

I single out Lasnik, one of the few linguists who rejects the ambiguity thesis, because his view is the specific target of an attack

---

[4] I should note that the assimilation thesis says not merely that there is no syntactic rule, such as a pronominalization transformation, underlying co-reference, but also, as Evans points out (1980, 350), that there is no interpretative rule of co-reference, which would also belong to grammar.

by Evans (1980), one of the few philosophers who have discussed anaphora and the only one I know of who has explicitly defended the ambiguity thesis. Because Evans appreciates why it might seem irrelevant to grammar that a pronoun should be used to refer to something mentioned previously in the sentence rather than to something else, he accepts the burden of showing that the anaphoric use is not merely a special case of the indexical use. To do this he poses an in-principle, theoretical objection to the assimilation thesis. Curiously, his objection echoes the very point I made above about linguistic coincidence.

Evans argues that assimilation renders unintelligible the fact that the same words that can be used anaphorically can also be used as 'bound variables' (he calls them this because he takes them to be bound by quantifier phrases). He argues that unless anaphoric pronouns are given a different semantic treatment from indexical ones, it can only be a linguistic accident that the same pronouns should be used as bound variables (not that he is proposing to assimilate bound to anaphoric uses). He recognizes the point made about (4) of the previous section,

Sam is broke. The muggers took his money.   (4)

that because 'his' and 'Sam' occur in different sentences any relation between them cannot be one of sentence grammar and that their relation in (1)

Sam lost his money.   (1)

seems essentially the same. However, Evans argues that it cannot be the same because the assimilation thesis 'precludes any explanation of the connection between pronouns [used anaphorically and those used as bound variables] and thus treats it as an accident that the same expression [can be used in both ways]' (1980, 351). The assimilation thesis leads to this result because it cannot explain what Evans claims to be the fact that when 'his' in (1) is used anaphorically, (1) is a substitution instance of (3),

Every gambler lost his money.   (3)

For this reason, Evans argues, the assimilation thesis cannot give the same grammatical treatment to the occurrences of 'his' in the two sentences. He concludes that we should distinguish in grammar the anaphoric use of 'his' from the indexical one, and reject the (Lasnik's) pragmatic account of co-reference (evidently Evans is unconcerned that on his own account it seems a linguistic accident that the same word 'his' has both an anaphoric and an indexical use).

What is meant by Evans's claim that (1) is a substitution instance of (3)? English is not a natural deduction system, and even if such a system could be imposed somehow on English, so that (1) could be derived from (3) logically, via universal instantiation, it would be absurd from a linguistic standpoint to suppose that (1) is somehow derived from (3) transformationally—they are two distinct sentences. Nevertheless, Evans adopts his 'Fregean' approach to bound pronouns because, he maintains, it renders the connection between bound and anaphoric pronouns not only intelligible but straightforward.

We know that 'Every man loves his mother' is true iff every man satisfies '( ) loves his mother', and, using the Fregean notion of satisfaction, we know that an arbitrary object x satisfies this predicate iff, interpreting 'b' as referring to x, the sentence '(b) loves his mother' is true. But at this point we are stopped, for it does not make sense, on Lasnik's view, to enquire into the truth value of a sentence of the form '(b) loves his mother' independently of information about a particular context of utterance. (Evans 1980, 351)

But this question is unavoidable in any case. Evans simply ignores the fact that in a sentence like (3) or 'Every man loves his mother', the pronoun 'his' can always be used indexically, just as in (1), to refer to some contextually identifiable male. When it is so used, 'his' in the Fregean predicate '( ) loves his mother' would not occur as an unbound pronoun ready either to be bound by a quantifier phrase like 'every man' or else to acquire an antecedent like 'John'. What Evans claims of 'his' might be true of 'his own', but it could apply to 'his' by itself only if 'his' were semantically ambiguous, with 'his own' not just as one of its uses but as one of its senses. Evans presents no evidence for its ambiguity, but even if he had he would not have succeeded in showing what he was trying to show.

Suppose that 'his' were ambiguous and did have 'his own' as one of its senses. Suppose too, contrary to what I will next argue, that Evans's Fregean approach did work at least for reflexives. Then just as the anaphoric use of 'his own' could be assimilated to its bound use, so the anaphoric use of 'his' (in its alleged reflexive sense) could be assimilated to *its* bound use. Thus if 'his' were ambiguous, there would be no assimilation of its anaphoric and indexical uses for Evans's argument to rend asunder. For even if 'his' did have a reflexive sense, if 'his' were used indexically this reflexive sense would no more be operative in (3) than in (1). In that case, it would not be Evans's argument that undermined the assimilation of anaphoric to indexical uses of personal pronouns but rather the (undefended) claim that these pronouns are ambiguous. In short, Evans's argument could be sound only if the ambiguity claim were correct, in which case the argument would be superfluous.

Even if these pronouns were ambiguous and did have a reflexive sense, would the Fregean approach work for them taken in that sense? To address this question it will be convenient to represent this sense with 'his own', as in (5) and (6),

Sam lost his own money. (5)

Every gambler lost his own money. (6)

Here Evans admits that he has 'consistently ignored the need for number . . . agreement' (1980, 358), as if that is merely a harmless complication. Yet if he had taken it seriously, he would have noticed a grammatical problem for his Fregean approach. Take a sentence like (7),

All the gamblers lost their own money. (7)

The Fregean approach involves extracting, so to speak, the Fregean predicate '( ) lost his own money' from both (5) and (6). (5) is true iff Sam satisfies that predicate, and (6) is true iff every gambler satisfies it. Now (7) has the same truth condition as (6), but the problem is that the required Fregean predicate cannot be extracted from (7), because of the occurrence of 'their own' instead of 'his own'. So it appears that the Fregean approach lacks full generality, in which case another approach is needed anyway.

A natural alternative is to use variables to represent the relevant open sentence, as in (8),

x lost x's money. (8)

(5) is the result of Sam's being the value of 'x', and both (6) and (7) are English equivalents of the universal closure of (8). Using variables in this way, we avoid the problem of number agreement that faces the Fregean approach thanks to the occurrence of 'his' in the Fregean predicate. Moreover, on the assumption (Evans's,

not mine) that (1), 'Sam lost his money', is ambiguous, we can straightforwardly represent the two predicates associated with the reflexive and the non-reflexive sense respectively as (8) and as (9),

$$x \text{ lost his money.} \tag{9}$$

Then if 'his' is used in the non-reflexive sense (to refer to some contextually identifiable individual), (3) and (10)

Every gambler lost his money. (3)

All the gamblers lost his money. (10)

would both be the English equivalents of the universal closure of (9).

In any event, I have not conceded that (1), or (3) for that matter, is ambiguous. So I am not advocating this alternative to the Fregean approach for non-reflexive pronouns. Instead of conceding ambiguity I suggest that we simply say that 'his' is univocal and can be used either anaphorically or indexically. Understanding an utterance of it is merely a matter of inferring the speaker's intention, not of disambiguating its linguistic meaning (besides, that would require inferring the speaker's intention anyway). Thus, we do not have to pay what Evans admits to be the

price of being able to recognize the obvious semantic connection between pronouns with singular and quantified antecedents, that we distinguish semantically between pronouns used as devices of coreference, and pronouns whose reference is secured in some other way, e.g. deictically. (1980, 352)

Indeed, Evans admits that his treatment of sentence-internal anaphora levies an excessive tax as well, for unlike anaphora across sentences, when

the previous reference is within the same sentence as the pronoun . . . the coreferential interpretation of the pronoun is secured, as one interpretation of the sentence, by a linguistic rule. (1980, 352)

But surely whether 'his' is anaphorically related to 'Sam' in a sentence like (1) is no less a matter of the speaker's communicative intention than in (4), where 'his' occurs in a separate sentence. So for want of a compelling argument, Evans's appeal to a linguistic rule, like his implicit commitment to ambiguity, does not appear to be warranted.

3. A RULE OF NON-CO-REFERENCE?

So far I have argued that Evans's argument for assimilating anaphoric to bound pronouns semantically does not succeed in undermining Lasnik's proposal to assimilate anaphoric to indexical pronouns pragmatically. Nevertheless, as we will see, Lasnik does propose a grammatical rule of non-co-reference (because it does not mention pronouns specifically, it does not contradict the assimilation thesis). I take up Lasnik's rule because it is the only rule of non-co-reference that Evans discusses. Moreover, it will serve to illustrate what is at stake when we ask whether any such rule belongs to sentence grammar, and Evans is the only philosopher I know of to have addressed this issue. It should be noted that the specific rule Lasnik proposed has been superseded by subsequent work on the syntax of anaphora, but it would take us too far afield to survey the more recent proposals here (see Reinhart 1983). In any case, for our purposes their differences in detail will not matter.

For anyone unfamiliar with the linguistic literature, a few preliminary comments are in order. Unlike Lasnik, most linguists believe that a rule of non-co-reference is needed specifically for anaphoric pronouns. Each of the many versions that have been proposed since Lasnik's paper appeared (1976) seems to have been designed to handle counter-examples to the previous one (much of the data appears in Reinhart 1983). The various formulations all seem to employ one version or another of the syntactic notion of 'command'. The most widely used version, which was introduced by Reinhart, is the notion of 'constituent'- or '*c*-command'. Since this is the one used by Evans, I should define it. Assume that tree structures are used as syntactic representations of sentences. Then one node *c*-commands another iff the branching node immediately dominating the first also dominates the second. The notion of domination, in turn, can be defined intuitively as follows: one node dominates another iff they are connected by branches that descend from the first to the second. Domination is immediate if there are no nodes in between.

So much for preliminaries. Evans is concerned to argue both that Lasnik's rule is inadequate and that even if it were adequate it would not belong to sentence grammar. I will argue that the same is true, and for Evans's own reasons, of the kind of rule of non-co-reference that Evans does endorse. Along with most linguists, Evans believes that there is a rule of grammar that constrains the anaphoric role of pronouns as well as of other singular terms. I will argue that such a rule cannot belong to sentence grammar.

Such a rule, claims Evans, applies to a sentence like (1),

He is happy when Oscar is in love. (1)

for there is a 'restriction on the case in which the pronoun precedes the term with which it is intended to be coreferential; in general, such a use is felicitous only if the pronoun does not *c*-command the term' (1980, 354). This restriction cannot be merely pragmatic, argues Evans, since one highly salient candidate for the reference of 'he' is Oscar. Lasnik agrees with Evans on this point, notwithstanding his pragmatic account of co-reference in the cases of the previous section. Lasnik avoids inconsistency by proposing the following grammatical rule of non-co-reference, as slightly modified by Evans (he replaces Lasnik's notion of kommand with that of *c*-command):

If NP_1 precedes and *c*-commands NP_2 and NP_2 is not a pronoun, then NP_1 and NP_2 are disjoint in reference.

(C-COM)

This rule does not conflict with Lasnik's pragmatic approach to anaphoric pronouns because, unlike other formulations of the rule of non-co-reference, it does not specify that NP_1 is a pronoun. So, for example, C-COM is supposed to apply to a sentence like (2),

Oscar is happy when Oscar is in love. (2)

and requires that the two 'Oscar's not be co-referential. However, as Evans points out, they can be co-referential, as when (2) is given as an answer to (3),

Who is happy when Oscar is in love? (3)

Another counter-example to C-COM that Evans gives is (4),

Oscar loves Oscar's mother. (4)

Not only does Evans regard (4) with co-reference as grammatical, he notes that in certain contexts its utterance can be pragmatically appropriate (it is generally inappropriate only because using 'his' in place of an 'Oscar' is stylistically preferable). Evans mentions one such context; another is in response to (5),

Does anyone at all love Oscar's mother?   (5)

Evans gives further examples to show that Lasnik's rule wrongly

predicts ungrammaticality when NP_1 is not a pronoun. Whereas the
appropriate conversational setting vastly increases the acceptability of such
sentences, . . . nothing can be done to increase the acceptability of
sentences which infringe the conditions upon when a pronoun can pick up
its reference from an NP elsewhere in the sentence. (1980, 357)

To illustrate that only the unacceptability of pronoun cases requires
a grammatical explanation, Evans contrasts examples like (6) and
(7),

> Everyone here admires someone on the committee. Joan
> admires Susan, Mary admires Jane, and Oscar admires
> Oscar.   (6)

> Everyone here admires someone on the committee. Joan
> admires Susan, Mary admires Jane, and he admires
> Oscar.   (7)

Evans finds (6) 'tolerable', but (7) is 'quite impossible, yet Lasnik's
grammar cannot distinguish between them' (1980, 357). But it is
easy to imagine a conversational context in which (7) is perfectly
acceptable, for example as a continuation of (8),

> What do you mean, unlike everyone else here Oscar
> doesn't admire anyone on the committee?   (8)

So Evans is right to think that Lasnik's rule does not distinguish
between (6) and (7) but wrong to think that it should. As I will
argue shortly, both are wrong to think that there is any
grammatical phenomenon to be explained here.

First consider Evans's next move, which leads him to propose a
rule rather different from Lasnik's. Evans observes that co-
reference is not the notion we need, since *fortuitous* co-reference by
the NPs mentioned in Lasnik's rule should be allowed. Evans also
points out that the required notion is not *intended* co-reference
either, because intended co-reference is possible in a sentence like
(1), when occurring in the context of (9),

> He is happy when Oscar is in love. Do you want to
> know why? Because he *is* Oscar!   (9)

Even though the speaker is using 'he' to refer to Oscar, in (9) the
utterance of (1) is perfectly acceptable. However, there is still

something wrong with (1), even if it is not intended co-reference, and a rule is needed to capture what that is. According to Evans, the rule that we need must employ not the notion of co-reference, actual or intended, but the notion of 'referential dependence': one expression is referentially dependent on another if its reference depends on the reference of the other. (1), which would ordinarily be unacceptable, is all right in a context like (9), despite intended co-reference, because the use of 'he' to refer to Oscar does not depend on the subsequent use of 'Oscar' to refer to Oscar. So Evans proposes the following rule, which I call RD,

A term can be referentially dependent upon an NP
if it does not precede and *c*-command that NP.   (RD)

Thus in the case of (7) above, which Evans found unacceptable but which proved acceptable once a suitable context was provided, RD is not violated because in that context 'he' is not referentially dependent on, even though it is intended to be co-referential with, the later occurrence of Oscar in the same sentence.

Evans insists that RD is a rule of grammar. Even though a pronoun that can be referentially dependent on other noun phrases can just as well 'be used to make independent reference to salient objects, the grammar must itself distinguish between [referentially dependent and independent uses, and] treat a sentence like ['Sam lost his money'] as ambiguous' (1980, 359). Unfortunately, Evans fails to give any argument to show that referential dependence is a grammatical relation or that sentences containing pronouns which can but need not be referentially dependent on other NPs are thereby ambiguous. Evans's own gloss on his rule casts serious doubt on such a claim. He asserts that (10),

I told him that John was a jerk.   (10)

'is *ungrammatical* if, and only if, the pronoun is *intended* to be referentially dependent upon the later occurrence of the name "John" '; generalizing, 'Strict ungrammaticality is produced when and only when the pronoun is *intended* to be referentially dependent upon that occurrence of the name which it precedes and *c*-commands' (1980, 360; my emphasis). Evans gives no explanation (apparently he sees no need for one) of how the grammaticality of a sentence could depend on the speaker's intention or, in this case, of how an otherwise grammatical sentence could be rendered ungrammatical on account of this intention.[5] In so far as referential dependence is a matter of the speaker's intention, as admittedly it is for non-reflexive pronouns, it cannot be a grammatical relation, unlike the case of reflexive pronouns where speaker intention plays no such role. And if referential dependence (for non-reflexive pronouns) is a pragmatic relation, then it is a relation not between terms, as RD says, but between particular uses of them. That is, the *use* of a pronoun is referentially dependent on the use of another expression iff the speaker intends the hearer to recognize that it is being used to refer to whatever the other expression is being used to refer to. Then Evans's rule could be recast as a pragmatic principle to the effect that the use of a term can be referentially dependent on the use of an NP iff it does not precede and *c*-command that NP.[6] Moreover, construing a rule like Evans's as pragmatic makes allowances for the fact that referential dependence (like co-reference) can cross sentence boundaries.

So Evans has not made a successful case for his claim that the difference between indexical and anaphoric uses of personal pronouns must be represented in the grammar and should be construed as semantic. In the course of defending Lasnik's pragmatic approach to pronominal co-reference from Evans's objections, I have argued, ironically, that the phenomenon which Lasnik's own grammatical rule of non-co-reference as well as Evans's reformulation are designed to explain is not a grammatical phenomenon at all. Even though the possibility of referential dependence between a pronoun and a noun phrase is constrained by the nature of their structural relationship, the rule that specifies this constraint (whether or not it is exactly captured by Evans's RD) belongs not to sentence grammar but to pragmatics. Of course to classify it as pragmatic is not to explain where it comes from. I can say only that this is but one of a number of clearly pragmatic phenomena which are sensitive to specific constructions (see note 6)

[5] Nor would it do to say that the grammaticality of the sentence depends on the context in which it is uttered, since grammaticality is a property of sentence types, not tokens.

[6] There is nothing in principle against there being pragmatic phenomena that are sensitive to grammatical relationships (other examples concern clefts, pseudoclefts, and inverted word order). Indeed, Farmer (1984) has given syntactic arguments showing that there are such pragmatic phenomena. In any case, the counter-examples given by Wasow (1979), McCray (1980), and others to alternative formulations of precede-and-(*c*-)command rules suggest that Evans's RD has plenty of exceptions too.

and that psycholinguistic research has, to the best of my knowledge, not yet explained any of them.

I will leave to the linguists the task of formulating the precise rule that specifies those structural relationships which preclude referential dependence between pronoun and noun phrase. Even without knowing what that rule is (the data strongly suggest that there must be one), I have argued that whatever its precise formulation, it must be a pragmatic rule, even though it adverts to intra-sentential structural relationships. Also, I have pointed out that if such a rule did belong to sentence grammar, any sentence in which a pronoun can but need not be used to refer to something mentioned elsewhere in the sentence would be structurally ambiguous. Now even if this were not a serious problem, there would be another problem, worth noting in its own right, with the supposition that the rule in question is one of sentence grammar.

On that supposition the relation of antecedency between noun phrase and pronoun would be a structural relation. However, as I will point out shortly, there are certain sorts of cases in which it seems that the relation of antecedency cannot be marked structurally. That is not a problem in a case like (1), for example,

Sam wants his cookies. (1)

where antecedency can be marked straightforwardly with indices,[7]

Sam_i wants his_i cookies. (1a)

with 'Sam' represented as the antecedent of 'his'. However, to mark this relation is implicitly to assume that (1) is structurally ambiguous, since another reading of (1) must be provided for in which this relation does not obtain, as represented in (1b),

Sam_i wants his_j cookies. (1b)

Thus, antecedency is marked in (1a) by *co-indexing* and its absence in (1b) by *free indexing*. Notice in (1b) that although who 'his' is used to refer to does not depend on who 'Sam' is being used to refer to, 'his' could still be used to refer to Sam, but it would not be referentially dependent on 'Sam'.

[7] This is Chomsky's (1981) technique, but there are others, such as the headed arrows used by Higginbotham (1983).

Antecedency can also be represented straightforwardly in the case of (2),

You can have the cookies after they cool.   (2)

where the plural pronoun 'they' (see the next chapter) can but need not be used to refer to the cookies (it might be used to refer to the plates the cookies are on). Indices can again be used to mark the structurally distinct readings (again assuming ambiguity) of (2):

You can have the cookies$_i$ after they$_i$ cool.   (2a)
You can have the cookies$_i$ after they$_j$ cool.   (2b)

In (2a), but not in (2b), 'the cookies' is represented as the antecedent of 'they', so that 'they' is being used to refer to whatever 'the cookies' is being used to refer to.

So far, so good. But now consider (3),

You can have some cookies after they cool.   (3)

where 'they' is being used anaphorically to refer to cookies (not to plates or whatever). Notice that 'they' is being used to refer to all the contextually relevant cookies, not just to some of them. So the antecedent of 'they' cannot be the full noun phrase 'some cookies', as indicated by the brackets in (3a),

You can have [some cookies]$_i$ after they$_i$ cool.   (3a)

but merely the noun 'cookies', as indicated by the brackets in (3b),

You can have some [cookies]$_i$ after they$_i$ cool.   (3b)

Then it would be clear that in its anaphoric use 'they' is being used to refer to whatever 'cookies' is being used to refer to, namely a contextually relevant batch of cookies. Of course if we do say this, then in consistency we should say the same thing about (2), and that seems harmless enough. For with (2) we can just as well let the index attach to 'cookies' as to 'the cookies'.

Unfortunately, this tactic does not work with sentence (4),

You can have a cookie after they cool.   (4)

again with 'they' being used to refer to the contextually relevant cookies. Inserting brackets and indices in the manner of (3b), we have (4a),

* You can have a [cookie]$_i$ after they$_i$ cool.[8]   (4a)

---

[8] In linguistics there is a convention of using an asterisk to indicate unacceptability.

but there is an obvious problem. 'Cookie' (or 'a cookie', for that matter) and 'they' disagree in number, and therefore one cannot be the antecedent of the other. Despite the fact that in (4) 'cookie' is not the antecedent of 'they', 'they' can still be used to refer to the relevant batch of cookies. In this case, the explanation cannot be structural (syntactic) and can only be pragmatic. The speaker has a certain batch of cookies in mind and, in the context of the utterance, intends the hearer to take him to be expressing an attitude about that batch of cookies. Indeed, he might just as well have uttered (5),

You can have one after they cool.   (5)

where there is no structural basis for the use of 'they' in (5) to refer to those cookies. This use in (5) has to be explained pragmatically, and the same sort of pragmatic explanation is available in the case of (4).

This point can be extended to (2) and to (3). Except for the difference in quantifier expression ('a' rather than 'the' or 'some') and the number of 'cookie', (4) is identical to (2) and (3). Accordingly, there is no need to regard 'they' as having an antecedent in (2) or (3) either. Again, if there is a pragmatic explanation for its use in (4) to refer to a contextually relevant batch of cookies and the same explanation is available for (2) and (3), a structural explanation in the latter cases would be superfluous at best. In my view, it is only because 'they' is used to refer to what 'cookies' refers to that there is any temptation in the first place to regard it as having an antecedent in the structural sense. For this reason I believe that there is really no explanatory role for the alleged structural relation of antecedency to play.

Except where reflexives are involved, we have found no reason to suppose that antecedency is a genuine structural relation. It seems that we should abandon the platitude of school grammar that pronouns have antecedents. In Chapter 12 these sceptical suggestions will be extended to so-called 'bound' pronouns.[9]

[9] Thanks are due to Ann Farmer for valuable advice on the linguistics of anaphora.

12

Quantifier Phrases and Pronouns: Plural Reference and Anaphora

As is usual in the study of reference, our discussion has focused on singular reference and singular terms, expressions used to make singular reference. Indeed, the definition of reference given in Chapter 3 was formulated only for the singular case. Yet if you can refer to one thing, surely you can refer to more. It might seem that the number of referents should make no theoretically interesting difference, but the phenomenon of PLURAL REFERENCE and the expressions used to make it do have important consequences. For one thing, the common identification of referring expressions with singular terms must be abandoned. Referring expressions are not limited to singular terms, since there are also plural pronouns and definite descriptions, and, as we will see, even QUANTIFIER PHRASES can be used to refer.

Let us extend to the plural case our definition of speaker reference as well as the distinction between objectual and descriptive reference. According to the original definition, 'to refer to something is to use a singular term with the intention (part of one's communicative intention) of indicating to one's audience the object of the attitude one is expressing' (recall that a communicative illocutionary act is simply the act of expressing an attitude, in the specific sense of Chapter 3). The changes needed to generalize this definition are straightforward. To refer to some thing or things is to use a noun phrase with the intention of indicating to one's audience the object(s) of the attitude one is expressing. Plural reference is descriptive if there is some condition, not necessarily made explicit, by way of which the audience is to identify the referents. It differs from singular descriptive reference only to the extent that there is no requirement of uniqueness on the satisfaction of the relevant condition. Plural reference is objectual if the speaker intends the audience to identify certain individuals, in one way or another, as the ones being referred to. As in the singular case, it can succeed only if the intended referents exist.

Expressions used to make plural reference come in two kinds, plural forms of singular terms and quantifier phrases. The former include pronouns ('we', 'these'), definite and demonstrative descriptions ('the/these trumpets'), and various combinations ('those trinkets of his'). The linguistic similarity of these plural forms to their singular counterparts might suggest that they require no special treatment, but quantifier phrases are another story, at least according to Fregean tradition. Commonly contrasted with referring expressions, as if they cannot be used to refer, quantifier phrases usually receive a distinctive logical treatment involving the use of quantifier symbols and variables. This is the traditional way of capturing the idea that even though quantifier phrases can and commonly do occur in grammatical subject position, they are not logical subjects. In the first section I will try to describe, without assuming any specific formalism, how quantifier phrases differ from other noun phrases. Then we will be better able to appreciate what it means to say that they can be used to refer, as a variety of examples to be given in the second section will illustrate. In the third section, we will survey plural pronouns.

The next two sections will take up the interaction of quantifier phrases with pronouns. So-called 'bound' pronouns are often likened to variables bound by quantifiers. However, despite the impressive influence of the Fregean tradition and of Chomsky's recent (1981) theory, I will argue that the bound variable approach to pronouns is unsatisfactory and unnecessary. Then I will extend the argument of the previous chapter, that the relation between a pronoun and its so-called antecedent is a not grammatical one, to so-called bound pronouns: the fact that the use of such a pronoun may or may not be referentially dependent on the use of a quantifier phrase does not make the pronoun ambiguous. I deny that when a pronoun functions as a 'bound' rather than as a 'free' pronoun it plays a different *semantic* role. Rather, the difference can be explained pragmatically with the help of the notion of referential dependence. In the final section, I will offer a pragmatic account of E-type pronouns used in environments containing quantifier phrases.

1. QUANTIFIER PHRASES

In the next section we will consider how quantifier phrases can be used to refer, but first we should take note of the phrases themselves. We should appreciate both their variety and what distinguishes them from other noun phrases. Then we will be in a position to characterize the special features of their referring uses.

Philosophers and linguists generally limit their attention to STANDARD quantifier phrases (it is only because of this that they are called 'standard'), namely existential and universal. Even standard ones come in a greater variety than is suggested by the logical notation commonly used to represent them. They can take singular or plural grammatical form, as illustrated by 'some boar', 'each goat', 'every roach', and 'a toad' (an INDEFINITE DESCRIPTION), and by 'some gazelles' and 'all giraffes'. Some are really single words, such as 'anyone', 'everybody', and 'something'. Then there are the commonly neglected NON-STANDARD quantifier phrases, such as 'few villages', 'many towns', and 'most cities', as well as numerical ones like 'two hamlets', 'more than half the townships', and 'all but three boroughs'. The last two phrases mentioned (as well as the one just used) contain several quantifier terms. These can occur in numerous combinations, such as 'some/few/many/three/nearly half/most/almost all of the jurors', 'all nine justices', and 'some/few/three of the many witnesses'.

When quantifier phrases are contrasted with singular terms,[1] the latter are often called 'referring expressions', as if quantifier phrases cannot be used to refer. But since they can be so used (as we will see), there must be something else to distinguish them from other noun phrases. It is, as Frege discovered, that when a quantifier phrase occurs in grammatical subject position, yielding what I will call a QUANTIFIER SENTENCE, it does not function logically as a subject expression. What this means is usually expressed, as it was by Frege, with the help of the formal device of quantifiers and variables. Thus sentences of the surface forms (1) and (2)

Some F is G.	(1)
Every F is G.	(2)

[1] To be sure, singular terms are ordinarily contrasted not with plural terms but with general terms (and both with mass terms, as in Quine 1960) and are represented in first-order predicate logic, which has no place for plural terms, as individual constants or variables (as opposed to predicate letters).

can be represented not by the subject-predicate form '*a* is G' but by the logical forms (1*f*) and (2*f*),

$$(Ex)(Fx \& Gx) \tag{1f}$$
$$(x)(Fx \supset Gx) \tag{2f}$$

The trouble with this familiar method of formalization, however, is that it produces what Barwise and Cooper (1981) have described as 'the notorious mismatch between the syntax of noun phrases in a natural language like English and their usual representations in traditional predicate logic' (1981, 165). They point out that quantifier phrases behave syntactically like other noun phrases—phrases of both sorts 'belong to a single syntactic category'[2]—and they would agree with Lycan that 'a theory of logical form must be compatible with syntax'[3] (1984, 15). Not only do Barwise and Cooper show that the traditional approach does not meet this requirement, they present various technical reasons why the traditional quantifier/variable approach cannot be extended to non-standard quantifier phrases. I cannot review the details of their argument here and will leave it as a challenge to the reader to extend the traditional approach to (3), for example.[4]

Few Fs are G. (3)

Even if a way of adapting traditional logical notation to non-standard quantifier phrases could be devised, it would still aggravate the problem of the 'notorious mismatch', for it would

[2] Hornstein (1984) has suggested certain syntactic differences between various quantifier phrases, and groups them into three separate categories.

[3] To appreciate this requirement, consider that it is one thing for a sentence in natural language to be capable of being represented by a logical formula and quite another for the sentence itself to have that form. If logical forms are ascribable to sentences themselves, there must be a straightforward mapping, exhibited by an adequate grammar of the language, between syntactic forms (at some level of linguistic description) and logical forms. It appears that the 'notorious mismatch' is inevitable if, for example, the form '$(x)(Dx \supset (Ey)(Cy \& Wxy))$' is attributed to 'Every dog wears a collar.'

[4] They try to show that sentences containing these phrases cannot be formalized using the standard quantifier symbols (existential and universal) and that the trouble with introducing non-standard quantifier symbols is that there seems to be no plausible way of combining them with variables and connectives to yield formulas that have the same truth conditions as the sentences being represented. Barwise and Cooper's approach handles all noun phrases in a uniform way, both syntactically and semantically. The same kind of notation is used for quantifier phrases as for other noun phrases, and quantifier phrases are also treated as denoting phrases. I will not discuss the elaborate formalism they devise, except to comment that to maintain uniformity they find it necessary to regard all noun phrases as denoting families of sets. This suits their technical purposes but is counter-intuitive.

produce formulas with vastly different structures from those of the sentences being formally represented.

At any rate, our interest in the difference between quantifier phrases and other noun phrases is informal. The usual way of describing the difference is that when a sentence contains a quantifier phrase it is not about anything; there seems to be no individual or individuals that the grammatical predicate is being applied to. For example, whereas (4)

Fred shaves.   (4)

seems to predicate something (shaving) of a certain individual,[5] Fred, sentence (5)

Some barber shaves.   (5)

clearly does not. There is no barber on whose shaving the truth of (5) depends. Similarly, in (6) or (7),

Many barbers shave.   (6)
Eleven barbers shave.   (7)

there are no specific barbers of whom shaving is being predicated; there are no barbers on whose shaving the truth of (6) or of (7) depends.[6] However, universal quantifier sentences, such as (8) and (9),

Every barber shaves.   (8)
All (the) barbers shave.   (9)

are exceptions to the apparent rule, since there are certain barbers, namely all barbers, on whose shaving the truth of these sentences depends.[7]

Further exceptions are provided by quantifier sentences containing what I call *limited* quantifier terms, such as 'few', 'exactly eleven', 'no more than three', and 'most but not all'. Consider (10),

Few barbers shave.   (10)

[5] Of course (1) does not *really* predicate something of a definite individual, since there are many people named 'Fred'. But here I am trying to describe the difference only pre-theoretically.

[6] There would be if there were only eleven barbers (similarly, if there were only one barber, the truth of (5) would depend on his shaving), but this does affect the general point about quantifier sentences.

[7] For this reason, as will be observed in the next section, universal quantifier phrases are generally used to refer, at least descriptively, namely to all the individuals denoted by the contained noun phrase.

for example. Even though (10) does not predicate shaving of all barbers, it is about all barbers. The reason is that evaluating (10) requires taking all barbers into account, not just those who shave. The ones who do not shave are as relevant to the truth of (10) as those who do. In general, a sentence of the form 'Q Fs are G', where 'Q' is a limited quantifier term, is true only if at least some Fs are not G.[8] However, there is no implication that any particular Fs are G and the rest are not. It is plausible to say, since each F's being or not being G is relevant to the truth of the sentence, that a limited quantifier sentence is about all Fs, considered as a class. Although such a sentence does not predicate G of all the Fs, it is *verified* (or falsified) by all the Fs, depending on how many (though not on which ones) are G.

Although this last observation does not apply to the other quantifier sentences given above, it does seem that each is about all barbers considered as a class[9] (I hesitate to say 'about the class of all barbers', since 'shaves' is not a predicate of classes). Regardless of which quantifier term occurs in a sentence of the form 'Q F is G' or 'Q Fs are G', the sentence is about all Fs. For this reason, I suggest that it is only the common noun in a quantifier phrase that denotes. If this suggestion is correct, it is immediately clear how a quantifier phrase differs from a logical subject term; as a whole it does not denote. For example, 'most barbers' does not denote, and only 'barbers' does; it denotes all barbers. Thus (8) and (9) are about certain barbers, namely all barbers, but not because of which quantifier terms they contain. Rather, they are about all barbers for the same reason that all the other sentences are: the quantifier phrase in each sentence contains 'barber(s)'. And, as we have seen, in some cases the truth of the sentence depends not only on how many barbers shave but also on how many do not. In every case, the sentence is about all barbers.

I am not suggesting that when we use such a sentence we must be talking about all barbers everywhere. We are likely to be talking

---

[8] Notice, incidentally, that unlike 'few', 'a few' is not a limited quantifier term; 'few' implies 'not most', but 'a few' does not. 'A few Fs are G' can be true even if most Fs are G—if there are not many Fs. Also, notice that '(a) few' can be used to mean either a small number or a small percentage.

[9] So is the description sentence (*i*),

The barber shaves.   (i)

at least if Russell was right about descriptions (see Chapter 5), for it implies that the class has only one member.

about some restricted class of barbers, such as all the barbers in town, but here we are not making fully explicit what we mean—we could have added the qualifying words, 'that is, all the barbers in town'. When we use a quantifier phrase to refer, we are also not making explicit what we mean, but in this case, as suggested in the next section, the implicit qualification begins not with 'that is' but with 'namely'.

So far I have tried merely to describe informally how quantifier phrases differ from other noun phrases. I have intended nothing weighty in suggesting that a quantifier sentence is 'about' the items denoted by the common noun in the quantifier phrase ('about' is a notoriously tricky term). The idea is simply that when a speaker is *not* using the quantifier phrase to refer, he is talking about those items considered as a class; if he were using it to refer, he would be talking about specific members of that class (or ones meeting some specific condition).

2. USING QUANTIFIER PHRASES TO REFER

It seems to me that quantifier phrases of virtually any kind can be used to refer. I will not try to prove this—there are too many cases to consider—but a look at a few seemingly unlikely cases will make it plausible. I propose a simple test: a speaker is using a quantifier phrase to refer (in uttering a quantifier sentence) if he could make his communicative intention explicit by uttering 'namely . . .' after the quantifier phrase, where the ellipsis is filled by terms specifying the individuals he is talking about. If I utter (1), for example,

> A few examples will show how plural reference is
> possible. (1)

I am using 'a few examples' to refer to the examples (of quantifier phrases being used to refer) that I am presently giving. I could make this explicit by using (2),

> A few examples, namely the ones I am giving here,
> will show how plural reference is possible. (2)

which contains the qualification introduced by 'namely'. In general, whenever a speaker makes such a qualification or at least intends the hearer to infer one, he is using the quantifier phrase thus qualified to refer.

Now referential intentions are like communicative intentions generally in the following way: a speaker can reasonably form a referential intention only if he can reasonably expect his audience to recognize it (Bach and Harnish 1979, 89–96). So when one is using a quantifier phrase to refer, one must not merely have certain individuals in mind but have reason to think one's audience will recognize this and, indeed, be in a position to identify them. In using 'a few examples' in (1), for instance, I expect you to infer that I am talking about the examples I am giving here, to which I am referring you descriptively, though not explicitly—I am not making the qualification given in (2). As the following examples show, various quantifier phrases can be used with inexplicit but recognizable referential intentions, be they descriptive or objectual.

Let us begin with the hard case of existential quantifier phrases, which might seem incapable of being used to refer. If someone returned home to find his house in a shambles and then uttered (3),

A burglar must have done this. (3)

he would probably be making merely an existential statement. He would not be using the indefinite description (an existential quantifier phrase) to refer.[10] But suppose that he and his wife had left their son alone for a few minutes and that upon seeing the mess he uttered (4),

A little boy must have done this. (4)

The speaker would then be using the indefinite description to refer to their son. Obviously, he would be exploiting the fact that under the circumstances it is clear that he has their son in mind, whom he intends his wife to identify as the little boy in question. Here the reference is objectual.

Even a quantifier expression as non-specific as 'someone' (or 'something') can be used to refer, as in (5),

Someone is happy. (5)

[10] Suppose the speaker went on to say 'He/the burglar stole the TV.' Now he would be referring. As the example illustrates, an indefinite description, even when not being used to refer, can be used to introduce an individual into a conversation for subsequent reference. This phenomenon is discussed by both Partee (1972) and Chastain (1975), who point out how indefinite descriptions can function, even across sentences, as antecedents (not in the grammatical sense, of course) for pronouns or for definite descriptions. When this occurs, the indefinite description functions as the first link in what Chastain calls an 'anaphoric chain'.

Imagine a roomful of disconsolate people in which somebody bursts out laughing. (5) might then be used not just to make an existential statement but to make a singular statement about that person.

Plural existential quantifier phrases can also be used to refer. If it has just been remarked that professional football players are in great shape, one might mention some players by name as counter-examples, and go on to utter (6),

> Some professional football players are in bad shape. (6)

using 'some professional football players' to refer objectually to the players named. Or, in a situation where some flabby place-kickers are conspicuous, one might utter (6) and be using 'some professional football players' to refer descriptively to all placekickers. In each case, it is obvious how the speaker could have inserted a 'namely' qualification.

Referring uses of non-standard quantifier phrases seem to raise no special problems. If someone uttered (7),

> Few philosophers understand quantum theory. (7)

he might be using 'few philosophers' to refer (descriptively) to the philosophers of physics, as would be made explicit by the 'namely' qualification in (8),

> Few philosophers, namely philosophers of physics,
> understand quantum theory. (8)

In the case of (9),

> Most/many professional football players are in good
> shape. (9)

probably one would be making a statement about professional players in general, but in the context of a remark about the pitiful condition of placekickers, one might use 'most/many professional football players' to refer descriptively to all players but placekickers. Something similar can happen with numerical quantifier phrases. In uttering a sentence like (10),

> 1,700 people got arrested at the anti-nuclear rally. (10)

one is not likely to be referring. 1,700 are far too many to refer to objectually, but one could use '1,700 people' to refer descriptively. One might have prefaced (10) with 'With the peaceful protestors assembled elsewhere, all 1,700 members of People against Peaceful

Uses of Nuclear Power threw hand-grenades at the nuclear reactor.' Objectual reference is more feasible with small numbers, as in (11),

Two US presidents almost got impeached. (11)

In all these examples, there is reference not merely because the speaker is thinking of certain definite individuals or, in the case of descriptive reference, individuals meeting a certain condition. Referring is expressing an attitude about certain individuals, and its success requires that this attitude be recognized. As usual, contextual information must be exploited, by the speaker in his intention and by the hearer in recognizing it. If one prefaced (11) with 'Considering that Andrew Johnson avoided impeachment by one vote and Richard Nixon resigned just before the impeachment process was completed', one would be using, and be taken to be using, 'two US presidents' to refer objectually to those two.

We have not yet discussed universal quantifier phrases, on which two observations may be made. First, they comprise a special case, albeit in a trivial way, because when they occur in grammatical subject position they cannot but be used to refer, at least descriptively. If one uttered (12),

All men are mortal. (12)

and was not referring to certain men in particular, one would still be referring descriptively to each and every man (in this case the qualification 'namely all men' would be redundant). Secondly, observe that grammatically plural quantifier phrases, such as 'all Fs' and 'the Fs', but not singular quantifier ones ('every/each F'), can be used to refer collectively as well as distributively to the Fs. A likely utterance of (13),

All the King's men couldn't put Humpty Dumpty
together again. (13)

would illustrate the collective use.

If we may generalize from the hard cases we have considered, it would seem that any quantifier phrase can be used to refer. To be sure, these referring uses are not strictly literal, for they include an inexplicit 'namely' qualification, but then most referring uses of proper names and of definite descriptions are not strictly literal either (the only ones that are, as argued in earlier chapters, involve descriptive reference with an unshared name or with a complete description). Semantically, quantifier phrases do not denote and are not referring expressions (strictly literal uses of quantifier sentences express general propositions), but our examples have shown that they also have referring uses.

3. PLURAL PRONOUNS

Singular or plural, pronouns are referring expressions *par excellence*. Plural pronouns are surely more akin to singular pronouns than singular pronouns are to other singular terms. Indeed, we should not expect to find any important difference (aside from number, of course) between plural and singular pronouns. Still, plural pronouns deserve mention in their own right, as do plural demonstratives and demonstrative descriptions.

Although referring is a pragmatic phenomenon, it is a semantic fact that pronouns are referring expressions and, indeed, that they are token reflexives. I suggested in Chapter 9 that what distinguishes one from another semantically is the particular REFERENTIAL CONSTRAINT associated with it, and that the constraint on each explains its specific token reflexive character. So let us extend this idea to plural pronouns. A token of 'we' is used to refer to a certain group to which the speaker (the producer of that token) belongs; a token of plural 'you' is used to refer to the members of the audience (of that very token) or to a certain group to which the audience belongs; and a token of 'they' is used to refer to any other group, presumably identifiable in the context of its utterance. A token of 'these (Fs)' or of 'those (Fs)' is used to refer to some contextually identifiable group (of Fs).[11]

Like their singular counterparts, plural pronouns can be used to refer either objectually or descriptively. For example, standing in front of the lion grotto, a zoo-keeper who utters (1)

They are getting hungry. (1)

might be using 'they' to refer objectually to the lions visible to him and his audience. He could just as well use it, say if no food had been delivered for several days, to refer descriptively to all the

---

[11] The difference between 'these' and 'those', like the one between 'this' and 'that', is a matter of relative proximity, but that, as we saw in Chapter 9, is a rather vague matter.

animals in the zoo. Either way, for his act of reference to succeed there must be mutual contextual beliefs for him and his audience to exploit, so that he can reasonably intend his audience to identify, and it can identify, the intended referents. If the zoo-keeper uttered (2),

> These animals are getting hungry. (2)

the same points would apply to an objectual or a descriptive use of the plural demonstrative description, 'these animals'.

Demonstrative descriptions need not be used demonstratively and, like pronouns, can be used instead to refer to individuals previously mentioned, as in (3),

> If you retain Simon & Shyster, those lawyers/
> they will steal you blind. (3)

Indeed, with plural pronouns even that is not always necessary for successful non-demonstrative reference. For example, one might utter (4),

> Have they caught the Night Stalker yet? (4)

and be using 'they' to refer (collectively) to the local police.

Plural pronouns can be used to refer to individuals mentioned either in the same sentence or in a previous one. When these individuals are mentioned in the same sentence, the reference is said to be anaphoric. The so-called antecedent can be a plural noun phrase, as in (5),

> The chumps from Oxford lost their hats. (5)

a 'conjunction'[12] of singular terms, as in (6),

> Laurel and Hardy wanted their hats back. (6)

or a plural quantifier phrase, as in (7),

> Most of the buyers wanted their money back. (7)

In each of these cases the plural pronoun can be used to refer either distributively or collectively. So, for example, (6) could be used to assert that Laurel wanted his hat(s) back and Hardy his or that they both wanted their jointly owned hats.[13] Similarly, (7) could be used to assert that of some majority of the buyers each wanted his own

---

[12] It cannot be a disjunction, since the pronoun would be singular, as in 'Laurel and Hardy wanted his hat back.'

[13] One could even assert both if, under the circumstances, it was mutually believed that some of the hats were individually owned and some collectively.

money back or that some majority of the buyers (all of whom went in on the deal together) wanted their collective money back. Notice, by the way, that in both cases 'their' is being used to refer to all the buyers, not just most of them. This illustrates the observation made earlier that sentences of the form 'Q Fs are G' are about all the Fs, not just about some subset of them.

4. QUANTIFIER PHRASES AND 'BOUND' PRONOUNS

In Chapter 11 we considered whether the relation between a pronoun and its so-called antecedent is a grammatical one. I argued that it is not. In this section I will extend that argument to so-called bound pronouns (personal pronouns, that is, not reflexives). I can make clear my position by comparing the different occurrences of 'their' in (1), (2), and (3),

Mugsy took their hats.	(1)
Laurel and Hardy lost their hats.	(2)
All the haberdashers lost their hats.	(3)

Notice that in an utterance of any of these sentences 'their' might be used to refer to Laurel and Hardy, and the mere fact that Laurel and Hardy happen to be mentioned in (2) but not in (1) does not require distinguishing grammatically the occurrences of 'their' in those two sentences. Similarly, there is no need to regard (2) as ambiguous just because 'their' can be used to refer either to Laurel and Hardy or to some other group of people. As we saw, the first use demands no special explanation, such as a supposed structural relationship between 'their' and 'Laurel and Hardy'.

Now I will extend the argument to sentences, such as (3), which contain quantifier phrases. It might seem that because 'their' can be used to refer either to all the haberdashers or to some other group of individuals, (3) is ambiguous, with 'their' having either of two semantic roles, one as a 'bound' and the other as a 'free' pronoun. Whether or not the traditional quantifier/variable method is used to represent binding (Chomsky (1981) uses a method of indexing[14]), is there any reason to regard as grammatical

---

[14] By this method the difference between the alleged bound and free readings of (3) would be captured by the co-indexing in (3b) and the free indexing in (3f):

All the haberdashers$_i$ lost their$_i$ hats.	(3b)
All the haberdashers$_i$ lost their$_j$ hats.	(3f)

the relationship between 'bound'[15] pronouns and the quantifier phrases that appear to bind them? Is there any *structural* sense in which quantifier phrases are antecedents of (non-reflexive[16]) pronouns?

Linguists commonly suppose that there is such a structural relationship, largely on the basis of apparent differences among sentences such as these (the asterisk indicates where 'binding' cannot occur):

Every employee thinks he should be promoted. (4)

As soon as he gets to work, every employee signs in. (5)

*He hates the company that every employee works for. (6)

Every employee is loyal to his company. (7)

Without his company's support, every employee would be insecure. (8)

*His company exploits every employee. (9)

Every employee has a window near him/*himself. (10)

*The company hired him because every employee is qualified. (11)

Every employee looks out for *him/himself. (12)

In each instance one must determine whether 'he', 'his', or 'him', as the case may be, can be 'bound' by (co-indexed with, in Chomsky's framework) 'every employee'. With such data in mind, linguists try to give a syntactic account of the linguistic environments in which a pronoun can or cannot be 'bound' by a quantifier phrase. The extensive linguistic research on this topic in recent years has produced a voluminous variety of data, of which the

---

(2) has two analogous representations. (1), of course, does not, because of the disagreement in number.

Notice that the indexing approach is quite different from the traditional quantifier/variable approach. The difference is evident with a sentence like 'All men are mortal.' Here there is no pronoun to be co-indexed with 'all men', hence no role for indexing to play. In the traditional formalization there is still a place for variables; to provide a place it breaks up the quantifier phrase and yields '(x)(if x is a man, then x is mortal)'.

[15] I put 'bound' in quotes both to indicate my doubt, which I will soon explain, that these pronouns are bound in any literal, i.e. structural sense and also to stay neutral on the possibility of some other account of the structural relation they supposedly bear to quantifier phrases.

[16] I do not mean to imply that with reflexives there is such a structural relationship, although it is true that reflexives admit only of a 'bound' interpretation. In the next section I will suggest an alternative to binding as an account of this relationship.

above is but a small sample, and an assortment of theories, whose conflicts I cannot hope to resolve here.[17] However, it is realistic to try to identify which questions are properly grammatical and which are pragmatic, for only then will it be clear what the linguistic dispute is really about.

Sentences (10) and (12) raise an interesting question about reflexives, which occur only in the accusative case (in English). Why should it be that 'himself' can occur in one environment but not in another that seems so similar? To answer this question linguists have proposed various structural hypotheses, but counter-examples have been produced to each. Still, the phenomenon does seem, even to a pragmaticist like me (not: 'myself'), to be a structural one. Fortunately, we do not need to discover the grammatical rule that captures it to be able to accept the following pragmatic hypothesis: whenever a reflexive *can* be used in an environment that 'binds' it to a quantifier phrase, if a pronoun were used in the same environment it would not be taken as 'bound'. For if the reflexive is available, a speaker cannot use a pronoun as 'bound' and have reason to expect it to be taken as such.[18] That is, the availability of a reflexive in a given position keeps a pronoun in that position from being construed as 'bound'. Notice that this fact (if it is a fact—perhaps there are exceptions) is pragmatic, not grammatical. Where a reflexive can occur is a grammatical question, but how the possibility of its occurrence can be exploited is a pragmatic one.

Since there is no nominative reflexive (in English), we must seek a different way of explaining the circumstances under which 'he' can or cannot be 'bound', as in sentences (4), (5), and (6),

> Every employee thinks he should be promoted.   (4)
>
> As soon as he gets to work, every employee signs in.   (5)
>
> *He hates the company that every employee works for.   (6)

To be bound 'he' does not have to follow the quantifier phrase, for it is capable of being 'bound' in (5) as well as in (4). Yet it cannot be 'bound' in (6). This might seem to be because 'he' c-commands 'every employee', but in (13),

---

[17] A good source of data and of theoretical approaches is Reinhart (1983).

[18] Analogously, in an utterance of 'I saw you with a woman last night' (to borrow an example from Grice), the use of 'a woman', because of the availability of 'your wife', is likely to be taken as excluding the hearer's wife.

*He arrived at work, and then every employee
signed in. (13)

where 'he' does not *c*-command 'every employee', the reason
appears to be that 'every employee' does not *c*-command 'he' (this
is true in (6) as well). Indeed, Chomsky's rule for co-indexing in his
syntactic explanation of 'binding' requires that the quantifier
phrase (or other noun phrase) *c*-command the pronoun. But is this
really necessary for 'binding'? Suppose we substitute a plural
quantifier phrase for 'every employee' and replace 'he' with 'they':

All the employees think they should be promoted. (4*p*)
As soon as they get to work, all the employees sign in. (5*p*)
*They hate the company that all the employees work for. (6*p*)
They arrived at work, and then all the employees
signed in. (13*p*)

In (13*p*), even though the *c*-command condition is not met, 'they'
can be 'bound' by 'all the employees'. So that condition is not
necessary for 'binding'. Now let us replace the quantifier phrase by
a proper name and put back the singular pronoun:

Sam thinks he should be promoted. (4*n*)
As soon as he gets to work, Sam signs in. (5*n*)
*He hates the company that Sam works for. (6*n*)
He arrived at work, and then Sam signed in. (13*n*)

In all but (6*n*), 'he' can be used to refer anaphorically to Sam.
Notice that just as in (13*p*) 'they' can be 'bound', in (13*n*) 'he' can
be used anaphorically, whereas in (13) 'he' cannot be 'bound'. So it
appears that the sentences with the plural quantifier phrase pattern
with those containing the proper name and not with those
containing the singular quantifier phrase. Moreover, because (13)
and (13*p*) are similar in structure but 'binding' is possible only in
(13*p*), perhaps the constraints on 'binding' are not syntactic after
all.

I believe we can explain the above pattern without having to
discover the syntactic constraints on 'binding' (assuming they are
purely syntactic), a task which continues to defy linguists. For
whatever the precise nature of these constraints, the above
examples support the following conjecture: plural 'binding' seems
to be possible wherever singular anaphoric reference is possible,
mutatis mutandis (pronoun number must be changed). Thus
'binding' is impossible in (6*p*), for example, for the very same

reason that anaphoric reference is impossible in (6*n*), *whatever* that reason might turn out to be. I could make this conjecture inductively plausible by taking up the literally hundreds of sentences discussed in the literature, but rather than use the space required for that I will only attest that I have yet to discover a counter-example.

In the linguistic literature many sentences have been presented to show that the syntactic constraints on 'binding' do not parallel those on anaphoric reference. However, I have noticed a curious fact about these examples, which I cannot try to document here, namely that all these examples, have a feature in common with (13): they all contain a singular pronoun followed by a singular quantifier phrase. For example, if in (13) we substitute 'they' for 'he', as in (13*t*),

They arrived at work, and then every employee
signed in.   (13*t*)

then 'binding' is possible. Accordingly, I offer a further conjecture: what makes 'binding' impossible in a sentence like (13) but not in (13*p*) or (13*t*) is not a matter of syntactic structure but of the number of the pronoun.

One might wonder how 'binding' is possible in (13*t*), since 'they' and 'every employee' do not agree in number, but keep in mind that I have not been taking 'binding' literally (thus my use of quotes). When a pronoun does not occur in the same clause as a quantifier phrase, it makes no syntactic sense to speak of number agreement, much less of binding. In saying this, I do not mean to suggest that when the pronoun does occur in the same clause as a quantifier phrase and does agree with it in number, it stands in some special relation to the quantifier phrase. Even in that case I doubt that there really exists such a relation. For just as we saw with pronouns and singular terms in Chapter 11, there is no reason to suppose that antecedency, which the relation of number agreement presupposes, is a genuine syntactic relation—except, of course, when reflexives are present. In other words, so-called number agreement (or gender agreement, for that matter) between pronoun and 'antecedent' is, as far as syntax is concerned, nothing more than an epiphenomenon. *Given* that pronoun and 'antecedent' co-refer, we *say* that they 'agree' in number (or gender), as if they are syntactically marked as co-referring.

That number and gender agreement appear to be syntactic phenomena gives rise to the illusion of ambiguity. For once it is supposed that agreement is syntactic, then it inevitably will seem that sentences which contain a pronoun together with a quantifier phrase or a singular term of the same number and gender, must be systematically ambiguous, with both indexical and bound or anaphoric readings. So too with the pronouns themselves. Two readings must be posited in order to account for the apparent fact that agreement may or may not be syntactically significant (on the indexical reading it is not). However, if we regard agreement as a mere epiphenomenon, in the way explained above, we can view bound and anaphoric uses of pronouns as nothing more than special cases of indexical uses.

So the constraints on 'binding' non-reflexive pronouns seem pragmatic, like the ones on 'co-reference'. Even though the rules capturing these constraints, whatever their precise formulation, are certain to be sensitive to syntactic factors, they do not thereby belong to sentence grammar. As observed in Chapter 11, there is no reason why pragmatic phenomena cannot be sensitive to structural relations, and Farmer (1984) has given syntactic reasons why there must be such phenomena. By denying that the constraints on 'binding' belong to sentence grammar, once again we can avoid multiplying meanings beyond necessity.

5. 'BINDING' AS REFERENTIAL DEPENDENCE

Contrary to popular linguistic opinion, the linguistic data do not show that antecedency is a syntactic relation. In my view it is merely a pragmatic epiphenomenon, and the relations of binding and anaphora are not syntactic. Also, I have conjectured that there is a way to explain away the specific data which seem to suggest that bound uses of pronouns are structurally constrained in ways that anaphoric uses are not. Those all seem to be sentences in which a plural rather than a singular pronoun can be 'bound' by a singular quantifier phrase. Even though I cannot begin to give a detailed treatment of these data, much less a precise formulation of the structural constraint that has eluded linguists, I must still address two further questions. If 'bound' pronouns are not really bound in any syntactic sense, how should their use be described in relation to their quantifier phrase 'antecedents'? And should reflexives still be regarded as bound variables (or, in Chomsky's framework, as involving obligatory co-indexing)? In answer to the first question, I will argue that the 'bound' use of pronouns is essentially the same as their anaphoric referential use, which I have interpreted as a kind of indexical use. I will suggest that the 'bound' use is referentially dependent on the common noun in the 'antecedent' quantifier phrase. As for the second question, I will argue that instead of regarding reflexives as bound variables, we can construe them as operators on verb phrases. What a reflexive does is, in a way to be explained, to 'reflexivize' the verb phrase with which it is in construction.

Earlier in this chapter I suggested that regardless of how quantifier sentences ought to be represented formally, it is plausible to treat the expression 'F(s)' contained in a quantifier phrase 'Q F(s)' as denoting all Fs, even though how we evaluate a sentence containing the quantifier phrase depends on the particular quantifier term 'Q'. For example, sentence (1)

> Most philosophers admire Kant.   (1)

is about all philosophers even though it does not predicate admiring Kant of them all. This suggestion can be extended to sentences containing 'bound' pronouns, such as (2),

> Most philosophers think they are clever.   (2)

if we think of the ('bound') use of 'they' as being referentially dependent, in the sense of Chapter 11, on 'philosophers' ('they' can also be used to make independent reference, say to linguists). This way of interpreting the connection of pronouns to quantifier phrases make it understandable why the 'bound' use of pronouns is so called even though they are not bound in a strict, structural sense. More importantly, it assimilates 'bound' pronouns to anaphoric pronouns, which we accounted for earlier by means of the notion of referential dependence. When the 'antecedent' of the pronoun is a quantifier phrase, the use of the pronoun is referentially dependent on the descriptive expression contained in that quantifier phrase.

In (2) the quantifier phrase is not being used to refer and 'they' is being used to refer to whoever 'philosophers' denotes, namely all philosophers. But suppose the quantifier phrase is being used to refer, as in (3),

> The philosophers moved their cars.   (3)

say to some philosophers congregating in a car-park. There is a different referential dependence in this case: 'their' is being used to refer to the specific philosophers 'the philosophers' is being used to refer to. The reference to them is distributive—to each philosopher one by one—but in an utterance of (4),

> The philosophers moved their refrigerators. (4)

reference would probably be collective—to these philosophers considered together (a speaker can make clear whether his referential intention is distributive or collective by adding the word 'individually' or 'together').

What if a reflexive rather than a pronoun is 'bound' by a quantifier phrase? Just as the use of a reflexive occurring with a singular term must be referentially dependent on the singular term, so the use of a reflexive occuring with a quantifier phrase must be a 'bound' use. Because it must be c-commanded by its antecedent the reflexive is bound by the quantifier phrase in a strict, structural sense. Thus in a sentence like (5),

> Most philosophers admire themselves. (5)

'themselves' is bound by 'most philosophers' or, to take Chomsky's (1981) approach, 'themselves' must be co-indexed with 'most philosophers'. What is the semantic import of reflexives? It seems plausible that their semantic role is to convert a two-place predicate into a reflexive predicate, so that (5) would be represented by (6),

> Most philosophers self-admire. (6)

In the example, 'admire' is 'reflexivized' by 'themselves'. Notice that this way of handling reflexives, unlike the traditional method with its quantifiers and variables, works straightforwardly with non-standard as well as with standard quantifier phrases.[19]

In any case, as far as non-reflexive pronouns are concerned, I have suggested that they require no special treatment at the level of

---

[19] We might take brief note of the case of the reciprocal 'each other/one another', as illustrated by (i) and by (ii),

> Most philosophers admire one another. (i)
> Most philosophers and most linguists admire
> each other. (ii)

Reciprocals have exercised Chomsky (1981) because there is a serious technical problem, not yet solved, of how to get right the indexing demanded by his theory. I will not spell out the details of the problem nor offer an alternative approach.

sentence grammar. Such a pronoun is 'bound' only in the sense that its use is referentially dependent on some 'antecedent' quantifier phrase. This is just a special case of an indexical use, and the apparent relation of antecedency has no syntactic significance.

6. QUANTIFIER PHRASES AND 'E-TYPE' PRONOUNS

Finally, let us examine an interesting and seemingly special case of pronouns in construction with quantifier phrases. Here the pronouns do not even seem to be bound. Evans (1980) contrasts them with what he takes to be bound pronouns, and calls these special ones E-TYPE pronouns. For example, in (1),

John owns some donkeys and feeds them at night. (1)

'them', though seemingly tied to the quantifier phrase 'some donkeys', does not even appear to be a bound pronoun (Evans had argued that bound pronouns do constitute a distinct grammatical class). Evans points out that if 'them' were bound by 'some donkeys', (1) would be interpreted incorrectly to mean that there are donkeys that John both owns and feeds at night. Moreover, Evans observes this interpretation would incorrectly fail to exclude the possibility of John's owning additional donkeys that he does not feed at night. Nor could 'them' function here as a 'pronoun of laziness', for then (1) would wrongly be taken to mean that John owns some donkeys and feeds some donkeys at night, perhaps not the ones he owns. Rather, (1) means that there are donkeys John owns and that John feeds (all) the donkeys he owns at night. From this Evans concludes that 'them' in (1) belongs to the special class of E-type pronouns.

In reaching this conclusion Evans is aware that 'them' in (1) admits of a purely pragmatic treatment. That is, 'them' could be used to 'refer to any group of entities salient in the context; one very likely (but, from the point of view of the semantics of the language, in no way privileged) group will be the donkeys which John owns' (1980, 353). But then Evans takes up (2),

Every villager owns some donkeys and feeds them
at night. (2)

and observes that it makes no sense to ask, assuming 'them' is not being used indexically, which group of donkeys 'them' is being used to refer to in (2). That is because 'every villager' has replaced the 'John' of (1), and presumably not every villager owns the same donkeys. So Evans proposes that a special linguistic rule is needed to explain how 'them' works in (2): the reference of an E-type pronoun 'is fixed by a description recoverable from the antecedent, quantifier-containing clause' (1980, 344). Evans goes on to assimilate the occurrence of 'them' in (1) to its occurrence in (2). Despite the fact that its occurrence in (1) would otherwise admit of a purely pragmatic treatment, Evans argues that because of the similarity in grammatical structure between (1) and (2), in consistency we must invoke his linguistic rule to account for the occurrence of 'them' in (1) as well.

In my view this appeal to a linguistic rule is superfluous in both cases. Even though it is only in (1) that 'them' is being used to refer to a certain group of donkeys, we can easily give the same pragmatic account of 'them' in (2) as in (1), in which case we need not construe it as a pronoun of a special (E-) type. In both (1) and (2) a speaker uses 'them' to refer descriptively, to the donkeys that John owns and to the donkeys that each villager owns. In effect, the speaker intends the hearer to take him as using 'them' to mean 'the donkeys that he owns', hence to take him as meaning (3),

John owns some donkeys and feeds the donkeys
that he owns at night. (3)

in uttering (1) and as meaning (4),

Every villager owns some donkeys and feeds
the donkeys that he owns at night. (4)

in uttering (2). (3) and (4) make explicit how utterances of (1) and (2) are to be taken when 'them' is being used in an E-type way, but this is merely a case of independent reference. No special account of E-type pronouns is needed, and (3) and (4) do not constitute special semantic readings of (1) and (2) in addition to their indexical readings. 'The donkeys that he owns' is just another way in which the speaker can intend his use of 'them' to be taken, and from a purely semantic standpoint this use is no more noteworthy than if he had uttered (1) or (2) ('John/every villager owns some donkeys and feeds them at night') and intended 'them' to be taken as 'the village piranhas', were this salient in the context. How the hearer actually does take 'them' depends, as with communication generally, on how he identifies the speaker's intention, on the basis of the utterance together with whatever mutual contextual beliefs may prevail. In one context the speaker might be using 'them' to mean 'the donkeys that he owns' (the seemingly special case of E-type pronouns), in another to mean 'the village piranhas', but in both cases he would be making an ordinary descriptive reference. We need not invoke a special linguistic rule to account for the E-type case, which seems special only because what the hearer is to exploit, in identifying what the pronoun is being used to refer to, happens to be the preceding quantifier phrase.

In any event, there is a serious problem for Evans's proposed linguistic rule, according to which the reference of an E-type pronoun is 'fixed by a description recoverable from the antecedent, quantifier-containing clause'. Presumably he means 'recoverable' in some technical, for example transformational, sense, for if he meant merely that the description is contextually inferable, he could not very well invoke a linguistic rule to explain the 'recovery' of this description. The phenomenon would be not semantic but pragmatic. What he does mean is that this description is the one which picks out 'the object(s), if any, which verify the antecedent, quantifier-containing clause', that is, the object(s) 'which satisfy the predicate in the antecedent clause and thereby make that clause true' (1980, 340). However, if we consider a sentence containing a limited non-standard quantifier, we can see that this appeal to what verifies the antecedent clause does not work. This is illustrated by (5),

> Few congressmen admire Kennedy, and they are
> very junior.   (5)

one of Evans's own examples. Again the pragmatic account works fine: 'they' is intended by the speaker as shorthand for 'the congressmen who admire Kennedy'. The trouble with Evans's account is that the clause 'few congressmen admire Kennedy' is verified not just by those congressmen who admire Kennedy but by the other congressmen as well. The latter contribute to the verification of 'few congressmen admire Kennedy' by *not* admiring Kennedy. Since the E-type use of pronouns is but a special case of their ordinary use, no linguistic rule is necessary to explain this use. So it is no calamity that Evans's proposed linguistic rule does not work.

We have found no reason to give E-type pronouns special syntactic or semantic consideration. They are ordinary pronouns used in a slightly special way, a way that is subject to straightforward pragmatic explanation.

13

Reference and Natural Kinds

Our study of reference has been limited to terms used to refer to individuals.[1] However, Kripke and Putnam have raised important questions about terms used to refer to so-called natural kinds. These include mass terms like 'water' and 'gold' and sortals like 'cat' and 'lemon'. Both Kripke and Putnam vehemently reject the Fregean view of these terms. On that view (at least in its simplest form) the meaning of a term, assumed to be the concept conventionally associated with it, determines its reference. Their reasons for rejecting this view in regard to natural-kind terms are in some ways similar to Kripke's reasons for rejecting description theories of proper names. Kripke even likens these terms to proper names (Putnam likens them to indexicals). Inasmuch as Kripke does not really develop a positive account of natural-kind terms while Putnam does propose a number of important doctrines about them, our discussion will focus on Putnam's views.

The case against Frege is best begun with Putnam's (1975, 139–42) famous Twin Earth thought experiment. In brief, we are to imagine a counterpart to Earth in which everything is the same except for the fact that the liquid that rains on Twin Earth and fills its lakes, rivers, and oceans is not H_2O but the chemically different yet superficially indistinguishable XYZ. The speakers of English on Twin Earth even call XYZ 'water'. However, in Putnam's view the extension of their word 'water' is not the same as the extension of ours. Their word applies to XYZ, ours to H_2O. Accordingly, as *we* use the word 'water', there is no water on Twin Earth.

This conclusion would be innocuous if we assumed that the *meaning* of 'water' were H_2O here and XYZ there, but Putnam does not assume that. To bring home the force of his conclusion, he rolls back the time to before the advent of chemistry, when no one could have associated the concept of a chemical compound with

[1] Actually, it has been more limited than that, namely to concrete individuals. I have not discussed reference to abstract entities because I believe that the real issues there lie not with reference itself but with the ontological and epistemological status of those entities. This is hardly the place to try to resolve those perennial issues.

'water'. Putnam claims that even then our term 'water' had a different extension than did theirs. This was so even though Twin Earthlings associated the same (phenomenal) concept with 'water' as Earthlings did. But since this one concept constituted the (Fregean) meaning of the term 'water' on both planets and yet its extension was not the same, its meaning could not have determined its extension (QED).

We will assess Putnam's thought experiment in due course. Suppose for now that we accept the claim that there is no water on Twin Earth. As Putnam himself points out, instead of giving up the Fregean view that meanings determine extension, we could equally well abandon the Fregean conception of meaning, that 'meanings are in the head'. This is the option Putnam chooses, 'thereby giving up the doctrine that meanings are concepts or, indeed, are mental entities of any kind', and construing extension itself as an aspect of meaning. Now his immediate conclusion from the experiment is that 'words like "water" have an unnoticed indexical component: "water" is stuff that bears a certain similarity relation to the water around here' (1975, 152). So it is puzzling that Putnam takes both options to be compatible with this conclusion, for, as Burge (1982, 105) and Putnam himself (1975, 151) are well aware, if 'water' is a true indexical then not its meaning but only its reference should vary with the context. But this entails that its meaning does not determine its reference, the option that Putnam rejects. If Putnam insists on the second option, that 'water' has a different meaning on Twin Earth than on Earth, he should not regard it as an indexical.[2]

I mention Burge's criticism because he goes on to interpret the thought experiment in a way that is even more radical than rejecting either the Fregean claim that meaning determines extension or the Fregean conception of meaning. Burge holds that the meaning of 'water' does determine its extension, hence that it has a different meaning on Twin Earth, *and* he holds that the meaning of a term is the concept conventionally associated with it.

---

[2] The idea is dubious anyway, since with ordinary indexicals what varies with context is token reference, whereas with natural-kind terms, at least as suggested by the thought experiment, what varies with context is type reference (extension). Also, there is an equivocation here on 'context'. The reference of an indexical varies with the context of the specific utterance. The reference of a natural-kind term is supposed to vary with global context, i.e. from planet to planet, not from utterance to utterance on each planet.

However, he takes the radical course of denying that *concepts* are in the head! Thus he is rejecting the 'methodological solipsism' endorsed by Putnam (1975, 136). So for Burge the Twin Earth experiment extends beyond the theory of the meaning to the theory of mental contents. He is rejecting what amounts to a Fregean conception of concepts. It will be convenient to take up Burge's position first, because the points to be made about identifying concepts and determining their extensions will be germane to our discussion later of Putnam's and Kripke's views about the meanings and extensions of terms.

1. BELIEF AND MEANING

Burge claims that the contents of propositional attitudes are not determined by internal psychological state. Now we saw in Chapter 1 that the *objects* of propositional attitudes are not always determined by psychological state, but that is not what Burge means. He means contents. Besides, he is talking not about *de re* attitudes, whose contents have indexical elements (and which are not propositional anyway), but only about attitudes with fully conceptual contents. Paradoxical as it may seem, his claim is that the contents of propositional attitudes, even with internal states fixed, can vary with certain social or physical differences in the environment. Devising Twin Earth experiments of his own, Burge has argued separately for the social (1979 and 1986) and the physical (1982) side of this claim. We will devote a section to each.

Burge makes the startling assertion that a person can 'incompletely understand' a notion that belongs to the content of an attitude he has. One would have thought that if a person incompletely understood a notion it could not be the one that figured in his attitude. Yet Burge denies that 'having a propositional attitude strictly implies full understanding of its content' (1979, 89). To support his view as well as to clarify it, Burge performs some Twin Earth experiments. Whereas Putnam's experiments concern only the meaning and extension (or 'reference') of natural-kind terms, Burge's experiments, which are not restricted to natural-kind terms, concern the use of various terms to express the contents of propositional attitudes. Burge does not ask us to imagine that there are any physical differences between Earth and Twin Earth. Instead, we are to imagine that certain terms are used somewhat differently on the two planets. For example, on Earth 'arthritis' means inflammation of the joints while on Twin Earth it means inflammation of either the bones or the joints. So Twin Earthlings apply the term where we withhold it, but that is only because 'arthritis' has a broader meaning there.[3] There is nothing interesting about the difference between Earth and Twin Earth so far, but Burge goes on to describe the case of a certain Earthling, whom we will call 'Criqui'. He has long suffered from inflammation of the knuckles, wrists, ankles, and knees. Doctors have diagnosed him as having arthritis and have given him considerable information about it to go along with what he has already figured out for himself. He has acquired such beliefs as that he has had arthritis for years, that it is hard to treat, and that it is preferable to cancer. Recently he has developed stiffness in the thigh and complained to his doctor that his arthritis has spread to his thigh. Evidently, he has never looked up the word 'arthritis' in the dictionary and no one has ever told him that arthritis is inflammation of the joints. In fact, he has misunderstood the word all along. Now far away on Twin Earth is Criqui's psychologically identical counterpart, whose name is the same. 'Arthritis' means the same to both of them, though of course Twin Criqui understands it correctly (on Twin Earth). Unfortunately, he is also physically identical to Criqui and goes to the doctor with the same complaint. The stage is set.

Burge now supposes that on both planets the same sentence is used to ascribe a belief.

Criqui thinks he has arthritis in the thigh.   (1)

Because of the difference in how 'arthritis' is used on the two planets, (1) describes a different belief on Twin Earth from what it does on Earth. And yet, Burge maintains, as used on their respective planets (1) correctly describes both Criqui's and his counterpart's beliefs. But whereas Twin Criqui has a true belief on Twin Earth, Criqui has a false belief on Earth. We could make up a

---

[3] The following situation would be more complex—and more suited to Putnam's purposes. Suppose that the Twin Earthlings originally used the term as we do but later discovered that bone inflammation was due to the spreading of joint inflammation or at least was essentially the same disease, whereas in us there is no connection between the two. Putnam would say that even prior to the discovery on Twin Earth, 'arthritis' had a different extension (and meaning) there.

term, say 'tharthritis', to mean here on Earth what 'arthritis' means on Twin Earth, and then we could describe Twin Criqui as believing that he has tharthritis in the thigh. Or we could simply describe him as believing that he has an arthritis-like disease in the thigh. Criqui may have such a belief too, but, Burge maintains, Criqui also has the belief described by (1). He believes, falsely of course, that he has arthritis in his thigh.

Burge anticipates the objection that because Criqui has a false metalinguistic belief about the meaning of 'arthritis', (1) is not literally true.[4] Insisting that (1) is literally true, Burge claims that Criqui's false metalinguistic belief merely tells against substitutivity of synonyms for synonyms in belief contexts. Since Criqui does not mistakenly think that thighs are joints, no belief of his is correctly described by (2),

> Criqui believes that he has inflammation of
> the joints in the thigh.   (2)

According to Burge, not only does Criqui's false metalinguistic belief about 'arthritis' not falsify (1), it helps explain why Criqui has the belief that (1) ascribes. Evidence that Criqui really does think he has arthritis in the thigh consists partly in the fact that (1) would ordinarily be used to describe Criqui's belief and partly in the fact that Criqui himself, when apprised of his mistake, would still allow that (1) had correctly described his belief.

Burge diagnoses our resistance to accepting (1) as stemming from the unwarranted assumption that

what a person thinks his words mean, how he takes them, fully determines what attitudes he can express in using them: the contents of his mental states and events are strictly limited to notions, however idiosyncratic, that he understands; a person cannot think with notions he incompletely understands. (1979, 102)

Burge often describes this and his other examples as involving 'incomplete understanding of concepts' or 'conceptual errors', even though they seem more aptly described as involving incomplete understanding of words or linguistic errors. Indeed, sometimes he seems to equate the two, as when he says that 'the

---

[4] A better formulation of the objection would be in terms of what the word 'arthritis' means to Criqui rather than in terms of what Criqui believes about the word. I will go along with Burge's formulation, but I think the objection would have seemed more forceful to Burge if he had taken it the other way.

error is linguistic or conceptual' (1979, 82), though surely these are distinct. At any rate, if Criqui misunderstands the word 'arthritis' and does not associate it with the concept of arthritis, there seems to be no reason to suppose that the concept of arthritis figures in his belief. Again, Burge rests his case on the fact that we would use (1) to describe Criqui's belief and that Criqui himself, once apprised of his (linguistic) error, would acknowledge the correctness of (1). Burge offers no positive account of what it is to think with a concept one incompletely understands or of what it is to believe a proposition that one does not understand.[5] As for me, I have no idea what it is to think with a concept that one incompletely understands. That is because I have no idea what it is to understand a concept over and above possessing it.

Instead of venturing into the mysterious realm of the epistemology and psychology of concepts, I will offer a direct reply to Burge's argument. Criqui is mistaken about what the word 'arthritis' means, but this does not show that he has an 'incomplete understanding' of the concept of arthritis. For although he may think that 'arthritis' designates any inflammatory disease of the bones or joints, he may also think that there is such a condition specific to the joints. He could very well have complete mastery of the concept of arthritis and, owing to his linguistic error, simply not use the word 'arthritis' to express it. Not only that, people would still use (1) to describe his belief about what he has in his thigh, and he would still acknowledge, once apprised of the meaning of 'arthritis', its correctness. But they, and he, would be wrong.[6]

In trying to explain why (1) merely seems to be correct, we should distinguish two versions of the example, as they require separate

---

[5] The latter is not to be confused with accepting a sentence that one does not understand, i.e. without knowing which proposition it expresses (notice that one could still understand the proposition). Probably millions of people would describe themselves and one another as believing that $e = mc^2$ without either understanding that proposition or the sentence (equation) that expresses it.

[6] Suppose there was a word, 'tharthritis', for inflammation of the joints or bones. Then people would describe Criqui as thinking that arthritis was tharthritis, and he himself, once corrected of his linguistic error, would acknowledge that he thought this. This way of describing his belief would be natural enough, but not thereby correct, at least if taken to express the content of his belief. For even if Criqui thinks that 'arthritis' expresses the concept of tharthritis and that 'tharthritis' expresses the same concept (in the manner of 'flammable' and 'inflammable'), still he does not think that the concept of arthritis and the concept of tharthritis are the same.

treatment. In the first the subject has 'some deviant notion in mind', while in the second he does not.

Regarding the first version Burge rightly remarks that (1) should not be rejected merely because the subject also believes that he has tharthritis in the thigh. Very well, for the sake of argument let us suppose that Criqui does believe that he has arthritis in the thigh. But then he has *two* beliefs, that he has tharthritis in the thigh and that he has arthritis in the thigh. Yet we, who according to Burge have been using (1) correctly, would surely deny that Criqui has two beliefs. If we maintained that he believes he has arthritis in the thigh, that would only be because we take him to believe that arthritis is inflammation of the joints or bones.

Nevertheless, Burge finds it is arbitrary 'to attribute a notion that just captures the misconception', since 'the appropriate restrictions on the application . . . of the patient's supposed notion are unclear' (1979, 93–4). Of course it is not necessary to make up a new word, like 'tharthritis', to express the patient's notion, but still,

It is simpler and equally informative to construe him as thinking that arthritis may occur outside joints. When we are making other attributions that do not directly display the error, we must simply bear the deviant belief in mind, so as not to assume that all of the patient's inferences involving the notion would be normal. (1979, 94)

But now Burge is being arbitrary, inasmuch as these very inferences constitute the evidence for attributing to the patient some other notion than that of arthritis. For example, one normal inference from the proposition that one has arthritis in the thigh is that one has inflammation of the joints in the thigh, hence that the thigh is a joint. The patient does not make that inference. Hence we have reason to think that the patient is not operating with the concept of arthritis. However, that leaves open the question of what concept he is operating with. Burge remarks that the patient himself

does not say (or think) that he had thought he had some-category-of-disease-like-arthritis-and-including-arthritis-but-also-capable-of-occurring-outside-of-joints in the thigh instead of the error commonly attributed. This sort of response would be disingenuous. . . . In examples like ours, he typically admits his mistake, changes his views, and leaves it at that. (1979, 95)

Of course the patient would not use an elaborate hyphenated locution to express his thought. But one way he might admit his mistake would be to say, 'OK, I thought you could have arthritis in your bones, but still, I have something like arthritis in my thigh.' The question here is whether he has admitted to a substantive or merely to a verbal mistake and whether he has really changed the belief he admitted to or merely his way of expressing it. Again, his failure to have made appropriate inferences is good evidence that even in using the word 'arthritis' he was not operating with the notion of arthritis. Besides, we have seen that he could have had the notion of arthritis without having used the word 'arthritis' for it. He would have expressed it with the phrase 'arthritis in the joints'. Indeed, his using such a redundancy would indicate that he was not using 'arthritis' to express the concept of arthritis.[7]

Now let us consider a case in which the person does not, as Criqui did with 'arthritis', have a deviant notion in mind. In this case Burge suggests that we 'count people who incompletely understand terms in ascribed content clauses as sharing true . . . attitudes with others who understand the relevant terms better' (1979, 96). He suggests also that the subject's 'willingness to submit his statement and belief to the arbitration of a dictionary indicates a willingness to have his words taken in the normal way' (1979, 101). Of course a person wants to use words that do express his concepts and not to use words that do not, but does the willingness just described show that he incompletely understands the concept or merely the term that expresses the concept? Often a person is fully aware of his incomplete understanding of technical terms. If he says 'My father suffered a myocardial infarction' and knows only that a myocardial infarction is some kind of heart attack, he has no deviant concept but is deferring to the experts. Then does he believe that his father suffered a myocardial infarction? Not if having this belief requires having the concept. Rather than say that he has the concept but understands it incompletely (if this could mean something other than that he understands the expression incompletely), we should say that he believes his father suffered the kind of heart attack that doctors call 'myocardial infarction'.

---

[7] Burge (1979, 95) tries to bolster his argument by suggesting that the patient, once enlightened on what arthritis is, would be relieved that the disease in his knee had not spread to his thigh. Evidently Burge assumes not only that if a disease spreads to a new area it must be the same disease, but also that if Criqui can get relief that easily the condition in his thigh is merely psychosemantic.

Even someone who does not even know that the term has anything to do with heart attacks could still say 'My father suffered a myocardial infarction' without having a belief with that content. He could make this explicit if he uttered 'My father suffered a myocardial infarction, whatever that is.' Still he would be using 'myocardial infarction' to refer to whatever his father suffered. It is common to use a term one does not understand to refer to whatever it denotes (assuming it does denote). One does not have precisely the belief being expressed, at least not if beliefs are individuated by their contents. Besides, as Burge himself observes, in practice we often identify beliefs without fully specifying their contents. However, he does not seem to appreciate that this practice undermines his argument, which depends, in my view, on reading too much about our psychological notions into our psychological discourse.

The same difficulty besets another thought experiment devised by Burge. It features 'not incomplete [linguistic] understanding . . . but nonstandard theory' on the part of the relevant protagonists (1986, 709), and is even intended to challenge the dogma that necessary truths like (3)

Sofas are pieces of furniture [of such and such
construction] made or meant for sitting.　　　　　　　　　(3)

cannot be doubted. The experiment does not depend on the choice of example, and Burge enumerates a wide variety of terms/notions to which it might be adapted. A certain person A has a normal mastery of English, understands the word 'sofa', and has acquired the normal truisms about sofas. However, he comes to doubt these truisms (e.g., he thinks that sofas would collapse under people's weight) and hypothesizes, contrary to (3), that sofas are really works of art or religious artifacts. He even devises an elaborate account of people's misconceptions about sofas. He is prepared to put his hypothesis to the test empirically, proposes some reasonable tests, and ultimately, once their results come in, even acknowledges that he was mistaken.

Then there is B, A's physically identical counterpart in another world, a world in which the things called 'sofas' really are works of art or religious artifacts. Burge calls them 'safos', but people in B's world use 'sofa' to refer to them. It so happens that B hears counterparts of the truisms heard by A, but they are, unbeknownst to *B*, jokes, lies, or figurative utterances. *B* takes them literally and accepts them at first, taking safos to be pieces of furniture . . . made for sitting, but eventually develops doubts much like *A*'s. Unlike *A*, however, *B* *mistakenly* thinks that he is challenging common opinion—like everyone else, he correctly thinks that safos are works of art or religious artifacts.

According to Burge, the experiment shows that even though *A* and *B* are physically similar and in a phenomenologically similar situation, their 'sofa'-thoughts do not have the same contents. Whereas '*A* mistakenly thinks that sofas do not function primarily to be sat upon, *B*'s counterpart thoughts do not involve the notion of sofa and could not correctly be ascribed with "sofa" in oblique position'; *A*'s thoughts can be so ascribed. In short, '*A* and *B* have different thoughts' (1986, 708).

Do they? Clearly *A* and *B* have thoughts about different things, sofas and safos respectively, but that is not at issue. Burge is claiming that whereas '*A* has numerous mental events involving the notion of sofa, *B*'s skepticism does not involve thinking of anything as a sofa' (1986, 708). Burge maintains that *A* thinks of the objects of the thoughts expressible or ascribable with the word form 'sofa' as sofas, but that *B* thinks of their counterparts as safos (his thoughts are expressible or ascribable in *B*'s world with the word form 'sofa'). We would attribute 'sofa'-thoughts to *A* with ascriptions of the form,

> *A* believes that sofas are . . . (4)

and we could, if we adopted the word 'safo', attribute 'sofa'-thoughts (i.e. thoughts expressible by the word form 'sofa' as used in *B*'s world) to *B* with ascriptions of the form

> *B* believes that safos are . . . (5)

Burge assumes that if one literally and correctly uses a term in the 'that'-clause of an attitude attribution, one is imputing to the subject the notion expressed by the term and is, further, including it in the content of the attitude being attributed. We commonly do this all right, but not always. When using a form of ascription such as (4), it is our standard practice to use a word like 'sofa' both to refer to sofas, thereby expressing our notion of sofa, and to impute the same notion to the subject in his thoughts about sofas. However, our standard practice must be modified when the situation is not standard, as in Burge's thought experiment. For in that situation, although *A* possesses the notion of sofa, the thought he expresses when he denies (3) by uttering (6)

> Sofas are not pieces of furniture . . . made for sitting.　　　(6)

does not involve the notion of sofa. To be sure, he possesses the notion of sofa and that is what the word 'sofa' means, even to him, but in using (6) to say something about sofas, he is not using the notion of sofa to think of sofas. We may be inclined to use the form (4) to attribute beliefs to *A*, as here,

> *A* believes that sofas are . . . religious artifacts.　　　(7)

but this inclination can be explained by the fact that *we* are employing the notion of sofa to think of sofas when we use the word 'sofas' to refer to sofas. It is perfectly consistent for us to cancel the implication that *A* thinks of sofas in the way that we do. We can add to (7), 'not that he takes them to be sofas'. It is not being denied that *A* possesses the notion of sofas but only that this notion figures in the content of the thought in question. However, if we said of *A*,

> *A* believes that sofas do not exist.　　　(8)

we *would* be using 'sofas' to impute the notion of sofa to *A* but we would *not* be referring to sofas, since we would not be attributing to *A* the belief that they, the things everyone else takes to be sofas, do not exist. Notice also that if *A* uttered (9),

> [I believe that] sofas are . . . religious artifacts.　　　(9)

he would not be speaking literally, since even though he is using 'sofas' to refer to what in fact are sofas, he does not take them to be sofas and is thinking of them as *what most people think of as sofas* (or as *so-called sofas*). However, if *A* uttered (10),

> [I believe that] sofas do not exist.　　　(10)

he would be speaking literally. He would not be denying the existence of the things that he takes to be . . . religious artifacts.

Burge considers several rejoinders to his interpretation of the thought experiment. They all challenge his claim that *A* literally doubts what he appears to doubt, and suggest that *A* does not really possess the notion of sofa but some other notion instead. One of these rejoinders is similar to mine, except that it refuses to impute to *A* the notion of sofa: '*A* thinks only that *what most people think of as sofas* are works of art or religious artifacts.'

(1986, 711) Burge does not consider the possibility that A not only thinks this but also possesses the notion of sofa and understands the word 'sofa'.

What makes plausible Burge's contention that ascriptions of the form of (4) literally describe A's beliefs (including the belief that sofas are not pieces of furniture . . . made for sitting) and impute to him the notion of sofa is that A does possess the notion of sofa, he does associate this notion with the word 'sofa', and he does use that word to refer to sofas. However, Burge does not realize that when A uses 'sofa' to refer to sofas, he does not intend to be using the word literally. For although 'sofa' means *pieces of furniture . . . made for sitting*, even to him, he does not take the things to which he is using 'sofa' to refer to be sofas. If he utters (6), he means that so-called sofas (what everybody else calls 'sofas') are not pieces of furniture . . . made for sitting. He is exploiting the common, but in his view mistaken, belief that those items are sofas. Indeed, he might well go on to say that he does not take those items to be sofas. Only then would he be using 'sofa' literally.

This way of describing the situation with A is perfectly natural, as can be seen if we change the example from sofas to witches. Imagine being in New England in the period when deranged women were called witches, where 'witch' meant *woman in league with the Devil* (or something of the sort). Suppose you began to doubt common opinion and came to believe that these women are not in league with the Devil. Your fellow New Englanders would use (11)

> S believes that witches are not in league with the Devil. (11)

to attribute this belief to you, but we would not—unless we put 'witches' in quotes. Your fellow New Englanders take it to be a necessary truth that witches are in league with the Devil, which they take you to reject, but we don't suppose there are any witches at all. Like you, we reject their belief in witches, though not their notion of witch. Yet Burge's position seems to require that (11) attributes a belief literally and correctly and implies that your belief involves the notion of witch. Then what you believe would be the negation of a necessary truth, in which case it could not be true. Here Burge might contend that it is not a necessary truth but false that witches are in league with the Devil and that witches are (really) insane women, but then he would be implying that witches exist. Clearly a better course is to say that (11) attributes to you a belief about so-called witches (in early New England), a belief which does not involve the notion of witch, and that you disagree with your fellow New Englanders about what these individuals are. This is not to deny that you possess the notion of witch; indeed, it figures in your belief that there are no witches.

Let us conclude our discussion of the thought experiment by considering the situation of A's counterpart B, whom we have been neglecting. Recall that B is relevantly similar to A. In particular, his experience of sofa-like items and his exposure to uses of the word form 'sofa' are the same. But of course, in B's world these objects are safos and this word form means *safo*. B is right about the objects but wrong about popular opinion. Moreover, according to Burge, B possesses the notion of safo, not that of sofa, and B's thoughts do not involve the notion of sofa and could not correctly be ascribed with 'sofa' in oblique position'; A's thoughts can be so ascribed. A and B have different thoughts; or so Burge maintains.

However, Burge's only reason for denying that B possesses the notion of sofa seems to be that in B's world the word form 'sofa' means *safo*, as in ascriptions of the form

$$B \text{ believes that sofas are } . . . \tag{12}$$

Now of course people in B's world do use 'sofas' to refer to safos, even in the context of (12), and use it to express the notion of safo. But it doesn't follow that they would use it, as in (12), to impute the notion of safo to B. Assuming they understood his views, they would realize that to him 'sofa' does not mean *safo* but *piece of furniture . . . made for sitting.* And although this is what it means to him, if he uttered (13),

$$\text{Sofas are not pieces of furniture } . . . \text{ made for sitting.} \tag{13}$$

he would not be using 'sofa' to express this notion but rather *so-called sofa*. As we saw earlier, the same goes for A. Indeed, Burge's experiment demonstrates no difference between them as to the contents of their beliefs.

2. CONCEPTS AND CONTEXT

The thought experiments discussed above, whatever they may show about our practice of ascribing beliefs, do not serve to establish Burge's claim about beliefs themselves. He has not shown that with internal states fixed, contents of beliefs (or of other propositional attitudes) can vary with differences in social environment. Burge has also (1982) used Putnam's (1975) original Twin Earth experiment in an effort to show that contents can vary with differences in the physical environment. Here Burge, like Putnam originally, applies the experiment only to natural kind terms, though unlike Putnam he is concerned not merely with their meaning and extension but with the concepts they are used to express. Again, that is because he is not challenging either the Fregean view that meaning determines extension or the Fregean conception of the meaning of a term as the concept associated with it. Rather, he is challenging the traditional view of concepts. He claims that having a natural-kind concept such as the concept of water is not simply a matter of being in a certain internal state. Whereas Putnam's entire discussion of the thought experiment presupposes that the relevant Earthling and his counterpart are psychologically the same, Burge interprets the experiment to show that they 'are in no sense exact duplicates in their thoughts' (1982, 102).

As usual, Earth and Twin Earth are supposed to be qualitatively identical except for a structural difference in the stuff or things to which a given natural-kind term applies. On Earth water is made up of H_2O, on Twin Earth XYZ. Or, to vary the example, our cats are animals, theirs are robots remotely controlled from Twin Mars.[8] Earthling Adam speaks English, and its terms, like 'water' and 'cat', can be used to 'express and characterize his way of thinking about the relevant stuff and things' (1982, 109), even if he is ignorant about the constitution of water and cats. Twin Adam speaks Twin English, in which, according to Burge, the words 'water' and 'cat' do not mean what they mean in English (nor are there terms in Twin English that mean what 'water' and 'cat' mean in English). Moreover, it is 'intuitively obvious' to Burge that the English words cannot legitimately be used to attribute Twin Adam's attitudes. Burge concludes that Twin Adam does not have the same relevant attitudes, for he could not have acquired the

---

[8] Actually, Putnam (1962) did not introduce feline robots as cat counterparts on Twin Earth. He supposed, rather, that the things we here on Earth have been calling 'cats' all along are really Martian robots. It was his intuition that if this supposition turned out to be true these Martian robots would have been cats. Anyway, I am using cats for Twin Earth purposes on account of my ignorance about the nature of elms and mackerel.

concepts of water or of a cat. Despite his internal identity with Adam, Twin Adam could not believe, for example, that cats drink water. The belief that he would express with those words, the belief that Twin Earthlings would ascribe to Twin Adam by saying 'Adam believes that cats drink water', would be a different belief (it would have a different content). We, speaking English, would be mistaken if we thought that Twin Adam believes that cats drink water, for we would be imputing to him concepts that he does not have.

This is Burge's view of Twin Adam's cognitive situation. One of his main reasons for denying that Twin Adam could have acquired the concept of water, at least in the normal way, is that

> There is no water on Twin-Earth, so he has never had any contact with water. Nor has he had contact with anyone else who has had contact with water. Further, no one on Twin-Earth so much as uses a word which means *water*. (1982, 109)

Burge's other main reason for denying that Twin Adam has the concept of water is that if we supposed that he did have that concept, many of Twin Adam's beliefs, such as that fish swim in water, would implausibly turn out to be false, inasmuch as 'there is no water on Twin-Earth'. Clearly both of Burge's reasons for denying that Twin Adam has the concept of water depend on the assumption that there is no water on Twin Earth, an assumption he does not try to justify. Confident that Putnam has made a good case for it, Burge regards it as 'pretty obvious, pretty widely shared, and stronger than arguments that might be or have been brought to buttress it' (1982, 100).

Not everyone shares Putnam's and Burge's intuitions that there is no water on Twin Earth. Instead of denying that there is water on Twin Earth, some people are inclined to say that there are two kinds of water, one kind here and one kind there. And a natural response to the cat-robot example is to say that if the things we have been calling 'cats' are not animals but robots, they are not cats at all. Indeed, Unger (1983) has recently devised a variety of ingenious variations on Putnam's thought experiments that support contrary intuitions.[9] Some even provoke pairs of

[9] Here is a variation of my own. Instead of XYZ being the only liquid superficially indistinguishable from H_2O, there are hundreds of such liquids on counterparts of Earth scattered all over the universe. Then we would be much less inclined to say that there is water only on Earth. We would think that what is essential to water is not its chemical make-up but its functional role.

conflicting intuitions. I will not repeat his examples here, for my concern is not with the conflicting intuitions but with what underlies their conflict.

Unger suggests that such conflicts indicate a tension, as revealed by the experiments, between our 'existential belief' and our 'property belief' about the kind in question. For example, we all believe that there are cats and that cats are animals, but if the things we have been calling 'cats' are Martian robots, either there are no cats or cats are not animals. Differences in intuitions reflect interpersonal differences in priorities enjoyed by the two beliefs. The latter differences, according to Unger, are psychologically significant but of no great philosophical import. Even if, in any particular case, one intuition is much more popular than another, the other deserves consideration too, enough (says Unger) to show that the greater appeal of the first does not establish Putnam's view. Its relative popularity shows only that, under the circumstances of the thought experiment in question, people tend to be less willing to give up one of the beliefs than the other.

What is at issue when people disagree on whether Martian robots are cats or on whether Twin Earth oceans are filled with water? The disagreement has the air of an empirical dispute, but of course everyone agrees on the facts, at least as long as the contested words are not being used (they can still be mentioned). We agree on the difference between the stuff we call 'water' and the stuff they call 'water'. We agree on the difference between feline animals and feline robots. We disagree on the existence of water and cats on Twin Earth. Yet to Putnam and Burge it is obvious that on Twin Earth there is neither water nor cats. They do not make the circular claim that 'water' *means* 'stuff that bears a certain similarity relation to the water around here',[10] but they do insist that water is stuff that bears a certain similarity relation to the water around here. XYZ does not bear that relation to H_2O, and so is not water.

Presumably there is a difference in meaning between 'XYZ is not water' as used by us and as used on Twin Earth. What is at issue here is whether XYZ is water in our sense of 'water'. Unfortunately, Burge gives no account of the sense of 'water', such that

---

[10] Searle's (1983, 204–8) main criticism of Putnam assumes that this claim is being made, since he thinks that giving Fregean account of such locutions (which he does) constitutes an objection to Putnam.

water is H_2O and XYZ is not water.[11] He just assserts that as used on Earth 'water' applies to water and means *water*, and that on Twin Earth it applies to twater (the stuff they call 'water') and means *twater* (1982, 101). However, what these two specifications of meaning specify is utterly obscure. Burge has not begun to explain what is at issue in asserting or denying that XYZ is water. So he is hardly in a position to explain why, for example, Twin Earthlings do not have the concept of water, so that what they express with the words 'Water quenches thirst' is not the belief that water quenches thirst but that twater quenches thirst.

The problem here is not just how to refer to but how to specify the relevant concepts. After all, unlike Putnam Burge maintains that the concept conventionally associated with a word constitutes its meaning. His claim is that Twin Earthlings associate a different concept with 'water' than we do. But what concept is that? Burge refers to it as the concept of twater, but he has not specified it in such a way as to make evident that it is not the same as the concept of water. He has merely labelled it differently.

Perhaps an embellishment of Putnam's thought experiment will help make clear the problem here. As we will see later, Putnam claims that the experiment works even if applied before the chemical composition of water or twater was discovered. So let us turn back the calendar to 1717, when Handel wrote his Water Music and Twin Handel his Water Music (he called twater 'water'), and nobody knew the molecular make-up of what anyone called 'water'. Miraculously, the two composers are talking by futuristic videophone about the première performances of their new works (on the Thames and Twin Thames, respectively). Each asks the other if the performance was as muddy as the water in the Thames (or Twin Thames, not that Twin Handel calls it that, any more than he calls himself 'Twin Handel'). Thus each uses 'water' to refer to the liquid in the other's river. We could ask whether each is unwittingly making a linguistic mistake or perhaps a factual mistake about the stuff in the other's river, but we will take up these questions when we get to Putnam. The question here is what

[11] Putnam's theory of the meaning of terms like 'water' provides a semblance of an account, but only because he includes extension in meaning. Only thus does meaning (trivially) determine extension. Contrary to Burge, Putnam claims that there is but one concept associated with the word (which however does not fully constitute its meaning), so that there is no difference between what we think about H_2O and what Twin Earthlings think about XYZ.

each believes about the contents of the other's river. Does each believe that the other's river contains water, or, as Burge would insist, does only Handel believe that? Each might have wondered whether the two liquids were really the same, but why is it only Handel and not Twin Handel who, according to Burge, could have wondered whether the other's liquid was really water? It would seem, rather, that if the two Handels supposed that there was a difference in composition between the two liquids, they could not reasonably argue about which liquid was really water, much less which one of them really had the concept of water. Yet Burge is committed to the view that only Handel had the concept of water, even though Handel had no reason to think that he was operating with a concept different from Twin Handel's.

If this is not enough of a problem, what if someone on a third planet were eavesdropping on Handel and Twin Handel's conversation? Where he lives they speak English but there is nothing like water and they have a different word for the common liquid there. What reason would he have for thinking that the two Handels were operating with different concepts, and how could he even formulate the question of which of the two really had the concept of water? Even if he knew that there was H_2O on one planet and XYZ on the other, he would have no reason for thinking that only Handel had the concept of water. What is more, even knowing what he knows, how could *he* form the concept of water? Do not forget that Burge is not claiming that 'water' *means* 'H_2O', so that having the concept of H_2O is not the same as having the concept of water.

We could add further embellishments to Burge's thought experiment, but we have gone far enough to conclude that he has not made clear, much less established, his claim that Adam but not Twin Adam has the concept of water.[12] The problem is not that he has failed to show that there is no water on Twin Earth but that, even granting this, he has failed to show what the difference is in

[12] One other difficulty should be noted. I have been going along with Burge who, as philosophers often do, speaks of *the* concept of water, as if there is only one concept of water. In a way, however, *any* concept (expressed by a word) coextensive with 'water' is also a concept of water. Of course, such a concept (e.g. the concept expressed by 'H_2O') would not be identified as the meaning of 'water'. Only the concept that is the meaning of 'water' qualifies as 'the' concept of water. The problem for Burge is that he has no way of specifying this concept without using the word 'water' and yet it is that very word whose meaning is to be specified.

the concepts that Adam and Twin Adam associate with the word 'water'. He has merely asserted that because there is the difference in the liquids on the two planets, Adam's and Twin Adam's concepts are not the same.

3. USES AND EXTENSIONS

No doubt Putnam would object to both Burge's and my concern with concepts. After all, he rejects the Fregean view that the concept associated with a term like 'water' gives its meaning or determines its extension. So he would not object to my resistance to Burge's suggestion that Adam and Twin Adam have different concepts. Now since Putnam denies that satisfying our concept of water is either necessary or sufficient for belonging to the extension of 'water', it is appropriate for him to call this concept the 'stereotype' of water. According to Putnam, for any natural-kind term 'K' it could turn out that most Ks do not satisfy the stereotype associated with 'K' and, as his thought experiments are supposed to show, that things satisfying the stereotype can fail to be Ks.[13] Since neither the stereotype nor any other concept determines the extension of 'K', it is incumbent on Putnam at this point to explain how the extension of 'K' is determined.

Putnam holds that the extension of a natural-kind sortal term 'K' is the set of all things that are called 'K' or are relevantly similar to them. For example, cats are those things that are called 'cats' and things with the same internal structure. Since the things called 'cats' are animals, Martian robots are not relevantly like them and are not cats. However, if the things called 'cats' really are Martian robots (contrary to what we believe, of course) then only feline robots[14] are cats. Now in saying that to be a cat is either to be so-called or to be relevantly similar to things so-called, Putnam is not suggesting that 'cat' *means* 'being called a cat or being relevantly similar to things that are so-called'. That would be a viciously circular definition. Putnam does not offer a definition at all, since

[13] This formulation applies to sortals, but a little rewording would make it apply to mass terms. We would then be talking about being K or a sample of K rather than being a K.

[14] Do they have to be *Martian* robots? Martian robots of a certain design? What if the Martians came up with a new, improved model that was radically different internally, though to us indistinguishable from the previous model?

he denies that any concept associated with the word 'cat' constitutes its meaning or determines its extension.[15]

The key question here concerns the operative notion of similarity and how it enables us, without relying on the concept associated with a given natural-kind term, to project from local samples to the complete extension of the term. We will take up that issue in the next section, but first we should look more closely at Putnam's suggestion that if, for example, the things called 'cats' really are Martian robots then only they are cats. Since he goes into much more detail in making essentially the same point about 'water', we will work with that example.

According to Putnam, no concept of stuff with the familiar superficial properties of water both constitutes the meaning of 'water' and determines its extension. That is because other substances than water could have the superficial properties of water. And not only is having those properties not sufficient for being water, it is not necessary either. A massive illusion might have caused us to have been mistaken all along about the look and feel of water. Putnam holds this even though

It could have turned out that the bits of liquid we call 'water' had no important common physical characteristics except the superficial ones. In that case the necessary and sufficient condition for being 'water' would have been possession of sufficiently many of the superficial characteristics. Incidentally, the last statement does not imply that water could have failed to have a hidden structure (or that water could have been anything but H_2O). When we say that it could have turned out that water had no hidden structure, what we mean is that a liquid with no hidden structure (i.e., many bits of different liquids, with nothing in common except superficial characteristics) could have looked like water, tasted like water, and have filled the lakes, etc., that are actually full of water. In short we could have been in the same epistemological situation with respect to a liquid with no hidden structure as we were actually with respect to water at one time. (1975, 159–60)

We may grant that any liquid with a hidden structure different from H_2O is a different liquid, and that, since water *is* H_2O, such a

---

[15] However, Putnam's view may seem to entail that being a cat requires the actual use of the word 'cat' to refer to cats, so that, for example, if there were no English language there would be no cats. I doubt that his view entails this, but it does seem to entail that if there were no cats, 'cat' would not and could not have the meaning that it has.

liquid is not water. In short, it is metaphysically necessary that water is H_2O. In-so-far as it is not epistemically necessary, that is because what we can imagine not being water is not water but what we would have called 'water', given our epistemological situation. Whether this liquid is XYZ or some heterogeneous mixture, whatever it is it is not water. And if it is indeed heterogeneous then, as Putnam says, 'the necessary and sufficient condition for being "water" would have been possession of sufficiently many of the superficial characteristics'. But this stuff would not be *water*.

Thus Putnam allows that in our ignorance we can associate the same concept with the word 'water' regardless of the sort of stuff the stuff we call 'water' is (if indeed it is a sort in any important way). Yet it qualifies as water only if it is H_2O. As we use the word 'water', water is necessarily H_2O since, as we use the word 'water', we use it to refer to the stuff that is H_2O. Thus, the concept we associate with 'water' does not determine its extension. It is epistemically possible that the extension of 'water' be a different stuff, but then 'water' would have meant something different.[16] The stuff called 'water' would not have been water, in the sense of 'water' as used by us. It would not have been a different kind of water, but water in a different sense.

Of course for Putnam the sense of a word like 'water' is not a matter of what is in the head but of how the word is used. 'Water' is used differently by Twin Earthlings than by us. And since what is in the head, the concept associated with 'water', can be the same while the uses differ, it seems that what distinguishes the uses of the word on the two planets are its different extensions. Putnam asserts that the extension of 'water' is H_2O on Earth and XYZ on Twin Earth, but since he claims that these extensions are not determined by any concept (do not forget that Twin Earthlings associate the same concept with 'water' that we do[17]) but by what is called 'water' on each planet, his implicit principle that extensions

[16] It would have meant something different only if meaning determines extension (in which case its meaning would not be in the head). Of course Putnam denies that meaning determines extension (except in the trivial sense in which, according to him, extension is part of meaning) and holds the strange view that terms like 'water' are indexicals. But if this were so, then there would be no such thing as water *simpliciter*. There would only be water relative to a context, e.g. Earth or Twin Earth.

[17] That is why it is not only paradoxical but inconsistent for Putnam to say that in 1750 'it would have taken their scientific communities about fifty years to discover that they understood the term "water" differently' (1975, 141).

individuate uses seems to have things backwards. It suggests that Twin Earthlings use 'water' differently because they call different stuff 'water'. One would have thought that they call different stuff 'water' because they use 'water' differently. It seems that Putnam's conception of use revolves in a circle: a use of a term is individuated by its extension (hence the different use of 'water'on Twin Earth), but specifying the relevant extension requires knowing what the use is. Putnam's *notion* of use seems strange as well. If Adam were unwittingly teleported to Twin Earth and called 'water' what the locals call 'water', would he be using the term 'water' differently from before?

In any case, how is it, according to Putnam, that here on Earth 'water' has, and always has had, H_2O as its extension? How did its extension get 'fixed' as H_2O long before anyone had any notion of chemical compounds? Evidently, it got so fixed because, whether people knew it or not, H_2O was called 'water' and nothing else was called 'water'. But how did that happen and how do we know that it did? Who's to say that H_2O was called 'water' all along? These questions seem to concern epistemological issues that Putnam dismisses as irrelevant, but the following story suggests otherwise.

Suppose that we are back in the eighteenth century, before we had the wherewithal to detect hidden chemical differences, and assume that all the samples of liquid that have thus far been called 'water' are made up of H_2O. However, there just happen to be many other samples of liquid that are not made up of H_2O but which, had we encountered them, we would have called 'water' anyway. These include bits of XYZ, and mixtures in various proportions of H_2O and XYZ. It is just an unlikely coincidence that all the stuff that has been called 'water' thus far, here in 1750, is H_2O.[18] What is the extension of 'water', pure H_2O or also XYZ and any mixture of H_2O and XYZ? According to Putnam, that is a question of how 'water' has been used, but how *has* it been used? To refer just to H_2O or also to XYZ and any mixture of H_2O and XYZ? In actual fact, it has been used to refer only to H_2O, but that is just a coincidence. If, after 1750, XYZ and mixtures were called

[18] Even today it is possible that there is a lot of XYZ around which we do not know about even though it *has* been encountered. This might be discovered and there might be an explanation for the fact that up until now all samples have been found to be H_2O: previous testing techniques caused the XYZ in the samples to evaporate unnoticed. If this sort of thing seems unlikely, it is no more unlikely than Putnam's tall tale about XYZ on Twin Earth.

'water', as they would have been called all along had they been called anything, would 1750 have marked a change in the use of 'water'? To say that its use would have changed seems arbitrary. The only real change would have been in what samples of liquid were actually called 'water'.

Perhaps Putnam would reply that in this hypothetical situation 'water' would have had a different meaning and that being 'water' in that sense would have been a matter of possessing sufficiently many of the superficial characteristics that we associate with water. He would insist that even in this situation only H_2O is water in *our* sense. That unlikely situation would not threaten his view so much as to provide a further illustration of the fact that extension is not fixed by what is in the head. Putnam could *say* this all right, but our hypothetical situation still exposes the obscurity of the notion of use with which he is operating. The situation is one in which the non-H_2O that would have been called 'water' (if it had been called anything) is *around*. It has not actually been called 'water' only because it has not yet been encountered. But why should it matter that the stuff is around? What if it were miles under the ground, at the bottom of the oceans, on Mars, or only on Twin Earth? People would still call that stuff 'water' if they had access to it. Surely this would not mean that they were using 'water' differently from how it was in fact used at least until 1750.[19]

The same point can be made in terms of the same-liquid relation, which he calls 'theoretical', that Putnam relies on in order to project the use of 'water' from actual cases of liquid called 'water' to the full extension of 'water'. It seems that in our hypothetical situation of 1750 this relation was indeterminate with respect to 'water'. It was not merely unknowable, since, given the skewed selection of samples available then, chemical theory and testing of samples would not have helped. Rather, the predicate 'is called

---

[19] In the context of his discussion of the term 'jade', which applies to two different minerals, Putnam remarks that 'if H_2O and XYZ had both been plentiful on Earth, . . . it would have been correct to say that there were two kinds of "water". And instead of saying that "the stuff on Twin Earth turned out not to really be water", we would have to say "it turned out to be the XYZ kind of water".' (1975, 160) He says, however, that this would not be *water*, since we would be using the term 'water' differently. As things are, we use 'water' to refer to H_2O. In general, 'if there is a hidden structure, then generally it determines what it is to be a member of the natural kind, not only in the actual world, but in all possible worlds'. Unfortunately, Putnam gives no account of why, just because the extension of 'water' is, in fact, a natural kind, the *word* belongs to a *semantic* natural kind.

"water" ' was unprojectible. Therefore, from Putnam's point of view the word 'water' had no determinate extension in 1750. But it did. Its extension was all of the stuff made up of any combination of H_2O and XYZ. Thus, in our imaginary situation the extension of 'water' is not fixed by what is called 'water'. That should come as no surprise: being called 'water' is not what makes water water.

4. RELEVANT SIMILARITY

The most obvious impurity in Putnam's 'water' treatment is the vagueness of the all-important similarity relation. It is supposed to provide the basis for projecting the predicate 'is called "water" ' and thereby determining the extension of 'water'. One problem is that the relevant similarity relation will vary, depending on the sort of term involved. It is different for 'cat' than for 'water'. Perhaps there are terms of the same sort which have been applied so far to exactly the same items and yet have different extensions. That could happen only if different similarity relations are involved. Then we would need an account of how each relation is determined, but for Putnam no appeal to the meanings of the terms would be allowed. Ignoring these problems, let us take up merely the problem of determining the relevant similarity relation in the case of 'water'.

According to Putnam, ' "water" is stuff that bears a certain similarity relation to water around here'[20] (1975, 152). What is the similarity relation such that any liquid bearing it to water around here, that is the stuff we call 'water', qualifies as water? XYZ is not relevantly similar. What about so-called heavy water? Pure heavy water, containing deuterium and no ordinary hydrogen, is different in various ways from every natural water sample. Yet it counts as water and presumably did so before it was discovered or ever called 'water'. Even rarer is heavy heavy water, containing radioactive tritium. It is very different from regular water. Yet it too counts as

---

[20] This formulation suggests that what qualifies as water around here is already determined. That is why I assume that Putnam means 'stuff called "water" around here'. But we must be careful even with that phrasing, because we cannot take it to include the bits of liquid that we have not actually encountered and called 'water'. They can be said to be called 'water' in this broader sense only if we assume that they belong to the extension of 'water', but what belongs to the extension of 'water' is precisely what is in question.

water. Is that because it is a form of H_2O or because of its superficial similarities to ordinary water?

Putnam says that being the same liquid as is a theoretical relation, so that it is a theoretical question whether a given sample of liquid is water, that is bears that relation 'to most of the stuff I and other speakers in my linguistic community have on other occasions called "water" ' (1975, 141–2). However, two samples of liquid could be the same according to one theory and different according to another. Indeed, according to just one theory they could be the same in one respect and different in another. According to present-day physical theory, heavy water is the same as water in one respect but different in another. It is not obvious from physical theory why *we* count heavy water as water. Physical theory is not semantics and is silent on the question of which relation (of being the same liquid as) is the one that counts for the purposes of applying a word like 'water'. Do not forget, 'water' is not a term of physical theory. Or suppose that there is a lot of XYZ scattered about on Earth and that this stuff is actually H_4O_2. Chemically it behaves pretty much like H_2O, even though its molecular make-up is different. We would have been calling it 'water' all along, despite the molecular difference. Physical theory does not tell us which similarity relations count and which do not. Putnam's theory is supposed to apply to natural-kind terms in common usage, not just in scientific usage, but there can be many similarity relations, each of which justifies grouping together certain items (or bits of stuff) for one theoretical purpose or another. So he should explain why one similarity relation rather than another is relevant to the common usage of such a term.

5. THE DIVISION OF LINGUISTIC LABOUR

Putnam does not offer such an account, but perhaps his notion of the 'division of linguistic labor' (1975, 144–6) is applicable here. The idea is that the criteria of application for certain terms are known only to the experts and that everyone else who acquires such a term defers to the these experts regarding its application. This idea seems plausible with technical terms like 'arthropod', 'deciduous', and 'molybdenum', of whose meanings most people are partially or totally ignorant, but it is less plausible with common terms like 'fish', 'elm', and 'aluminium'. Many people regard dolphins and whales as fish, even though they do not belong to the class Pisces but are mammals. A lot óf people, including biologists (to whom others presumably defer), deny that dolphins and whales are fish. Who is correct? One possibility is that biologists, in so far as they use the word 'fish' at all, mean something more specific by it than do the masses. The interesting question is what 'fish' means to those who do defer to the biologists and agree, without knowing why, that dolphins and whales are not fish. What does 'fish' mean to them? They would seem to have the ordinary concept of fish, yet they think 'fish' means something more specific than that. They do not know what, but they do believe that biologists know. In disbelieving that dolphins and whales are fish but without knowing why, they must believe that fish are whatever biologists say fish are. Evidently, they use 'fish' to mean whatever it means to biologists. But of course to these laymen the word 'fish' does not itself mean 'whatever "fish" means to biologists'. 'Fish' really has no definite meaning to them, though of course they are confident that it has a definite meaning to biologists. Putnam just seems to assume that a person who defers to the experts on a term like 'fish', 'elm', or 'aluminium' nevertheless understands the term. Yet it is perfectly possible for people to use a word without fully understanding it. Perhaps that is all the division of linguistic labour amounts to.

In considering whether it amounts to anything more than that, we must keep in mind that if a speaker really defers to the experts on what, say, aluminium is, he is effectively acknowledging his own ignorance of what counts as aluminium. Now Putnam thinks that such a person has 'acquired' the word 'aluminium'; surely in some sense he has. But the question is whether he understands it in the sense in which he acknowledges the authority of the experts. Putnam remarks,

Whenever a term is subject to the division of linguistic labor, the 'average' speaker who acquires it does not acquire anything that fixes its extension. In particular, his individual psychological state certainly does not fix its extension; it is only the sociolinguistic state of the collective linguistic body to which the speaker belongs that fixes the extension. (1975, 146)

It is true that the average speaker who acquires such a term does not acquire anything that fixes its extension.[21] No concept that the

---

[21] It is not exactly clear how, according to Putnam, the 'sociolinguistic state of the collective linguistic body' fixes the extension, since it is anything but clear what a

speaker associates with the term fixes its extension, and if meaning determines extension this concept cannot constitute the meaning. But Putnam does not ask whether the speaker who acquires the term understands it, evidently because he equates acquiring a term with understanding it. As I will now argue, the distinction between the two deprives the division of linguistic labour of its apparent significance.

Each of us knows of terms in English that we do not understand at all. Have we 'acquired' these terms, in Putnam's sense? Presumably not, since we cannot use them with any comprehension but only mouth them. What about terms that we but partially understand? Before I looked up 'mauve' and 'puce' in the dictionary, I knew only that they were colour words. I did not know whether they were shades of red, green, or what. Had I acquired them? I am inclined to say that I had not, although I could use those terms in a limited way. What then about Putnam's examples of 'beech' and 'molybdenum'? He claims to have acquired these terms even though he does not know the difference between beech trees and elm trees or the difference between molybdenum and aluminium. All he claims to know about 'molybdenum', for example, is that it designates a metallic element somewhat similar to aluminium. He does not know whether pots and pans can be made out of molybdenum or, if so, whether they could be distinguished easily from ones made out of aluminium. Indeed, he supposes that they can be distinguished only by an expert and that this 'could be true for all I know by virtue of "knowing the meaning" of the words *aluminium* and *molybdenum*' (1975, 142). However, he has not shown that he does know the meaning of the word 'molybdenum'. Ditto for 'beech'. Putnam is quite right to say that the concepts he associates with these terms do not fix the extensions of these terms, but those concepts are not even candidates for being their meanings inasmuch as he does not fully understand the terms.

Evidence for his lack of full understanding of 'elm' and 'beech', for example, consists precisely in the admitted fact that he associates the same concept with both and yet believes that beeches

socio-linguistic state is. Evidently Putnam believes that the notions of language in a community and of linguistic meaning are not reducible to idiolect and meaning to a person, but he never defends his view. This view does not obviously follow from the claim that extension is fixed communally.

are not elms.[22] I conjecture that what disinclines Putnam to deny that he understands these words is that he can use them, for example to express the belief that beeches are not elms. However, being able to use them in this way does not demonstrate understanding them. Indeed, the belief Putnam has, as opposed to the one he would express, in saying 'Beeches are not elms' does not contain the concepts that constitute the meanings of 'elm' and of 'beech', inasmuch as he is thinking of beeches/elms under the concepts 'trees of the kind that experts call "beeches"/"elms" '. These concepts are coextensive with the concepts expressed by 'beeches' and 'elms', but they hardly constitute the meanings of those words.

Thus Putnam's own examples show that acquiring a word is a matter of degree. On one extreme is merely knowing of a certain word. On the other is understanding it fully. In between is knowing its syntactic category, knowing its semantic type, and roughly understanding it. No one fully understands all the words of English. Like most languages English is a mass production, and there is nothing particularly interesting or startling about the division of linguistic labour. The fact that people often defer to others on words they do not understand at all or not fully, not to mention the fact that they are willing to acknowledge linguistic errors, does not show that what determines extension is the sociolinguistic state of the linguistic community. We could just as well take it as showing (Putnam gives no reason for denying) that the notion of a language is an idealization of the notion of an idiolect.[23]

Putnam (and also Kripke 1980, 118) is reluctant to allow that such terms as 'water', 'gold', 'fish', and 'tiger' are ambiguous, with both a vulgar and a scientific meaning. Even if this is correct, it implies that people who need to defer to scientists on the (unitary) meaning of a term do not understand it themselves. Nothing important for the theory of meaning follows from that. Of course

---

[22] The same point is made by Searle (1983, 202).

[23] The idea here is that the idealization constituting a natural language factors out interpersonal variations in lexicon, syntax, and semantics. Also, allowances have to be made for the fact that no user of a language knows it fully, either lexically or syntactically. This does not mean, however, that a language, unless considered as an abstract entity (say as a mapping from forms to meanings), somehow has an existence apart from its users. Facts about English seem to reduce to facts about users of English, including facts about the way they defer to experts and acknowledge errors.

the meaning of a term is not in the head of a person who does not
understand it.

Not only does Putnam claim that a term like 'water' has but one
meaning today, he maintains that it had that meaning way back
when the chemical constitution of water was not yet known. He
cheerfully allows that people did not fully understand the term,
and asserts that if there were a lot of XYZ around here, 'water'
would not mean what it means in fact. This would not be a case
of two kinds of water in our sense of 'water'. We have addressed
these claims already, but now I want to raise a more fundamental point about the semantic relevance of natural-kind
terms.

Recall the conversation between Handel and Twin Handel, who
complained that the première performances of their respective
compositions of 'Water Music' were as muddy as the rivers on
which the music was played. According to Putnam, they used
'water' differently, but what about the word 'mud'? If Handel
meant by it a mixture of dirt and water, Twin Handel must have
meant something else, yet obviously he did not. Putnam would
explain this by saying, quite correctly, that 'mud' is not a natural-
kind term, but what entitles him to say this? Why should not
Putnam take the same position about 'mud' as he does about
'water'? In 1750 the epistemological situation with 'mud' was the
same as with 'water'. Putnam should say that people did not fully
understand 'mud' and that if, contrary to fact, what was called
'mud' contained XYZ, 'mud' would not have meant what it did in
fact. There would not have been two kinds of mud in our sense of
'mud'.

What reason is there for claiming a semantic difference between
'water' and 'mud'? Water may be a natural kind in a way in which
mud is not, but this is a matter of empirical fact that could not have
affected the meaning of the word 'water' in Handel's time. That
water is a natural kind and mud is not does not establish a
difference in semantic category between 'water' and 'mud'.
Putnam is implicitly making the undefended assumption that
because a term applies to a natural kind, it belongs to a special

semantic category, the category of natural-kind terms. He has given no reason for claiming that the terms that refer to natural kinds make up a natural kind for semantics.

Bibliography

Ackerman, D. (1979), 'Proper names, propositional attitudes, and non-descriptive connotations', *Philosophical Studies* 35: 55–9.

Atlas, J. (1977), 'Negation, ambiguity, and presupposition', *Linguistics and Philosophy* 1: 321–36.

Austin, J. L. (1962), *How to Do Things with Words*, Cambridge, Mass.: Harvard University Press.

Bach, K. (1982), '*De re* belief and methodological solipsism' in A. Woodfield (ed.), *Thought and Object*, Oxford: Oxford University Press.

—— (1984), 'Default reasoning', *Pacific Philosophical Quarterly* 65: 35–56.

—— and R. Harnish (1979), *Linguistic Communication and Speech Acts*, Cambridge, Mass.: MIT Press.

—— —— (1982), 'Katz as Katz can', *Journal of Philosophy* 79: 168–71.

Barwise, J., and R. Cooper (1981), 'Generalized quantifiers and natural language', *Linguistics and Philosophy* 4: 159–219.

—— and J. Perry (1983), *Situation Semantics*, Cambridge, Mass.: MIT Press.

Beebe, M. (1979), 'How beliefs find their objects', *Canadian Journal of Philosophy* 9: 595–608.

Bertolet, R. (1980), 'The semantic significance of Donnellan's distinction', *Philosophical Studies* 37: 281–8.

Boer, S. (1975), 'Proper names as predicates', *Philosophical Studies* 27: 389–400.

—— and W. Lycan (1975), 'Knowing who', *Philosophical Studies* 28: 299–344.

Burge, T. (1973), 'Reference and proper names', *Journal of Philosophy* 70: 425–39.

—— (1977), 'Belief *de re*', *Journal of Philosophy* 74: 338–62.

—— (1979), 'Individualism and the mental', *Midwest Studies in Philosophy* 4: 73–121.

—— (1979a), 'Sinning against Frege', *Philosophical Review* 88: 398–432.

—— (1982), 'Other bodies' in A. Woodfield, (ed.), *Thought and Object*, Oxford: Oxford University Press.

—— (1986), 'Intellectual norms and foundations of mind', *Journal of Philosophy* 83: 697–720.

Chastain, C. (1975), 'Reference and context' in K. Gunderson (ed.), *Language, Mind, and Knowledge*, Minneapolis: University of Minnesota Press.

Chisholm, R. (1957), *Perceiving: A Philosophical Study*, Ithaca, NY: Cornell University Press.

—— (1980), 'The logic of believing', *Pacific Philosophical Quarterly* 61: 31–49.

Chomsky, N. (1981), *Lectures on Government and Binding*, Dordrecht, Holland: Foris Publications.

Cooper, R. (1983), *Quantification and Syntactic Theory*, Dordrecht, Holland: Reidel.

Cresswell, M. (1985), *Structured Meanings: The Semantics of Propositional Attitudes*, Cambridge, Mass.: MIT Press.

Dennett, D. (1982), 'Beyond belief' in A. Woodfield (ed.), *Thought and Object*, Oxford: Oxford University Press.

Devitt, M. (1974), 'Singular terms', *Journal of Philosophy* 71: 183–205.

—— (1980), *Designation*, New York: Columbia University Press.

—— (1981), 'Donnellan's distinction', *Midwest Studies in Philosophy* 6: 511–24.

Donnellan, K. (1966), 'Reference and definite descriptions', *Philosophical Review* 75: 281–304.

—— (1968), 'Putting Humpty Dumpty together again', *Philosophical Review* 77: 203–15.

—— (1974), 'Speaking of nothing', *Philosophical Review* 83: 3–32.

Evans, G. (1980), 'Pronouns', *Linguistic Inquiry* 11: 337–62.

—— (1982), *The Varieties of Reference*, edited by J. McDowell, Oxford: Oxford University Press.

Farmer, A. (1984), *Modularity in Syntax*, Cambridge, Mass.: MIT Press.

Fodor, J. (1980), 'Methodological solipsism considered as a research strategy in cognitive psychology', *The Behavioural and Brain Sciences* 3: 63–73.

Frege, G. (1892), 'On sense and reference', in P. Geach and M. Black (eds.) (1966), *Translations of the Philosophical Writings of Gottlob Frege*, Oxford: Blackwell.

—— (1918), 'The thought: a logical inquiry', trans. by A. and M. Quinton, *Mind* 65 (1956): 289–311.

Geach, P. (1967), 'Intentional identity', *Journal of Philosophy* 64: 627–32.

Grice, H. P. (1957), 'Meaning', *Philosophical Review* 66: 377–88.

—— (1968), 'Utterer's meaning, sentence-meaning and word meaning', *Foundations of Language* 4: 225–42.

—— (1969), 'Vacuous names' in D. Davidson and J. Hintikka (eds.), *Words and Objections*, Dordrecht, Holland: Reidel.

—— (1975), 'Logic and conversation' in D. Davidson and G. Harman (eds.), *The Logic of Grammar*, Encino, Calif.: Dickenson Publishing Co.

Harman, G. (1973), *Thought*, Princeton, NJ: Princeton University Press.

Heny, F. (ed.) (1981), *Ambiguities in Intensional Contexts*, Dordrecht, Holland: Reidel.

Higginbotham, J. (1983), 'Logical form, binding, and nominals', *Linguistic Inquiry* 14: 395–420.

Hornstein, N. (1984), *Logic as Grammar*, Cambridge, Mass.: MIT Press.

Kaplan, D. (1968), 'Quantifying in', *Synthese* 19: 178–214.

—— (1979), 'Dthat' in P. French *et al.* (eds.), *Contemporary Perspectives in the Philosophy of Language*, Minneapolis: University of Minnesota Press.

Katz, J. (1977), *Propositional Structure and Illocutionary Force*, New York: Crowell.

—— (1978), 'The theory of semantic representation', *Erkenntnis* 13: 63–109.

Kim, J. (1977), 'Perception and reference without causality', *Journal of Philosophy* 74: 606–20.

Kripke, S. (1971), 'Identity and necessity', in M. Munitz (ed.), *Identity and Individuation*, New York: New York University Press.

—— (1977), 'Speaker's reference and semantic reference', *Midwest Studies in Philosophy* 2: 255–76.

—— (1979), 'A puzzle about belief' in A. Margalit (ed.), *Meaning and Use*, 239–83, Dordrecht, Holland: Reidel.

—— (1980), *Naming and Necessity*, Cambridge, Mass.: Harvard University Press.

Lasnik, H. (1976), 'Remarks on coreference', *Linguistic Analysis* 2: 1–22.

Lewis, D. (1983), 'Truth in fiction', in *Philosophical Papers*, vol. 1, Oxford: Oxford University Press.

Loar, B. (1972), 'Reference and propositional attitudes', *Philosophical Review* 80: 43–62.

—— (1976), 'The semantics of singular terms', *Philosophical Studies* 30: 353–77.

—— (1980), 'Names and descriptions: a reply to Michael Devitt', *Philosophical Studies* 38: 85–9.

Lycan, W. (1984), *Logical Form in Natural Language*, Cambridge, Mass.: MIT Press.

McCray, A. (1980), 'The semantics of backward anaphora', in T. Jensen (ed.), *Proceedings of the Tenth Annual Meeting of the North Eastern Linguistics Society*, 10, Ottawa.

McGinn, C. (1982), 'The structure of content' in A. Woodfield (ed.), *Thought and Object*, Oxford: Oxford University Press.

Martin, C., and M. Deutscher (1966), 'Memory', *Philosophical Review* 75: 161–96.

Mill, J. (1872), A System of Logic, definitive 8th edition, London.

Montague, R. (1974), 'The proper treatment of quantification in ordinary English' in R. Thomason (ed.), *Formal Philosophy*, New Haven: Yale University Press.

Nunberg, G. (1979), 'The non-uniqueness of semantic solutions: polysemy', *Linguistics and Philosophy* 3: 143–84.

Partee, B. (1972), 'Opacity, coreference, and pronouns' in G. Harman and D. Davidson (eds.), *Semantics of Natural Language*, Dordrecht, Holland: Reidel.

Peacocke, C. (1975), 'Proper names, reference, and rigid designation' in S. Blackburn (ed.), *Meaning, Reference and Necessity*, Cambridge: Cambridge University Press.

—— (1979), *Holistic Explanation*, Oxford: Clarendon Press.

Perry, J. (1979), 'The problem of the essential indexical', *Nous* 13: 3–21.

—— (1980), 'A problem about continued belief', *Pacific Philosophical Quarterly* 61: 317–32.

Pollock, J. (1980), 'Thinking about an object', *Midwest Studies in Philosophy* 5: 487–99.

Putnam, H. (1962), 'It ain't necessarily so', *Journal of Philosophy* 59: 658–71.

—— (1975), 'The Meaning of meaning' in K. Gunderson (ed.), *Language, Mind, and Knowledge*, Minneapolis: University of Minnesota Press.

Quine, W. V. (1956), 'Quantifiers and propositional attitudes', *Journal of Philosophy* 53: 177–87.

—— (1960), *Word and Object*, Cambridge, Mass.: MIT Press.

Reinhart, T. (1983), *Anaphora and Semantic Interpretation*, London: Croom Helm.

Russell, B. (1905), 'On denoting', reprinted in R. Marsh (ed.) (1956), *Logic and Knowledge*, London: George Allen & Unwin.

—— (1918), 'The philosophy of logical atomism', reprinted in R. Marsh (ed.) (1956), *Logic and Knowledge*, London: George Allen & Unwin.

—— (1919), 'Descriptions', chapter 16 of *Introduction to Mathematical Philosophy*, London: George Allen & Unwin.

Salmon, N. (1982), 'Assertion and incomplete definite descriptions', *Philosophical Studies* 42: 37–45.

Schiffer, S. (1977), 'Naming and knowing', *Midwest Studies in Philosophy* 2: 28–41.

—— (1978), 'The basis of reference', *Erkenntnis* 13: 171–206.

—— (1981), 'Indexicals and the theory of reference', *Synthese* 49: 43–100.

Searle, J. (1958), 'Proper names', *Mind* 67: 166–73.

—— (1968), 'Austin on locutionary and illocutionary acts', *Philosophical Review* 77: 405–24.

—— (1969), *Speech Acts*, Cambridge: Cambridge University Press.

—— (1979), 'Referential and attributive' in *Expression and Meaning*, Cambridge: Cambridge University Press.

—— (1983), *Intentionality*, Cambridge: Cambridge University Press.

Soames, S., and D. Perlmutter (1979), *Syntactic Argumentation and the Structure of English*, Berkeley and Los Angeles: University of California Press.

Stich, S. (1978), 'Autonomous psychology and the belief–desire thesis', *The Monist* 61: 573–91.

Strawson, P. F. (1950), 'On referring', reprinted in J. Rosenberg and C. Travis (eds.) (1971), *Readings in the Philosophy of Language*, Englewood Cliffs, NJ: Prentice–Hall.

—— (1952), *Introduction to Logical Theory*, London: Methuen.

—— (1959), *Individuals: An Essay in Descriptive Metaphysics*, London: Methuen.

Unger, P. (1983), 'The causal theory of reference', *Philosophical Studies* 43: 1–45.

Walton, K. (1978), 'On fearing fictions', *Journal of Philosophy* 75: 5–27.

Wasow, T. (1979), 'Problems with pronouns in transformational grammar' in F. Heny and H. Schnelle (eds.), *Syntax and Semantics* vol. 10, New York: Academic Press.

Wettstein, H. (1979), 'Indexical reference and propositional content', *Philosophical Studies* 36: 91–100.

—— (1981), 'Demonstrative reference and definite descriptions', *Philosophical Studies* 40: 241–57.

Wittgenstein, L. (1953), *Philosophical Investigations*, trans by G. E. M. Anscombe, Oxford: Blackwell.

Glossary

Listed below for convenient reference are expressions which were introduced by small capital letters in the text. A brief explanation is given of my use of each item, be it a common technical term or part of my own terminology.

ANAPHORIC reference: reference to something previously mentioned.

ATTRIBUTIVE USE: use of a definite description to make a descriptive reference (intuitively, to make a statement about a unique individual of a certain sort).

CAUSAL THEORY OF REFERENCE: theory of linguistic reference (by proper names) in terms of causal/historical chains.

C-NON-LITERAL utterance: utterance of a sentence involving the non-literal use of a specific constituent of that sentence.

COLLECTIVE reference: (plural) reference to several individuals considered together.

COMMUNICATION-BASED *de re* thought: *de re* belief (or other thought) whose object is represented by a name acquired through communication.

COMMUNICATIVE PRESUMPTION: in a speech situation, presumption (mutual belief) among participants that each utterance is made with a recognizable communicative intention.

COMPLETION (of a definite description): result of inserting qualifying material into an incomplete definite description to make it complete.

DE DICTO (DESCRIPTIVE) BELIEF: belief about an object in virtue of the object's uniquely falling under a certain concept (satisfying a certain definite description) in the content of the belief.

DEFERRED reference: indirect and non-literal reference to an object.

DEMONSTRATIVE reference: reference, typically by gesturing, to something in the perceptual environment.

DENOTATION: linguistic reference.

DE RE BELIEF: intuitively, belief about some object in particular; in my view, belief (token) whose object is determined by a special relation to that very belief token.

DESCRIPTION SENTENCE: sentence containing a definite description in subject position and expressing a uniqueness proposition; the primary target of Russell's theory of descriptions.

DESCRIPTIVE reference: reference with the intention to be talking about whichever individual uniquely satisfies a certain individual concept.

DISTRIBUTIVE reference: (plural) reference to several individuals considered separately.

E-TYPE PRONOUN: pronoun whose antecedent is a quantifier phrase but which is not bound by that phrase.

EXPRESSING AN ATTITUDE: intending (reflexively) one's audience to take one's utterance as reason to think one has that attitude; the type of attitude individuates the type of communicative illocutionary act being performed.

FALL-BACK DESCRIPTION: in a referential use of a definite description, another description which, though not used, is intended to pick out the referent.

FILE: set of beliefs, often labelled with a name, stored together and about a single (actual or putative) individual; basis for implicit identity beliefs, under different modes of presentation, about that individual.

ILLOCUTIONARY ACT: act performed in saying something (in performing a locutionary act); can be conventional or communicative.

INCOMPLETE definite description: definite description whose predicative content is not uniquely satisfied.

INDEFINITE DESCRIPTION: common noun preceded by the indefinite article.

INDEXICAL SENTENCE: sentence containing an indexical or demonstrative term or phrase in subject position.

INDIRECT reference: reference to one thing by way of reference to another.

INEXPLICIT reference: reference in which the expression used, even accompanied by a gesture, does not pick out the referent uniquely, so that the referent must be identified on the basis of other factors as well.

LINGUISTIC PRESUMPTION: in a speech situation, presumption (mutual belief) among participants that they share the language being used.

LINGUISTIC REFERENCE: designation of something by an expression.

LOCUTIONARY ACT: act of saying something, whose content is determined by (a) meaning of the uttered sentence.

MEMORY-BASED *de re* thought: *de re* belief (or other thought) whose object is represented by a memory, which is a trace of a perception (or of a prior memory) of that object.

MERGING (of files): joining of files on putatively distinct individuals when one comes to believe that they are one and the same.

MODE OF PRESENTATION: way of thinking of something, whether descriptively or in a *de re* way.

MUTUAL CONTEXTUAL BELIEF: salient contextual information in a communicative situation; a belief which the participants share, believe one another to share, and believe one another to believe one another to share.

NOMINAL DESCRIPTION THEORY (NDT): thesis that a proper name 'N' is semantically equivalent to the description 'the bearer of "N" '.

NON-LITERAL reference: reference in which the expression used does not apply to the referent.

NON-STANDARD QUANTIFIER: quantifier term which cannot be represented formally by the existential and/or universal quantifiers of ordinary logic.

OBJECTUAL reference: reference to a certain individual with no specific intention as to how the audience is to identify that individual.

PERCEPT: content of a perceptual state individuated by a way in which an object can appear; hence a perceptual mode of presentation.

PERCEPTION-BASED *de re* thought: *de re* belief (or other thought) whose object is represented by a percept.

PLURAL reference: reference to more than one individual.

PRAGMATICS: theory of language use, that is, of communication and speech acts.

PRESUMPTION OF LITERALITY: in a speech situation, presumption (mutual belief) among participants that a given utterance is to be taken literally—unless there is reason to take it otherwise.

PRIORITY: in a referential use of a definite description, the ability of another phrase (such as a fall-back description), which is not uttered, to determine the referent.

PSYCHOSEMANTICS: theory of contents of propositional attitudes.

QUANTIFIER PHRASE: noun phrase introduced by a quantifier term.

QUANTIFIER SENTENCE: sentence with a quantifier phrase in subject position.

REFERENTIAL CONSTRAINT: restriction on what a given pronoun can be used to refer to literally.

REFERENTIALLY INDETERMINATE sentence: sentence lacking a determinate truth condition because of containing a referring expression, such as an indexical, whose meaning cannot determine the intended referent.

REFERENTIAL OPACITY: property of an occurrence of an expression such that existential generalization or substitution of a co-referring expression may affect truth value.

REFERENTIAL TRANSPARENCY: occurrence of an expression where existential generalization and substitution of a co-referring expression cannot affect truth value.

REFERENTIAL USE: use of a definite description to make an objectual reference (intuitively, to make a statement about some individual in particular).

REFERRING EXPRESSION: expression capable of being used to refer, either to one or more individuals.

RELATIONAL determination of an object of a belief (token): determination a matter of which individual stands in the appropriate causal connection to the belief token.

SATISFACTIONAL determination of an object of a belief: determination a matter of which individual uniquely falls under a certain concept (expressed by a definite description) in the content of the belief.

SEMANTICALLY INDETERMINATE sentence: sentence lacking a determinate truth condition, even modulo indexicality; sentence not expressing a complete thought.

SEMANTICS: theory of linguistic meaning (of expression/sentence types, not tokens).

SHARED NAME: proper name with more than one bearer.

SINGULAR: reference: reference to a single individual.

SINGULAR TERM: expression capable of being used to refer to an individual.

SINGULAR STATEMENT: statement about a certain individual, which is referred to objectually.

S-NON-LITERAL utterance: non-literal use of a sentence without any of its constituents being used non-literally.

SPEAKER REFERENCE: use of a term or phrase in an utterance to indicate to one's audience who/what one is expressing an attitude about.

STANDARD QUANTIFIER: quantifier term which can be represented formally by the existential or universal quantifiers of ordinary logic.

TRACE: memory of an object derived from a perception of that object.

UNIQUENESS PROPOSITION: a general proposition implying the existence of a unique object of a certain sort.

UNSPECIFIED REFERENCE: inexplicit reference to something under the description 'what I have mind'.

Postscript
to the Paperback Edition

All the main topics of this book have received considerable attention since the book first appeared. The main purpose of this postscript is to provide an update on relevant developments, with references to important recent work, particularly as it bears, either explicitly or by implication, on views proposed here. In some cases this work sheds new light on these topics, whether by offering new ideas or by clarifying the issues, and in some cases it raises difficulties that need to be resolved or at least acknowledged. In the course of identifying these recent developments, I hope to clarify my views and the reasons for them. This postscript is divided into sections corresponding to the four parts of the book, with subsections in the order of main topics. Page and section references are to this book unless otherwise indicated. All other references are new and collected at the end.

I should begin with the general observation that there has been a growing appreciation of the importance of separating problems of singular thought from those of singular reference and of distinguishing questions of pragmatics from those of semantics. So, for example, it is now widely recognized that singular thoughts are to be characterized by relations between thinkers and objects rather than by how their objects are referred to. It is also widely recognized that singular terms of all sorts (definite descriptions, proper names, demonstratives, and indexicals) can, despite their diverse semantic features, play similar roles in the expression of singular thoughts. On the other hand, they all can also occur in the expression of non-singular thoughts, by being used to refer in but a weak, descriptive sense, that is, to a unique individual of a certain kind rather than to a certain individual in particular.

1. SINGULAR THOUGHT

The problem of singular thought, as part of the general philosophical problem of intentionality, is to explain how some thoughts can be about particular things external to oneself. These thoughts contrast with those whose contents are uniqueness propositions (propositions whose truth conditions require merely the existence of a unique object of a certain sort), which are general, not singular. That is, it does not count as singular thought to think of an object under a description, as the item which satisfies a certain definite description. My account of singular thought is not satisfactional but relational. It identifies three types of *de re* relation, corresponding to the information sources of perception, memory, or communication, that cạn determine a thought's object. Relying on the notion of *de re* mode of presentation, this account is Fregean rather than Russellian in three respects. First, it denies that singular thoughts are simply relations to singular propositions. Second, it rejects (2.3) what Evans calls Russell's Principle, that the thinker must be able to identify the object of a singular thought. Third, it does not entail that the existence of a singular thought is dependent on that of its object. In the last two respects it differs from Evans's account, which though billed as Fregean is anything but. This billing was based on Evans's Russellian reading of Frege, but, as David Bell (1990) has argued in his aptly titled 'How "Russellian" was Frege?', that reading is quite at odds with Frege's texts.

What singular thought is not. My account of singular thought does not lead to the provocative view, championed by John McDowell (1984, 1986) following Evans, that singular thoughts are object-dependent. This view has been resisted by a number of philosophers (Blackburn 1984, ch. 9, Carruthers 1987, Segal 1989, and Noonan 1991), but lately it has been defended by Adams, Fuller, and Stecker (1993). However, their counter-arguments depend on the supposition that non-object-dependent thoughts are either 'incomplete or general' (1993, 101). They are correct to suppose that genuine singular thought is different from and not reducible to general or descriptive thought, but they are wrong to infer from this that singular thoughts without objects can be represented simply by open sentences, with no indication of how the object is contextually determined (1.3). They fail to consider that singular thoughts are indexical and that the (causal–historical) relation that determines the object of a thought token relative to its context is itself determined by the form of the thought. On my account the object of a singular thought token is the item which stands in this relation to that very thought token (of course this applies only to concrete objects, not to abstract objects or to places and times—singular thoughts of times and places are relational, but the relation in question is not causal–historical). Consequently, singular or *de re* modes of presentation, which function as mental indexicals, can be individuated independently of their objects, so that the singular thoughts they belong to are themselves not object-dependent.

My reasons for denying that singular thought is reducible to general or descriptive thought are complemented by Tyler Burge (1991) and by McDowell (1991) in their criticisms of John Searle's descriptive theory. Searle's (1991) reply is subtle, especially in how he explains that his view does not require that contextual relations be explicitly represented. However, he does not seem to appreciate the complaint, which I had previously registered (p. 19 n.), that the object of a singular thought need not be represented descriptively *as* the item which stands in a certain relation to that very thought (token), i.e., that the object is not determined satisfactionally.

François Recanati (1993, 98–106) utilizes the relational conception of singular thoughts to explain how they can be non-descriptive without being object-dependent. Objecting specifically to McDowell's concept of *de re* senses, which are individuated by their objects, he argues that the non-descriptiveness of *de re* modes of presentation consists in their 'truth-conditional irrelevance'. Recanati's idea here is that an object must be thought of and referred to under some aspect or other but that this aspect does not enter into truth-conditional content. If it did, then the thought in question would be general (i.e. descriptive), not singular.

Mental indexicals. Although I did not articulate the notion of truth-conditional irrelevance, I think it is fair to say that this notion is built into my characterization of *de re* modes of presentation as mental indexicals (Chapter 1) and, for that matter, into my account of the semantics of natural language indexicals in terms of referential constraints (9.4). This is clear in the latter case, for the referential constraint on a pronoun or any other indexical in natural language is not synonymous or interchangeable with the pronoun. For example, 'the person I am now addressing' gives the referential constraint on 'you' but is not interchangeable with it. Why *de re* modes of presentation are truth-conditionally irrelevant is a more subtle manner. As explained in 1.3, a *de re* mode of presentation determines the relation which determines the object that a thought of a certain form is about in a given context. The truth condition of the thought token involves the object itself, rather than the operative way of thinking of it.

The notion of mental indexicals has been utilized lately by several philosophers, notably Recanati and Graeme Forbes (1989, 1990), both of whom have developed the conception of mental names as labels attached to files on individuals (2.2). Both accounts are very interesting but too complex to summarize here. I might mention that Recanati develops my suggestion (p. 36) that we operate with temporary files labelled with indexicals or demonstratives and that Forbes incorporates the idea of files into a model of the 'mental operating system' at the centre of our 'cognitive architecture'. Also, Forbes mentions an interesting phenomenon that I over-looked. He suggests, as I do (p. 37), that when one comes to believe an identity, two files on ostensibly distinct individuals come to be merged, but he also points out that after the merging one can, at least for a while, distinguish what one believed about the individual in question under each of the two modes of presentation. That is, the merging does not immediately obliterate the two original files. Even so, the two files have effectively merged because anything one comes to believe of the individual under one mode of presentation one automatically believes of that individual under the other.

2. SINGULAR REFERENCE

Singular thought and singular reference. Singular reference, as something that speakers do, is characterized in Chapter 3 in terms of referential intentions (they are constituents of communicative intentions). This point needs to be stressed, because philosophers have continued to speak loosely when describing referential intentions. A referential intention is not just any intention to talk about or call one's audience's attention to something (3.1). For example, in the context of demonstrating something it is the intention for one's audience to think of a certain item *as* that which one is pointing at and thereby intending to be talking about (see 'Intending and demonstrating' at the end of the next section). Also, singular reference need not involve the expression of a singular thought. What is relevant here is not how one thinks of the object but whether it, rather than the way in which one refers to it, enters into the truth condition (3.5). As Recanati explains (1993, 46–8), when the mode of referring is truth-conditionally irrelevant to an utterance, the object itself must be identified if the utterance is to be understood. However, complete communicative success requires that the hearer think of the object in the same sort of way as the speaker. So the way of referring to the object can be communicationally relevant despite being truth-conditionally irrelevant. Also, what is relevant to communication partly depends on the form of referring expression, as illustrated by the hierarchy of cognitive statuses constructed by Gundel, Hedberg, and Zacharski (1993).

Semantics and pragmatics. Several critics have complained about my formulation of the semantics/pragmatics distinction, which is introduced in Chapter 4 and later exploited in my account of definite descriptions and proper names. The complaint seems to be that I am inattentive to common philosophical usage and formulate the distinction to suit my own purposes. Like most linguists I characterize semantics in terms of linguistic types (not tokens—see 4.6) and the information competent speakers can glean from them apart from particular contexts of utterance. Whatever a hearer infers from collateral information about the context of a particular utterance of a linguistic type counts for me as non-semantic information. Here I am restricting semantic to linguistic information: what speakers know in virtue of their linguistic competence (see Chomsky 1986, 43–5). Even so, I have no objection in principle to the conception of semantics, shared by many philosophers, on which a systematic account of truth conditions (or of determinants of truth conditions, i.e. propositions) can count as semantic even though many (assertoric) utterances are true or false only relative to a context of utterance. Under this conception semantics is concerned not just with (in Kaplan's terms) character, as determined by linguistic meaning, but also with content, which is sensitive also to context (other philosophers, such as Salmon (1986), Soames (1987), and Richard (1993), speak of truth conditions of sentence types 'with respect to' contexts). But the question for me is precisely how context enters in. In Chapter 9 I reject Kaplan's claim that 'character is a function from context to content', at least if the word 'function' is taken seriously. The meanings of a great many indexicals are not rules that determine reference as a function of context but merely impose referential constraints on their use (9.4). This will be amplified at the end of the next section, but the present point is that although Kaplan's conception of semantics is not objectionable in principle, in practice it does not work. The reference of most indexicals (given their meanings) is context-relative but not context-determined.

Conversational impliciture. No one disputes that there are various ways in which what is communicated in an utterance can go beyond sentence meaning. The problem is to catalogue the ways. It is generally recognized that linguistic meaning underdetermines speaker meaning because of the need for disambiguation and reference assignment and because people can speak figuratively or indirectly. It is coming to be recognized that these are not the only ways. Unfortunately, philosophers and linguists sometimes confuse context sensitivity in general with indexicality in particular. And sometimes they assume that inexplicitness is invariably a case of conversational implicature (Sperber and Wilson (1986) are an important exception). However, in my view we need to distinguish not only the implied from the explicit but the implicit from the implied—Grice's distinction between what is said and what is implicated is not exhaustive. In recent work (Bach 1994*a* and 1994*b*), where the discussion of Chapter 4 is extended, I describe two ways in which a speaker can, without using any ambiguous or indexical expressions and without speaking figuratively or indirectly, mean something without making it fully explicit. The first occurs when the linguistic meaning of the sentence, even after disambiguation and reference fixing, does not determine a complete proposition (4.2). If a sentence is in this way *semantically underdeterminate* (in the book the term 'indeterminate' is used), understanding an utterance of it requires a process of *completion* to produce a full proposition. Semantic underdetermination is not ambiguity (see Atlas 1989)—ambiguity is semantic overdetermination. The second way occurs when the utterance does express a complete proposition (possibly as the result of completion) but some other proposition, yielded by what I call the process of *expansion*, is being communicated by the speaker. This is what I call *s*(entence)-non-literality (4.1). In both cases the speaker is not being fully explicit. Rather, he intends the hearer to read something into the utterance, to regard it as if it contained certain conceptual material that is not in fact there. The result of completion and/or expansion is what I call *conversational impliciture*. Impliciture is distinct from Grice's conversational *implicature*, for in implicature one says and communicates one thing and thereby communicates something else in addition. Impliciture, however, is a matter of saying one thing but communicating something else instead, something closely related to what is said. Unlike metaphorical and other sorts of non-literal utterance impliciture is not a case of using particular words in some figurative way. Rather, part of what is communicated is only implicit in what is explicitly expressed, either because the utterance is semantically underdeterminate and completion is required or because what is being communicated is an expanded version of the proposition expressed.

These ideas, though not all the labels, were presented in Chapter 4 but have been misunderstood. As a result, my application of them to singular terms (see the next section) has received some misconceived objections. For example, Recanati (1993, 248–9) does not appreciate how s-non-literality differs from figurative speech, where constituents are used non-literally, and William Taschek (1990, 45) mistakes s-non-literality for a kind of indirection. These misunderstandings lead to misconstruals of my account of uses of incomplete definite descriptions and of proper names, which relies on the notion of s-non-literality. In such cases the linguistic content of the utterance does not make fully explicit what the speaker means, and yet nothing in the uttered sentence is being used non-literally. S-non-literality is to be contrasted with c(onstituent)-non-literality: it is simply a matter of intended additional conceptual material to be read into one's audience, a process that generally occurs so routinely as not to be noticed. That is why it does not pass Recanati's intuitive test for non-literality. Intuitively, people would not classify as non-literal typical utterances of sentences like 'Let's go to Chez Panisse [together]' or 'I haven't taken a shower [today]', where the unuttered word in brackets indicates what needs to be filled in by the hearer. In my view, even though we may not intuitively regard such utterances as non-literal when we reflect on them metalinguistically, in practice we take them non-literally when we hear them. They are not literal even though they may seem to be because, as in the above examples, the conceptual material that we unreflectively insert into the utterance does not correspond to anything in the sentence being uttered. In such cases what is meant is not strictly what is said but some expansion thereof. These examples, as well as the cases of incomplete definite descriptions and shared proper names cited below, are not special cases. S-non-literality is a pervasive phenomenon, for we generally do not make fully explicit what we mean.

The doctrine of direct reference remains popular despite its difficulties with Frege's four puzzles (8.4). To be sure, serious attention has been paid to the problems of belief reports (see Salmon 1986 and Crimmins 1992) and of identity statements (see Ramachandran 1991) as they arise for direct reference theories, but controversy still rages on both. On the other hand, Michael Devitt's (1989) complaint remains valid that the 'Emptiness Problem' (the meaningfulness of vacuous names) and the 'Existence Problem' (the non-triviality of true existence statements and the meaningfulness of true negative ones) continue to be neglected. Another problem for direct reference theories is that both names (7.4) and indexicals (9.5) can be used to make descriptive reference, where what enters into what is said is not the referent but its distinguishing property. Stephen Neale (1990, ch. 6) and Recanati (1993, ch. 16) have both examined descriptive uses of indexicals.

Recanati, though recognizing the descriptive uses of names and indexicals, claims that they are semantically marked as referential expressions—their meaning includes the feature 'REF' (1993, 17). REF is supposed to distinguish names and indexicals from quantified noun phrases. However, he provides no linguistic evidence for this feature. Indeed, from a linguistic point of view names and pronouns are distinguished by the fact that they do not take overt determiners. For example, the phrases 'the Recanati' and 'one he' are ill-formed. Moreover, as Neale (1993) suggests, at the level of LF (the linguistic counterpart of philosophy's logical form) names and pronouns occupy argument positions, whereas quantified noun phrases are represented as variable-binding operators, with the variable occupying the argument position at LF. For example, (1) is represented as (1_{LF})

Most philosophers are near-sighted. (1)

[Most x: philosopher x] (x is near-sighted). (1_{LF})

Neale uses restricted quantifier notation, as exemplified by '[Most x: philosopher x]' in (1_{LF}), for two reasons. First, it is suited to non-standard quantified noun phrases (12.1), such as 'most philosophers'. Second, it avoids the syntactic contortions characteristic of the usual representations of standard quantified noun phrases in first-order logic, so that what is described in 5.1 as the misleadingness of grammatical form as to logical form is merely an artifact of notation. At any rate, as far as Recanati's claim is concerned, if quantified noun phrases are treated as variable-binding operators, then referential terms may be distinguished from them by the absence of that feature rather than by the presence of REF. So we may accept Recanati's and Neale's distinction between referential terms and quantified noun phrases. But it is one thing to accept that distinction and quite another to agree on which expressions belong to which category.

Definite descriptions. Russell's theory of descriptions is first defended (Chapter 5) and then incorporated (Chapter 6) into a pragmatic account of the referential/attributive distinction. Neale (1990) has independently done likewise, giving Russell's theory a book-length defence within a rigorous semantic framework. We both employ Kripke's pragmatic strategy (discussed in 5.3) to show that definite descriptions are quantified noun phrases and to undermine the suggestion that they are systematically ambiguous expressions with referential readings as well. Ludlow and Neale (1991) have extended the argument to indefinite descriptions, which also have been thought to have referential readings.

Russell's theory, as a semantic account of sentences containing definite descriptions, is not obliged to explain referential uses, where the referent itself enters into the content of the speaker's statement. It is important to note here that a pragmatic account of referential uses does not imply that they are not literal. Ordinarily when one uses a definite description referringly, one does intend the description to apply to the referent. So, as I argue in 6.3, referential uses of definite descriptions, at least complete ones, are literal but not direct. Non-literal referential uses are a special case, because the description is not intended to be taken to apply to the referent (6.5).

Non-literal uses of description sentences, such as occur when the description is incomplete, are another matter. Here the distinction between *s-* and *c*-non-literality comes into play. On Russell's theory, a sentence like 'The book is open' is ordinarily used *s*-non-literally, since there are many books. But this is not a case of *c*-non-literality because no constituent (i.e. 'the', 'book', or 'the book') is being used non-literally (6.4). So Taschek's complaint that on my view 'we only rarely mean what we say!' (1990, 40) when using incomplete definite descriptions sounds more serious than it is. My claim is not that any word or phrase in the sentence is being used non-literally but rather that the sentence as a whole does not make fully explicit what is meant. So when the utterance does not make explicit which F is being referred to, which F that is has to be inferred. And though that is a contextual matter, it is a case not of indexicality. Nor is it implicature. It is what I now call impliciture, and in this regard I should have made clearer the reason why an utterance of a sentence like 'The book is open' is taken as being about a certain book rather than as expressing a general proposition of the sort given by Russell's theory. The reason is not that the utterance is obviously false, as in typical cases of Gricean implicature, but that it is blatantly uninformative, given the mutual knowledge that there is more than one book in creation.

Proper names. My theory of proper names (Chapters 7 and 8), the 'nominal description theory' (NDT), has met with less than whole-hearted enthusiasm. A typical objection is that a sentence like

Tipper Gore loves rock-and-roll. (2)

does not seem to say the same thing as

The bearer of 'Tipper Gore' loves rock-and-roll. (2N)

especially not if the latter is unpacked as

There is one and only one bearer of 'Tipper Gore',
and she loves rock-and-roll. (2Q)

This objection is supported by the argument that utterances of (2), (2N), and (2Q) would not have the same force in 'otherwise pragmatically identical circumstances' (Taschek 1990, 43). Such an argument is weak, however, since it ignores the fact that choice of words (from among semantically equivalent alternatives) can matter pragmatically. Compare, for example, 'I know that Caesar crossed the Rubicon' with 'I have an ungettiered justified true belief that Caesar crossed the Rubicon'. In general, substituting a long paraphrase for a word can make a big pragmatic difference.

Part of the aim of NDT (or any descriptive theory of names) is to show how a name does not have to denote anything to be mean-

Postscript

ingful and can retain its usual meaning in existence, identity, and belief contexts. David Freedman finds NDT plausible but worries that it 'leaves the notion of being the bearer of a name unexplained' (1989, 169). I take bearing a certain name to be a matter of convention, rather like having a certain licence number. However, there is no one way in which a name can be acquired, and some ways are less formal than others. When responding to Kripke's circularity objection (8.3), where I argued that it is one thing for an individual to be referred to by a name and quite another for it to bear the name, I was not particularly concerned with the latter relation. The relevant point was that we can immediately understand a sentence containing a name we have never heard before, so that understanding a name as a linguistic item does not require knowing who its (intended) bearer is. That is not a semantic but a pragmatic matter. To appreciate this consider that proper names, because they can be shared, generally do not carry the information needed to determine the referent in a particular case. That is one reason why I argued (8.5) against the view that a shared name is semantically ambiguous (with as many meanings as it has bearers), as well as against the more radical claim, made recently by Kaplan (1990), that a shared name is really a set of distinct but phonologically identical words, one for each bearer.

NDT has struck some as a desperate, rearguard action in defence of Russell's thesis that ordinary names are not logically proper names but disguised descriptions. NDT has not been refuted but merely ignored, probably because the Mill–Kripke view is so widely accepted (despite its well-known difficulties with Frege's four puzzles). At any rate, I tried to defend NDT (Chapter 8) against Kripke's objections to descriptional theories generally and to NDT in particular, and to account for the 'illusion of rigidity' by explaining away the intuitions supporting the Mill–Kripke view of names. However, I should have been clearer on the distinctness of certain theses: that names are directly referential, that they are rigid, that they are not descriptional, and that their reference is explained by the causal theory of reference. Fortunately, philosophers are coming to appreciate that these theses are distinct and do not all stand or fall together. Devitt (1989), for example, not only distinguishes these theses but considers which entails which. He is particularly concerned to show that the strongest (and simplest) of the direct reference theories of names, the 'Fido'–Fido theory (defended, for example, by Wettstein 1986 but rejected by Devitt because it unjustifiably ignores cognitive content), is not entailed by the above theses. Recanati's concept of truth-conditional irrelevance is helpful here, because it clears the way for claiming that names can be directly referential and yet have semantic properties (senses) that determine their references. A direct reference theory can hold that these senses are descriptional but claim that they are truth-conditionally irrelevant and that only the referents enter into truth conditions. The claim that names are rigid designators also does not preclude this possibility. Of course, NDT is incompatible with such claims if they are taken, as is customary, as strictly semantic theses, but it can accommodate a pragmatic construal of direct reference and rigid designation (8.5) and incorporate a non-descriptional causal theory of names at the cognitive level (Chapter 1).

Reference, pronouns, and context. In my view there is a fundamental difference between mental and linguistic indexicals. As explained earlier, I take *de re* modes of presentation to function as mental indexicals, by determining the relation between a thought (token) and an object that must obtain in the context for the former to be a thought of the latter. From this it follows that for them reference is a function of context: the object is that which stands in the relevant relation to the thought. But this is generally not the case for the pronouns and other linguistic indexicals. Except for special cases like 'I' and 'now', indexical reference is, though context-relative, not strictly context-dependent. That is, it is not a *function* of context. With words like 'she', 'they', 'this', and 'then', singular indexical reference depends on the speaker's intention, and intention does not count as a parameter of context. This is because the speaker's intention is not part of the input to the audience's inference but part of what is to be inferred (9.1).

Intending and demonstrating. Even if it is agreed that the contribution of the speaker's intention is not on a par with other contextual contributions, there remains the following question, which is addressed in 9.3 but has received further attention lately: when you refer to something demonstratively, what determines the reference, your demonstration or your intention? David Kaplan used to think it is the demonstration but now, in his 'Afterthoughts' (1989), he says the intention. Marga Reimer (1991*a*, 1991*b*) thinks he was right the first time and produces various counterexamples designed to show that the intended demonstratum is not automatically the actual demonstratum. She argues that something else—or nothing at all—may be the actual demonstratum, in which case the speaker's intention is overridden. In reply (Bach 1992*a*, 1992*b*) I have defended the priority of intentions over demonstrations by showing that there is more to a referential intention than having something in mind and intending to refer to it. Not just any intention to refer to something counts as a specifically referential intention. A referential intention is part of a communicative intention intended to be recognized by one's audience (for more on the reflexive character of communicative intentions, see Bach 1987). As such, it is the intention for one's audience to identify a certain individual by thinking of it in a certain identifiable way (3.1). Such an intention is not fulfilled if the audience fails to identify the right individual in the right way, that is, the one intended in the way intended (not that the latter is part of the truth-conditional content). If one has mistaken beliefs about which object that is, as in Reimer's counterexamples, then any intention one has to be referring to what is in fact not the demonstratum will not be fulfilled. But such an intention is not a specifically referential intention. The intention to refer to the object one is demonstrating is the controlling intention, because it is one's demonstration on which one intends the audience to rely in identifying the referent.

The claim that referential intentions determine reference might suggest that they succeed by magic or are somehow self-fulfilling. So it is important to appreciate that this claim does not lead to the absurd consequence that one can utter any old thing and gesture in any old way and still manage to refer to whatever one has in mind. To think that it does would be to misunderstand the role of referential intentions and their relationship to the utterances used to express them. You do not say something and then, as though by an inner decree (an intention), determine what you are using it to refer to. You do not just have something 'in mind' and hope that your audience is a good mind-reader. Rather, you decide to refer to something and try to select an expression whose utterance will enable your audience, under the circumstances, to identify that object. Referential intentions, if they are to be fulfilled, must satisfy the rational constraints on communicative intentions generally.

Singular terms in belief contexts. In my view the distinction between transparent and opaque occurrences of singular terms in belief contexts is not semantically grounded (10.1). In particular, the semantics of belief sentences do not determine the extent to which true belief ascriptions impute concepts to the ascribee (see Loar 1988). A singular term in the embedded clause, the so-called content clause, can be used to refer to an individual or to impute a conception of an individual (similarly, a general term can be used to indicate a property or relation or to impute a concept). However, this is not a case of semantic ambiguity but of underdetermination. Understanding the full import of an utterance of a belief sentence requires the pragmatic process of completion.

The pragmatic dimension of belief reports is central to the theories put forward in three important books by Nathan Salmon (1986), Mark Richard (1990), and Mark Crimmins (1992). All three recognize that there is more to a belief report than meets the eye (or ear), so that part of what enters into it is determined pragmatically. However, they disagree on what that is and on how it enters in. Salmon claims that imputed ways of thinking are not part of the literal content of belief reports but are merely 'pragmatically imparted'. Richard claims that 'believe' is an indexical whose reference is to a context-dependent relation that involves a particular translation function (roughly, from words used to ascribe beliefs to imputed ways of thinking). And Crimmins claims that belief reports involve a hidden indexical reference to ways of thinking (these do not depend on the reference of 'believes' but are 'unarticulated constituents' of belief reports). All three authors offer numerous insights about belief reports, but Stephen Schiffer (1987, 1992) has raised serious problems for such pragmatic approaches (but see Salmon's 1989 defence). In my opinion pragmatic accounts could benefit from the notions of semantic underdetermination and conversational impliciture, and I hope to develop my rather sketchy account of belief reports (Chapter 10) in more detail.

4. OTHER KINDS OF REFERENCE

Anaphoric reference. I argue (Chapters 11, 12.4, and 12.5) that anaphoric reference, the use of pronouns to refer to individuals previously mentioned, deserves no special semantic or syntactic consideration: being previously mentioned is simply one way of being salient. Unless the anaphoric reference is explicitly marked, by dedicated anaphors like reflexives and reciprocals, it is not a syntactic phenomenon. So there is no need for linguistic theory to make special provisions for the anaphoric use of ordinary pronouns or to treat the relation between them and their 'antecedents' as a syntactic relation, as with the device of co-indexing. Indeed I gather that many linguists now agree in downplaying the importance of principle B of the binding module of government-binding theory (roughly, principle B requires that pronouns be free in 'local domains', whereas principle A requires that anaphors be bound in local domains—see Chomsky 1986, 164 ff.).

In the case of so-called E-type pronouns there is even less reason to regard the relation of antecedency as syntactic (12.6). Such pronouns do not require any special syntactic or semantic treatment and can be handled pragmatically. In an example like

> Many drivers don't use seat belts, and they are
> very foolish. (3)

'they' functions as a descriptive pronoun, whose intended descriptive content is 'the drivers who don't use seat belts'. A descriptive approach to such pronouns has been worked out in detail by Neale (1990, 187–91, 196–204, and ch. 6), who calls them 'D-type pronouns' to indicate that they go proxy for descriptions, contrary to Evans's contention that they are referential, with their references fixed by descriptions.

Plural reference. There is not much new to say on plural reference, which can be made with the use of quantified noun phrases (12.2) as well as with plural pronouns (12.3) and conjunctions of singular terms. To my knowledge what little there has been written on this topic has done nothing to suggest that it is relevantly or interestingly different from singular reference, except that it admits of the linguistically interesting distinction between distributive and collective reference. It is worth reiterating the benefits of Neale's use of restricted quantifier notation to represent both standard and non-standard quantified noun phrases. Not only does this notation provide a uniform way of representing quantified noun phrases, but it does so in a way that minimizes the fracturing of syntax characteristic of first-order representations (12.1). Moreover, it lends itself to straightforward incorporation into the analysis of L(ogical) F(orm) in syntactic theory.

Reference and natural kinds. The arguments in Chapter 13 against Burge's externalism about concepts and Putnam's externalism about meanings of natural kind terms have been supplemented by those in Crane 1991 and Elugardo 1993 (also, Putnam's claims about natural kinds have been debunked on empirical grounds in Dupré 1993, ch. 1). However, all these arguments are primarily concerned with the import of philosophical thought experiments. Philosophers are now becoming more interested in substantive questions about concept attribution (see Crimmins 1992, 93–8, and Woodfield 1993, for example) and concept possession and individuation (see Peacocke 1992). They are paying attention to the extensive research in the psychology of concepts, which is already too large to document here (for references and discussion see Smith 1990 and Kornblith 1993).

In philosophy as in romance one thing leads to another. So I have had to limit this discussion to recent developments closely tied to issues raised in the book. Nothing has been said about such far-reaching issues of current interest as the nature of propositions, the relation between language and thought, and the status of mental content. I have not staked out a position on these issues, but I believe that the views put forth here are neutral on them.

REFERENCES

Adams, F., G. Fuller, and R. Stecker (1993), 'Thoughts without objects', *Mind & Language* 8: 90–104.

Atlas, J. D. (1989), *Philosophy Without Ambiguity*, Oxford: Oxford University Press.

Bach, K. (1987), 'On communicative intentions', *Mind & Language* 2: 141–54.

—— (1992a), 'Paving the road to reference', *Philosophical Studies* 67: 295–300.

—— (1992b), 'Intentions and demonstrations', *Analysis* 52: 140–6.

—— (1994a), 'Conversational impliciture', *Mind & Language* 9.

—— (1994b), 'Semantic slack: what is said and more' in S. L. Tsohatzidis (ed.), *Foundations of Speech Act Theory*, London: Routledge.

Bell, D. (1990), 'How "Russellian" was Frege?', *Mind* 99: 267–77.

Blackburn, S. (1984), *Spreading the Word*, Oxford: Oxford University Press.

Burge, T. (1991), 'Vision and intentional content' in Lepore and Van Gulick (1991).

Carruthers, P. (1987), 'Russellian thoughts', *Mind* 96: 18–35.

Chomsky, N. (1986), *Knowledge of Language*, New York: Praeger.

Crane, T. (1991), 'All the difference in the world', *Philosophical Quarterly* 41: 1–25.

Crimmins, M. (1992), *Talk about Beliefs*, Cambridge, Mass.: MIT Press.

Devitt, M. (1989), 'Against direct reference', *Midwest Studies in Philosophy* 14: 206–40.

Dupré, J. (1993), *The Disorder of Things*, Cambridge, Mass.: Harvard University Press.

Elugardo, R. (1993), 'Burge on content', *Philosophy and Phenomenological Research* 53: 367–84.

Forbes, G. (1989), 'Cognitive architecture and the semantics of belief', *Midwest Studies in Philosophy* 14: 84–100.

—— (1990), 'The indispensability of sinn', *Philosophical Review* 99: 535–63.

Freedman, D. (1989), 'Review of K. Bach, *Thought and Reference*', *Mind* 98: 167–9.

Gundel, J., N. Hedberg, and R. Zacharski (1993), 'Cognitive status and the form of referring expressions in discourse', *Language* 69: 274–307.

Kaplan, D. (1989), 'Afterthoughts' in J. Perry, J. Almog, and H. Wettstein (eds.), *Themes from Kaplan*, Oxford: Oxford University Press.

—— (1990), 'Words', *Proceedings of the Aristotelian Society* 64: 93–119.

Kornblith, H. (1993), *Inductive Inference and its Natural Ground*, Cambridge, Mass.: MIT Press.

Lepore, E., and R. Van Gulick (eds.) (1991), *John Searle and his Critics*, Oxford: Blackwell.

Loar, B. (1988), 'Social content and psychological content' in R. Grimm and D. Merrill (eds.), *Contents of Thought*, Tucson, Ariz.: University of Arizona Press.

Ludlow, P., and S. Neale (1991), 'Indefinite descriptions: in defense of Russell', *Linguistics and Philosophy* 14: 171–202.

McDowell, J. (1984), '*De re* senses' in C. Wright (ed.), *Frege: Tradition and Influence*, Oxford: Basil Blackwell.

—— (1986), 'Singular thought and the extent of inner space', in P. Pettit and J. McDowell (eds.), *Subject, Thought, and Content*, Oxford: Oxford University Press.

—— (1991), 'Intentionality *de re*' in Lepore and Van Gulick (1991).

Neale, S. (1990), *Descriptions*, Cambridge, Mass.: MIT Press.

—— (1993), 'Term limits' in J. Tomberlin (ed.), *Philosophical Perspectives* 7, Atascadero, Calif.: Ridgeview Publishing Co.

Noonan, H. (1991), 'Object-dependent thoughts and psychological redundancy', *Analysis* 51: 1–9.

Peacocke, C. (1993), *A Study of Concepts*, Cambridge, Mass.: MIT Press.

Ramachandran, M. (1991), 'Sense and schmidentity', *Philosophical Quarterly* 41: 463–71.

Recanati, F. (1993), *Direct Reference: From Language to Thought*, Oxford: Blackwell.

Reimer, M. (1991*a*), 'Demonstratives, demonstrations, and demonstrata', *Philosophical Studies* 63: 187–202.

—— (1991*b*), 'Do demonstrations have semantic significance?', *Analysis* 51: 177–83.

Richard, M. (1990), *Propositional Attitudes*, Cambridge: Cambridge University Press.

—— (1993), 'Attitudes in context', *Linguistics and Philosophy* 16: 123–48.

Salmon, N. (1986), *Frege's Puzzle*, Cambridge, Mass.: MIT Press.

—— (1989), 'Illogical belief' in J. Tomberlin (ed.), *Philosophical Perspectives 3*, Atascadero, Calif.: Ridgeview Publishing Co.

Schiffer, S. (1987), 'The "Fido"–Fido theory of belief' in J. Tomberlin (ed.), *Philosophical Perspectives 1*, Atascadero, Calif.: Ridgeview Publishing Co.

—— (1992), 'Belief ascription', *Journal of Philosophy* 89: 499–521.

Searle, J. R. (1991), 'Response: reference and intentionality' in Lepore and Van Gulick (1991).

Segal, G. (1989), 'The return of the individual', *Mind* 98: 39–57.

Smith, E. E. (1990), 'Categorization' in D. N. Osherson and E. E. Smith (eds.), *Thinking*, Cambridge, Mass.: MIT Press.

Soames, S. (1987), 'Direct reference, propositional attitudes, and semantic content', *Philosophical Topics* 15: 47–87.

Sperber, D., and D. Wilson (1986), *Relevance*, Cambridge, Mass.: Harvard University Press.

Taschek, W. (1990), 'Review of K. Bach, Thought and Reference', *Journal of Philosophy* 87: 38–45.

Wettstein, H. (1986), 'Has semantics rested on a mistake?', *Journal of Philosophy* 83: 185–209.

Woodfield, A. (1993), 'Pragmatic aspects of talk about concepts', presented at the European Congress of Analytic Philosophy, Aix-en-Provence, April 1993.

Index

Ackerman, D. 154
ambiguity 64–5, 69, 74, 77–8
 and pronouns 223–9
 and proper names 137–8, 155, 168
 and scope 207–11
anaphoric reference 221–37, 249
Atlas, J. 99 n.
Austin, J. 181 n.

Bach, K. 34 n., 51–3, 77 n., 98 n.,
 121, 180 n., 181 n., 245
Barwise, J. 179 n. 241
Beebe, M. 19 n., 29 n.
belief ascriptions 16–17, 198–9, 265–74
belief sentences 57, 96, 165–7,
 195–214
Berkeley, G. 28 n.
Boer, S. 43, 139
Brand, M. 142
Burge, T. 13, 17, 19 n., 65 n., 139,
 140 n., 263–80

causal theory of reference 7–8, 13,
 34 n., 161, 173
Chastain, C. 245 n.
Chisholm, R. 16, 20
Chomsky, N. 76 n., 223, 235 n., 250,
 253, 255, 257
communicative intentions 51–3, 66,
 119 n.
Communicative Presumption 53, 215
concepts 264–80
 individual concepts 21, 27, 31, 131,
 133–4
context 5, 13, 65 n., 70, 175–82, 263,
 275
Cooper, R. 224, 241
Cresswell, M. 58 n., 62 n., 64, 69 n.,
 195 n.

de dicto (descriptive) thought 7, 11,
 16–17
definite descriptions 59–60, 91–129,
 195–202
 fall-back 112, 115, 127–8

in belief contexts 195–203, 209–14
 incomplete 82–5, 103–8, 116, 124–6
Dennett, D. 30 n., 39 n.
denotation see linguistic reference
de re modes of presentation 13–15,
 18, 25–6, 33, 43–5
de re relations 12–13, 17, 19–26
de re thought (belief) 6–8, 11–45,
 111–12, 173, 197–8
 communication-based 24–6, 31–9
 memory-based 23–4, 27–31
 perception-based 20–3
Descartes, R. 20 n.
descriptive reference 66–7, 193–4, 238
Devitt, M. 34 n., 87, 101 n., 137 n.,
 161, 162 n., 171 n., 216–17
Donnellan, K. 69 n., 98–102, 109–14,
 123, 126–8, 162 n.

Evans, G. 14 n., 19 n., 35 n., 39,
 41–3, 50, 119 n., 137 n., 138,
 156 n., 225–34, 258–60
existence sentences 56–8, 95, 163–4
expressing attitudes 51–2, 64

Farmer, A. 234 n., 255
fictional reference 214–18
files 29, 34–7, 43–4, 215–16
Frege, G. 7, 57 n., 65, 91–2, 164,
 211 n., 240, 262

grammar 4–5, 62
 and anaphora 221–5, 230–5
 and bound pronouns 250–5
Grice, H. P. 29 n., 77, 121 n., 252 n.

Harnish, R. 51–3, 77 n., 98 n., 121,
 180 n., 181 n., 245
Heny, F. 211 n.
Higginbotham, J. 235 n.
Hornstein, N. 241 n.

identity sentences 95–6, 164–5
illocutionary acts 51, 73, 113, 180–2
indexicals see pronouns

Kant, I. 94
Kaplan, D. 16, 87, 111 n., 177–9,
    182–6
Katz, J. 70
Kim, J. 16
Kripke, S. 34 n., 35, 37, 69, 83–4,
    100, 105–6, 130, 133–6, 138,
    144 n., 149–61, 167–73, 193,
    203 n., 262

Lasnik, H. 225–6, 230–2, 234
Lehrer, K. 141
Lewis, D. 214–18
linguistic meaning 4–5, 62–6, 69–72,
    262–4, 280–3, 286–90
    see also semantics
Linguistic Presumption 53
linguistic reference 3–4, 6–7, 39–40,
    49, 52, 61, 85–7, 195
    and natural-kind terms 262–91
Loar, B. 112 n., 135, 149–50, 161,
    173, 199
locutionary acts 51, 113–14, 180–3
    and referring 179–82
Lycan, W. 43, 178 n., 241

McCray, A. 234 n.
McGinn, C. 13
mental indexicals 13, 18, 26
    see also de re modes of presentation
mental names 25–6, 32–6
Mill, J. S. 130, 133, 135
modes of presentation *see de re* modes
    of presentation
Montague, R. 4 n.

Nominal Description Theory (NDT)
    34–5, 135–51, 156–61, 167, 173–4,
    204
non-literality 68–72
    standardized 77–85

objectual reference 66–7, 118–20,
    129, 169, 172–3, 193–4, 238–9

Partee, B. 245 n.
Peacocke, C. 21 n., 162–3
percepts 20–1, 28, 35, 43–4
Perry, J. 15 n., 29 n., 179 n.
plural reference 238–9, 244–50
    collective vs. distributive 67, 247,
    249, 257
Pollock J. 16
pragmatics 4–6, 61, 69, 85–6

Presumption of Literalness 53
pronouns 175–82
    anaphoric uses of 221–37
    antecedents of 235–7, 250–1, 254–5,
        260
    E-type 258–61
    in belief contexts 205–6
    plural 248–50
    referential constraints on 186–92,
        248
    reflexives 257
proper names 7–8, 33, 60, 130–174
    descriptive 33
    in belief contexts 203–5
    in fictional contexts 214–16
    logically proper 14, 131–3
    shared 153–6
    vacuous 162–3
Putnam, H. 262–4, 265 n., 275–8,
    280–90

quantifier phrases 239–44
    and bound pronouns 250–5
    non-standard 240–3, 246
    referential uses of 244–8
Quine, W. V. 57, 62 n., 97 n., 196–7

reference *see* linguistic reference;
        speaker reference
referential/attributive distinction
    98–103, 109–29
referential opacity/transparency
    196–214
referring expressions 40, 55–62, 240
Reichenbach, H. 187
Reinhart, T. 230, 252 n.
relational determination 12, 18, 21,
    26, 28, 32, 35
Rigid Designator Thesis (RDT) 130–1,
    149, 151–6, 162–74
Russell, B. 14–15, 32, 59–61, 91–4,
    97, 99, 130–5, 164
    theory of descriptions 59–60, 91–108

Salmon, N. 101 n., 104 n.
satisfactional determination 12, 21, 32
saying *see* locutionary acts
Schiffer, S. 14, 21, 22 n., 28 n., 36 n.,
    63, 165–6
scope 144–8, 194, 207–11
Searle, J. 17, 19 n., 50, 115–17, 134,
    180 n., 216, 277 n., 289 n.
semantic indeterminacy 74–7, 202,
    210–14

semantics 4–6, 61–4, 69, 82, 85–8, 290–1
singular thought *see de re* thought
speaker reference 3–4, 6–7, 39, 49–53, 55, 61, 85–7
  and demonstrating 182–6
  definition of 52
  referential intentions 176–86, 245
  types of 66–8
Speech Act Schema (SAS) 53–5, 66
Stich, S. 15 n.
Strawson, P. F. 32 n., 39–40, 50, 61, 92, 93 n., 96–8, 132–4

trace (memory) 23, 28
truth 4–6, 63–4
  in fiction 217–18
type/token distinction 5–6, 15, 62 n., 70, 86–8

Unger, P. 276–7

Walton, K. 214
Wasow, T. 234 n.
Wettstein, H. 83–4, 101 n., 106, 122, 193
Wittgenstein, L. 2